# GMAT®

# All the Verbal

This essential guide takes the guesswork out of grammar by presenting all of the major grammatical principles and minor grammatical points known to be tested on GMAT Sentence Correction.
It also teaches you all of the critical and logical reasoning you need for the Reading Comprehension and Critical Reasoning sections of the GMAT.

## Acknowledgements

A great number of people were involved in the creation of the book you are holding.

Our Manhattan Prep resources are based on the continuing experiences of our instructors and students. The overall vision for this edition was developed by Stacey Koprince and Andrea Pawliczek, who determined what strategies to cover and how to weave them into a cohesive whole.

Stacey Koprince (SC, RC), Andrea Pawliczek (CR), and Daniel Fogel (SC) were the primary authors; they were supported by a number of content experts. Chelsey Cooley and Daniel Fogel served as the primary editors during the writing phase. Mario Gambino, Helen Tan, and Patrick Tyrrell served as a sounding board during the writing phase, vetting both ideas and content. Patrick Tyrrell deserves special mention as the source of multiple new ideas for the CR unit of the guide. Mario Gambino managed production for all images, with Derek Frankhouser and Israt Pasha lending their design expertise.

Matthew Callan coordinated the production work for this guide. Once the manuscript was done, Naomi Beesen and Emily Meredith Sledge edited and Cheryl Duckler proofread the entire guide from start to finish. Carly Schnur designed the covers.

# GMAT® Strategy Guides

**GMAT All the Quant**

**GMAT All the Verbal**

**GMAT Integrated Reasoning & Essay**

## Strategy Guide Supplements

<u>Math</u>

**GMAT Foundations of Math**

**GMAT Advanced Quant**

<u>Verbal</u>

**GMAT Foundations of Verbal**

September 3, 2019

Dear Student,

Thank you for picking up a copy of *All the Verbal*. I hope this book provides just the guidance you need to get the most out of your GMAT studies.

**At Manhattan Prep, we continually aspire to provide the best instructors and resources possible. If you have any questions or feedback, please do not hesitate to contact us.**

Email our Student Services team at gmat@manhattanprep.com or give us a shout at 212-721-7400 (or 800-576-4628 in the United States or Canada). We try to keep all our books free of errors, but if you think we've goofed, please visit manhattanprep.com/GMAT/errata.

Our Manhattan Prep Strategy Guides are based on the continuing experiences of both our instructors and our students. The primary authors of the 7th Edition All the Verbal guide were Stacey Koprince, Andrea Pawliczek, and Daniel Fogel. Project management and design were led by Matthew Callan, Mario Gambino, and Helen Tan. I'd like to send particular thanks to instructors Chelsey Cooley, Emily Meredith Sledge, and Patrick Tyrrell for their content contributions.

Finally, we are indebted to all of the Manhattan Prep students who have given us excellent feedback over the years. This book wouldn't be half of what it is without their voice.

And now that *you* are one of our students too, please chime in! I look forward to hearing from you. Thanks again and best of luck preparing for the GMAT!

Sincerely,

Chris Ryan
Executive Director, Product Strategy
Manhattan Prep

# TABLE OF CONTENTS

**ix**

# The GMAT Mindset

The GMAT is a complex exam. It feels like an academic test—math, grammar, logical reasoning—but it's really not! At heart, the GMAT is a test of your *executive reasoning skills*.

Executive reasoning is the official term for your ability to make all kinds of decisions in the face of complex and changing information. It makes sense, then, that graduate management programs would want to test these skills. It's crucial for you to understand *how* they do so because that understanding will impact both how you study for the GMAT and how you take the test.

You do need to know various math and grammar facts, rules, and concepts in order to do well on the GMAT—and this makes the test feel similar to tests that you took in school. There's one critical difference though: When your teachers gave you tests in school, they tested you on material they expected you to know how to handle. Your teachers wouldn't put something on the test that they *expected* you to get wrong. That would be cruel!

Well, it would be cruel if the main point of the exam was to test your mastery of those facts, rules, and concepts. But that isn't the main point of the GMAT. Rather, the GMAT wants to know how well you make decisions regarding when to invest your limited time and mental energy—and when *not* to.

In other words, the GMAT wants to know how you make business decisions. And no good businessperson invests in every single opportunity placed in front of them, just because it's there. A good businessperson evaluates each opportunity, saying yes to some and no to others. That's what you're going to do on the GMAT, too. You'll invest in a majority of the problems presented to you, but you *will* say no to some—the ones that look too hard or seem like they'll take too long to solve. These are literally bad investments.

So, the GMAT will offer you questions that it thinks you will not be able to do. How does it accomplish this? The GMAT is an adaptive test; that is, it adapts to you as you take it, offering easier or harder questions based on how you're doing on the test. Ideally, you'll do well on the material that you know how to answer in a reasonable amount of time. Your reward? You'll earn questions that are too hard for you to do—either they'll take too long to answer or they'll be so hard that you wouldn't be able to do them even if you had unlimited time.

Then what? If you try to use a "school mindset" on the test, you'll keep trying to answer the questions even though you really can't do them. You'll waste a bunch of time and then, later, you'll have to rush on other questions. As a result, you'll start to miss questions that you actually do know how to answer and your score will go down. This is the business equivalent of spending most of your annual budget by August...and then not having enough money left to run the business well from September through December.

Instead, use your "business mindset" to carry you through the exam. When the test finds your limit, acknowledge that! Call it a bad investment and let that problem go (ideally before you've spent very much time on it). Choose an answer, any answer, and move on.

Extend the business mindset to your studies as well. If there are certain topics that you really hate, decide that you're not going to study them in the first place. You're just going to bail (guess quickly and move on) when one of those "opportunities" comes up. (One caveat: You can't bail on huge swaths of content. For example, don't bail on all of grammar; that represents too great a portion of the Verbal section. You can, though, bail on a subset of grammar—say, pronouns and idioms.)

Start orienting yourself around your business mindset today. You aren't going to do it all. You're going to choose the best opportunities as you see them throughout the test. When you decide not to pursue a particular "investment," you're going to say no as quickly as you can and forget about it—don't waste precious resources on a poor investment opportunity! Move on to the next opportunity, feeling good about the fact that you're doing what you're supposed to do on the GMAT: making sound investment decisions about what to do and what *not* to do.

## Verbal Reasoning on the GMAT

The Verbal Reasoning (or Verbal) section of the GMAT consists of three different question types: Sentence Correction (SC), Reading Comprehension (RC), and Critical Reasoning (CR).

Sentence Correction (SC) questions test the proper usage of grammar and meaning. Reading Comprehension (RC) questions test your ability to comprehend and to infer from complex information. Critical Reasoning (CR) questions test your ability to understand, analyze, critique, and infer from arguments.

You'll need to average a bit less than 2 minutes per question in the Verbal section, though your timing for individual questions will likely range from almost no time at all to approximately 3 minutes. The "almost no time at all" questions will be your *bail* questions: questions that look way too hard or that you know are a big weakness of yours (in other words, bad investment opportunities!). On other questions, you'll choose to invest some extra time—perhaps on a harder question in an area of strength.

You'll learn more about time management, as well as other test details, both in this guide and in the online resources associated with this guide. You can also test your skills using official GMAT problems that are published by the test makers in *The GMAT Official Guide* (also known as "the big OG" or "the OG"). These problems appeared on the official GMAT in the past, so they're a fantastic resource to help you get ready for the real test. (Note: The OG is sold separately from the Manhattan Prep strategy guides.)

# Sentence Correction

**In this unit, you will learn** an efficient and effective solving process for all Sentence Correction problems. You will also learn the underlying grammar rules tested on the GMAT, as well as how to handle the various types of meaning issues (such as redundancy, ambiguity, and faulty logic) that come into play.

## In This Unit:

# The Sentence Correction Process

## In This Chapter:

**In this chapter, you will learn** a 4-step process to use on all Sentence Correction (SC) problems. You'll also learn how to take advantage of the way SC works in order to save time and how to study to improve your SC skills.

# CHAPTER 1 The Sentence Correction Process

Sentence Correction (SC) is one of three question types found in the Verbal section of the GMAT. Sentence Correction tests your mastery of both grammar and meaning as they apply to conventional written English.

SC questions typically comprise about one-third of the questions in the Verbal section. They tend to be the fastest of the three question types that appear in the Verbal section, so learning to work efficiently is especially important. To that end, you'll need to build a strong process for working through SC problems.

## Question Format

Take a look at this SC problem:

> Although William Pereira first gained national recognition for his set designs for <u>such movies as *Reap the Wild Wind* and *Jane Eyre*, he was more commonly remembered now</u> as the architect of the Transamerica Tower and the designer of the master plan for the city of Irvine, California.
>
> (A)  such movies as *Reap the Wild Wind* and *Jane Eyre*, he was more commonly remembered now
>
> (B)  such movies as *Reap the Wild Wind* and *Jane Eyre*, he is now more commonly remembered
>
> (C)  such movies as *Reap the Wild Wind* and *Jane Eyre*, but now he will be more commonly remembered
>
> (D)  movies such as *Reap the Wild Wind* and *Jane Eyre*, he would be more commonly remembered now
>
> (E)  movies such as *Reap the Wild Wind* and *Jane Eyre*, but he is now more commonly remembered

The question consists of a given sentence, part of which is underlined. The underlined segment may be short or it may comprise most or even all of the original sentence. The five answer choices are possible replacements for the underlined segment.

In all SC questions, choice (A) is exactly the same as the underlined portion of the sentence above it; in other words, you would select answer (A) if you think nothing is wrong with the original sentence. The other four choices will always offer different options. Your task is to select the answer that creates the best sentence *of the choices given*, in terms of both grammar and meaning. (It might not be the best way that you can think to write the sentence yourself.)

By the way, each of the five answer choices is correct approximately 20 percent of the time, including answer choice (A)—that is, the original sentence is correct approximately 20 percent of the time (though that's not the case on this particular problem). Because the original sentence is wrong about 80 percent of the time, you may find yourself unconsciously avoiding it closer to 100 percent of the time; just remember that every answer choice has an approximately equal chance of being the correct answer.

## The Sentence Correction Process

Because the other two Verbal question types, Critical Reasoning (CR) and Reading Comprehension (RC), require so much reading, you're going to have to move quickly on Sentence Correction (SC). In fact, you'll need to average about 1 minute and 20 seconds per SC question.

As a result, you'll need a standard process to help you work through any SC question efficiently and effectively.

Here's the basic process:

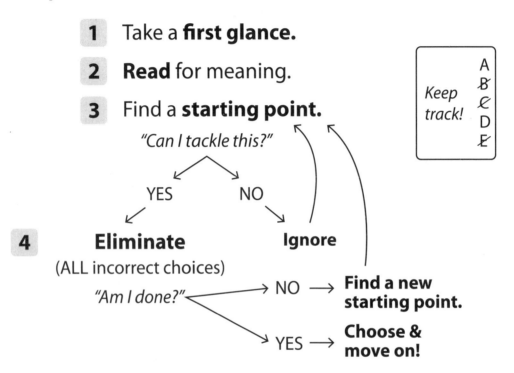

Try the process with the William Pereira example:

> Although William Pereira first gained national recognition for his set designs for <u>such movies as Reap the Wild Wind and Jane Eyre, he was more commonly remembered now</u> as the architect of the Transamerica Tower and the designer of the master plan for the city of Irvine, California.

(A) such movies as *Reap the Wild Wind* and *Jane Eyre*, he was more commonly remembered now

(B) such movies as *Reap the Wild Wind* and *Jane Eyre*, he is now more commonly remembered

(C) such movies as *Reap the Wild Wind* and *Jane Eyre*, but now he will be more commonly remembered

(D) movies such as *Reap the Wild Wind* and *Jane Eyre*, he would be more commonly remembered now

(E) movies such as *Reap the Wild Wind* and *Jane Eyre*, but he is now more commonly remembered

### Step 1: Take a First Glance

Don't start reading yet. Just take a *first glance* to spot clues that may help you answer the question. You may not notice much at first; you'll get better with practice!

How long is the underline? What's happening where the underline starts?

In the Pereira problem, the underline is relatively short. It starts after the word *for* and the first underlined word is *such*.

The word *such* by itself isn't a huge clue, so read a couple more words: *such movies as*. The phrase *such as* is used to introduce examples of something. Now you know that the sentence is going to give examples and discuss something about movies.

This is the equivalent of noticing right away on a quant question that there's a diagram of a triangle or that the problem text contains a quadratic equation. You don't have enough information to solve the problem, of course, but you have some context about what it is testing. In the Pereira problem, you now know something about the overall meaning and at least part of the organization of the sentence.

You can take this first glance one step further. On SC, the beginning of the five answers will *always* contain at least one difference, so glance at the first word or two of each choice. The "split," or difference among the answers, is *such movies as* vs. *movies such as*.

People more commonly say *movies such as*, but it's also acceptable to say *such movies as*, as long as that word in the middle (*movies*, in this case) is the category for which you're about to give examples. In other words, both variations are fine.

When the test gives you a split for which both variations are okay, it's called a **Red Herring**. A red herring is a distraction—the test is trying to get you to waste time debating two (or three or more!) variations, when the different forms are all acceptable.

So, you've taken your first glance; now what? The last word of the five answers will also always contain at least one difference. Most of the time, glancing at the beginning of the choices will be enough to give you your first clue and then you'd go to step 2. In this case, though, the beginning of the choices contained a red herring, so glance at the end of each choice as well.

At the end, the split is between *remembered now* and just plain *remembered*. It could be that the word *now* moves around in other choices or that the word *now* disappears entirely from some choices. The movement or disappearance of a time marker often affects the meaning of a sentence.

So, with the investment of perhaps 5 to 10 seconds, you know several things. The sentence is going to be about movies and give examples of movies. You won't waste time debating the *movies such as* and *such movies as* split, but you will keep an eye on the meaning of the sentence—in particular, *when* are things happening (now vs. some other time)?

## Step 2: Read the Sentence for Meaning

Next, read the entire original sentence. It's natural to focus on grammar as you solve SC problems; the title of this step emphasizes meaning because most people forget to think about the meaning, even though meaning is just as important as grammar!

A sentence can be grammatically correct and yet illogical or ambiguous:

> Anne and Millie went to the movies in her car.

Wait a minute whose car did they take? Anne's? Millie's? Someone else's? The sentence is ambiguous.

As you read, pay attention to *both* the overall meaning and the underlying grammar. Don't think about how to fix anything yet; just notice what the possible issues are.

**1**

What does the William Pereira sentence say?

> Although William Pereira first gained national recognition for his set designs for <u>such movies as *Reap the Wild Wind* and *Jane Eyre*, he was more commonly remembered now</u> as the architect of the Transamerica Tower and the designer of the master plan for the city of Irvine, California.

The sentence begins with a contrast word (*although*), and that word is not part of the underline, so it can't change. As you read the rest of the sentence, pay attention to the contrast that it's trying to convey.

Extract the "core" of the sentence:

> Although WP first gained recognition for one thing, he was remembered for other, quite different things.

That basic meaning does make sense. Did anything else jump out at you? The end of the sentence says this:

> . . . he was more commonly remembered now . . .

*Was remembered* is in the past, but *now* is in the present. Using those two time markers together is illogical.

When something jumps out as a possible issue, jot down a word or two to help you remember, then keep reading. In this case, you might jot down something like "was . . . now?"

## Step 3: Find a Starting Point

Most SC problems test multiple issues, and those issues can appear anywhere in the sentence. Your task at this stage is to decide where to start.

If you've spotted an issue in the original sentence that you know for sure is incorrect, you can cross off answer (A), as that answer always repeats the text of the original sentence.

For example, let's say that you start with the "was . . . now?" issue. It doesn't make sense to say that he *was remembered* in the present (*now*), so the original sentence is incorrect. Cross off answer (A).

## Step 4: Eliminate All Incorrect Choices

Make that first issue keep working for you. Whenever you find an error in one choice, your next step is to check the remaining answer choices for that exact same error or a closely related error. Do any of the other choices have a similar illogical meaning?

Work efficiently. Scan the five answer choices vertically *only for that portion of the text*. In other words, do *not* read the full text of all five answers:

> (A)  . . . he was more commonly remembered now
> (B)  . . . he is now more commonly remembered
> (C)  . . . but now he will be more commonly remembered
> (D)  . . . he would be more commonly remembered now
> (E)  . . . but he is now more commonly remembered

~~A~~
B
~~C~~
~~D~~
E

1

The word *now* moves around, but it is always in the sentence, so the verb tense needs to be consistent with the meaning of *now*.

The hypothetical *he would be…remembered now* is illogical in this sentence, so answer (D) is incorrect. It's also not great to say *now he will be remembered*, as in answer (C). While you might hear someone say something like, "Now, I will go to the store," that person should really say, "I am leaving now" (as she leaves) or "In a few minutes, I will leave for the store."

So answers (A), (C), and (D) are out. Three down, two to go!

## Repeat!

Find another starting point and repeat steps 3 and 4. After a repetition or two, you'll either get down to one answer or get stuck. Either way, pick an answer and move on to the next problem.

Now, where are you going to find these new starting points? You have two main options:

1.  Tackle other errors that you've already spotted.

2.  Compare the remaining answer choices vertically, looking for differences, or splits.

Spot a difference, then ask yourself whether you think that difference is straightforward to address. If so, go for it. If not, *ignore* that difference and look for a different one that you think is more straightforward—don't waste time agonizing over an annoying split. SC questions will almost always offer you multiple paths to the correct answer, so take the path that is easiest and fastest for you.

In the Pereira example, answers (B) and (E) remain. Compare them vertically—what's different? Answer (E) starts with the word *but*; this word is not present in answer (B).

*But* indicates a contrast; this is a meaning issue, so remind yourself of the big picture of the sentence:

> Although WP first gained recognition for one thing, he was remembered for other, quite different things.

The word *although* already conveys the contrast. A second contrast word would be redundant:

> Although WP first gained recognition for one thing, *but* he was remembered for other, quite different things. ??

Eliminate answer (E). The correct answer is (B).

## Step 3 Redux

Let's go back to step 3 for a moment. What if you think a particular thing *may* be wrong but you're not sure?

Go straight to the answers and scan vertically for the text that you think might be an issue. Compare all five answers: What alternative wordings do the others contain for that text? These are your splits, or differences, for this particular issue. Use those splits to help you decide how to evaluate the issue (or whether to look for a different, easier issue).

Other times, you may spot a potential issue but not feel confident addressing it. In that case, forget about it—don't waste any time agonizing about it. Go look for something else that is easier for you. (Most SC problems offer at least three splits.)

What if you don't spot anything at all in the original sentence? (After all, that one is correct 20 percent of the time!) In this case, go straight to the answers and scan vertically to compare, looking for any splits. Use these splits to figure out what the sentence is testing. If you don't feel comfortable handling any particular split, move on to the next one.

Sometimes, you may think you've spotted an issue in the original sentence, but when you check the answers, all five are identical (for that specific issue). In that case, go look for something else.

In all of these scenarios, regardless of whether you spot an error in the original sentence, you'll always end up at the same next step: Compare the answers vertically, focusing on shorter "chunks" of the sentences to spot the differences. Use the splits to figure out your next steps.

There is one thing you do *not* want to do: Do not think about how you would rewrite the sentence yourself. There are many ways that a faulty sentence could be fixed, and you could waste a lot of time thinking of different ways to do so. Instead, let the splits drive your process.

## The SC Process

Here's a summary of the process:

### 1. Take a First Glance

Look for an early clue that will help orient you to the problem—similar to noticing a certain math symbol on a quant problem. Don't spend more than 5 to 10 seconds on this step.

Glance at the beginning of the underline. Notice the word (including punctuation marks) just before the underline and the first one to three words of the underline itself. Then, glance at the beginning of each answer choice to see how the beginning of the underlined text changes.

Most of the time, this will be enough to give you an early clue. If it's not, try one more place: the end of the underline. Then, go to step 2, even if you still haven't found any early clue (you won't find a hint 100 percent of the time).

### 2. Read the Sentence for Meaning

Read the entire original sentence. Don't get so focused on grammar that you forget to process the meaning of the sentence.

Jot down words (possibly abbreviated) when something jumps out at you as a possible issue. Don't actually try to decide anything about that issue yet—just note the possibilities.

### 3. Find a Starting Point

Start with anything that feels straightforward to you. Often, you will spot something in the original sentence that you feel comfortable evaluating; immediately check the splits in the answer choices to see what your options are to fix the issue.

Sometimes, you will not spot anything in the original sentence that you want to use; in this case, scan the answers vertically to find the differences.

Make your first decision—most of the time, this will be a choice between keeping or eliminating answer choice (A)—and then...

### 4. Eliminate All Incorrect Choices

Reuse your work! Check all of the remaining answers to see whether they have the same error (or a very similar one). On occasion, you can cross off all four wrong answers based on your first issue!

Most of the time, though, you will still have more than one answer remaining after you address your first issue.

### (As Needed) Repeat Steps 3 and 4

So, most of the time, you'll need another starting point. By this time, you will likely have spotted multiple potential issues to investigate. Don't review them in order. Choose whatever you think is easiest and repeat steps 3 and 4.

At some point, you'll either have one answer left (choose it—you're done!) or you'll have more than one answer left but you'll realize that you don't feel comfortable with any of the remaining splits. In the latter case, don't keep throwing time at this problem. Make the executive decision to pick an answer and move on. You'll likely have narrowed down your answers, so you'll be in position to make a strong guess.

## "Best" Does Not Mean Ideal

SC questions ask for the best option *among those given*, not the best option in the universe. Sometimes you may feel—rightly so—that all the answers, including the correct one, aren't very good. Correct GMAT SC answers never break strict grammatical rules, but these answers can seem formal or even awkward. Expect that, at times, a correct answer won't sound or feel very good to you—it will merely be the best *of the options given*.

## Sentence Correction Timing

In order to have adequate time for longer Reading Comprehension and Critical Reasoning questions, you'll need to average about 1 minute and 20 seconds per Sentence Correction problem. Some longer SCs might take up to 2 minutes, so you'll answer some SCs in a minute or less.

How can you possibly move that quickly and still reliably get the right answer? Here's how:

- Most wrong answers contain more than one error, but you only need one valid reason to cross off any wrong answer.
- The same error is often repeated in two or more choices.
- The SC process described earlier capitalizes on the first two points above to get you through the problem as efficiently as possible: Always work with whatever issue you find easiest, and when you do spot an error, eliminate as many answer choices as possible.

Although you have to work efficiently on SC, don't go so quickly that you make careless mistakes. Follow the process and you'll be able to work through the problem systematically, spending enough time but not too much.

If you're approaching the 2-minute mark, wrap up the problem. If you need longer than that to narrow down to one answer, chances are good that you're missing something and that this time would be better spent on another problem. Guess from among the remaining answers and move on.

In fact, if you can narrow it down to two answers, your 50-50 guess should barely be considered a guess. Because the GMAT is an adaptive test, you're only going to answer about 60 percent of Verbal questions correctly overall. Practically speaking, then, a 50 percent chance on any problem isn't bad; that's a legitimate answer on an adaptive test. Choose one of the remaining two answers and move forward with confidence.

## Using and Improving Your Ear for Sentence Correction

When answering practice questions, if you are *completely confident* that an answer is wrong (as in, you'd bet someone $20 that you're right!), even though you can't articulate exactly why, go ahead and cross that answer off. When you review your work, ask yourself which specific words in the sentence sound funny or incorrect. Then, see whether you can articulate what was really going on—and make this open book (you can look up anything you want in the SC unit of this guide or any of your other study materials). Finally, check the solution.

First, were you right that that answer was wrong? Second, was your reason valid? If both of those things are true, then your "ear" may already be accurate for this specific type of issue—and now you know how to check whether it is. (Of course, if you want to improve your performance in this area, then you are still going to need to learn more than you know right now about the grammar or meaning of this issue.)

If you discover that you were wrong*, though, then you will need to dive into the grammar or meaning issues in that area, including possibly learning some technical grammar terminology and rules. Think of this process as retraining your ear so that you get that issue right the next time you see it.

*Wrong* can mean two things. It could mean that you thought (B) was the right answer when it was really (C). It could also mean that you correctly chose answer (B) but that your reason for choosing (B) was faulty—so the next time you see a similar issue, you might get that problem wrong. If this happens, consider the problem "wrong" for study purposes; that is, there's something here that you definitely need to learn in order to get a similar problem right in the future.

The first two chapters of this guide cover strategy and overall lessons for SC, while subsequent chapters teach specific grammar and meaning concepts that you need to know for the GMAT. The next section of this chapter provides you with some techniques to hone your SC process. As you progress through the guide, return to the next section periodically to remind yourself how to drill the process in the context of the grammar that you're learning.

Beginning with Chapter 2, the end of each chapter contains a problem set that tests your skills. Try some of the problems now and save some for later review. After you complete each problem, check the answer. Whenever necessary, return to the lessons in the chapter to solidify your understanding before trying the next problem.

You can also use *Official Guide* problems published by the makers of the official test, to further hone both your SC process and your SC ear. (Note: The *Official Guide* is sold separately from this guide.)

## How to Get Better at the Sentence Correction Process

### First Glance

Your first glance at a problem is, by definition, quick and superficial. If you get good at this step, though, you can pick up some useful clues that will help you read the original sentence with an idea already in mind of one topic the sentence may be testing.

For SC, pay attention to three issues during your first glance:

| Clue | Possible Implication |
|---|---|
| 1. Is the underline very long? Very short? | Very long underlines often signal issues with sentence structure, meaning, modifiers, or parallelism. |
| | Very short underlines (less than five words) may lead you to compare the answers in full before reading the original sentence. |
| 2. What is the first underlined word? What is the word right before? | The nature of the first underlined word (or the word just before the underline) can give you a clue about one of the issues tested in the sentence. For example, if the word *has* is the first underlined word, the sentence is likely testing either subject–verb agreement or verb tense, since *has* is a verb. |
| 3. What are the differences among the first word or two of each answer choice? | There will always be at least one difference at the beginning of the answers (as well as one at the end). Glance at the first word or two of each answer. For example, if the first word switches between *has* and *have*, then you know the sentence is testing singular vs. plural. Now, you can actively look for the relevant subject when you go to step 2 and read the original sentence. |

After you've studied SC for a few weeks and tried some problems from the *Official Guide* material or other sources, add a first glance drill to your study regimen. Find some lower-numbered (easier) problems that you've already tried. Give yourself a few seconds (5 to 10 max!) to glance at a problem, then look away and say out loud what you noticed in those few seconds.

Afterwards, look at the full problem and remind yourself what it tests. Did your first glance unearth any of those issues? Examine the first underlined word, the one just before the underline, and the first one to three words of each choice more carefully, and ask yourself whether there are any clues, or markers, that you missed. If so, write them down on a flash card. Here's an example:

| (front) | (back) |
|---|---|
| When I see:<br><br>**and** | I'll think:<br><br>Parallelism: X and Y<br>X, Y, and Z<br><br>Could be: a list, a modifier, compound subject or verb, two independent clauses |

Sometimes, there are no good clues at the first glance level, so don't expect that this strategy will always help you. Still, don't skip this step; good clues exist for more than 50 percent of problems, so this quick step can be quite valuable.

## Read the Sentence for Meaning

Your default strategy is to read the entire original sentence all the way to the period, noting possible grammar or meaning issues along the way. The non-underlined portion contains valuable information that can help you decide how to proceed. Once you're done reading, decide which issue to tackle first. If you think you've spotted an error in the original, verify, then cross off answer (A) as well as any other answers that repeat that error.

You might, though, choose to break this strategy for one very good reason: You spot an early error in a longer underline and you are 100 percent sure that you've found an error. In that case, go ahead and eliminate choice (A) immediately, then glance through the remaining answers to eliminate any with that same error. At that point, though, return to the original sentence and finish reading it, keeping an eye out for any additional errors that you could use to eliminate other answers.

Either way, read the entire original sentence so that you can spot overall issues with meaning or sentence structure. If you don't, you'll be much more likely to fall into a trap.

To drill yourself on meaning, pull out your *Official Guide* again and look at some problems you've done in the past. Read only the original sentence (not the answers), then look away and try to articulate aloud, in your own words, what the sentence is trying to say. (You don't need to limit your rephrase to a single sentence.)

Do actually talk out loud. You'll be able to hear the conviction in your own voice when you know what the sentence is trying to say, and when you don't know what the sentence means, you'll also be able to hear that you're not sure.

In the latter case, examine the problem again. Either you just didn't understand it, or there was actually an issue with the meaning of that sentence. Which is it? Check the solution: Does it say that there is a meaning problem? If so, great! No wonder you had trouble rephrasing it. If not, then the explanation itself may help you understand what the sentence is trying to say. (If you find the official solution hard to follow, you can find Manhattan Prep solutions to *Official Guide* problems in our *GMAT Navigator* program.)

## Find a Starting Point

Most of the time, you'll have to find multiple starting points on SC problems—one of the annoying things about this problem type. There are two primary ways to find a starting point: 1) Read the original sentence and 2) compare answers.

To drill the latter skill, open up your *Official Guide* again and look at some problems you have done before. This time, do *not* read the original sentence. Instead, cover it up and go straight to the answers.

Compare the answers and, based on the splits that you spot, try to articulate all of the things that the problem might be testing.

You usually won't be able to pick the correct answer, but you can often tell *what* is being tested even when you can't tell *how* to answer. For example, you might see a verb switching back and forth between singular and plural. If the subject isn't underlined, then you can't know which verb form is required (because you haven't read the sentence!), but you do know that subject–verb agreement is an issue.

When you're done, read the full sentence or check the solution. How good were you at figuring out what the problem was testing? What clues did you miss? Consider making flash cards for those clues.

## Eliminate All Incorrect Choices

One of the most frustrating moments in SC problems is when you've narrowed down the answers to two…and then you don't know how to decide. When this happens to you, don't waste time going back and forth repeatedly, agonizing over the answers. Pick one of the two and move on.

Afterward, review the problem to learn how to make that choice. Add the following analysis to your overall review of SC problems:

1. Why are each of the four wrong answers wrong?

2. How would someone (mistakenly) justify *eliminating* the right answer? What is the trap that would lead someone to cross out the correct answer?

3. How would someone (mistakenly) justify *picking* any of the wrong answers? What is the trap that would lead someone to pick a wrong answer?

4. Why is the right answer right? (Mostly, it's right because it doesn't make any of the mistakes made in the four wrong answers. But if you were tempted to eliminate it for some reason, make sure you understand why that part was actually okay.)

When you learn how you (or someone) would fall into the trap of thinking that some wrong answer looks or sounds or feels better than the right one, you'll be a lot less likely to fall into that same trap yourself in the future. In other words, you're getting into the minds of the test writers and figuring out how to avoid the traps that they're setting for you.

Throughout this guide, you will encounter both wrong and right examples to teach you the precise differences:

| | |
|---|---|
| Wrong: | SINCE the company failed to meet its earnings forecast, CONSEQUENTLY the stock dropped as soon as the numbers were released. |
| Right: | SINCE the company failed to meet its earnings forecast, the stock dropped as soon as the numbers were released. |
| Right: | The company failed to meet its earnings forecast; CONSEQUENTLY, the stock dropped as soon as the numbers were released. |

Don't just glance over those examples. Cement the wrongness of the wrong options in your brain by saying aloud why they're wrong or adding a note:

| | |
|---|---|
| Wrong: | SINCE the company failed to meet its earnings forecast, CONSEQUENTLY the stock dropped as soon as the numbers were released. |

This is redundant! Use *since* or *consequently*, not both.

There are many steps to the SC process—and so there are many opportunities to learn to work more efficiently and effectively. As you complete subsequent SC chapters, return to this section to remind yourself how to hone your process as you increase your SC expertise.

Advanced material for the SC unit can be found in Atlas, your online learning platform, on the Manhattan Prep website. Use the online material only if you feel that you have mastered everything in the SC unit of this strategy guide and you are aiming for a Verbal section score of 42 or higher.

# Grammar and Meaning

## In This Chapter:

- Grammar: A Closer Look
- Meaning: A Closer Look
- Connect, or Match, the Words
- Say It Once: Avoid Redundancy
- Place Your Words
- Choose Your Words

**In this chapter, you will learn** how grammar and meaning work together on the GMAT, including the primary ways the GMAT will try to sneak errors past you.

# CHAPTER 2 Grammar and Meaning

Sentence Correction (SC) appears on the GMAT because business schools want to be sure that their admitted applicants grasp the two principles of good business writing:

1. **Grammar:** Does the sentence adhere to the rules of standard written English?

2. **Meaning:** Does the sentence clearly indicate the author's intended meaning?

These principles are equally important and actually overlap quite a bit. Certain grammar rules exist in order to convey a logical and unambiguous meaning. You'll learn some of these principles in this chapter and others as you work your way through the SC unit.

**Grammar:** Much of the language that you hear in everyday speech actually violates one rule or another. The GMAT tests your ability to distinguish between good and bad grammar, even when the bad grammar seems natural.

Consider this example: *As a long-time member of this team, it's really gratifying that we won the championship.* You likely hear similar sentences all the time, but the sentence actually violates the rules of standard written English. It should read: *As a long-time member of this team, I am really gratified that we won the championship.* You'll learn why later in this unit.

**Meaning:** Confusing writing is bad writing. If you have to read a sentence more than once to figure out what the author is saying—or if the sentence lends itself to multiple interpretations—it is not a good sentence.

What about the often-cited principle of concision? It is true that the GMAT does not like to waste words. If an idea expressed in 10 words can be expressed clearly and grammatically in 6, the GMAT prefers 6. However, this is a *preference*, not a rule.

Often, test-takers focus far too much on concision. As a result, the GMAT often makes the right answer *less* concise than an attractive wrong answer. Furthermore, *Official Guide* explanations often label a sentence *wordy* or *awkward* without additional explanation. In fact, these sentences have a meaning problem or an idiom error—but the explanation does not spell out the specific issue. In general, focus your efforts on grammar and meaning; ignore concision by itself.

## Grammar: A Closer Look

This unit will steer you through the major points of standard written English on the GMAT. Each chapter presents a major grammatical topic in depth: sentence structure, modifiers, parallelism, comparisons, pronouns, verbs, and idioms. You will learn the overarching principles of each grammatical topic. You will also learn the nitty-gritty details that will help you differentiate both correct grammar from poor grammar and clear and logical meaning from ambiguous or illogical meaning. In addition, you will complete practice exercises designed to hone your skills in the various topics.

2

For your reference, a glossary of common grammatical terms appears in Appendix B of this guide. Do not be overly concerned with memorizing the names of the grammatical terms, as the GMAT will never require you to know what the rules are called. Focus on understanding and applying these rules—that's what really matters. In fact, when the formal grammar term is obscure, this guide may substitute a made-up name, abbreviation, or nickname that will be easier to remember.

One more thing: For every grammar rule, there is an exception to the rule. This can be really annoying when you're studying grammar! The rules you will learn are valid in more than 90 percent of cases, so you really can rely on them. Every now and then, however, you'll run across an exception. If the exception is discussed in this guide, make an effort to remember it. If the exception is not mentioned in this guide (but you still see it in an *Official Guide* problem), we made the judgment that the exception is rare enough that learning it is not a good return on your investment. If SC is a stronger area for you, feel free to memorize such exceptions as you see them; if SC is not a strength, it's probably better to shrug and let that issue go. You don't need to get everything right to get a good score.

## The Five Grammar Terms You Need to Know

We try to keep fancy terms to a minimum in this book, but there's no way to discuss grammar without using at least a few actual grammar terms. Here are the five terms you absolutely need to know:

### 1. Clause

A **Clause** is a set of words that contains a subject and a working verb. Here is an example of a clause:

> She applied for the job.

|  |  |
|---|---|
| *She* | *applied* |
| Who applied for the job? She did. | What did she do? She applied. |

*She* is the **Subject** because she is the one performing the action. *Applied* is the **Working Verb** because it describes what the subject did. For any sentence, you could ask, "Who (or what) did what?" and the (correct) answer will point to the subject and working verb.

Together, the subject and working verb create a complete, stand-alone sentence, or an **Independent Clause**. Independent clauses have, at the very least, a subject and a working verb. Every correct sentence must have at least one independent clause.

More complex sentences will also include something else: a second independent clause, a dependent clause, or other modifiers.

A **Dependent Clause** also contains a verb but cannot stand alone as a sentence:

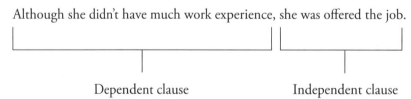

Although she didn't have much work experience, she was offered the job.

| Dependent clause | Independent clause |

Only the second part of that sentence is independent: *She was offered the job.*

If you took just the first part by itself, you'd have a **Sentence Fragment**: *Although she didn't have much work experience.*

A sentence fragment is not a complete sentence. On the GMAT, the correct answer is always a complete sentence; if you spot a sentence fragment, cross off that answer.

You'll learn more about clauses in the Sentence Structure chapter of this unit.

## 2. Modifier

A **Modifier** provides additional information in a sentence, beyond the core subject and verb. The simplest example is an adjective. For example, in the phrase *the happy child*, the word *happy* is an adjective, modifying (or describing) the word *child*.

Modifiers can also be more complex:

> The large dog, which has black fur, is a Labrador.

The modifier *which has black fur* is called a **Nonessential Modifier**. If you remove it from the sentence, the core of the sentence still makes sense: The large dog is a Labrador.

Compare that to this sentence:

> The job that she started last week is much harder than her previous job.

In this sentence, *that she started last week* is called an **Essential Modifier**. Why is this one essential? Look what happens when you remove it from the sentence:

> The job is much harder than her previous job.

Which *job*? Her current job? Someone else's job? If you haven't already specified a particular job, then the meaning of the sentence is ambiguous. This is why *that she started last week* is an essential modifier: The modifier is necessary in order to understand the meaning of the core sentence.

You can find a full discussion of essential and nonessential modifiers in Chapter 4.

## 3. Sentence Core

The **Core** of a sentence consists of any independent clauses along with some essential modifiers. This is the bare minimum needed in order to have a coherent sentence.

Remember this sentence?

> Although she didn't have much work experience, she was offered the job.

The core sentence is *she was offered the job*. The part before the comma is a modifier—it's providing additional information about the core of the sentence. If you take that part out, you can still understand the basic meaning of the core (she got the job!), so this is a nonessential modifier. When you're looking for the core of the sentence, you can ignore any nonessential modifiers.

You'll learn more about the sentence core in the Sentence Structure and Modifiers chapters.

**4. Conjunction**

**Conjunctions** are words that help stick parts of sentences together. Here's an example:

> He worked hard, **and** a raise was his reward.

Coordinating conjunctions, or **Co-Conjunctions**, such as *and*, can glue two independent clauses together (among other things). Both *he worked hard* and *a raise was his reward* are independent clauses because each one can function as an independent sentence: He worked hard. A raise was his reward. Co-conjunctions connect two parts of a sentence that are at the same level or serve the same function (hence, the prefix *co*).

The most common co-conjunctions are the FANBOYS: *for, and, nor, but, or, yet, so.*

Modifiers can be connected to independent clauses by subordinating conjunctions, or **Sub-Conjunctions**. This is an example:

> **Although** she didn't have much work experience, she was offered the job.

The word *although* is a sub-conjunction. Other examples include *because, while, though, unless, before, after,* and *if.* Sub-conjunctions start a subordinate clause; the clause has a subject and verb but it cannot stand alone as its own sentence. As a result, these sub-clauses must be connected to an independent clause in order for you to have a valid sentence.

You'll learn more about conjunctions in the Sentence Structure and Modifiers chapters of this unit.

**5. Marker**

This one is not a grammar term, but it is important. A **Marker** is a clue that a certain grammatical topic is being tested. As you work through this unit, you will learn about various kinds of markers. For example, the word *unlike* is a comparison marker; when you see *unlike*, ask yourself what comparison is being made.

Let's say you read an explanation and think, "Hmm, I didn't know that that word was a marker for that topic." Immediately write that marker down! Keep a list, make flash cards, record it however you prefer— but do record the fact that when you see this particular marker, you should think about a particular grammar issue.

That's your quick-start grammar guide. (Yes, technically, we did sneak more than five terms into that list. The "extra" terms are all related, though.)

If you run across other unfamiliar terms, look them up in the glossary at the end of this guide.

# Meaning: A Closer Look

For a sentence to be considered correct on the GMAT, it must be logical and unambiguous. If a choice is illogical or has more than one reasonable interpretation, cross it off. Consider this example:

> Tomorrow, she bought some milk.

This sentence doesn't violate any grammar rule, but it doesn't make any sense! Either she bought the milk in the past or she will buy the milk in the future. You know the sentence is wrong because the *meaning is illogical.*

Try another example:

> Animation filmmaker Hayao Miyazaki is arguably more famous than any animation filmmaker in the history of the art.

This sentence may appear to be just fine—in the real world, it probably would be—but there's something illogical about it. Miyazaki cannot be more famous than *any* animation filmmaker, because Miyazaki is himself a member of the group of animation filmmakers. The sentence currently says that he is more famous than anyone in a group that *includes himself.* Someone could claim that he is more famous than any *other* animation filmmaker, but not *all* animation filmmakers (including himself).

Consider this sentence:

> Falsehoods can be exposed using a polygraph device by a law enforcement professional.

Again, this sentence would probably be fine in the real world. Technically, though, the last part of the sentence is ambiguous: Was the *device* created *by a law enforcement professional?* Or can the falsehoods be exposed *by a law enforcement professional?* Remove the ambiguity by restructuring the sentence. Here's one possibility:

> Falsehoods can be exposed by a law enforcement professional using a polygraph device.

Now, the meaning is unambiguous: The law enforcement professional uses the device to expose the lie.

If the original sentence is confusing in some way, you will need to determine a logical and unambiguous meaning—but you don't have to come up with your own sentence from thin air! The possible answers will be sitting right in front of you, and they will help guide you to the proper meaning.

Most meaning issues fall into one of three major categories:

1.  Words or phrases don't properly *match* in meaning (e.g., Yesterday she will buy milk).

2.  Words are *redundant* (e.g., She loves movies, and she's a big fan of indie films in addition).

3.  Words are in the wrong *place* (e.g., She tended to the gardens daily vs. She tended to the daily gardens).

## Connect, or Match, the Words

Most sentences contain multiple words or groups of words that must connect, or match, in some way. For example, a singular subject must be paired with a singular verb in order to be grammatically correct. This requirement to pair certain words or phrases can also impact meaning; as you saw in an example earlier in this chapter, a verb tense must match the time frame of the overall sentence.

What's wrong with the following comparison?

> Unlike northern Canada, where the winter is quite cold, the temperature in Florida rarely goes below freezing.

Though it's probably clear that the author is trying to say that northern Canada and Florida are dissimilar, technically the sentence says that *Canada* and the *temperature* (in Florida) are dissimilar. It's illogical to compare a geographic location to the *temperature* in a different location.

A similar matching principle holds for other grammatical connections (e.g., pronouns and the nouns to which they refer). Future chapters will explore each type of connection in turn; for now, remember to test the *meaning* of any potential connection. Connected words must always make sense together.

# Say It Once: Avoid Redundancy

Another aspect of meaning is redundancy. Each word in the correct choice plays some important role in the overall meaning of the sentence—but you don't need to say something twice. Redundancy can actually confuse the meaning, causing the reader to ask: Did I read that right? Is the author trying to say something other than what I first thought the sentence was trying to say?

A common redundancy trap on the GMAT is the use of two words or phrases that convey the same meaning:

| | |
|---|---|
| Wrong: | The value of the stock ROSE by a 10 percent INCREASE. |
| Right: | The value of the stock INCREASED by 10 percent. |
| Right: | The value of the stock ROSE by 10 percent. |

Since *rose* and *increase* both imply growth, only one is needed. Here's another example:

| | |
|---|---|
| Wrong: | The three prices SUM to a TOTAL of $11.56. |
| Right: | The three prices SUM to $11.56. |
| Right: | The three prices TOTAL $11.56. |

Pay attention to expressions of time. It is easy to sneak two redundant time expressions into an answer choice (especially if one expression is in the non-underlined part, or if the two expressions do not look like each other):

| | | | | |
|---|---|---|---|---|
| Past: | Previously | Formerly | In the past | Before now |
| Present: | Now | Currently | Presently | At present |
| Yearly: | Annual | Each year | A year (e.g., *three product launches a year*) | |

If a sentence includes more than one time marker from the same category, check for redundancy:

| | |
|---|---|
| Wrong: | AT PRESENT, the customer service department is NOW in the process of analyzing complaints. |
| Right: | AT PRESENT, the customer service department is in the process of analyzing complaints. |
| Right: | The customer service department is NOW in the process of analyzing complaints. |

In the wrong example, *at present* and *now* are referring to the same action (*in the process of analyzing*), so it is redundant to use both time markers.

It is possible for there to be a valid reason to introduce a second time marker from the same category. For example:

| | |
|---|---|
| Right: | AT PRESENT, the customer service department is in the process of analyzing complaints to determine how customer satisfaction has changed from last year until NOW. |

In the final correct example, there are two present-tense time markers, but they are serving different functions. The first one indicates what the department is doing at the moment; the second one contrasts two different time frames (*last year* and *now*).

Also pay attention to transition words, such as contrast words. What is wrong with the sentence below?

> Although she studied night and day for three months, yet she did not do well on her exam.

The word *although* already conveys the coming contrast; it is redundant to introduce the contrast a second time with the word *yet*.

Throughout this unit, you will see additional examples of redundant language.

## Place Your Words

Another common meaning issue has to do with where words are placed in a sentence. If you see that words are moving from one position to another in different answer choices, check the sentence for meaning issues.

The placement of a single word can alter the entire meaning of a sentence. For example:

> ALL the children are covered in mud.

> The children are ALL covered in mud.

In these sentences, changing the placement of *all* shifts the intent from *how many* children are covered in mud (all of them) to *how* the children are covered in mud (they have mud all over themselves). Consider another example:

> ONLY the council votes on Thursdays.

> The council votes ONLY on Thursdays.

In the first sentence, *only* indicates that the council alone votes on Thursdays (as opposed to the board, perhaps, which can vote any other day, but not Thursdays). According to that first sentence, the council could also vote any other day of the week. In the second sentence, however, the placement of *only* indicates that the council cannot vote on any day except for Thursday.

When a word changes its position in the answer choices, consider whether the change has an impact on the meaning of the sentence. Look out for short words (such as *only* and *all*) that quantify nouns or otherwise restrict meaning.

At a broader level, pay attention to overall word order. All of the words in a sentence could be well-chosen, but the sentence could still be awkward or ambiguous. For example:

> The council granted the right to make legal petitions TO CITY OFFICIALS.

What does the phrase *to city officials* mean? Did the city officials receive the right to make legal petitions? Or, did someone else receive the right to make petitions *to the officials*? Either way, the correct sentence should resolve the ambiguity:

> The council granted CITY OFFICIALS the right to make legal petitions.

> OR

> The right to make legal petitions TO CITY OFFICIALS was granted by the council.

You will learn more about how word placement affects meaning throughout the rest of this unit.

## Choose Your Words

The GMAT doesn't explicitly test vocabulary, but on occasion, it may try to set a trap based on word choice.

An SC problem might try to mix up a particular word and its cousin. For example:

> My decision to drive a hybrid car was motivated by ECONOMIC considerations.

> ECONOMICAL considerations motivated my decision to drive a hybrid car.

**2**

The second sentence, which is shorter and in active voice, may sound preferable. Unfortunately, it is wrong! *Economical* means "thrifty, efficient." Notice that this meaning is not too distant from what the author intends to say: He or she wants an efficient automobile. But the appropriate phrase is *economic considerations*—that is, *monetary* considerations.

Consider the following pairs of "cousin" words and expressions, together with their distinct meanings:

> *aggravate* (worsen) vs. *aggravating* (irritating)

> *known as* (named) vs. *known to be* (acknowledged as) vs. *known for* (famous for a particular thing)

> *loss of* (no longer in possession of) vs. *loss in* (decline in value)

> *mandate* (command) vs. *have a mandate* (have authority from voters)

> *native of* (person from) vs. *native to* (species that originated in)

> *range of* (variety of) vs. *ranging* (varying)

> *rate of* (speed or frequency of) vs. *rates for* (prices for)

> *rise* (general increase) vs. *raise* (a bet or a salary increase in American English)

> *try to do* (seek to accomplish) vs. *try doing* (experiment with)

Some of these pairings are examples of idioms that can have different meanings depending upon the small word attached to the "main" word. For example:

> Charles "Buddy" Bolden, known as King Bolden, is considered one of the founders of jazz and was known for his improvisational skills and for combining elements from ragtime, blues, and gospel.

Bolden's nickname was King Bolden; he was *known as* this name; it would be incorrect to say he was *known for* this name. Similarly, he was *known for* certain musical traits; it would be incorrect to say he was *known as* these traits.

The list above is not comprehensive; English has plenty of pairs of cousin words whose meanings depend on context and the surrounding words. You'll learn more as you work your way through this unit, but if you run across unfamiliar examples in *Official Guide* problems, jot them down on a flash card.

# Problem Set

In this chapter, you learned to avoid redundancy that muddles the meaning. In problems 1–4, circle the pair or pairs of redundant words.

1. Though canals have experienced a severe decline in barge traffic over the past several decades, yet with the rise in fuel costs, "shipping" by actual ships may once again become an important means of exporting goods outside the country.

2. After the test format was changed, scores subsequently dropped by more than a 25 percent decrease.

3. It is possible that the earthquake may have caused the building's collapse.

4. The retail sector has shrunk by a staggering margin each of the past five years, posting annual losses of at least 5 percent or more compared with the previous year.

Problems 5–7 are multiple choice with one correct answer. As on the real GMAT, answer (A) repeats the original sentence. Unlike the real GMAT, though, these problems have only two answer choices. Keep an eye out for issues with meaning discussed in this chapter.

5. No matter how much work it may require, getting an MBA is an investment that pays off for most people.

    (A) No matter how much work it may require

    (B) Though it does not require much work

6. Many people believe that crime is on the rise but that, despite what is depicted on television, crime is actually at its lowest rate in decades.

    (A) Many people believe that crime is on the rise but that, despite what is depicted on television, crime is actually at its lowest rate in decades.

    (B) Contrary to what many people believe and what is depicted on television, crime is at its lowest rate in decades.

7.  Rising costs of raw materials may result in <u>fewer employees on the assembly line or product volume</u>.

    (A)  fewer employees on the assembly line or product volume

    (B)  a decrease in product volume or the number of employees on the assembly line

**2**

In this chapter, you learned about the importance of word placement as it relates to meaning. Modifiers, which you'll learn more about later, can completely change the meaning of the sentence as they move around. For example, these two sentences have very different meanings: 1) *Only* Ashanti plays tennis; 2) Ashanti plays *only* tennis.

8.  In how many different places could you add the word *nearly* to the following sentence? How does the meaning change with each placement?

    The car did a 360-degree turn as it rolled off the track, colliding with some of the one thousand bystanders who had gathered to watch the race.

9.  In how many different places could you add the phrase *in the first half* to the following sentence? How does the meaning change with each placement?

    The offense played well, and they showed significant progress even after they fell behind 23–0.

# Solutions

1. ⟨Though⟩ canals have experienced a severe decline in barge traffic over the past several decades, ⟨yet⟩ with the rise in fuel costs, "shipping" by actual ships may once again become an important means of ⟨exporting⟩ goods ⟨outside the country.⟩

   Using two contrast words such as *though* and *yet* is redundant. In this case, it is preferable to keep *yet* in order to delineate the contrast clearly; otherwise, a reader might mistakenly consider the phrase *with the rise of fuel costs* to be part of the first clause.

   *Export* means "to send goods *outside the country*"; using these phrases together is redundant.

2. ⟨After⟩ the test format was changed, scores ⟨subsequently⟩ ⟨dropped⟩ by more than a 25 percent ⟨decrease.⟩

   The words *after* and *subsequently* convey the same idea. Similarly, you do not need both *dropped* and *decrease.*

3. It is ⟨possible⟩ that the earthquake ⟨may⟩ have caused the building's collapse.

   *It is possible that* and *may* both express the same level of uncertainty, so you can remove one of them without changing the intended meaning.

4. Sales for many stores in the retail sector have shrunk by staggering margins ⟨each of the past five years⟩, posting ⟨annual⟩ losses of ⟨at least⟩ 5 percent or ⟨more⟩ compared with the previous year.

   *Each of the past five years* describes something that happens each year for a certain period of time. The word *annual* conveys part of that same meaning: Something happens each year. Since the word *annual* by itself does not also convey the idea of a five-year period, it would be preferable to drop this word from the sentence.

   *At least 5 percent* and *5 percent or more* both express the same idea, so you can remove one of them without changing the intended meaning.

5. **(A):** The original sentence indicates that getting an MBA might be a lot of work, but it still turns out to be a good investment for most people. Answer (B) loses this contrasting idea: Getting an MBA is not a lot of work, *though* (or *but*) it still turns out to be a good investment. It would be more logical to connect two positives with *and*, not the contrast word *though*: It's not a lot of work *and* it's a good investment.

6. **(B):** The original sentence indicates that people believe two things: 1) Crime is on the rise and 2) crime is at its lowest rate in decades. These two ideas are contradictory. While people can certainly believe contradictory things, if the sentence had intended to convey that meaning, it would have connected the two ideas with the word *and*. Instead, it uses the word *but*, signaling a different intended meaning: People believe one thing, but the opposite is actually true. Eliminate choice (A) for meaning issues.

   Choice (B) provides a logical and clear meaning: *Contrary* to popular belief, *crime is at its lowest rate* in a long time.

7. **(B):** The original sentence contains a subtle error; many people, in fact, will prefer answer (A) because it is more concise than (B). Try to avoid using concision to make your choice.

Logically, the sentence is trying to convey two things that may result from rising costs: 1) The company will employ *fewer employees* or 2) the company will have to reduce *product volume*. The original sentence can be read in one of two ways. First, *rising costs…may result in…product volume*. This is illogical; the rising costs should result in some *change* in product volume. Second, *rising costs…may result in fewer…product volume*. This is an error; *product volume* is an uncountable noun, so it would have to be paired with an uncountable modifier (e.g., *lower product volume*). Either way, the original sentence is incorrect. You can learn more about countable and uncountable nouns in the Modifiers chapter.

8. There are (at least!) six different meanings that can be created by moving the word *nearly* around in the sentence:

   1. The car *nearly* did a 360-degree turn. The car came close to starting to spin, but it did not actually spin.

   2. The car did a *nearly* 360-degree turn. The car turned almost a full circle, but not quite.

   3. …as it *nearly* rolled off the track. The car almost started rolling, but it didn't actually roll.

   4. …as it rolled *nearly* off the track. The car did roll, and it rolled so far that it almost went off the track.

   5. …off the track, *nearly* colliding with some…bystanders. The car came very close to the bystanders, but did not collide with them (thankfully!).

   6. …some of the *nearly* one thousand bystanders. There were almost—but not quite!—one thousand bystanders at the track.

9. There are (at least) three different meanings that can be created by moving the words *in the first half* around in the sentence:

   1. *In the first half*, the offense played well. The offense played well *in the first half*. In both of these cases, the offense played well specifically for the first half of the game. It's not clear whether the action in the second part of the sentence (*showed significant progress…*) occurred in the first half or the second half.

   2. …showed significant progress *in the first half*. The offense now appears to have played well for the entire game. The offense showed significant progress specifically during *the first half* of that game, which is also when they fell behind 23–0.

   3. …they fell behind 23–0 *in the first half*. The offense played well for the entire game. The score was 23–0 at some point during the first half. Sometime after that, the offense showed significant progress, though it's not clear whether this was during the first half or the second (or both).

In all of these cases, the time marker *in the first half* indicates when a particular action took place. The placement of a time marker can significantly change the meaning of a sentence because it changes when a specific event occurs.

# CHAPTER 3

# Sentence Structure

## In This Chapter:

- Subject and Verb Must Both Exist
- Subject and Verb Must Agree in Number
- Eliminate the Middlemen and Skip the Warm-Up
- Use Structure to Decide
- Mid-Chapter Quiz: Test Your Skills
- The Sentence Core
- Two Independent Clauses
- Adding Modifiers

**In this chapter, you will learn** about core sentence structures, from the elements required in a valid sentence structure to the ways the GMAT attempts to camouflage sentences with invalid structure. You'll learn about complex sentence structures, subject–verb agreement, and punctuation, among other topics.

# CHAPTER 3 **Sentence Structure**

Every sentence must have a **Subject** and a **Verb**. The subject is the noun that performs the action expressed by the verb:

The DOG with the gray ears RUNS out of the house.

|                                         |

Subject                    Verb

The subject, the *dog*, performs the action of *running*. The subject and the verb must agree in number: In this case, both *dog* and *runs* are singular.

How does the GMAT make things more complicated?

## Subject and Verb Must Both Exist

If a sentence is missing the subject or the verb, the sentence is a **Fragment**; in other words, it is not a complete sentence. On the GMAT, the correct answer must be a complete sentence, or **Independent Clause**. (The previous chapter introduced independent clauses; if you skipped or skimmed that chapter, go take a look now.)

The GMAT might disguise the error by dropping the verb:

      Wrong:    The cat sitting by the stairs.

Wait a minute, what about *sitting*? *Sitting* certainly looks like a verb. It is not, however, a **Working Verb**, a verb that can run a sentence by itself. Here's an example of a working verb:

      Right:    The cat sitting by the stairs WATCHED the mouse.

In this sentence, the word *watched* is a working verb. Here's another example of a working verb:

      Right:    The cat WAS SITTING by the stairs.

In this sentence, the words *was sitting* make up the full verb form. The word *sitting* is called a **Present Participle** and you'll see more of these *–ing* words throughout this book. For now, just remember that an *–ing* word is only a verb when it is preceded by a helping verb such as *is*, *was*, *will be*, and so on. *The cat sitting by the stairs* is not a complete sentence.

These are also not complete sentences:

      Wrong:    BECAUSE the dog was never mine.

      Wrong:    WHICH will be approved tomorrow.

*Because* and *which* are connecting words. They add extra information to a sentence, but they are not sentences by themselves. They're examples of **Modifiers**, which you will learn about in the next chapter.

The correct answer must contain at least one independent clause; if an answer choice does not, eliminate it!

# Subject and Verb Must Agree in Number

A singular subject requires a singular verb form:

> The <u>dog runs</u> out of the house.

A plural subject requires a plural verb form:

> The <u>dogs run</u> out of the house.

You already know this; you would never write *the dog run out* or *the dogs runs out*. The GMAT, therefore, has to try to obscure these errors to get people to fall into a trap.

How? The GMAT might hide the subject so that you are unsure whether the subject is singular or plural. If you do not know the number of the subject, then you will not be able to select the verb form that agrees with it. Consider this example:

> The discovery of new medicines (was/were) vital to the company's growth.

What is the subject, *discovery* or *new medicines*? If you ask yourself, "What is/are vital to the company's growth?" you may be able to talk yourself into either choice. It makes as much sense to say the *discovery was vital* as it does to say the *new medicines were vital*.

In this case, *the discovery…was* is the correct subject–verb pair because the noun *medicines* is part of the **Prepositional Phrase** *of new medicines*. A noun in a prepositional phrase will *not* be the subject of the sentence. Note: There is an exception here, which you'll learn about in the advanced material associated with this chapter (located online in your Atlas learning platform). This is an example of one of those "for every grammar rule, there is an exception" cases mentioned earlier in this guide.

The plural *medicines* is a trap; the test writer deliberately inserts a noun that is both physically closer to the verb and the opposite in number from the actual subject, just hoping to catch you. Train yourself not to rely on physical proximity when finding the subject; check the actual sentence structure.

Are these sentences both correct?

> Lin and Guy drive to work.

> Lin, as well as Guy, drive to work every day.

The first sentence is a correct example of a **Compound Subject**: Lin and Guy together function as the subject of the sentence. Compound subjects are always plural because at least two nouns function together as the subject.

A compound subject *must* be connected by the word *and*, but the second sentence uses the modifier *as well as Guy*. This sentence, as written earlier, is incorrect because only Lin qualifies as the subject. It should read:

Right:     LIN, as well as Guy, <u>drives</u> to work every day.

             Subject   Modifier     Verb

A sentence can also contain a **Compound Verb** (two or more verbs that all point to the same subject). For example:

Right:    Lin *drove* to work *and said* hello to his coworker.

    Subject  Verb    Conjunction    Verb

Right:    Lin and Guy *drive* to work together every morning *and greet* their coworkers cheerfully.

    Subject   Conjunction  Subject   Verb        Conjunction   Verb

That last sentence contains both a compound subject (*Lin and Guy*) and a compound verb (*drive and greet*). If the writer inserts enough distance between the two portions of a compound subject or verb, it could be easy to make a mistake. Read on to learn how the GMAT does this.

# Eliminate the Middlemen and Skip the Warm-Up

The most common way to hide a subject is to insert words between the subject and the verb; we call these words the **Middlemen**. If you learn to ignore these words when looking for a subject, you'll be much less likely to pick the wrong noun as the subject.

To further obscure things, the GMAT often puts a significant number of words in front of the subject. In these cases, you have to ignore the **Warm-Up** that comes before the subject of the sentence.

There are a few common types of middlemen and warm-ups.

### 1. Prepositional Phrases

A prepositional phrase (or prep phrase, for short) is a group of words headed by a **Preposition**. For example:

| | | |
|---|---|---|
| <u>of</u> mice | <u>for</u> milk | <u>by</u> 1800 |
| <u>in</u> Zambia | <u>with</u> her | <u>at</u> that level |
| <u>to</u> the store | <u>on</u> their orders | <u>from</u> the office |

The underlined prepositions are among the most common in the English language. A list of common prepositions is included in the Glossary at the end of this guide. If you think something is a preposition but you're not sure, try making a prep phrase with *the house*:

| | |
|---|---|
| dig <u>under</u> the house | fly <u>over</u> the house |
| the car <u>by</u> the house | walk <u>to</u> the house |

Prepositions are followed by nouns or pronouns, which complete the phrase. Prep phrases modify or describe other parts of the sentence. A noun in a prep phrase will not be the main subject of the sentence. For example:

Near Galway, the houses on the road to Spiddle is/are gorgeous.

~~Near Galway~~, the HOUSES ~~on the road to Spiddle~~ ARE gorgeous.

In the example above, the subject is *houses* (plural) and the correct verb is *are* (also plural).

### 2. Dependent Clauses

Dependent clauses, which begin with connecting words such as *while* or *because*, cannot stand alone as sentences. They do not contain the main subject or main verb; rather, they are always attached to independent clauses. Look back at the first sentence in this paragraph: Can you find the dependent clause? (Hint: Examine the commas.)

> The dependent clause: which begin with connecting words such as *while* or *because*

> The independent clause: Dependent clauses cannot stand alone as sentences.

If a dependent clause is stripped out of a sentence, what remains is still a complete sentence.

Try another example:

> Because she studied hard, she earned a good score on the test.

What is the dependent clause? What is the independent clause (complete sentence)?

> Dependent: Because she studied hard

> Independent: She earned a good score on the test.

### 3. Other Modifiers

Other words can also function as modifiers, which add extra information to the sentence. Modifiers will be covered in depth in the next chapter.

## Use Structure to Decide

Consider the following sentence:

> In the waning days of the emperor's life, the conquest of new lands on the borders of the empire was/were considered vital.

To find the subject of the verb *was* or *were considered*, you might be tempted to ask yourself, "What *was* or *were considered* vital?" This method will get rid of obviously inappropriate subjects, such as *the emperor's life* or *the waning days*, but you could fall into the trap of thinking that *new lands* is the subject. However, *new lands* is in a prep phrase modifying the noun *conquest*. Since a noun in a prep phrase cannot be the subject of the sentence (with very limited exceptions that you'll learn about later), the subject must be *conquest*:

> Wrong:   ~~In the waning days of the emperor's life,~~ the CONQUEST ~~of new lands~~
>
> ~~on the borders of the empire~~ WERE CONSIDERED vital.

> Right:   ~~In the waning days of the emperor's life,~~ the CONQUEST ~~of new lands~~
>
> ~~on the borders of the empire~~ WAS CONSIDERED vital.

Certain tempting nouns, such as *new lands*, will be inserted purposely to distract you. Use the structure of the sentence to eliminate the middlemen and find the subject.

Now consider this example:

> The tidal forces to which an object falling into a black hole is/are subjected is/are sufficient to tear the object apart.

You have to match up two subject–verb pairs in this one. First, find the main subject and match it with the appropriate verb:

Better:     The tidal FORCES ~~to which an object falling into a black hole is/are~~ ~~subjected~~ ARE sufficient to tear the object apart.

Next, match up the subject and the verb in the dependent clause:

Right:     The tidal forces to which an OBJECT ~~falling into a black hole~~ IS SUBJECTED are sufficient to tear the object apart.

# Mid-Chapter Quiz: Test Your Skills

The following problems are multiple choice with one correct answer. As on the real GMAT, answer (A) repeats the original sentence. Unlike the real GMAT, though, these problems have only two answer choices. Keep an eye out for issues with sentence structure, discussed in this chapter.

When you're done, you may want to pause for a day or two to let this material sink in before you continue with the second half of this chapter.

1. The recent string of burglaries, in addition to poor building maintenance, have inspired the outspoken resident to call a tenants' meeting.

    (A)  The recent string of burglaries, in addition to poor building maintenance, have

    (B)  Recently, the string of burglaries, along with the poor building maintenance, has

2. The computer science instructor assigned a new textbook focused on recent advances in artificial intelligence.

    (A)  The computer science instructor assigned a new textbook focused on recent advances in artificial intelligence.

    (B)  A new textbook that is focused on recent advances in artificial intelligence assigned by our instructor.

3. Some of the earliest computer games designed to involve many players at once and first developed before the widespread availability of high-speed internet connections.

    (A)  Some of the earliest computer games designed to involve many players at once and first developed before the widespread availability of high-speed internet connections.

    (B)  First developed before the widespread availability of high-speed internet connections, some of the earliest computer games were designed to involve many players at once.

1. **(B):** Properly identifying the subject of this sentence can be tricky; remember to eliminate the middlemen!

   *The recent string ~~of burglaries, in addition to poor building maintenance~~, have…*

   The subject of the sentence is *string*, which is singular. Since the subject and verb must agree in number, the singular *has* is correct.

2. **(A):** The original sentence contains a correct subject (*instructor*) and verb (*assigned*) pair.

   In choice (B), however, the only verb (*is*) lies within a dependent clause (*that…intelligence*); no main verb exists, so this sentence structure is a fragment. The sentence could be fixed by adding *was* before *assigned* to turn that modifier into a working verb (*a textbook…was assigned*). You'll learn more about modifiers in the next chapter.

3. **(B):** Similar to choice (B) in question 2, answer (A) contains participles (*designed* and *developed*) that masquerade as verbs but are actually modifiers. There's no main verb at all in answer (A), so this sentence is a fragment. Choice (B) fixes this mistake by using the main verb *were designed*.

# The Sentence Core

SC sentences can be very complex, so it is useful to learn how to strip out the extraneous text (mentally, since you can't write on the test screen) and get yourself down to the sentence core. You've already started to learn how to do this by stripping out middlemen and skipping the warm-up.

The core sentence consists of at least the main subject and verb—but more complex sentences, such as the ones found in SC, can have a lot more going on in the core. Take a look at this example:

> Despite some initial concerns, the teacher is confident that her students mastered the lesson.

The core structure of the sentence is this:

> The teacher is confident that her students mastered the lesson.
>
> Subject     Verb     THAT     Subject     Verb     Object

When the word *that* appears just after a working verb, it often acts as a reset button in the sentence: A new subject–verb(–object) structure will follow. When this occurs, both subject–verb pairs are part of the core sentence. (Not every sentence has an object.)

Note: The word *that* can also serve other roles, which you'll learn about throughout this guide.

In the real world, people will often drop the word *that* from the sentence structure:

> Wrong on the GMAT:     The teacher is confident her students mastered the lesson.

This is acceptable in the real world, but it doesn't follow the strictest grammar conventions. Technically, the missing *that* can make the sentence ambiguous or confusing; consider these sentences:

| Right: | I know Lupita Nyong'o, who won an Academy Award for her role in *12 Years a Slave*. |
|---|---|
| Wrong on the GMAT: | I know Lupita Nyong'o, who won an Academy Award for her role in *12 Years a Slave*, was born in Mexico City. |
| Right: | I know that Lupita Nyong'o, who won an Academy Award for her role in *12 Years a Slave*, was born in Mexico City. |

Someone reading the middle sentence will initially think that you personally know Ms. Nyong'o. That reader will only realize much later in the sentence that you are trying to say that you know something *about* her. A good sentence is clear from start to finish; it doesn't make you change your interpretation of the meaning halfway through.

The word *that* signals to the reader that more information is coming—it's literally a signal to the reader to wait for that information before trying to interpret the meaning. The teacher isn't just confident in her students in general. She is confident *that they mastered the lesson.* You don't personally know Lupita Nyong'o; you know *that she is an actor.*

## Two Independent Clauses

Two complete sentences can be connected into one extra-long sentence. For example:

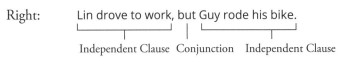

Right:

Lin drove to work, but Guy rode his bike.

Independent Clause   Conjunction   Independent Clause

*Lin drove to work* is a complete sentence. So is *Guy rode his bike.* Two complete sentences can be connected using a comma plus a co-conjunction (such as *but*) to create a **Compound Sentence**. In this kind of sentence, you have two main subject–verb pairs and both are part of the core sentence.

*But* is part of a group of seven co-conjunctions called the FANBOYS:

For

And

Nor

But

Or

Yet

So

The English language contains many conjunctions; these seven are special because they are very common in the English language and because they can be used to connect two independent clauses into one complex, or compound, sentence.

It is not acceptable, however, to connect two sentences using only a comma:

Wrong:

Lin drove to work, Guy rode his bike.

Independent   Comma without   Independent
Clause        Conjunction!    Clause

This is called a **Run-On Sentence** or a comma splice. Any GMAT answer choice that connects two independent clauses via only a comma is incorrect.

Pop quiz! What is the error in the sentence below?

Wrong:   The latest statistics released by the Labor Department indicate that producer prices rose rapidly last month, despite a generally weakening economy, some analysts contend that the economic slowdown in the euro zone and in Asia will stem the rise in commodity prices, reducing inflationary pressures in the United States.

The sentence above is a run-on. The example below strips the sentence to its core subject and verb components and adds the necessary conjunction:

> Right: The latest statistics ~~released by the Labor Department~~ indicate that producer prices rose ~~rapidly last month, despite a generally weakening economy~~, BUT some analysts contend that the economic slowdown ~~in the euro zone and in Asia~~ will stem the rise in commodity prices~~, reducing inflationary pressures in the United States~~.

Here's just the core of the corrected sentence:

> Core: The latest statistics . . . indicate that producer prices rose, . . . BUT some analysts contend that the economic slowdown . . . will stem the rise in commodity prices.

Here's another type of error the GMAT might throw at you:

> Wrong: The term *Eureka*, which means "I have found it" in ancient Greek and was famously uttered by Archimedes, and ever since then, scientists have exclaimed the same word upon making important discoveries.

What's the problem with that sentence? It does contain a comma along with the conjunction *and* connecting the two parts.

Unfortunately, the first half is not a complete sentence. Try to make it stand alone:

> Wrong: The term *Eureka*, which means "I have found it" in ancient Greek and was famously uttered by Archimedes.

*The term Eureka* could be a subject, but the rest is only a modifier; it does not contain a working verb.

You could fix the sentence by turning the first part into an independent clause:

> Right: The term *Eureka*, which means "I have found it" in ancient Greek, WAS famously uttered by Archimedes, and ever since then, scientists have exclaimed the same word upon making important discoveries.

In sum, use a comma plus a co-conjunction to connect independent clauses. (The most common co-conjunctions are the FANBOYS.) Cross off any answers that connect two independent clauses using only a comma.

## Semicolon

You can also connect two independent clauses with a semicolon. For instance:

> Right: Earl walked to school; he later ate his lunch.

Note that the part before the semicolon is a complete sentence, as is the part after the semicolon. Consider another example:

> Wrong: Arya and Nymeria are inseparable; doing everything together.

The second part of this sentence cannot stand on its own. Therefore, the two parts cannot be connected by a semicolon.

> Right: Arya and Nymeria are inseparable; they do everything together.

In the corrected example above, the two sentence parts can each stand alone. Therefore, you're allowed to connect them using a semicolon.

The semicolon is often followed by a transition expression, such as *however, therefore,* or *in addition.* For example, the two sentences in the previous paragraph can be combined in this way:

> Right:  In the corrected example above, the two sentence parts can each stand alone; therefore, you're allowed to connect them using a semicolon.

Note that these transitional elements are not co-conjunctions like *and.* As a result, you must use semicolons, not commas, to join the sentences:

> Wrong:  Arya and Nymeria are inseparable, THEREFORE, we never see them apart.

> Right:  Arya and Nymeria are inseparable; THEREFORE, we never see them apart.

From a practical standpoint, commas and semicolons are never interchangeable. If a sentence is correctly written using a comma, you can't replace that comma with a semicolon without making other changes. Likewise, if a sentence is correctly written using a semicolon, you can't replace that semicolon with a comma without making other changes.

When you see a split in the answers between a comma and a semicolon, check whether each half of the sentence can stand on its own. If one cannot, don't use a semicolon. If both can, the correct answer will use either a semicolon or a comma *plus* a co-conjunction. If a choice has two independent sentences connected only by a comma (with no co-conjunction), cross off that choice.

A rare but correct use of the semicolon is to separate a list of items that themselves contain commas:

> Ambiguous:  I listen to *Earth, Wind & Fire, Wow, Owls,* and *Blood, Sweat & Tears.*

> Right:  I listen to *Earth, Wind & Fire; Wow, Owls;* and *Blood, Sweat & Tears.*

The GMAT might also test colons and dashes; these punctuation marks are less common, so learn them if you are aiming for a higher score on the Verbal section of the GMAT. They are addressed in the additional material located online in your Atlas learning platform on the Manhattan Prep website.

# Adding Modifiers

Quick quiz: What do you remember about dependent clauses? (You first learned about them in detail earlier in this chapter, in the Eliminate the Middlemen section.) Glance back through that section if you need to.

Dependent clauses are modifiers; they add extra information to the sentence. GMAT SC sentences will often include dependent clauses in order to make these sentences as complex as possible.

You'll learn all about these and other types of modifiers in the next chapter. For now, concentrate on learning the core sentence structures discussed in this chapter so that you are fully prepared to add even more complexity when you move to the Modifiers chapter.

# Problem Set

For problems 1–4, box the $\boxed{\text{verb}}$ and underline the <u>subject</u>. Then, determine whether the subject agrees in number with the verb. If there is a mistake, rewrite the sentence to correct the mistake. If the sentence is correct as it is, mark it with the word CORRECT.

1.  <u>Jack</u>, along with some of his closest friends, is ⟨sharing⟩ a limo to the prom.  *C*

2.  After all the gardening we did, the <u>sun</u> shining on the flowerbeds ⟨make⟩ a beautiful sight.  *makes*

3.  The <u>decision</u> to ⟨place⟩ the beautiful artifacts in out-of-the-way nooks around the mansion's various rooms was inspiring.  *C*

4.  A national <u>supermarket chain</u> and a <u>locally owned bakery</u>, which ⟨has⟩ won awards for its croissants, ⟨has⟩ seen a significant decrease in revenues since the biggest employer in the area shut down.  *have*  *have*

Problems 5–7 are multiple choice with one correct answer. As on the real GMAT, answer (A) repeats the original sentence. Unlike the real GMAT, though, these problems have only two answer choices.

5.  <u>The sports governing body recently revamped the rules about hits to the head, a change intended to increase player safety, ever since then</u> players have, somewhat paradoxically, suffered more concussions.

    (A) The sports governing body recently revamped the rules about hits to the head, a change intended to increase player safety, ever since then

    (B) Ever since the sports governing body revamped the rules about hits to the head, a change intended to increase player safety,

6.  <u>Disappointed by the narrow loss after a long and grueling campaign, Governor Schuster, with counsel from her family, is</u> considering whether to run for Governor again next election.

    (A) Disappointed by the narrow loss after a long and grueling campaign, Governor Schuster, with counsel from her family, is

    (B) Although the narrow loss after a long and grueling campaign was disappointing, Governor Schuster and her family are

7. The lighthouse down by the bay overlooks both a <u>vast stretch of coastline and a number of fisheries that are owned by the local government</u>.

   (A) vast stretch of coastline and a number of fisheries that are owned by the local government

   (B) number of fisheries that are owned by the local government and a vast stretch of coastline

Bonus exercise! For problems 8–12, identify the error(s) and try to write a correct sentence. Note that there are many ways to fix any sentence, so on the GMAT itself, don't try to fix the sentence without examining your options in the answer choices.

8. The music company was afraid of the accelerating decline of sales of compact discs would not be compensated by increased internet revenue.

9. The petroleum distillates were so viscous, the engineers had to heat the pipe by nearly 30 degrees.

10. The municipality's back-to-work program has had notable success, nevertheless, it is not suitable for a statewide rollout for several reasons.

11. Historically, the Isle of Man had an economy based primarily on agriculture and fishing; now, one based on banking, tourism, and film production.

12. The Bentley trench, situated more than a mile and a half below sea level and completely covered by Antarctic glaciers, and it is the lowest point on the planet not under the oceans.

# Solutions

1. **Correct.** The phrase *along with* is a middleman; don't count *some of his closest friends* as part of the subject. Only Jack is the subject.

   <u>Jack</u>, along with some of his closest friends, is sharing a limo to the prom.

2. **Incorrect.** The singular subject *the sun* must be paired with the singular verb *makes*.

   After all the gardening we did, the <u>sun</u> shining on the flowerbeds makes a beautiful sight.

3. **Correct.** Ignore prep phrases and other middlemen when looking for the subject. The sentence contains three middlemen in a row: 1) *to place the beautiful articles*, 2) *in out-of-the-way nooks*, and 3) *around the mansion's various rooms*.

   The <u>decision</u> to place the beautiful artifacts in out-of-the-way nooks around the mansion's various rooms was inspiring.

4. **Incorrect.** The word *and* creates a compound subject (the *supermarket chain* and the *bakery*), so the subject is plural, but the verb (*has*) is singular. There are two other subject–verb pairings in the sentence, both of which are correct: *bakery…has won* and *employer … shut down*.

   A national supermarket <u>chain AND</u> a locally owned <u>bakery</u>, which has won awards for its croissants, have seen a significant decrease in revenues since the biggest employer in the area shut down.

5. **(B):** The original sentence is a run-on; it connects two independent clauses with nothing but a comma. Strip out the modifiers to find the (incorrect) core sentence: *The sports governing body revamped the rules, ever since then players have suffered more concussions.*

   Two independent clauses connected by a comma must also use a co-conjunction. Answer (B) corrects this error by changing *ever since then* to *ever since*. Now, the sentence begins with a dependent clause (*ever since…the head*); it's acceptable to connect a dependent clause to an independent clause with a comma and nothing else.

6. **(A):** Skip the middlemen and eliminate the warm-up to strip the sentence down to its core: *Governor Schuster is considering whether to run again next election.*

   The core of choice (B) says that *Governor Schuster and her family are considering whether to run for Governor again next election*. The subject changed from a singular subject (*Governor Schuster*) to a compound subject (*Governor Schuster and her family*), and the verb correctly changed from singular (*is*) to plural (*are*) to match. However, the compound subject introduces a meaning error: Governor Schuster is the person who ran for Governor last time and who may or may not run again this time. Her family members may have supported her, but they did not all run for Governor. You could fix this error by saying *Governor Schuster and her family are considering whether she should run* or by maintaining a singular subject, as the original sentence does.

7. **(B):** This is a tricky one. The original sentence is grammatically correct, but the meaning is ambiguous. What does the government own? *A number of fisheries*? Or both *a vast stretch of coastline and a number of fisheries*? That ending modifier (*that are owned by the local government*) could apply just to the second of the two parallel items, but it could also apply to both of the parallel items.

   The second sentence fixes this ambiguity by switching the order of the two phrases. Now, the sentence conveys a single, clear meaning. When more than one possible interpretation is acceptable, it doesn't matter which meaning the correct answer conveys; it matters only that the meaning is unambiguous. In this case, it's clear that the local government owns only the *fisheries*, not the *coastline*.

8. The original sentence has one independent clause (*the music company was afraid of* something) and then includes another main verb (*would not be... revenue*), but there is no conjunction to create a compound verb, so that second verb doesn't have the same subject (*company*). Logically, the subject for the second verb should be *the decline of sales*, but this noun is in a prep phrase, so it can't function as a subject of the sentence. One way to fix the sentence is to replace the preposition *of* with *that*:

   The music company was afraid THAT the accelerating decline of sales of compact discs would not be compensated by increased internet revenue.

9. Not sure what *viscous* means? It doesn't matter! Just think "they were so *something*" and keep going. The original sentence is a run-on. Here are some ways to fix it:

   The petroleum distillates were so viscous THAT the engineers had to heat the pipe by nearly 30 degrees.

   The petroleum distillates were EXTREMELY viscous; AS A RESULT, the engineers had to heat the pipe by nearly 30 degrees.

10. The word *nevertheless* is not a FANBOYS conjunction (such as *and*), so it cannot be used with a comma to connect two independent clauses. Here are two ways to fix the sentence:

    The municipality's back-to-work program has had notable success; nevertheless, it is not suitable for a statewide rollout for several reasons. [Change comma to semicolon.]

    The municipality's back-to-work program has had notable success, BUT it is not suitable for a statewide rollout for several reasons.

11. A semicolon connects two independent clauses. In the original sentence, the second part of the sentence does not form a valid independent clause. Here is one way to fix the sentence:

    Historically, the Isle of Man had an economy based primarily on agriculture and fishing; now, IT HAS one based on banking, tourism, and film production.

12. The original sentence begins with what could be the subject, followed by a modifier. After the modifier, the co-conjunction *and* starts a new independent clause; there is no main verb to pair with the first subject, *trench*. The first half of the sentence is a fragment. Here is one way to fix it:

    The Bentley trench, situated more than a mile and a half below sea level and completely covered by Antarctic glaciers, IS the lowest point on the planet not under the oceans.

# CHAPTER 4

# Modifiers

## In This Chapter:

- Adjectives and Adverbs
- Modifier vs. Core Part 1
- Noun Modifiers
- Noun Modifier Markers: *Which, That, Who,* and More
- Adverbial Modifiers
- Modifier Markers: Prepositions
- Modifier Markers: *–ing* and *–ed* Words
- Modifier vs. Core Part 2
- Modifier Markers: Subordinators
- Quantity

**In this chapter, you will learn** about how modifiers—extra information—fit into and elaborate on the sentence core that you learned about in the previous chapter. You'll learn what markers indicate noun and adverbial modifiers and how to use these markers to spot and fix commonly tested GMAT modifier errors.

# CHAPTER 4  Modifiers

A **Modifier** (or mod, for short) describes extra information about something else in the sentence. Although modifiers can be as simple as a single word (an adjective or an adverb), GMAT sentences often contain several complex modifiers. For example:

> Tired out from playing basketball, CHARLES DECIDED to take a nap.

The modifier *tired out from playing basketball* provides additional context as to *why* Charles decided to take a nap. Many modifiers answer the questions *who, what, which, when, where, how,* or *why.* Incorrectly used modifiers can lead to ambiguity or illogical meaning.

There are two broad categories of modifiers: **Noun** and **Adverbial**. Noun modifiers modify only a noun (including pronouns, a type of noun). Adverbial modifiers do *not* modify plain nouns or pronouns. Instead, they modify almost anything else: verbs, adjectives, prepositional phrases, even entire clauses. Note that adverbial modifiers can modify nouns + other stuff (such as a clause)—just not stand-alone nouns. Most of the time on the GMAT, adverbial modifiers modify some sort of action (and a noun could be part of that broader action).

Some types of words, such as adjectives, can only be noun mods; some types, such as adverbs, can only be adverbial mods.

Many structures, though, can be either noun or adverbial mods, depending upon how they're used. The three structures of this type that are most commonly used on the GMAT are prep phrases, *–ing* words, and *–ed* words. You will learn about all of these in this chapter.

## Adjectives and Adverbs

Let's start with the most basic modifiers. An **Adjective** modifies *only* a noun, so these are always noun mods. An **Adverb**, on the other hand, modifies almost anything *but* a plain noun, so these are always adverbial mods. Neither of these is tested all that much on the GMAT, but they're a good introduction to help you understand the broader topic.

For example:

The smart STUDENT WORKS quickly.

Here, the adjective *smart* modifies the noun *student*, while the adverb *quickly* modifies the verb *works*. Many adverbs are formed by adding *–ly* to the adjective.

Adjectives and adverbs are typically the simplest types of modifiers in a sentence—and perhaps that's why the GMAT doesn't test them all that frequently. Sometimes, you'll see a sentence in which an adverb (or occasionally an adjective) moves around in the different answer choices. For example:

> The company makes only one kind of bicycle.

> The company only makes one kind of bicycle.

In the first sentence, the company makes exactly one kind of bicycle, but it may also make other things (perhaps it makes scooters and skateboards as well). In this sentence, *only* modifies *one kind*.

In the second sentence, by contrast, the company makes exactly and only one thing: a kind of bicycle. It makes nothing else. In this sentence, *only* modifies *makes*.

The placement of a modifier is one of the most important things the GMAT tests, because the placement can completely change the meaning of the sentence. In some cases, as in the examples about the bicycles, the two meanings are both acceptable; they're just different.

Sometimes, though, one of the placements creates an ambiguous or outright illogical meaning. Compare these two sentences:

> The flower is so rare that it is found in only one type of habitat, rain forests at the highest humidity levels.

> The flower is so rare that it is found in one type of habitat, rain forests at only the highest humidity levels.

The first sentence conveys a clear and logical meaning: The *flower is so rare that it is found only* in a certain type of place. The second sentence, by contrast, is less clear. The word *only* now applies to the *humidity level* rather than the *type of habitat*, so the sentence appears to leave open the possibility that the flower can be found in other habitats, too. Logically, though, the word *only* should complete the *so rare that* meaning: It is *so rare that* it is found in *only* one area.

The GMAT will sometimes offer answers that use an adjective where an adverb is required, or vice versa. Consider this example:

> Max's great-grandmother, from whom he inherited his curly hair, is his supposed Irish ancestor.

> Max's great-grandmother, from whom he inherited his curly hair, is his supposedly Irish ancestor.

In the first option, the adjective *supposed* points to the noun *ancestor*, implying that Max's great-grandmother might not actually be his ancestor. In the second option, the adverb *supposedly* points to the adjective *Irish*, implying that Max's great-grandmother might not actually be Irish.

Max's great-grandmother is his relation, so she is by definition his ancestor. Only the second option has a sensible meaning: Max's grandmother is *supposedly Irish*, but she may not be after all.

Adjectives that have been observed alternating with their corresponding adverbs in released GMAT problems include *corresponding, frequent, independent, rare, recent, seeming, separate, significant, supposed,* and *usual*. If you spot an answer switching back and forth between the adjective and adverb forms of the same word, examine the meaning.

In order to do this, first decide what the word is modifying. If the choice uses the adjectival form of the word, the adjective must be modifying a noun; if the choice uses the adverbial form, the adverb must be modifying something other than a noun. Once you have that straightened out, you can decide which meaning is logical.

# Modifier vs. Core: Part 1

Most modifiers are not part of the core sentence, so when you are trying to pay attention just to the core, you can mentally ignore many—but not all—modifiers.

Imagine a friend is giving you directions to her house. What's the difference between these two sets of directions?

> Turn left on Mayberry Street, and stop at the first house, which is red.

> Turn left on Mayberry Street, and stop at the first house that is red.

In the first example, the direction is to stop at the first house, period. The sentence also provides some extra information in the form of a modifier: That first house happens to be red. If you took that modifier out of the sentence, you would still know the proper meaning of the main part of the sentence and you'd stop at the correct house (the first one!). This is an example of a **Nonessential Modifier**, and these types of modifiers are *not* a part of the core sentence (since the information really is just extra).

The second sentence, by contrast, tells you to stop at the first red house. This is not necessarily the same house as the first house on the street. It could be that the first red house is actually the fifth one down the street. In other words, if you remove *that is red* from the sentence, you might show up at the wrong house. This is an example of an **Essential Modifier**, and you will usually want to keep these as part of the core sentence.

Why are these two meanings so different? In the second sentence, *that is red* is an essential mod, so it is part of the core description of the *house*. As a result, the adjective *first* applies to the whole description: First what? First *house that is red*.

By contrast, *which is red* is nonessential; it is not part of the core description of the house. In this case, the adjective *first* applies just to the *house* alone: First what? First *house* (which happens to be a certain color).

Nonessential mods are usually separated out from the rest of the sentence by commas, while essential mods typically are *not* separated out by commas, so you can use the presence or absence of a comma as a good clue as to whether the modifier is nonessential or essential. (You can also pay attention to the meaning.)

How do essential vs. nonessential modifiers map to noun vs. adverbial modifiers? These are two separate types of classifications. Both essential and nonessential modifiers can be either noun or adverbial mods. Whether there are commas will help you to classify essential vs. nonessential, but the distinction is a bit more intricate for noun vs. adverbial.

Start by noticing the specific marker that signals a modifier; the marker itself will usually tell you whether the modifier is noun vs. adverbial. For example, a *comma which* marker signals a nonessential noun mod. By contrast, when the word *that* is used to introduce a noun modifier, it is never set off by a comma; it is always an essential noun mod.

Next, scan the answers. If, for example, you see a *which* vs. *that* split, you now know that you need to think about whether this is essential or nonessential. (Since they're both noun modifiers, you don't need to think about the noun vs. adverbial issue.)

The three most commonly tested types of modifiers on the GMAT (prep phrases, *–ing* words, and *–ed* words) can be either noun or adverbial depending upon how they're used in a sentence.

## Prep Phrases

For the first type, prep phrases, there isn't an easy clue as to whether the mod is noun or adverbial. It can be useful to ask a question about the modifier to figure out what it's modifying: What does (this modifier) describe? Take a look at these examples:

| Marker | Example | What is it modifying? What does (the prep phrase) describe? |
| --- | --- | --- |
| Prep Phrase (preposition + noun) | Three companies have made offers to buy the PLOT <u>of land</u>. | Noun: What does *of land* describe? A *plot* (plain noun). |
| | The ACQUISITION HAS BEEN APPROVED <u>by regulators</u>. | Adverbial: What does *by regulators* describe? How the *acquisition has been approved* (not just a noun). |
| | <u>In some countries</u>, MERGERS between the top two companies in an industry ARE NOT ALLOWED. | Adverbial: What does *in some countries* describe? Where *mergers are not allowed* (not just a noun). |

When you see a prep phrase, but you're not sure what it's referring to, pull yourself back to the meaning of the sentence. What does (this mod) describe? If it describes a noun, it's a noun mod. If it describes anything other than a stand-alone noun, it's an adverbial mod. If it could refer to more than one thing or action in the sentence, cross that choice off for ambiguity. If whatever it refers to is illogical, cross off that choice for not making sense.

## *–ing* and *–ed*

The other two types of commonly tested modifiers, *–ing* and *–ed* mods, have a simple clue you can use to identify whether they are noun or adverbial. If they are *not* set off from the rest of the sentence by commas, they are noun mods. If they *are* set off from the rest of the sentence by a comma or commas, they are adverbial mods. Here are some examples:

| Marker | Example | What is it modifying? |
| --- | --- | --- |
| *–ing* | The ENGINEER <u>running this meeting</u> fixed the problem. | Noun: An *–ing* mod without a comma is a noun mod. |
| | The ENGINEER FIXED THE PROBLEM, <u>earning herself a promotion</u>. | Adverbial: A *comma –ing* mod is an adverbial mod. The comma could be before the mod (as here), after, or both. |
| *–ed* | The CANDIDATE <u>interviewed last week</u> has accepted the job. | Noun: An *–ed* mod without a comma is a noun mod. |
| | <u>Excited by the new opportunity</u>, the CANDIDATE HAS ACCEPTED THE JOB. | Adverbial: A *comma –ed* mod is an adverbial mod. Again, the comma could be before, after (as here), or both. |

As always, the first step is to spot the marker in the original sentence and then check the splits in the answers to see the given differences. If you have an *–ing* mod that is sometimes split out by a comma and sometimes not, then the problem is asking you to determine whether the modifier is referring to a noun (in which case, you don't want a comma) or an entire action (in which case, you do want a comma).

Bonus question: Which of the mods in the table are essential and which are nonessential? This quiz is open book; feel free to reread the earlier material to remind yourself how to distinguish between the two.

Ready? Okay: The *–ing* and *–ed* mods without any commas are essential mods. The ones with commas are nonessential mods. Most of the time, commas = nonessential and no commas = essential. (One tip: When stripping out the modifiers to get to the core sentence, you may sometimes be able to ignore all *–ing* and *–ed* mods, even if they are essential. Use meaning as your guide; if you can still understand the basic sentence without including the mod, go ahead and strip it out.)

Let's summarize the information about prep phrases, *–ing* mods, and *–ed* mods.

When you have a *comma prep phrase*, a *comma –ing*, or a *comma –ed*, then you have both an adverbial modifier and a nonessential modifier. (Note: The comma can appear before the mod, after the mod, or both before and after the mod.) You can ignore these mods when you are looking just for the sentence core.

When the modifier is *not* split out by a comma, things are a little more complicated. First, these are usually noun mods. (There are technically a decent number of exceptions here but, luckily, you can ignore the vast majority for the purposes of the GMAT.) Further, these no-comma mods are often essential—but they can also be nonessential. Use your best judgment based on the meaning of the sentence; when in doubt, call it essential and, if stripping to the core, leave it in.

You'll learn more about each of these forms throughout the rest of this chapter.

## Which vs. *–ing*

*Comma which* modifiers and *comma –ing* modifiers serve different roles in a sentence; the former modifies nouns while the latter modifies actions. As such, they can't be used interchangeably. Sentences such as the following are common in speech, but they are actually grammatically incorrect:

> Wrong:    Crime has recently decreased in our neighborhood, which has led to a rise in property values.

A *comma which* mod has to refer to a very nearby noun—but the *neighborhood* didn't lead to a *rise in property values*. Rather the action *crime decreased* led to the *rise in property values*. A noun modifier won't work here.

One way to correct the sentence is to use an adverbial modifier to refer to the whole clause:

> Right:    CRIME HAS recently DECREASED in our neighborhood, <u>leading to a rise in property values</u>.

You could also flip it around, eliminating the *which* modifier altogether:

> Right:    The recent DECREASE in crime in our neighborhood HAS LED to a rise in property values.

In speech, people often break these rules, incorrectly using *which* to refer to a previous thought that is *not* a noun. In fact, the GMAT has made the same mistake in Sentence Correction explanations and even in a Reading Comprehension passage! Do not use your ear for this one. When you see a *comma which* vs. *comma –ing* split in the answers, examine the meaning. If the modifier should refer to a noun, use *comma which*. If the modifier should refer to an action, use *comma –ing*.

# Noun Modifiers

Noun modifiers answer a specific question that you can ask about a noun. For example:

> The CAT <u>on the couch</u> loves dogs.

What does *on the couch* describe? The cat. When you ask the question What does (the modifier) describe? and the answer points to a stand-alone noun, you have a noun mod.

Long sentences typically have many nouns, so a noun modifier has to be placed in such a way that the reader knows exactly which noun is being modified. The practical result is that nouns and noun modifiers must be placed very close together (most of the time—though not always—they are right next to each other). Remember this rule:

> **Place a noun and its modifier as close together as the sentence allows.**

Adverbial modifiers are more flexible; they don't necessarily have to be placed near what they're modifying.

Here's what can happen when a noun and its modifier are separated by too much other text:

> Wrong:     A hard worker and loyal team player, the new project was managed by Sue.

The sentence begins with an **Opening Modifier** set off from the rest of the sentence by a comma. You can identify it as a modifier because it cannot stand as its own sentence. Further, it's singled out as an *opening* mod not just because it starts the sentence but because it doesn't tell you who or what it's talking about.

What does *a hard worker and loyal team player* describe? Logically, it should refer to Sue, but Sue is as far away as she can get in the sentence.

It's possible to move Sue closer to her mod:

> Right:     <u>A hard worker and loyal team player</u>, SUE managed the new project.

Since opening modifiers don't tell you who or what they're talking about, they need to refer to the main subject of the sentence. Most of the time, this noun will appear very soon after the comma at the end of the opening modifier.

More than half of the time, a noun and its modifier will be placed right next to each other, with no other words intervening. This isn't true 100 percent of the time, though. The most common exception occurs when you have two modifiers that both describe the same noun. For example:

> The BOX <u>of nails</u>, <u>which is nearly full</u>, belongs to Jean.

The noun *box* has two modifiers: *of nails* and *which is nearly full*. They can't both be placed right after the noun; one has to come before the other. The other order would look like this:

> Wrong:     The BOX, <u>which is nearly full</u>, <u>of nails</u> belongs to Jean.

In general, an essential modifier takes precedence over a nonessential modifier. *Of nails* is an essential modifier—it is not separated out by a comma—so it is placed immediately after *box*. The *comma which* modifier is a nonessential modifier, so it is placed second, even though it also refers to *box*.

A *comma which* mod is always nonessential, so it will always come after a prep phrase if both modifiers are describing the same noun.

Which of the options below is better?

> Jim biked along an old dirt road to get to his house, which cut through the woods.

> To get to his house, Jim biked along an old dirt road, which cut through the woods.

A *comma which* mod is always a noun mod. What does *cut through the woods* describe? The *road*. The second option places *road* closer to its modifier, so it's the better option.

One more thing: The first option isn't just worse than the second. The first option is incorrect. Why isn't it okay for there to be a little separation between the noun and the *comma which* modifier, as there was in the box of nails example? In this example, *to get to his house* is not a noun modifier referring to *road*. What does *to get to his house* describe? Why *Jim biked*.

When the sentence places text that is referring to something other than a noun in between a noun and its modifier, it's generally better to move that text elsewhere so that the noun and its modifier can be closer together. The second option accomplished this by moving *to get to his house* to the beginning of the sentence.

SC questions are multiple choice; you will never have to rewrite the sentence yourself. If two options both appear correct, but one choice gives you the option to place the noun and its modifier closer together, go with that option.

## Possessive Nouns Are Not Actually Nouns

Can you spot the error in the sentence below?

> Wrong:    Happy about his raise, Bill's celebration included taking his friends out to dinner.

Logically, the opening modifier *happy about his raise* should describe *Bill*. However, possessive nouns are technically adjectives, not nouns. (Whose celebration? Bill's celebration.) As it stands, the sentence technically says that *Bill's celebration* is *happy about his raise*. Here is one way to fix the sentence:

> Right:    <u>Happy about his raise</u>, BILL celebrated by taking his friends to dinner.

# Noun Modifier Markers: *Which, That, Who,* and More

Noun modifiers are often introduced by **Relative Pronouns** such as the following:

> Which   That   Who   Whose   Whom

The words in that list that start with *w* always signal noun modifiers; they are called *noun modifier markers*. Whenever you see this type of marker, think about noun modifiers.

The word *that* can also signal a noun modifier—but it doesn't always. A noun followed immediately by the word *that* signals a noun modifier. A verb followed immediately by the word *that* usually signals the more complex sentence structure subject–verb–THAT–subject–verb (see the Sentence Structure chapter for more).

The pronouns *who* and *whom* must modify people. On the other hand, the pronoun *which* cannot modify people.

Perhaps surprisingly, the pronoun *whose* can modify both people and things:

> . . . the TOWN <u>whose water supply was contaminated</u>.

The words *which* or *whom* sometimes follow prepositions:

> . . . the CANAL <u>through which water flows</u>.

> . . . the SENATOR <u>for whom we worked</u>.

A lot of people think these types of structures (*through which, for whom*) sound "off" and, as a result, mistakenly cross off a correct answer. When you see this *preposition–which* or *preposition–whom* structure, check whether it is correct by inverting the text to create a complete sentence:

> Original text: the CANAL <u>through which water flows</u>

> Inverted text: Water flows through the canal.

The noun and verb inside the prepositional phrase (*water flows*) become the subject and verb of the inverted sentence. Then, use the preposition (*through*) and finish up with the noun that started the original phrase (*the canal*). (Note that the marker *which* is dropped from the inverted sentence.) If the inverted sentence is a valid sentence, then the original structure was also correct.

The words *where* and *when* can be noun or adverbial modifiers (and the test doesn't typically make you distinguish). The word *where* can be used to modify a noun that is a place, such as *area, site, state/province,* or *country*. For example:

> Though most of the Nobel Prizes are awarded in Stockholm, where Alfred Nobel was born, the Peace Prize is awarded in Oslo.

However, w*here* cannot modify a metaphorical place, such as a *condition, situation, case, circumstance,* or *arrangement*. In these cases, use *in which* rather than *where*:

> Wrong:    We had an <u>arrangement</u> WHERE he cooked and I cleaned.

> Right:    We had an <u>arrangement</u> IN WHICH he cooked and I cleaned.

Invert that second sentence to verify that the usage of *in which* is correct: *He cooked and I cleaned in* [the] *arrangement*. You may sometimes have to change the article (*a, an, the*) that leads into the final noun; that's okay.

The word *when* can be used to modify a noun that is an event or a time, such as *period, age, 1987,* or *decade*. In these circumstances, you can also use *in which* or *during which* instead of *when*:

> Right:    The three-century span of the Renaissance, a PERIOD <u>when artists such as Leonardo da Vinci and Michelangelo thrived</u>, marked the European transition from the middle ages to modern times.

> Right:    The three-century span of the Renaissance, a PERIOD <u>during which artists such as Leonardo da Vinci and Michelangelo thrived</u>, marked the European transition from the middle ages to modern times.

## Adverbial Modifiers

**Adverbial Modifiers** answer a *how, when, where, why,* or *how much* question about some other information in the sentence. They do not have the same placement constraints as noun modifiers. A sentence typically contains only a few clauses, so adverbial modifiers can be placed more freely without creating meaning issues in the sentence. As long as the adverbial modifier clearly points to one particular verb or clause, the placement is acceptable.

It is still possible to place adverbial modifiers poorly, though. What's wrong with this sentence?

> Amar filled in his timesheet in order to make the payroll deadline rapidly.

Did he *fill in his timesheet rapidly* or did he *make the deadline rapidly*? The modifier is closer to the latter option, but that meaning doesn't make much sense—you either make a deadline or you don't. Here are two ways to fix the sentence:

> Right:     Amar FILLED in his timesheet <u>rapidly</u> in order to make the payroll deadline.

> Right:     Amar <u>rapidly</u> FILLED in his timesheet to make the payroll deadline.

In both cases, it's clear that *rapidly* modifies the first action—and this is a logical meaning.

## Modifier Markers: Prepositions

**Prepositions** can signal noun or adverbial modifiers. On the GMAT, you'll most often be tested on the noun modifier form.

Here's an example of the noun form:

> The executive DIRECTOR <u>of the company</u> resigned three days ago.

What does *of the company* describe? The *director*. When a prepositional phrase is a noun modifier, it will almost always directly follow the noun that it is modifying.

One fairly common issue tested is whether a particular preposition is the right one to match the other words in the sentence. For example, you can say *the team is capable of succeeding* but not *the team is capable for succeeding*. These idioms (*capable of* but not *capable for*) have to be memorized; see the Idioms chapter for more on this topic.

You can have two prep phrases in a row. For example:

> The board of directors had a vigorous DEBATE <u>about the EFFICACY of the new strategy</u>.

The prep phrase *about the efficacy* modifies the noun *debate*. The prep phrase *of the new strategy* modifies the noun *efficacy*. It's fairly common to have two prepositional phrases in a row, but three or four in a row can be dangerous; the more you have, the more likely you are to create meaning issues.

A sentence can test meaning as the result of the placement of a prep phrase. For example:

> Wrong:     The departmental director addressed the team's recent success in the memo.

> Right:     <u>In the memo</u>, THE departmental DIRECTOR ADDRESSED the team's recent success.

What does *in the memo* describe? Because a prep phrase can be noun or adverbial, the first sentence could be read in one of two ways, one of which is that the team's recent success occurred *in* the memo. (They wrote a great memo? Logically, that's probably not what the sentence is trying to say.)

Ambiguity is bad. The second sentence separates out the modifier by a comma to create one logical meaning: The team had success and the director addressed that success in a memo.

In general, prep phrases that explain *how*, *when*, *where*, or *why* an action occurred or that answer a *how much* question are adverbial modifiers. Here's another example of an adverbial prep phrase:

> The TEAM ATTENDS staff meetings <u>on Mondays</u>.

What does *on Mondays* describe? When *the team attends* (the meetings).

The following sentence contains multiple *noun* modifiers. See how many you can spot:

> Researchers discovered that the most common risk factor resulting in cholera epidemics is the lack of a clean water supply.

The adjective *common* describes the *risk factor*. (The adverb *most* refers to *common*, so this is an adverbial modifier.) What about the more complex noun modifiers?

> Researchers discovered that the most <u>common</u> RISK FACTOR <u>resulting in cholera epidemics</u> is the LACK <u>of a clean water supply</u>.

The prepositional phrase *of a clean water supply* modifies the noun *lack*.

What about *resulting in cholera epidemics*? The word *resulting* is an *–ing* word and the word *in* is a preposition. When you see this, go with the first word first: the *–ing* word. This word is not preceded by a comma, so *resulting in cholera epidemics* signals a noun modifier; it refers to the *risk factor*.

## Modifier Markers: *–ing* and *–ed* Words

**4**

When an *–ing* mod is not set off by a comma, then you have a noun modifier, as in this example from the previous section:

> Researchers discovered that the most common RISK FACTOR <u>resulting in cholera epidemics</u> is the lack of a clean water supply.

By contrast, when an *–ing* or *–ed* word is set off from the rest of the sentence by a comma, it is an adverbial modifier. Even though these are called *comma –ing* and *comma –ed* mods, it's also possible for that mod to be at the beginning of a sentence and followed by a comma.

Here's an example from earlier in this chapter:

> The ENGINEER FIXED THE PROBLEM, <u>earning herself a promotion</u>.

Both *–ing* and *–ed* words are called participles (though you don't need to know the official terms for the test):

| Verb | Present Participle (*–ing*) | Past Participle (*–ed*) |
| --- | --- | --- |
| to play | playing | played |
| to manage | managing | managed |
| to begin | beginning | begun |

Present participles always end in *–ing*. Past participles most commonly end in *–ed*, but there are a number of irregular verb forms, such as the example shown in the table above (*begun*).

Most people are used to thinking of –*ing* words as verbs, but they only function as verbs in one specific circumstance. Most of the time, –*ing* words are modifiers; they can even be nouns! Here are some examples of –*ing* words:

| She is running. | *is running* = verb |
|---|---|
| Running is fun. | *running* = subject (noun) |
| The GIRL <u>playing soccer</u> is my sister. | *playing soccer* (no commas) = noun modifier |
| SHE STAYED all day, <u>playing soccer until she was the only one left on the field</u>. | *, playing soccer…field* = adverbial modifier |

Any –*ing* word functioning as a verb will always have another verb immediately before it, as shown in the *is playing* example. If no other verb is right next to the –*ing* word, then the –*ing* word is not a verb.

Any –*ing* words that are *not* verbs and *not* separated from the rest of the sentence by a comma will either be a noun, as in the example *playing soccer is fun*, or modify another noun, as in the example *the girl playing soccer is my sister*.

Any –*ing* words that are *not* verbs and *are* separated from the rest of the sentence by a comma will be an adverbial modifier. (There is one semi-common exception here: The structure *comma including* is a noun modifier. For example: *She likes many types of puzzles, including sudoku, hitori, and skyscrapers.* Synonyms for the word *including* can also trigger this exception.)

Past participles, or –*ed* words, are not tested as frequently as –*ing* words, but you will still probably see them on the GMAT. They can fall into one of three categories:

| She played the lottery yesterday. | *played* = verb |
|---|---|
| She accidentally bought an <u>expired</u> lottery TICKET. | *expired* (no commas) = noun modifier |
| <u>Exhausted from her job</u>, SHE BOUGHT A lottery TICKET with hopes of winning big. | *exhausted…job,* = adverbial modifier |

Unlike –*ing* words, –*ed* words are commonly used as verbs and they can be verbs all by themselves. The comma rule still holds though: When the –*ed* word is separated by commas from the rest of the sentence, it is an adverbial modifier.

When either a *comma –ing* or a *comma –ed* modifier is an opening modifier (at the beginning of a sentence), the modifier needs to refer to the main subject after the comma, as shown in the last example in the table.

The rest of the sentence matters, too, though. A sentence such as *exhausted from her job, she has red hair* would not be acceptable on the GMAT because the opening modifier does not have anything to do with the fact that she has red hair. Both *comma –ing* and *comma –ed* modifiers have to make sense with the whole clause that they modify: *She bought a lottery ticket* because she was *exhausted from her job*.

## Check the Sequence in Participle Modifiers

The examples illustrate an additional requirement for *comma –ing* and *comma –ed* modifiers: The first piece of information leads to or results in the second piece of information.

For example:

The ENGINEER FIXED THE PROBLEM, <u>earning herself a promotion.</u>

Main Clause        *Comma –ing* Modifier

*Because* the engineer fixed the problem, she earned a promotion. Fixing the problem resulted in earning the promotion. Consider this example:

<u>Exhilarated by the successful product launch,</u> the TEAM CELEBRATED after work.

*Comma –ed* Modifier        Main Clause

*Because* the launch was successful, the team celebrated. The exhilaration about the success led to the celebration.

Picture a woman ice skating. She loses her balance, crashes to the ice, and then clutches her ankle in pain. Which of these three sentences correctly describes this scenario?

> Slipping on the ice, she broke her ankle.
>
> Breaking her ankle, she slipped on the ice.
>
> She slipped on the ice, breaking her ankle.

The first and third sentences both correctly describe what happened: The woman slipped on the ice, and this action caused her to break her ankle.

The middle sentence is illogical because it implies that she broke her ankle first (for no reason at all, apparently!), and then slipped on the ice. While that may be possible, it's not very likely.

# Modifier vs. Core: Part 2

What's going on in this sentence?

> The CEO declared that everyone had to work through the holidays to make the production deadline, but in calling for such an extreme measure, the company's employees were upset to the point of mutiny.

The phrase *in calling for such an extreme measure* is a modifier. Is it a prep phrase because it starts with *in* or a *comma –ing* because it has the word *calling*? Thankfully, you don't actually have to distinguish between those categories. What you do need to figure out is whether it's a noun or adverbial mod.

Since the text is separated out by a comma from the rest, it's an adverbial modifier. It needs to address the clause to which it is attached.

Which clause is that? The sentence has two:

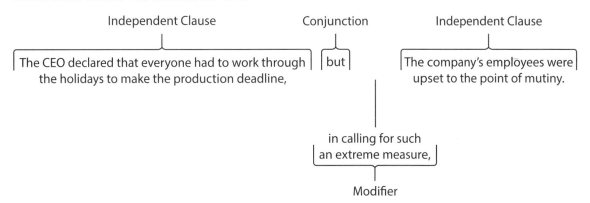

Because the *in calling* modifier falls after the conjunction connecting the two clauses (*but*), the modifier refers to the second part of the sentence—the *employees*, not the *CEO*. The employees didn't call for this extreme measure, though! The CEO did.

The sentence could be fixed in multiple ways:

> Right:     In an extreme measure, the CEO DECLARED that everyone had to work through the holidays to make the production deadline; her employees were upset to the point of mutiny.

> Right:     The CEO declared that everyone had to work through the holidays to make the production deadline, but in calling for such an extreme measure, SHE UPSET her employees to the point of mutiny.

Both of the correct sentences properly attribute the extreme move to the CEO, not to the employees.

Earlier, you learned that you can put two modifiers in a row. Remember this example?

> The BOX of nails, which is nearly full, belongs to Jean.

This sentence is okay because both noun mods refer to the same noun, *box*. The essential mod (*of nails*) is placed closest to the noun and the nonessential mod (*which is nearly full*) is a little farther away.

What if you have one noun mod and one adverbial mod? Consider this sentence:

> Wrong:     George Carlin, both shocking and entertaining audiences across the nation, who also struggled publicly with drug abuse, influenced and inspired a generation of comedians.

The first modifier, *shocking and entertaining*, is an adverbial modifier referring to the core clause *George Carlin influenced and inspired*. The second modifier, *who also struggled*, is a noun modifier referring just to Carlin himself. Noun mods are supposed to be placed as close to the noun as they can get, while adverbial mods are less restricted. So placing the adverbial mod in between the noun mod and Carlin is not a good sentence structure.

Here's a better way to convey the same information:

> Right:     GEORGE CARLIN, who also struggled publicly with drug abuse, INFLUENCED AND INSPIRED a generation of comedians, both shocking and entertaining audiences across the nation.

In the better sentence, the adverbial modifier is moved to the end of the sentence; now, the noun modifier can be placed right after *Carlin*.

On harder questions, the GMAT might even rephrase the sentence so that one of the modifiers becomes part of the core of the sentence; that is, it is no longer a modifier at all. Here's an example:

> Right:  Both shocking and entertaining audiences across the nation, GEORGE CARLIN INFLUENCED AND INSPIRED a generation of comedians YET STRUGGLED publicly with drug abuse.

Here's the core sentence:

> Carlin influenced and inspired (people) yet struggled (with drug abuse).

The *drug abuse* portion is now part of the core sentence, not a modifier. The sentence no longer separates the subject from the verbs *influenced and inspired*, making the opening modifier more clear as well.

If your first glance reveals a long underline, expect portions of the sentence to move around or even change roles completely in the answers. Here are two examples of correct sentences in which the core and modifier portions change:

> Right:  Employing the new lab equipment, the ENGINEER IDENTIFIED the problem within minutes.

> Right:  The ENGINEER EMPLOYED the new lab equipment, identifying the problem within minutes.

Both of these sentences convey the same information, but the first sentence begins with an opening modifier and then provides the core, while the second starts with the core and finishes with a modifier. Neither one is better than the other; both would be acceptable on the GMAT (and you won't have to choose between the two).

Here's another set of correct examples:

> Right:  Pushed to justify his decision, the MANAGER FROZE AND WAS UNABLE TO TALK,
> Modifier                                        Core
>
> eventually breaking down in tears.
> Modifier

> Right:  The MANAGER FROZE AND WAS UNABLE TO TALK when he was pushed to justify
> Core                                        Modifier
>
> his decision; he eventually broke down in tears.
> Core

In both of these sentences, the grammar is correct and the meaning is logical and unambiguous.

# Modifier Markers: Subordinators

Take a look at this sentence:

> Although the economy is strong, the RETAIL INDUSTRY IS STRUGGLING.

The first part of the sentence is called a **Subordinate Clause**, or sub clause. It is almost exactly like a complete sentence, but it has a subordinator (*although*) at the beginning.

Subordinate clauses are *not* complete sentences:

> Wrong:    Although the economy is strong.

Sub clauses modify the main clause to which they are attached; they are always adverbial modifiers. In the correct example presented first in this section, the subordinate clause provides additional information about the main clause: Despite the fact that the overall economy is doing well, one particular industry is not.

Sub clauses can look very similar to opening modifiers, but they are not actually opening mods for one specific reason. Sub clauses are actual clauses—they contain their own subjects. Openings mods do not. Compare these two correct examples:

> Opening Mod:   Although strong at the moment, the economy is showing signs that it may slow down soon.

> Sub Clause:   Although the economy is strong, the retail industry is struggling.

Take a look at just the portions of the sentence up to the comma:

> Opening Mod:   Although strong at the moment, . . .

> Sub Clause:   Although the economy is strong, . . .

In the opening mod example, you literally cannot tell what the sentence is talking about until you see the noun after that comma. An opening mod, by definition, does not tell you what noun it is talking about. Therefore, the noun has to be the subject/main word right after the comma; otherwise, you won't understand the meaning of the sentence.

By contrast, a sub clause tells you what noun it is talking about. Since you already know, the main clause can then start talking about a different subject.

If you see what looks like an opening mod at the beginning of a sentence, check whether it tells you what noun it's talking about. If not, that noun has to be the subject of the sentence, after the comma. If the opening text does tell you what noun it's talking about, though, then you don't have an opening mod after all, and you don't need to check whether the main subject matches.

Common subordinator markers include:

| after | although | because | before | if | since |
|-------|----------|---------|--------|-----|-------|
| so that | that | unless | until | when | while |

Pay attention to the meaning of the chosen word. If it indicates a contrast, for example, then make sure the sentence actually conveys a contrast:

> Wrong:    Although the economy is strong, the retail industry is doing well.

Use only one connecting word per "connection":

> Wrong:    ALTHOUGH I need to relax, YET I have so many things to do!

> Right:    ALTHOUGH I need to relax, I have so many things to do!

> Right:    I need to relax, YET I have so many things to do!

Subordinators are similar to the FANBOYS conjunctions: In both cases, make sure that the chosen word logically connects the two pieces of information. (The two types of conjunctions are not interchangeable, though; see the Sentence Structure chapter to remind yourself how to use FANBOYS.) The GMAT will test you to make sure that you are paying attention to this kind of meaning.

Here is a FANBOYS example that doesn't make sense:

> Wrong: She is not interested in playing sports, AND she likes watching them on TV.

In this example, the word *and* is not sensible, because the two independent clauses are in opposition to each other. This meaning error can be corrected in multiple ways:

> Right: She is not interested in playing sports, BUT she likes watching them on TV.

> Right: ALTHOUGH she is not interested in playing sports, she likes watching them on TV.

The first example uses a different FANBOYS conjunction, one that has the appropriate meaning. The second example changes the sentence structure. Now, the first part of the sentence is a sub conjunction; the chosen word (*although*) conveys the correct meaning.

Finally, be on the lookout for sentences that join a main clause to something that should be a clause but is not:

> Wrong: Citizens of many countries are expressing concern about the environmental damage— such as flooding and wildfires—caused by the widespread release of greenhouse gases may be impossible to reverse.

The main clause in this sentence is *citizens of many countries are expressing concern about the environmental damage caused by the widespread release of greenhouse gases*. There is nothing wrong with this main clause.

What about the rest of the sentence? The part between the dashes is okay, but the main verb at the end (*may be impossible to reverse*) has no subject. The GMAT wants you to think that *environmental damage* is the subject of *may be impossible to reverse*, but *environmental damage* is part of a prep phrase (*about the environmental damage*). Nouns in prep phrases cannot also be subjects.

One way to fix the sentence is to change the preposition *about* to the subordinator *that*:

> Right: Citizens of many countries are expressing concern THAT the environmental damage— such as flooding and wildfires—caused by the widespread release of greenhouse gases may be impossible to reverse.

You learned about this sentence structure in the Structure chapter: subject–verb–THAT–subject–verb. In this correct version, the main clause is *citizens…are expressing concern*. The sub clause begins with the word *that* and extends to the end of the sentence.

Another way to fix the sentence is to put *may be impossible to reverse* inside a modifier:

> Right: Citizens of many countries are expressing concern about the environmental damage— such as flooding and wildfires—caused by the widespread release of greenhouse gases, DAMAGE THAT may be impossible to reverse.

In this correct version, the main clause ends right before the comma. The words *damage that may be impossible to reverse* provide additional information about the damage mentioned earlier in the sentence.

This kind of structure sounds funny to many people (because no one talks this way), but it is a valid structure in more formal written English. The writer wants to provide additional information about *the environmental damage*, but that noun is pretty far away from the end of the sentence. In addition, there are other nouns (such as *release* and *gases*) between *damage* and the end of the sentence, so putting another noun mod referring to *damage* at the end of the sentence is likely to confuse the reader.

One way to get around that is to include a noun at the beginning of the mod. You can literally repeat the exact noun, as this sentence does: *the environmental DAMAGE...caused by the widespread release of greenhouse gases, DAMAGE that may be impossible to reverse.*

You may also be able to use a synonym for the original noun, such as: *the environmental DAMAGE...caused by the widespread release of greenhouse gases, DESTRUCTION that may be impossible to reverse.*

# Quantity

In the English language, words and expressions of quantity are subject to strict grammatical rules.

**Rule 1: Words Used for *Countable* Things vs. Words Used for *Uncountable* Things**

Some nouns in the English language are countable, such as *hat(s)*, *feeling(s)*, and *person/people*. Other nouns are uncountable, such as *patience*, *water*, and *furniture*. During the test, if you are unsure whether a particular word is countable, literally try to count it out:

For *hat*:     **One hat, two hats, three hats.** This works. *Hat* is countable.

For *patience*:     **One patience (?), two patiences (?), stop.** This does not work. *Patience* is not countable.

Here are some examples of words and expressions that modify countable things and those that modify uncountable things:

| Countable Modifiers | Uncountable Modifiers |
|---|---|
| MANY hats | MUCH patience |
| FEW stores | LITTLE merchandise |
| FEWER children | LESS money |
| FEWEST shoes | LEAST greed |
| NUMBER of chairs | AMOUNT of furniture |
| NUMEROUS books | GREAT courage |

*More, most, enough,* and *all* work with both countable (plural) and uncountable (singular) nouns: *more hats, more patience, most people, most furniture, enough hats, enough patience, all people, all furniture.*

Do not use the word *less* with countable items. This error has become common in speech and in the signs above express lines in grocery stores: *10 items or less.* Since the noun *item* is countable, the sign should actually read *10 items or fewer.* For example:

Wrong:     There were <u>less</u> Numidian KINGS than Roman emperors.

Right:     There were <u>fewer</u> Numidian KINGS than Roman emperors.

Be careful with unit nouns, such as *dollars* or *gallons*. By their nature, unit nouns are countable: *one dollar, two dollars, three dollars.* Thus, they work with most of the countable modifiers. However, unit nouns represent uncountable quantities: *money, volume.* (You can count money, of course, but you cannot count the <u>noun</u> *money*: *one money (?), two moneys (?), stop!*) Use *less* with unit nouns when you really want to indicate something about the underlying quantity:

Right:     We have less than 20 DOLLARS.

The amount of *money*, in whatever form, totals less than $20. If you write *we have FEWER THAN 20 dollars*, you would mean the actual pieces of paper. (You would probably say *fewer than 20 dollar <u>bills</u>*, to make the point even clearer.)

### Rule #2: Words Used to Relate *Two* Things vs. Words Used to Relate *Three* or More Things

To relate two things, use comparative forms of adjectives and adverbs (*better, worse, more, less*). For example, the rabbit is *faster* than the toad. Use superlative forms (*best, worst, most, least*) to compare three or more things or people. For example, the rabbit is the *fastest* of all of the animals at the farm.

In addition, use *between* only with two things or people. When you are talking about three or more things or people, use *among*:

> Right:    I mediated a dispute BETWEEN Maya and Kalen.

> Right:    I mediated a dispute AMONG Maya, Logan, and Kalen.

### Rule #3: The Word *Numbers*

If you wish to make a comparison using the word *numbers*, use *greater than*, not *more than* (which might imply that the quantity of numbers is larger, not the numbers themselves):

> Right:    The rare Montauk beaked griffin is not extinct; its NUMBERS are now suspected to be much GREATER than before.

### Rule #4: *Increase* and *Decrease* vs. *Greater* and *Less*

The words *increase* and *decrease* are not the same as the words *greater* and *less*. *Increase* and *decrease* express the change of one thing over time. *Greater* and *less* signal a comparison between two things. For example:

> Wrong:    The price of silver is 10 dollars GREATER.
> (Than what it used to be? Than the price of something else?)

> Right:    The price of silver INCREASED by 10 dollars.

> Right:    The price of silver is five dollars GREATER than the price of copper.

Watch out for redundancy in sentences with the words *increase* and *decrease*:

> Wrong:    The price of silver FELL by a more than 35 percent DECREASE.

> Right:    The price of silver DECREASED by more than 35 percent.

> Right:    The price of silver FELL by more than 35 percent.

*Decrease* already includes the notion of falling or lowering, so *fell* is redundant. Similarly, *increase* includes the notion of rising or growing, so *rise* or *growth* would be redundant as well.

# Problem Set

Problems 1–6 contain one or more underlined modifiers. For each of these modifiers, 1) identify the word or words, if any, that it modifies, and 2) indicate whether the modifier is correct. If the modifier is incorrect, suggest one possible way to correct the error.

1.  A <u>recent</u> formed militia, consisting of <u>lightly</u> armed peasants and a few <u>retired</u> army officers, is fighting a <u>bitterly</u> civil war against government forces.

2.  Angola, <u>which was ravaged by civil war for many years after it gained independence from Portugal</u>, <u>which is now one of Africa's success stories</u>, has an economy that grew by 21 percent last year, <u>where parliamentary elections are to be held later this week</u>.

3.  Mary buys cookies made with SugarFree <u>an artificial sweetener</u>, <u>which tastes as sweet as the corn syrup that her brother loves</u> but <u>having fewer calories than in an equivalent amount of corn syrup</u>.

4.  People <u>that are well-informed</u> know that Bordeaux is a French region <u>whose most famous export is the wine which bears its name</u>.

5.  <u>Unaccustomed to the rigors of college life</u>, James's grades dropped.

6.  The air conditioner broke in the middle of a heat wave, <u>which caused great consternation</u>.

Problems 7–10 contain boxed words or punctuation marks, some of which may be incorrect. Use the rules from this chapter to correct any errors that you can find in the boxed areas; do not change anything that is not boxed.

7.  The negotiations | between | the company, the union, and the city government were initially contentious but | ultimately | amicable.

8. Jim is trying to reduce the [number] of soda that he drinks, at last night's party, however, his resolve to drink [fewer] soda was sorely tested, he found himself quaffing [many] of sodas.

9. [Between] 1998 and 2003, there was heavy fighting in Parthia [between] numerous armed factions [yet] this conflict, so much more complicated than a conventional war [between] two states, involved no [less] than 8 countries and 25 militias.

10. Most legislators—including [much] in the governor's own party—realize that the governor's budget would imperil the state's finances, nonetheless, the budget is likely to be approved, [because] few legislators want to anger voters by cutting spending or raising taxes.

4

Problems 11–13 are multiple choice with one correct answer. For the rest of this guide, any problems may test anything you have learned to this point in the guide. As on the real GMAT, answer (A) repeats the original sentence. Unlike the real GMAT, though, these problems have only three answer choices.

11. Upon setting foot in the Gothic cathedral, the spectacular stained-glass windows amazed the camera-wielding tourists.

   (A) Upon setting foot in the Gothic cathedral, the spectacular stained-glass windows amazed the camera-wielding tourists.

   (B) Upon setting foot in the Gothic cathedral, the camera-wielding tourists were amazed by the spectacularly stained-glass windows.

   (C) The camera-wielding tourists were, upon setting foot in the Gothic cathedral, amazed by the stained-glass windows, which were spectacular.

12. Mt. Everest, which is the tallest mountain on Earth, lies on the border of Nepal and Tibet, first summited by Tenzing Norgay and Edmund Hillary in 1953.

   (A) Mt. Everest, which is the tallest mountain on Earth, lies on the border of Nepal and Tibet, first summited by Tenzing Norgay and Edmund Hillary in 1953.

   (B) First summited in 1953 by Tenzing Norgay and Edmund Hillary, the tallest mountain on Earth, which is Mt. Everest, and lies on the border of Nepal and Tibet.

   (C) First summited by Tenzing Norgay and Edmund Hillary in 1953, Mt. Everest, the tallest mountain on Earth, lies on the border of Nepal and Tibet.

13. The population <u>of San Antonio increased more than it did in any other U.S. city in 2016, adding almost</u> 66 people per day.

    (A) of San Antonio increased more than it did in any other U.S. city in 2016, adding almost

    (B) increased more in San Antonio than it did in any other city in the United States in 2016, adding almost

    (C) of San Antonio increased more than the population of any other U.S. city in 2016, almost adding

# Solutions

1.  *Recent*: INCORRECT. The adjective *recent* modifies *militia*, whereas logic calls for an adverb, *recently*, to modify *formed*.

    *Lightly*: CORRECT. The adverb *lightly* modifies the past participle *armed*, which is being used as an adjective (*armed* modifies the noun *peasants*).

    *Retired*: CORRECT. *Retired* is an adjective that modifies *army officers*. (You can also argue that *retired* is a past participle being used as an adjective.)

    *Bitterly*: INCORRECT. The adverb *bitterly* modifies *civil*, but the writer surely meant to use an adjective (*bitter*) to modify the noun phrase *civil war*.

    | Correction: | A <u>recently</u> formed militia, consisting of <u>lightly</u> armed peasants and a few <u>retired</u> army officers, is fighting a <u>bitter</u> civil war against government forces. |
    | --- | --- |

2.  *Which was ravaged…from Portugal*: CORRECT. This relative clause modifies the noun *Angola*.

    *which is now one of Africa's success stories*: INCORRECT. This relative clause illogically modifies *Portugal* (which is in Europe).

    *where parliamentary…this week*: INCORRECT. A relative clause that begins with *where* must modify a noun that names a physical place, so this clause cannot modify *year*. The clause is too far away from *Angola*, however, to perform its intended role of modifying *Angola*.

    Repairing this deeply flawed sentence involves rearranging its components and incorporating some of the modifiers into main clauses. Here is one possible way to fix it:

    | Correction: | <u>Ravaged by civil war for many years after it gained independence from Portugal</u>, Angola <u>is now one of Africa's success stories</u>; its economy grew by 21 percent last year, <u>and parliamentary elections are to be held later this week</u>. |
    | --- | --- |

3.  *an artificial sweetener*: CORRECT, but could be better. This appositive noun phrase modifies *SugarFree*; it is the first of two nonessential modifiers in a row, both of which modify SugarFree.

    *which tastes…brother loves*: CORRECT, but could be better. This modifier also modifies *the artificial sweetener SugarFree*. If an option exists to allow you to have both modifiers closer to SugarFree, that would be ideal.

    *having…corn syrup*: INCORRECT. Bonus point! The *–ing* modifier *having…corn syrup* is meant to be parallel to the relative clause *which tastes…brother loves*. When relative clauses are parallel, they should start with the same relative pronoun. You'll learn more about parallelism in the next chapter.

    | Correction: | Mary buys cookies made with <u>the artificial sweetener</u> SugarFree, <u>which tastes as sweet as the corn syrup that her brother loves</u> but <u>which has fewer calories than does an equivalent amount of corn syrup</u>. |
    | --- | --- |

4.  *that are well-informed*: INCORRECT. This clause uses the relative pronoun *that* to refer to people. Use *who* to refer to human beings.

    *whose most famous…bears its name*: CORRECT. This clause modifies *region*. Notice that *whose*, unlike *who* and *whom*, can correctly modify nonhuman entities.

*which bears its name*: INCORRECT. The context of this sentence calls for an essential clause to modify the wine, since the point of the clause is to identify *the wine*. If the sentence ended with the wine, it would be incomplete (*...whose most famous export is the wine.* Which wine?). The clause should therefore begin with *that* rather than *which*.

> Correction:    <u>Well-informed</u> people know that Bordeaux is a French region <u>whose most famous export is the wine that bears its name</u>.

5. *Unaccustomed to...college life*: INCORRECT. As an opening modifier, *unaccustomed...life* needs to refer to the main noun after the comma. Logically, however, James's *grades* are not *unaccustomed to college life*. James himself is.

> Correction:    <u>Because James was unaccustomed to the rigors of college life</u>, his grades dropped.

6. *which caused great consternation*: INCORRECT. A *comma which* modifier refers to a noun, but the *heat wave* itself didn't cause the *consternation*. Rather, the trouble was the full action: that the *air conditioner broke* during the heat wave. This meaning requires some type of adverbial modifier.

> Correction:    The air conditioner broke in the middle of a heat wave, <u>causing great consternation</u>.

7. Use the word *between* when talking about two things. Use the word *among* to describe relationships of three or more things. *Ultimately* is an adverb and correctly modifies the adjective *amicable*.

> Correction:    The negotiations AMONG the company, the union, and the city government were initially contentious but ultimately amicable.

8. *Number*: Here *soda* is an uncountable substance—otherwise, *soda* would be *sodas*—so change *number* to something uncountable, such as *amount*. (In the real world, you could keep the word *number* and make *soda* plural, but the instructions said to change only circled items.)

*Commas:* The sentence contains multiple independent clauses connected only by commas. For both circled commas, decide whether to connect the clauses by semicolons or by commas and appropriate conjunctions.

*Fewer*: Once again, *soda* is singular so it is an uncountable substance. Change *fewer* to *less*.

*Many*: This time, *sodas* is plural, so they are countable—presumably servings of soda. One possible fix is to use *a number of*.

> Correction:    Jim is trying to reduce the AMOUNT of soda that he drinks; at last night's party, however, his resolve to drink LESS soda was sorely tested, AND he found himself quaffing A NUMBER of sodas.

9. *Between*: The first *between* is correct, since only two dates are mentioned. The second *between*, however, should be *among*, since the fighting involved more than two factions. The third *between* is correct, since only two states are mentioned.

*Yet*: There are two problems here. First, *yet* is illogical because the action in the second clause (*this conflict...militias*) did not happen despite the action in the first clause (*Between...factions*), as the word *yet* suggests. Second, there are two independent clauses, but no comma before the conjunction (*yet*). Replace *yet* with either a comma plus a different conjunction or a semicolon.

4

*Less*: Countries and militias are countable entities, so change *less* to *fewer*.

> Correction: Between 1998 and 2003, there was heavy fighting in Parthia AMONG numerous armed factions; this conflict, so much more complicated than a conventional war between two states, involved no FEWER than 8 countries and 25 militias.

10. *Much*: Legislators are countable, so change *much* to *many*.

*Nonetheless*: This word connects two clauses but it is not a co-conjunction or sub-conjunction. Use a semicolon, or change to a comma plus a FANBOYS with a contract meaning, such as *yet*.

*Comma because*: This is correct. *Because* is a subordinating conjunction; therefore, it can be separated from a main clause by a comma.

> Correction: Most legislators—including MANY in the governor's own party—realize that the governor's budget would imperil the state's finances; nonetheless, the budget is likely to be approved, because few legislators want to anger voters by cutting spending or raising taxes.

11. **(C):** *Upon setting foot in the Gothic Cathedral* is an opening modifier; it describes something but doesn't tell you what it's describing, so it must describe the main noun following the comma. It is the *tourists*, not the *stained-glass windows*, who set foot in the cathedral, so eliminate answer (A).

Answer (B) contains the same opening modifier but fixes the mistake by putting the *camera-wielding tourists* after the comma. However, there is a subtle but important word change between answers (B) and (C): Choice (B) describes the *windows* as *spectacularly stained-glass*. Choice (C), on the other hand, describes the *windows* as *spectacular* (no *ly* at the end of that word).

*Spectacular* is an adjective; adjectives describe nouns (such as *window*). *Spectacularly* is an adverb—adverbs describe anything other than a stand-alone noun—so it can't apply to the noun *window*. You could say that something was spectacularly stained (as in, someone did a really good job of staining it). But it's not logical to say *spectacularly stained-glass* because stained-glass is just naming the type of window; it is not an action that could have been performed particularly well. Logically, the *windows* were *spectacular*.

12. **(C):** The full-sentence underline provides an early clue that the answer choices are likely to change pretty substantially in structure. Pay attention to the core vs. the modifiers, as well as the overall meaning of the sentence.

In the original sentence, two different modifiers (*which is the tallest mountain on Earth* and *first summited by...*) describe *Mt. Everest*. The first one is right next to *Everest*, but the second is so far away that it appears the two men summited *Tibet* (or perhaps *the border of Nepal and Tibet*). Eliminate choice (A) for faulty modifier placement.

Choice (B) fixes that initial error by rearranging the sentence but introduces a new error. The core sentence reads: *the tallest mountain AND lies on the border*. The subject and verb should not have a conjunction in between. It is also a bit clunky to set the subject as *the tallest mountain* and only later name it (*Mt. Everest*); while it is true that *the tallest mountain* was *first summited* by the two men, the meaning would be more immediately clear to the reader by using *Mt. Everest* as the subject, as correct answer (C) does.

13. **(B):** In the original sentence, the pronoun *it* refers back to the entire subject, *population of San Antonio*, implying that somehow the population of this city increased more than itself. Compare that to the structure in answer (B), which separates *population* from the city name; now *it* refers back just to the word *population*, and you can talk about the population of San Antonio separately from the population of any other U.S. city. (You'll learn more about both comparisons and pronouns later in this unit.)

Answer (C) also fixes the original illogical meaning, in this case by repeating the word *population*, but it introduces a different error at the end. *Adding almost 66 people* means that nearly 66 new people every day were in fact added to the population. *Almost adding 66 people* means that the city almost, but not quite, added people—so really, no new people were added at all. This doesn't fit with the meaning of the rest of the sentence; if the population increased more than that in other cities, then San Antonio must have added at least some people.

# CHAPTER 5

# Parallelism

## In This Chapter:

**In this chapter, you'll learn** how to spot the markers that indicate parallelism in a sentence and how to confirm that the parallel elements really are parallel.

# CHAPTER 5  **Parallelism**

Certain sentence structures require pieces of a sentence to be in the same form as, or parallel to, each other. One of the most common parallel structures is a list:

> Damian traveled to Argentina, Uruguay, and the Galapagos Islands.

The sentence above provides a list of three places. Notice that all three are not countries; to be parallel to each other, the **Elements** just have to be matching parts of speech. Since all three elements in this list are nouns, the sentence satisfies the rules of parallelism.

## Markers and Elements

Fortunately, parallel structures always have a **Marker** that tells you that parallelism is required. Spotting the marker is step 1 in the 3-step parallelism process. If you see a marker, check for parallelism. If you don't see a marker, then parallelism is not at issue. In the previous example sentence, *comma comma and* tells you that there are three parallel elements. In fact, the word *and* always indicates parallelism!

The first step in any SC question that tests parallelism is to recognize what's being tested. Memorize the common parallelism markers in the following table. (Use flash cards to help!)

|  | Marker | Structure | Example |
|---|---|---|---|
| **Open** | And | X and Y | Apples AND pears |
|  |  | X, Y, and Z | Apples, pears, AND bananas |
|  | Or | X or Y | Happy OR sad |
|  | But | X but Y | She stumbled BUT kept her balance |
|  | Rather than | X rather than Y | Play tennis RATHER THAN climb a mountain |
| **Closed** | Both/And | Both X and Y | BOTH men AND women |
|  | Either/Or | Either X or Y | EITHER she works OR she plays |
|  | Not/But | Not X but Y | NOT running BUT jogging |
|  | Not only/<br>But also | Not only X but also Y | NOT ONLY the manager BUT ALSO her team |
|  | From/To | From X to Y | FROM the house TO the end of the driveway |

In the *not only X but also Y* marker, for example, the marker itself consists of the words *not only* and *but also*. *X* and *Y* represent the two elements that must be parallel to each other. When you see the structure *not only X but also Y*, parallelism is required.

Sometimes SC questions contain an error in the marker itself, such as: *either X and Y* or *both X as well as Y*. If you see a mistake in the marker itself, cross that answer off.

Some of the markers in the table are labeled "closed," while some are labeled "open." Closed markers are markers that have two (or more) separate parts, like *either* and *or*; sentences with closed markers tend to be less complicated, because the the markers tell you exactly where the *X* and *Y* elements are—directly after each marker.

Try the following sentence:

> The sales rep determined that she would either have to increase the number of calls per hour or she would have to earn more per customer interaction.

### Step 1: Identify the Parallelism Marker

> Either *X* or *Y*

### Step 2: Identify the Elements

Since this is a closed (two-part) marker, the elements come directly after each piece:

> The sales rep determined that she would EITHER *X* (have to increase the number of calls per hour) OR *Y* (she would have to earn more per customer interaction).

The *X* element is a verb (*have*); the *Y* element is a clause (*she would have*). This sentence breaks the rules of parallelism, which require the elements to be the same parts of speech.

This table contains examples of parallel nouns, adjectives, working verbs, and more.

| Element | Example | Marker (open or closed) |
|---|---|---|
| Nouns | Her expression reflected BOTH anger AND relief. | *both X and Y* (closed) |
| Adjectives | The park was NEITHER accessible NOR affordable. | *neither X nor Y* (closed) |
| | We collected BOTH second- AND third-grade books. | *both X and Y* (closed) |
| Working Verbs | The custodian cleaned the basement AND washed the windows. | *X and Y* (open) |
| Infinitive Verbs | We would like NOT ONLY to hear your side of the story BUT ALSO to provide a response. | *not only X but also Y* (closed) |
| Participle Modifiers | The actor left quickly, waving to fans BUT ducking into a car. | *X but Y* (open) |
| Prepositional Phrases | It was important to leave the money in the drawer RATHER THAN on the table.<br><br>(Note: The prepositions do *not* necessarily have to be the same.) | *X rather than Y* (open) |
| Subordinate Clauses | They contended that the committee was biased BUT that it should not be disbanded. | *X but Y* (open) |

The majority of parallelism errors on SC questions occur when elements are not parallel parts of speech. However, there can still be an error even if the elements are parallel to each other. Consider the sentence from earlier with a slight tweak:

> The sales rep determined that she would EITHER (have to increase the number of calls per hour) OR (would have to earn more per customer interaction).

Now, both elements are verbs, satisfying the first requirement of parallelism, but there's still a mistake. Can you find it?

## The Root Phrase

The remaining error can be dealt with via the final step of the process.

### Step 3: Identify the Root Phrase and Distribute It to Each Element

The **Root Phrase** is the portion of the sentence that leads up to the first word of the parallelism marker. The root phrase of this sentence is shown in capital letters:

> THE SALES REP DETERMINED THAT SHE WOULD either have to increase the number of calls per hour or would have to earn more per customer interaction.

The root phrase needs to properly lead in to each element:

> Root phrase + *X* element: *The sales rep determined that she would have to increase the number of calls per hour.*

This makes perfect sense. On the GMAT, the root phrase typically properly leads into the first element, because an error there would be easier to spot.

> Root phrase + *Y* element: *The sales rep determined that she **would would** have to earn more per customer interaction.*

Once you remove the first element, the word *would* effectively appears twice in a row. There are two ways to fix this classic GMAT error. You could keep *would* in the root phrase and remove it from the second element:

> The sales rep determined that she would either have to increase the number of calls per hour or have to earn more per customer interaction.

Alternatively, you could remove *would* from the root phrase and add it into the first element:

> The sales rep determined that she either would have to increase the number of calls per hour or would have to earn more per customer interaction.

As you saw with *would either have*, a marker (*either*) can fall in between two-word verb structures (*would have*). When you have this construction with an open marker, look at the totality of the sentence to determine what the root phrase is.

Consider these three versions of the same sentence:

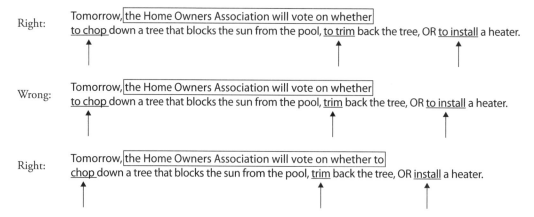

Each sentence contains a 3-item list, but the form of the elements in the list varies a bit from sentence to sentence. In the first sentence, the root phrase *the Home Owners Association will vote on whether* leads properly into the three parallel elements *to chop*, *to trim*, and *to install*. The third sentence is also properly parallel, but it extends the root phrase to include the word *to*; in this case, the three parallel elements are *chop*, *trim*, and *install*.

The second sentence, though, messes up the structure. The first and third elements both include *to* (*to chop*, *to install*), but the second element is missing the *to* (*trim*). Either all three elements need to begin with the word *to*, as in the first sentence, or the word *to* is part of the root phrase and it can't be repeated in any of the three elements, as in the third sentence.

## Closed vs. Open Markers

As shown in the last example (*X, Y, or Z*), open markers are trickier because the first element (*X*) has no marker word immediately preceding it to tell you exactly where it begins.

When working with open markers, start with the final element and work backwards from there. Use the 3-step process to evaluate the following sentence for parallelism issues:

> The doctor analyzed her patients' vital signs with a new device that simplified the process and logged the results in each patient's electronic medical records.

Step 1: Identify the Parallelism Marker

> *And*

Step 2: Identify the Elements

> *Y* element: *logged*

> *X* element: *?*

Hmm. There are multiple verbs in the first part of the sentence; which verb is parallel to *logged—analyzed* or *simplified*?

> The doctor <u>analyzed</u> (?) her patients' vital signs with a new device that <u>simplified</u> (?) the process AND <u>logged</u> the results in each patient's electronic medical records.

Step 3: Identify the Root Phrase, and Distribute It to Each Element:

> Option 1 root phrase + elements: *the doctor <u>analyzed</u> . . . AND (the doctor) <u>logged</u>*

> Option 2 root phrase + elements: *a device that <u>simplified</u> . . . AND (a device that) <u>logged</u>*

Did *the doctor* log *the results in each patient's electronic medical records* or did the *new device* log *the results in each patient's electronic medical records*? Nothing about the sentence structure indicates which of these two reasonable interpretations is intended, so this sentence is ambiguous.

Here are some ways the GMAT might fix the sentence:

> The doctor analyzed her patients' vital signs with a new device that BOTH <u>simplified</u> the process AND <u>logged</u> the results in each patient's electronic medical records.

> Using a new device that simplified the process, the doctor <u>analyzed</u> her patients' vital signs AND <u>logged</u> the results in each patient's electronic medical records.

In the first example, the closed marker *both X and Y* removes any ambiguity about the root phrase. Now, it is the *new device that both simplified the process and logged the results.*

In the second example, the sentence structure flips completely. You may not have anticipated this sort of fix—remember, stay flexible! Now, *a new device* is part of an opening modifier. *The doctor* uses the *new device*, but it is *the doctor* herself who is the subject for *analyzed* and *logged*.

How about the following example?

> Every night after the lights go out, the campers attempt to sneak out of their bunks and steal candy from the kitchen.

Step 1: Identify the Parallelism Marker

> *And*

Step 2: Identify the Elements

> *Y* element: *steal*

> *X* element: *?*

*Steal* is a verb, so look for a verb in the first clause. Again, there are two: *attempt* and *sneak*. Which one is parallel to *steal*?

> The campers <u>attempt</u> (?) to <u>sneak</u> (?) out of their bunks AND <u>steal</u> candy from the kitchen.

Option 1:

> *X* element: *attempt*

> *Y* element: *steal*

Option 2:

> *X* element: *sneak*

> *Y* element: *steal*

Step 3: Identify the Root Phrase, and Distribute It to Each Element:

> Option 1 root phrase + elements: *the campers <u>attempt</u> (one thing) . . . AND (the campers) <u>steal</u> (another)*

> Option 2 root phrase + elements: *the campers attempt to <u>sneak</u> . . . AND (the campers attempt to) <u>steal</u>*

Option 2 says that the campers *attempt to . . . steal candy*—but it isn't clear that they succeed. The first option implies that the campers are successful. However, there's only one logical interpretation here: It's nonsensical to say that *the campers attempt to sneak out of their bunks*—implying that they don't necessarily succeed—but that they definitely *steal candy from the kitchen.* If they don't succeed in sneaking out, then they can't steal the candy!

Thus, Option 2 is the only coherent meaning; *the campers attempt to* do two things: 1) *sneak out* and 2) *steal candy.*

## The Many Parallel Structures of the Word *And*

Many of the examples in this chapter contain the marker *and*. When *and* lacks a preceding comma, it can connect two of almost any part of speech, as shown in these correct sentences:

| | | |
|---|---|---|
| The <u>manager</u> AND her <u>team</u> were praised by the CEO. | → | compound subject |
| In one terrible day, the account manager <u>lost</u> a client AND <u>greeted</u> the CEO of her company by the wrong name. | → | compound verb |
| A rapid improvement <u>in motor function</u> AND <u>in vision</u> was observed. | → | prepositional phrase |
| Sal applied himself in his new job, <u>arriving</u> early every day AND <u>leaving</u> late every night. | → | adverbial modifier |

When *and* is preceded by a comma, there are a few possible scenarios. If it's preceded by exactly one comma, the word *and* connects two independent clauses. Recall from the Sentence Structure chapter that to create a compound sentence, you need both a comma and a co-conjunction between the two independent clauses:

> Right:     The driver swerved to avoid the oncoming car, and he barely missed colliding with a tree.

When *and* is preceded by exactly two commas, there are two possibilities. Often, two commas will convey a list of three things:

> Right:     George Washington, John Adams, and Thomas Jefferson were the first three presidents of the United States.

However, the two commas may also be there to offset a modifier:

> Right:      The baker looked at the wedding cake, which stood over four feet high, and beamed proudly.

Strip out any modifiers before you evaluate the parallel structure.

> The baker <u>looked</u> at the wedding cake~~, which stood over four feet high,~~ AND <u>beamed</u> proudly.

Finally, you may sometimes see three commas followed by *and*. This can introduce a list with four elements, but there is another tricky structure that the GMAT will sometimes test. Remember Sal from the earlier example, the one who was arriving early and leaving late every day? Take a look at what happens when a third modifier is added to *arriving* and *leaving*:

> Sal applied himself in his new job, arriving early every day, skipping lunch regularly, and leaving late every night.

The first comma separates the core sentence from the modifiers; the other two commas separate the three items in the list ($X$, $Y$, and $Z$). Imagine that the test also provides you with this choice:

> Sal applied himself in his new job, arrived early every day, skipped lunch regularly, and left late every night.

What's the difference between the two options? Is one preferable?

The second sentence is a list of four separate things that Sal did ($W$, $X$, $Y$, and $Z$), and the verbs are all properly parallel to each other. However, this version gives all four activities equal emphasis; at this level, the three latter activities do not need to have any connection to Sal's job. For example, the sentence could mean *Sal applied himself in his new job, arrived early every day at the gym, skipped lunch regularly on the weekend, and left the bar late every Saturday night.* While the sentence is grammatically correct, its meaning is less logical than the other option.

If you focus too rigidly on the $W$, $X$, $Y$, and $Z$ structure, you might misinterpret the first sentence to be a list of four things, the first of which is not parallel to the three that follow. In fact, however, that first sentence contains a properly parallel list of three modifiers that all describe how *Sal applied himself in his new job*. The first comma separates the main clause (*Sal applied himself in his new job*) from the adverbial modifier (*arriving early every day*). The three *comma –ing* modifiers are all properly parallel to each other. As always, you can check the elements with the root phrase to verify that they all make sense:

> Root phrase + $X$ element: *Sal applied himself in his new job, arriving early every day.*

> Root phrase + $Y$ element: *Sal applied himself in his new job, skipping lunch regularly.*

> Root phrase + $Z$ element: *Sal applied himself in his new job, leaving late every night.*

This sentence is grammatically correct and conveys a more logical meaning than the other option, relating each part of the sentence to the fact that Sal applied himself in his new job. The structure *clause, adverbial modifier, adverbial modifier, and adverbial modifier* can be particularly tricky to parse. Identify the modifiers before you eliminate an answer that appears to break the rules of parallelism, and pay careful attention to the meaning of the sentence.

## Idioms with Built-In Parallel Structure

Remember, check for parallelism *only* when you see a parallelism marker. A few examples of idioms with built-in parallel structure are shown below; you can find more in the chapters on Comparisons and Idioms.

| | | |
|---|---|---|
| Between *X* and *Y* | Distinguish *X* from *Y* | Neither *X* nor *Y* |
| Consider *X Y* | Estimate *X* to be *Y* | View *X* as *Y* |
| In contrast to *X, Y* | Mistake *X* for *Y* | Whether *X* or *Y* |

What's wrong with the following sentences?

The launch of the new product line was neither a success or a failure.

Producing a paper bag requires between 20 to 25 times as much water as producing a plastic bag.

In the first sentence, the proper idiom is *neither X nor Y*. In the second sentence, the proper idiom is *between X and Y*. If an answer contains an idiomatic error in the parallelism marker itself, cross that choice off and save the 3-step process for the remaining answers.

# Problem Set

In problems 1–4, box the open markers, circle the closed markers, put brackets around the [root phrase], and underline the elements in the parallel structure.

1. Researchers have found a correlation between exercising and learning good grades.

2. Although the nonprofit could not offer a high salary or a pension, it was able to offer not only four weeks of annual vacation but also full health benefits.

3. Many teachers choose to seek employment in the suburbs or private schools rather than face low salaries in the city.

4. A good night's sleep not only gives your body a chance to rest and to recover but also energizes you for the following day.

There is almost always more than one correct way to write a parallel structure. Problems 5–7 have at least one correct answer; some have more. Apply the 3-step process you learned about in the chapter, and select all the correct answers.

5. The corruption both at the city level and at the state level is dispiriting.

    (A) both at the city level and at
    (B) both at the city level and
    (C) at both the city level and at
    (D) at both the city level and

6. When the sales manager gets wind of the recent slump, she likely will fire some members of the sales team and blame the marketing team.

    (A) team and blame the marketing team
    (B) team and the marketing team
    (C) team, blaming the marketing team
    (D) and marketing teams

7.  The recently hired director of marketing has been an abject <u>failure; she neither understands principles of design nor</u> search engine optimization.

    (A)  failure; she neither understands principles of design nor

    (B)  failure, understanding neither principles of design nor principles of

    (C)  failure, lacking understanding in principles of design and

    (D)  failure; she understands neither principles of design nor

Problems 8–10 are multiple choice with one correct answer. As on the real GMAT, answer (A) repeats the original sentence. Unlike the real GMAT, though, these problems have only three answer choices.

8.  Voters want to elect a president who <u>not only genuinely cares about health care, the environment, and the travails of ordinary men and women,</u> <u>but also has</u> the experience, wisdom, and strength of character required for the job.

    (A)  not only genuinely cares about health care, the environment, and the travails of ordinary men and women, but also has

    (B)  genuinely cares about health care, the environment, and the travails of ordinary men and women, as well as

    (C)  genuinely cares not only about health care, the environment, and the travails of ordinary men and women, but also about

9.  The consultant is looking for a café <u>where there are</u> comfortable chairs and that provides free internet access.

    (A)  where there are

    (B)  that has both

    (C)  that has

10. The blizzard deposited more than a foot of snow on the train tracks, <u>which prompted the transit authority to shut down service temporarily and caused</u> discontent among commuters who were left stranded for hours.

    (A)  which prompted the transit authority to shut down service temporarily and caused

    (B)  prompting the transit authority to shut down service temporarily, causing

    (C)  prompting the transit authority to shut down service temporarily and causing

# Solutions

1.  [Researchers have found a correlation] (between) exercising (and) earning good grades.

2.  [Although the nonprofit could not offer] a high salary [or] a pension, [it was able to offer] (not only) four weeks of annual vacation (but also) full health benefits.

3.  This sentence has one parallel structure within another. The main pairing is [Many teachers choose to] seek [rather than] face. The parallelism within that is [in] the suburbs [or] private schools.

    [Many teachers choose to] seek employment [in] the suburbs [or] private schools [rather than] face low salaries in the city.

4.  Like question 3, this sentence has one parallel structure within another. The main pairing is [A good night's sleep] (not only) gives (but also) energizes. The pairing within that is [a chance] to rest [and] to recover.

    [A good night's sleep] (not only) gives your body [a chance] to rest [and] to recover (but also) energizes you for the following day.

5.  **(A) and (D):** The closed marker *both X and Y* requires the *X* and *Y* elements to be parallel parts of speech. Answer choices (B) and (C) commit a classic GMAT error, incorrectly placing a prep phrase (starting with *at*) parallel to a stand-alone noun. In choice (B), the given pairing is *both* (prep phrase) *and* (noun). In choice (C), the given pairing is *both* (noun) *and* (prep phrase).

    Answers (A) and (D) correct this error in different ways. In choice (A), the *X* and *Y* elements are parallel prep phrases (*at the city level* and *at the state level*). In choice (D), the *X* and *Y* elements are parallel nouns (*the city level* and *the state level*), as the preposition *at* has been moved to the root phrase, before the word *both*.

6.  **(A), (B), and (D):** When you have an open parallelism marker such as *X and Y*, start with the element that follows the marker. Since *blame* is underlined in the original sentence, the final element can (and does) change from answer to answer.

    In answer choice (A), the verb *blame* is properly parallel to the verb *fire*: *She likely will fire . . . and blame.*

    The *Y* element in choice (B) is *the marketing team*, which is properly parallel to *the sales team*: *She likely will fire some members of . . . the marketing team.*

    Choice (C) changes up the structure, removing the word *and* as well as the parallel structure that comes with it. *Blaming* is now an adverbial modifier, pointing back to *she likely will fire*. However, this meaning is illogical; *blaming the marketing team* does not describe *how* the sales manager *will fire some members of the sales team*. The two actions are related but separate; the parallel structure in the other answers properly conveys this.

    Notice that answer (D) changes *team* to *teams*. In this correct sentence, the adjectives *sales* and *marketing* both modify *teams*. Adjectives come before the nouns that they modify, so in this construction, the root phrase comes after the elements, not before. For example, in the sentence *The black and white photograph is beautiful*, the parallel adjectives *black* and *white* both describe the root word *photograph*.

7.  **(B), (C), and (D):** The closed parallelism marker *neither X nor Y* requires the *X* and *Y* elements to be parallel parts of speech. Answer choice (A) violates this requirement by placing a verb (*understands*) parallel to a noun (*search engine optimization*).

    Choice (B) correctly satisfies this parallel requirement, matching *principles of design* with *principles of search engine optimization*.

    In answer (C), the root phrase extends through the words *principles of*. The *X* and *Y* elements, *design* and *search engine optimization*, are both nouns.

    What about answer choice (D), in which *principles of design* is placed parallel to *search engine optimization*? The *X* and *Y* elements do not have to be exactly the same; they just need to be the same part of speech, and *X* and *Y* are both nouns here. The root phrase still logically leads into both elements: *She understands neither principles of design* and *she understands neither…search engine optimization*. Both elements are things the *director of marketing* does not understand.

8.  **(A):** This tricky sentence contains a list within the parallel structure *not only X but also Y*. The list is the same in all three answers, so investigate the *not only X but also Y* structure in answers (A) and (C).

    The *X* and *Y* elements in answer (A) are *genuinely cares* and *has*. Even though the first element has an attached adverb (*genuinely*), that does not break the parallelism between these two verbs.

    Answer (C) shifts the placement of *not only*; the *X* element is now *about health care* and the *Y* element is *about the experience*. These prep phrases are parallel, too. However, the meaning of (C) is illogical: *Voters want to elect a president who genuinely cares…about the experience, wisdom, and strength of character required for the job?* That's not what the sentence intends to say; it's trying to say that voters want a president who, as answer choice (A) says, *has the experience, wisdom, and strength of character required for the job*. Eliminate answer choice (C) for this meaning error.

    Answer choice (B) removes the *not only X but also Y* structure, but it maintains the meaning error discussed in answer (C). Voters want a president who *has* experience, not one who *cares about* experience.

9.  **(C):** The open marker *and Y* indicates parallelism. When you see an open marker, let the *Y* element guide you. Since *and* is in the non-underlined part of the sentence, the first element must be parallel to *that provides free internet access*.

    Answer choice (A) tries to make *where there are* parallel to *that provides*, but *where* introduces a full clause (*there are chairs*), while *that* has only a verb (*provides*), not a subject–verb pairing.

    Answer choice (B) does start with *that has*, but it adds in *both*, which is part of the closed parallelism marker *both X and Y*. The two elements in this marker are *comfortable chairs* and *that provides free internet access*. A noun cannot be parallel to a subordinate clause; eliminate this answer for violating parallelism.

    Answer (C) maintains the open parallel structure; *that has comfortable chairs* is properly parallel to *that provides free internet access*.

10.  **(C):** In the original sentence, the *comma which* noun modifier incorrectly implies that *the train tracks* are what led to the discontinuation of service and angered the commuters. In fact, the entire situation (*the blizzard deposited more than a foot of snow on the train tracks*) is what *prompted the transit authority to shut down service*. Thus, the sentence requires the adverbial modifier *prompting*, used in answers (B) and (C).

The construction in answer choice (B), exactly two *comma –ing* modifiers in a row, is almost never acceptable because it leads to an ambiguous meaning. Is it the case that the *blizzard deposit[ing] snow* caused *discontent* or is it the case that the *transit authority shut[ting] down service* caused *discontent*? Either interpretation is logical. Answer (C) avoids this ambiguity by employing a parallel structure (*X and Y*), signaling that each modifier (*prompting* and *causing*) refers back to the main clause.

5

# CHAPTER 6

# Comparisons

## In This Chapter:

- Comparison Markers
- Omitted Words
- *Like* vs. *As*
- The Many Uses of the Word *As*
- Comparative and Superlative Forms

**In this chapter, you will learn** about a subset of parallelism: comparisons. You'll learn the markers associated with comparisons and the stricter parallelism rules that comparisons must follow.

# CHAPTER 6 Comparisons

**Comparisons** are a subset of parallelism, but they get their own chapter because they require an additional check in order to ensure that they are valid.

For example, what's wrong with the sentence below?

Wrong: Like Mary, Adam's car is green.

Poor Mary. She must be pretty sick if she's green, like Adam's car!

Right: LIKE Mary's car, Adam's car is green.

Comparisons require parallelism between the two elements being compared (nouns with nouns, for example), but that's rarely the mistake in an SC question that tests comparisons. Instead, the mistakes tend to be in the meaning (is it logical to compare the two elements?) or in the comparison marker itself. As soon as you see a comparison marker, check the meaning and the marker.

## Comparison Markers

Like parallelism, comparisons always have a marker that alerts you to the comparison:

Right: John, LIKE his mother, has fiery red hair.

Right: LIKE his mother, John has fiery red hair.

This comparison can have the structure *X, like Y or like X, Y.* Here is a list of some common comparison markers and their associated structures:

| Marker | Sample Structure |
|---|---|
| Like, Unlike | Jane, LIKE her parents, has green eyes. <br> UNLIKE the cat, the dog is friendly. |
| As | Dhivya is smart, AS is Abby. |
| Than | You have earned a BETTER score THAN I have. <br> Cisco's revenues are considerably HIGHER THAN Starbucks's. |
| As (adjective) as | Mira is AS likely AS Sam to win the promotion. |
| Different from, Similar to | My current job is quite DIFFERENT FROM my last one. (Pronoun *one* refers to *job*.) <br> Ferraris are SIMILAR TO Lamborghinis. |
| In contrast to/with | Canada's housing market did not suffer many difficulties during the economic downturn, IN CONTRAST TO the housing market in the United States. |

How can the GMAT break a comparison? Consider what's being compared in the following sentence:

> John's hair, like his mother, is red and fiery.

Now *John's hair* is being compared to *his mother*, and that's illogical. The GMAT loves to trap students with these sorts of nonsensical comparisons, and the GMAT often fixes these broken comparisons by using a pronoun or apostrophe to stand in for the missing noun:

> Right:        John's hair, LIKE that of his mother, is red and fiery.

> Right:        John's hair, LIKE his mother's, is red and fiery.

In fact, fixing a broken comparison with *that of* or *those of* is so common that you can think of these phrases as comparison markers!

In the correct examples, both the pronoun *that* and the apostrophe in *mother's* refer to *hair*. Note that it is acceptable for an apostrophe to imply a noun—you do not have to say *his mother's hair*.

What comparison is made in the sentence below?

> Beethoven's music, which broke a number of established rules with its structure and melodic form, is considered more revolutionary than Bach.

The comparison structure in this sentence is *X more than Y*. As with open markers, comparisons are often most easily tackled by finding the second element first, since it follows the comparison marker: *more revolutionary than Bach*. So, what is more revolutionary than Bach? The subject of the sentence: *Beethoven's music*. This comparison is not parallel.

In everyday speech, this sentence would likely sound fine, since people often talk about the music of Bach as "Bach" (e.g., *I like to listen to Bach on the radio)*. Grammar rules demand, however, that if the sentence has referred to Beethoven's music with the word *music*, then the sentence should do the same with Bach's music:

> Right:        Beethoven's music, which broke a number of established rules with its structure and melodic form, is considered MORE revolutionary THAN BACH'S.

As before, you do not have to repeat the word *music*, as long as the second element, *Bach's*, clearly refers back to music. The sentence could also use *that of Bach* as the second element.

## Omitted Words

As shown earlier in this chapter, comparisons can sometimes omit words in the *Y* element and still be considered properly parallel. Both of the following sentences are correct:

> Right:        My car is bigger than Brian's [*car*].

> Right:        My house is smaller than the Smiths' [*house*].

You can also omit units, verbs, and even whole clauses from the second term, as long as there is no ambiguity in the comparison:

> Right:        Whereas I drink two quarts of milk a day, my friend drinks three [*quarts of milk a day*].

> Right:        I walk faster than Brian [*walks*].

> Right:        I walk as fast now as [*I walked*] when I was younger.

In general, include the omitted words or appropriate helping verbs (such as *be*, *do*, and *have*) if the sentence would otherwise be ambiguous. For example:

      Ambiguous:      I like cheese more than Yvette.

Do you like cheese more than Yvette likes cheese? Or do you like cheese more than you like Yvette?

      Right:      I like cheese more than Yvette DOES. (*more than* Yvette *likes cheese*)

      Right:      I like cheese more than I DO Yvette. (*more than I like* Yvette)

The GMAT occasionally allows unnecessary helping verbs:

      Right:      Apples are more healthy to eat than caramels.

      Right:      Apples are more healthy to eat than caramels ARE.

The second sentence is not considered redundant or incorrect. If you see this on the test, ignore it and find some other difference on which to base your decision.

## *Like* vs. *As*

*Like* and *as* are two very common comparison signals.

*Like* is used to compare nouns. Never put a clause or a prepositional phrase after *like*. (Reminder: A clause contains a working verb, one that can be the main verb in a sentence.)

Consider the following examples:

      Right:      LIKE her brother, Ava aced the test.

      Wrong:      LIKE her brother did, Ava aced the test.

Start with the easier element to spot: the one that directly follows the comparison marker. In the first sentence, *like* is followed by the noun phrase *her brother*, so *her brother* is the first element. The second element is the noun following the comma, *Ava*. It's logical to compare one person to another, so this choice is fine.

Note two things. First, the element immediately following the word *like* is a noun. This part should always have just a noun or noun phrase—no main verb. The incorrect example is incorrect precisely because the portion following *like* includes a verb (*her brother DID*).

Second, the other noun in the comparison (the one *not* following the word *like*) will be attached to a verb. In this case, the other element is the noun *Ava*, but *Ava* also functions as the subject of the main part of the sentence. Any legal sentence core does need a subject and verb; the part of the comparison that doesn't connect to the marker *like* will provide that subject and verb.

When you see *like*, think noun-to-noun comparison. The noun attached to *like* should never have its own verb.

*As*, on the other hand, can only be used to compare clauses, not nouns. In other words, each element of the comparison needs its own verb:

      Right:      AS her brother DID, Ava aced the test.

      Wrong:      AS her brother, Ava aced the test.

Notice that this comparison can be made correctly using either *like* or *as*, so stay flexible as you move through the answer choices. Don't assume that the correct answer will compare two nouns simply because the original sentence compares two nouns. It's not unusual for the GMAT to change the comparison marker in the correct answer—and that can change the form of the comparison elements as well.

Occasionally, you may see an *–ing* word that is functioning as a noun. For example:

> Right:      LIKE <u>swimming, skiing</u> is great exercise.

This comparison still pairs two nouns; the nouns just happen to be in *–ing* form. An *–ing* word is not a verb unless it has another verb directly attached to it (such as *is swimming*).

## The Many Uses of the Word *As*

*As* is a remarkably versatile word. It can do more than just compare clauses. In fact, it has as many uses as almost any other word that you'll encounter. It can be used as a prepositional (prep) phrase. It has other uses, such as introducing examples. Did you notice all the different instances of the word *as* as you read this paragraph?

1.  *As X as* (comparing clauses)

    One of the most common uses of *as* on the GMAT is in the two-part phrase *as X as*, where *X* is an adjective or adverb:

    > Indian food is *as spicy as* Mexican food (is).

    > Cheetahs can run almost three times *as fast as* the fastest human (can run).

    If you see a double-*as* on the GMAT, you've usually got a comparison; there are some other valid uses of *as X as*, though, so pay attention to the meaning. For example:

    > The temperature may drop *as low as* 20 degrees.

    The words *as low as* convey a quantity, not a comparison. *As X as* can be a quantity modifier:

    > The new product may be available *as soon as* next week.

    The words *as soon as* convey a time frame, not a comparison. *As X as* can also be a time marker.

2.  Prep phrase (modifying clauses)

    *As* can also be the preposition that starts a prep phrase:

    > Liat worked *as a consultant* for seven years.

    > Barry Bonds retired *as the all-time home run leader*.

    When *as* starts a prep phrase, it's always an adverbial modifier.

3.  Conjunction (connecting clauses)

    *As* can also function as a conjunction, connecting two clauses. In this context, it most often means *at the same time that*:

    > He looked down at his phone *as he crossed the street*.

    > Shoshana ate her breakfast *as she watched the news*.

4. Idioms

   *As* can be used in a number of idioms; here are some that are common on the GMAT. See the Idioms chapter and the Idioms appendix for a more comprehensive list.

   4a.  *X such as/ Such X as*

        *As* can be used as part of the phrase *such as* to introduce examples:

        > Recent environmental regulations have banned *items such as* plastic straws and single-use plastic bags.

        > Recent environmental regulations have banned *such items as* plastic straws and single-use plastic bags.

        The sentences are both correct. You can say *such X as* or *X such as*, where *X* is the category of examples (in this case, the category is *items*).

   4b.  *So as to*

        The phrase *so as to* means *in order to*:

        > He made up an excuse so as to avoid suspicion.

   4c.  *As* vs. *than*

        As discussed in the Parallelism chapter, the GMAT will sometimes use incorrect markers, such as *either X and Y*, rather than the correct *either X or Y*. This type of mistake is relatively common with comparison markers as well, and since *as* has so many uses, the GMAT will sometimes try to sneak it into places where it doesn't belong. For example:

        | Wrong: | The speed limit is *higher* in the state of Texas *as* it is anywhere else in the United States. |

   The correct idiom is *higher…than*; the pairing *higher…as* is incorrect.

## Comparative and Superlative Forms

When comparing two things, use the comparative form (*–er*) of an adjective or adverb. When comparing more than two things, use the superlative form (*–est*) of an adjective or adverb. For example:

| Comparative: | She is SHORTER than her sister. |
| Superlative: | She is the SHORTEST of her five siblings. |
| Comparative: | You are MORE INTERESTING than he is. |
| Superlative: | You are the MOST INTERESTING person here. |

Do not take an adverb that ends in *–ly* and make it a comparison by changing the ending to *–er*. This error is common in speech. Instead, add *more*:

| Wrong: | Adrian runs QUICKLY. He runs QUICKER than Jacob. |
| Right: | Adrian runs QUICKLY. He runs MORE QUICKLY than Jacob. |

However, some adverbs that do not end in *–ly* are made into comparatives by adding *–er*:

| Right: | Adrian runs FAST. He runs FASTER than Jacob. |

Do not use a comparative word, such as *higher*, unless the word *than* completes the comparison. The GMAT often incorrectly pairs comparative words with words besides *than*. Examples seen on SC include *more likely . . . as*, *higher . . . over*, and *less . . . compared to*. It is also incorrect to drop *than* entirely:

Wrong:      With winter coming, I will have HIGHER energy bills.

The sentence *implies* the comparison *than before*. On the GMAT, however, you must make that comparison explicit, using the word *than*:

Right:      With winter coming, I will have HIGHER energy bills THAN I did over the summer.

6

# Problem Set

In problems 1–9, underline all comparison signals and all comparative or superlative forms. If the sentence is fine, write CORRECT. If not, correct the errors in the sentence. For an ambiguous sentence, express each possible meaning of the sentence with a correct sentence of your own.

1. Like many other states, Virginia is technically a commonwealth.

   *Correct*

2. I scored three goals in yesterday's game, as did Suzanne.

   *Correct*

3. The rapid development of India in the twenty-first century is like England in the eighteenth century.

4. A leopard cannot run as fast as a cheetah.

5. A leopard cannot catch a wildebeest as fast as a cheetah.

6. In contrast to the trapeze artists, who fumbled their routine, the antics of the circus clowns kept the audience entertained for hours.

7. The clothes looked more appealing inside the store than on the racks outside.

8.   The <u>clothes inside</u> the store looked more <u>appealing</u> than on the racks outside.

9.   Hugo is widely acknowledged to be our best employee, because he works harder and more creatively than anyone else in the company.

Problems 10–12 are multiple choice with one correct answer. As on the real GMAT, answer (A) repeats the original sentence. Unlike the real GMAT, though, these problems have only three answer choices.

10.   Although the towers appear <u>to be identical, the east tower is the tallest, reaching</u> 20 feet higher than the west tower.

   (A)   to be identical, the east tower is the tallest, reaching

   (B)   to be identical heights, the taller east tower reaches

   (C)   identical, the east tower reaches

11.   Trends in popular music come and go, and the genres that are mainstream today <u>are more likely to be forgotten tomorrow, as have many similar styles</u> before them.

   (A)   are more likely to be forgotten tomorrow, as have many similar styles

   (B)   more likely will be forgotten tomorrow, as many similar styles have

   (C)   are likely to be forgotten tomorrow, as were many similar styles

12.   Courtney's experience at Haleford, a large research university <u>with renowned professors, affluent students, and imposing buildings, were unlike her</u> high school in a small town.

   (A)   with renowned professors, affluent students, and imposing buildings, were unlike her

   (B)   that employs renowned professors, affluent students, and imposing buildings, was unlike her experience at

   (C)   known for its renowned professors, affluent students, and imposing buildings, was nothing like her experience at

# Solutions

1. <u>Like</u> many other states, Virginia is technically a commonwealth.

   **CORRECT.** The noun phrase *many other states* follows the comparison signal *like*. This noun phrase is being compared to the noun *Virginia*, which is the subject of the sentence.

2. I scored three goals in yesterday's game, <u>as</u> did Suzanne.

   **CORRECT.** The word *as* sets up a comparison between two clauses: *I scored three goals in yesterday's game* and *did Suzanne*. The verb *did* in the second clause stands for the entire phrase *scored three goals in yesterday's game*, which thus does not need to be repeated.

3. The rapid development of India in the twenty-first century is <u>like</u> England in the eighteenth century.

   This sentence incorrectly compares the *rapid development of India* to *England*. The easiest way to fix the sentence is to include the phrase *that of* to make it clear that the comparison is between the rapid developments of both countries:

   Correction:  The rapid development of India in the twenty-first century is <u>like</u> that of England in the eighteenth century.

4. A leopard cannot run <u>as fast as</u> a cheetah.

   **CORRECT.** The phrase *as fast as* sets up a comparison between two clauses. Since *can run* is implied after *as fast as a cheetah*, the clause *a leopard cannot run* is properly parallel to *a cheetah (can run)*.

   Another acceptable version of this sentence is *a leopard cannot run as fast as a cheetah can*. Here the helping verb *can* stands for the full phrase *can run*.

5. A leopard cannot catch a wildebeest <u>as fast as</u> a cheetah.

   This sentence is ambiguous because it's unclear what is being compared to what. Does it mean that the wildebeest is as fast as a cheetah?

   Correction (1):  A leopard cannot catch a wildebeest that runs <u>as fast as</u> a cheetah (runs).

   Or does it mean that the leopard catches the cheetah?

   Correction (2):  A leopard cannot catch a wildebeest <u>as fast as</u> it can (catch) a cheetah.

   Or does it mean that the cheetah catches the wildebeest?

   Correction (3):  A leopard cannot catch a wildebeest <u>as fast as</u> a cheetah can (catch a wildebeest).

   In these corrected versions, the text in parentheses is implied. The GMAT considers these sentences acceptable with or without the implied text.

6. <u>In contrast to</u> the trapeze artists, who fumbled their routine, the antics of the circus clowns kept the audience entertained for hours.

   This sentence makes an illogical comparison between *trapeze artists* and *antics*. A more logical comparison would be between *trapeze artists* and *circus clowns*.

   Correction:  <u>In contrast to</u> the trapeze artists, who fumbled their routine, the circus clowns kept the audience entertained for hours with their antics.

7. The clothes looked <u>more appealing</u> inside the store <u>than</u> on the racks outside.

   **CORRECT.** This sentence compares how some clothes looked *inside the store* to how the same clothes looked *on the racks outside*.

8. The clothes inside the store looked <u>more appealing than</u> on the racks outside.

   This sentence seems to compare some clothes (*the clothes inside the store*) to a location (*on the racks outside*). It is hard to tell whether the author wants to compare two separate sets of clothes or one set of clothes in two display locations.

   One way to correct the sentence would be to rewrite it as the sentence in the previous question.

   Correction (1):  The clothes looked <u>more appealing</u> inside the store <u>than</u> on the racks outside.

   This version makes sense because it puts the phrase *inside the store* after the comparison signal *more appealing*, making that phrase available for a comparison with *on the racks outside*. In this version, there is one set of clothes, and the comparison is between how these same clothes looked *inside the store* and how they looked *on the racks outside*. (Perhaps a customer brought the clothes into the store and is describing the different appearance of the same clothes before and after the move.)

   Correction (2):  The clothes inside the store looked <u>more appealing than</u> (did) those on the racks outside.

   This version compares two sets of clothes: *the clothes inside the store* and *those on the racks outside*. The word *did* is optional.

9. Hugo is widely acknowledged to be our <u>best</u> employee, because he works <u>harder</u> and <u>more creatively than</u> anyone else in the company.

   **CORRECT.** In the first clause, Hugo is being singled out from among a group (employees), so use a superlative (*best*) to modify *employee*.

   In the second clause, there is a comparison between *X* and *Y*, so use the comparative forms rather than the superlative forms. (The comparison is between how *he works* and how *anyone else in the company works*.) The comparative form of the adverb *creatively* is *more creatively*. The comparative form of the adverb *harder* is simply *harder*, because *harder* is a short adverb that does not end in *–ly*.

10. **(C):** The original sentence says that *the east tower is the tallest*; this superlative form (*tallest*) indicates that there are at least three towers. However, the sentence describes only two towers—*the east tower* and *the west tower*—so the comparative form (*taller*) should be used instead.

    Answer choice (B) correctly replaces *tallest* with *taller*; however, the sentence already says that this *tower reaches 20 feet higher than* the other one. Describing *the east tower* as *taller* is redundant. Even the word *heights* is redundant in conjunction with *taller* and *higher than*. It might be acceptable to say that the two buildings were thought to be identical *heights* but one is actually *taller*. But all three descriptions (*heights, taller, higher than*) together are overkill.

    Choice (C) changes *appear to be identical* to *appear identical*. These idioms are both correct. This choice removes *taller* and *heights*, eliminating the redundancy.

11.  **(C):** The word *more* indicates a coming comparison that should be in the form *X more than Y*. However, answers (A) and (B) use *more* without the second piece of the comparison idiom, *than*. *The genres that are mainstream today are more likely* than what *to be forgotten tomorrow*? Since there is no second piece of the comparison, eliminate answers (A) and (B) for this comparison error.

Answer (C) fixes this by removing the word *more* altogether. Now, there's no comparison in the first half of the sentence, simply a statement that these mainstream genres *are likely to be forgotten*.

12.  **(C):** This sentence is filled with modifiers, and there's no verb before the underline. Strip out the modifiers to find the core sentence: *Courtney's experience…were unlike her high school*. Since *experience* is singular, the verb must be singular to match. In addition, this choice compares *Courtney's experience* to *her high school*; these are not the same kind of thing. Eliminate choice (A) for a mismatched subject–verb and a mismatched comparison.

Answers (B) and (C) correctly change the verb to *was*. Choice (B) uses *unlike*, while choice (C) uses *nothing like*. Although *unlike* is the more common comparison marker, these markers are both correct. Find another split.

Both sentences have a list (*renowned professors, affluent students, and imposing buildings*), which requires parallelism, but the list is the same in each answer. The lead-in, however, is different. The root phrase in answer choice (B) is *that employs*. While Haleford *employs renowned professors*, it certainly does not *employ…imposing buildings*. Eliminate choice (B) for this meaning error.

6

# Pronouns

## In This Chapter:

- The Antecedent Must Exist and Be Sensible

- The Antecedent and Pronoun Must Agree in Number

- The Deadly Five: *It, Its, They, Them, Their*

- *This, That, These,* and *Those*

- Some Ambiguity Is Acceptable

**In this chapter, you will learn** how to recognize pronouns and how to test that they are logical and reflect the appropriate number. You'll also learn how to deal with pronoun ambiguity—and when to ignore that issue and concentrate on something else instead.

# CHAPTER 7 **Pronouns**

A **Pronoun** is a word that takes the place of a noun so that you do not have to repeat that noun elsewhere in the sentence. For example:

> GASOLINE has become so expensive that it now consumes as much as 16 percent of personal income in some rural areas.

In the sentence above, the pronoun *it* takes the place of the noun *gasoline*. In other words, *it* refers to *gasoline*. The noun that a pronoun replaces is known as its **Antecedent**.

On the GMAT, it is not unusual to think that a pronoun error exists, only to discover that the pronoun is correct after all. As soon as you think that you may have a pronoun issue, check the answer choices to see what the differences are.

Do the answers split between singular and plural? Between a pronoun and a regular noun? If there are differences, then you can apply the rules and possibly cross off some answers. Occasionally, you may discover that the pronoun does not change in all five answers; in this case, look for some other issue to tackle instead.

If you think a non-underlined pronoun may be problematic, find the antecedent (you'll learn how in this chapter). If the antecedent is also not underlined, then the pronoun is fine; look for some other split. If the antecedent is underlined, check the answers to see what other options are offered.

In short, whenever you think a pronoun might be problematic, immediately check the splits in the answers to see whether there is an issue at all.

## The Antecedent Must Exist and Be Sensible

If the answer choices do offer different pronouns, then find the antecedent:

> Due to the ongoing drought, emergency wildfire prevention measures must be implemented immediately in all national parks in order to ensure that they don't inadvertently start fires.

What noun does *they* refer to? The *prevention measures*? That doesn't make sense. Logically, it should refer to the *visitors* or *people using the parks*. However, no noun exists in the sentence for those people. This answer choice would be incorrect on an SC problem because it never says who *they* are.

Be careful not to gloss over the meaning. For example:

> Although the term "supercomputer" may sound fanciful or exaggerated, it is simply an extremely fast mainframe that can execute trillions of calculations every second.

The antecedent appears to be *the term "supercomputer."* Look what happens when the pronoun is replaced with this noun:

> ... the TERM "supercomputer" is simply an extremely fast mainframe ...

*The term* is not a *mainframe* itself; rather, the term *refers to* a mainframe. In addition, the word *supercomputer* is not used to refer to an actual supercomputer; it is referring just to the term or class of item. Therefore, you must change the verb or make some other edit to refer to the term or class:

> Right:    Although the TERM "supercomputer" may sound fanciful or exaggerated, it simply *refers to* an extremely fast mainframe that can execute trillions of calculations every second.

Pronoun issues center around *meaning*. The GMAT tries to trick you into "assuming away" little wrinkles in meaning. Always replace the pronoun with its antecedent to make sure that the sentence still makes sense.

## The Antecedent and Pronoun Must Agree in Number

If the answers switch between singular and plural *pronouns*, check the antecedent to see whether it is singular or plural. If the answers switch between singular and plural *nouns*, the issue could be one of two things: pronouns or verbs (for subject–verb agreement). Consider this example:

> Confronted by radical changes in production and distribution, modern Hollywood studios are attempting various experiments in an effort to retain its status as the primary arbiter of movie consumption.

The antecedent of *its* is intended to be *studios*. However, *its* is singular, while *studios* is plural. Either the noun or the pronoun has to change (depending upon which portion is underlined in the problem):

> Right:    Confronted by radical changes in production and distribution, modern Hollywood STUDIOS are attempting various experiments in an effort to retain their status as the primary arbiters of movie consumption.

> Right:    Confronted by radical changes in production and distribution, THE modern Hollywood STUDIO is attempting various experiments in an effort to retain its status as the primary arbiter of movie consumption.

The GMAT tends to test number agreement when you can easily express the relevant concepts either in singular or in plural form (*studio* or *studios*). Use the underline placement and the differences in the answers as your guide.

As you learned in the Sentence Structure chapter, the GMAT can separate a subject from its verb in various ways in order to get you to miss a singular–plural mismatch. The same disguises apply to pronoun antecedents.

# The Deadly Five: *It, Its, They, Them, Their*

The most common pronoun mistakes involve the singular *it* and *its*, as well as the plural *they*, *them*, and *their*. Whenever you see one of these five pronouns, check the answers; if differences exist, find the antecedent and check its viability.

$$
\left.\begin{array}{l} \text{it} \\[4pt] \text{its} \end{array}\right\} \text{singular}
$$

$$
\left.\begin{array}{l} \text{they} \\[4pt] \text{them} \\[4pt] \text{their} \end{array}\right\} \text{plural}
$$

If you see one of these words in the non-underlined portion, the sentence may or may not be testing pronouns. In that case, it's worth noting that the pronoun is there. If a noun switches from singular to plural in the answer choices, check whether that noun is the antecedent for the non-underlined pronoun. If so, the pronoun will dictate whether that noun must be singular or plural.

# *This, That, These,* and *Those*

*This*, *that*, *these*, and *those* can be used as adjectives in front of nouns:

> New "NANO-PAPERS" incorporate fibers that give <u>these materials</u> strength.

You may also use *that* or *those* to indicate a "new copy" of the antecedent:

> The MONEY spent by Cersei's parents is less than <u>that</u> spent by her children.

In this example, *that spent by her children* means *the money spent by her children*, but the two pots of money are *not* the same. One pot of money is spent by the parents; another pot of money, spent by the children, is the new copy. In contrast, when you use *it*, *they*, or other personal pronouns, you mean the same actual thing as the antecedent. Consider this example:

> The MONEY SPENT BY CERSEI'S PARENTS is more than <u>it</u> was expected to be.

In this example, *it* refers to the actual money spent by her parents.

When a sentence uses *that* or *those* to indicate a new copy or copies, the pronoun must include a modifier that describes how the new copy is different from the previous version. For example:

> The MONEY spent by Cersei's parents is less than <u>that spent by her children</u>.

> The company's DIGITAL WATCH OFFERING is outperforming <u>that of its competitor</u>.

7

Official GMAT questions have required that this new-copy usage of *that* or *those* agree in number with the previous version:

> Wrong: The company's DIGITAL WATCH OFFERING is outperforming <u>those of its competitors</u>.

> Right: The company's DIGITAL WATCH OFFERING is outperforming <u>the offerings of its competitors</u>.

The correct option has a bonus pronoun lesson: The pronoun *its* refers to the possessive noun *company's*; technically, *company's* is an adjective, not a noun. This is an exception to the general rule that a pronoun refers to a noun: It is possible for a pronoun to refer to a possessive noun.

Finally, on the GMAT, do not use *this* or *these* in place of nouns. A sentence such as *This is great* is unacceptably vague to the GMAT. Also, do not use *that* or *those* in place of nouns, unless you modify *that* or *those* to make them new copies. Instead, use *it, they,* or *them*:

> Wrong: Tal's PRODUCTS are unusual; many consider <u>these</u> unique.

> Right: Tal's PRODUCTS are unusual; many consider <u>them</u> unique.

## Some Ambiguity Is Acceptable

In theory, every pronoun in a well-written sentence should clearly refer to one antecedent. If a sentence uses the exact same pronoun multiple times, every instance should refer to the same antecedent. If the first *it* refers to one noun and the second *it* refers to another, the sentence is going to be confusing.

It is also preferable to have pronouns of the same class refer to the same noun. *It* and *its* are one class, and *they, them,* and *their* are another class. This is a preference, however, not an absolute rule; some correct GMAT sentences do use different pronouns of the same class to refer to different nouns. What are the antecedents for the pronouns in this sentence:

> Researchers claim to have developed new "nano-papers" incorporating tiny cellulose fibers, which <u>they</u> allege give <u>them</u> the strength of cast iron.

Logically, the pronoun *they* refers to *researchers* (who *claim* something) and the pronoun *them* refers to the *nano-papers*. If another grammatically correct option exists without this mild ambiguity, choose the other option. If, however, the other four choices all contain other errors, then this choice would be correct.

An answer choice could avoid potential ambiguity by not using a pronoun in the first place:

> Right: Researchers claim to have developed new "NANO-PAPERS" incorporating tiny cellulose fibers, which give <u>these materials</u> the strength of cast iron, according to the researchers.

In this example, the sentence inserts a new noun, *materials*, to refer back to the nano-papers, so it isn't necessary for the reader to find the antecedent. (It also repeats the word *researchers* to avoid using the pronoun *they*.)

If you spot a split between a sentence that uses a pronoun and one that inserts a regular noun instead, there's a good chance that the answer with the regular noun is correct. Removing the pronoun prevents any possible ambiguity around the antecedent.

What if the sentence contains more than one possible antecedent with the right plurality for a given pronoun? Sometimes, these answers are wrong; sometimes, the GMAT accepts a mild ambiguity. In general, if you run up against this issue, ignore it and use some other split to decide. If you are really gunning for a top score, your Atlas learning platform provides an advanced pronoun lesson on this topic.

7

## Problem Set

In problems 1–8, box all the pronouns and underline each pronoun's antecedent, if there is one. If you notice any pronoun errors in a sentence, correct the sentence by altering the pronoun(s). Explain what rules are violated by the incorrect sentences. If a sentence is correct, mark it with the word CORRECT.

1. When the guests finished their soup, they were brought plates of salad.

2. Meg left all her class notes at school because she decided that she could do her homework without it.

3. Some people believe that the benefits of a healthy diet outweigh that of regular exercise.

   *those*

   *those*

4. Oil traders have profited handsomely from the recent increase in its price.

   *its what?*    *wrong*

5. The players' helmets need to be repainted before they are used in Sunday's game.

6. A few Shakespearean scholars maintain that he borrowed some of his most memorable lines from Christopher Marlowe.

   *who?*

7. The Smiths avoid the Browns because they dislike their children.

8. Samantha took her laptop and her books with her on the airplane because she thought that she could use these to get some work done.

   *them*

Problems 9–11 are multiple choice with one correct answer. As on the real GMAT, answer (A) repeats the original sentence. (Unlike the real GMAT, though, these problems have only three answer choices.)

9.   When tetrapods developed <u>lungs capable of surviving on land, they became the first amphibians</u>.

  (A)   lungs capable of surviving on land, they became the first amphibians

  (B)   lungs capable of surviving on land, tetrapods became the first amphibians

  (C)   lungs, they became the first amphibians capable of surviving on land

10.   The <u>bite of the king cobra delivers such strong neurotoxins that they</u> can kill an Asian elephant.

  (A)   bite of the king cobra delivers such strong neurotoxins that they

  (B)   king cobra's bite delivers such strong neurotoxins that it

  (C)   neurotoxins delivered by a king cobra's bite are so strong that it

11.   Television writer Aaron Sorkin is known for writing <u>dialogue that is wittier than that in</u> most real-world interactions.

  (A)   dialogue that is wittier than that in

  (B)   wittier dialogue than

  (C)   dialogue that is wittier than it is in

# Solutions

1.  When the <u>guests</u> finished their soup, they were brought plates of salad.

    **CORRECT.** *Guests* is the antecedent of *their* and *they*.

2.  <u>Meg</u> left all her class <u>notes</u> at school because she decided that she could do her homework without them.

    *Meg* is the antecedent of *her* and *she*. *Notes* is the antecedent of *them*. (In the original sentence, the pronoun *it* is incorrect because *notes* is plural.)

3.  Some people believe that the <u>benefits</u> of a healthy diet outweigh those of regular exercise.

    *Benefits* is the antecedent of *those*. (In the original sentence, *that* is incorrect, because *benefits* is plural.)

4.  Oil traders have profited handsomely from the recent increase in the price of oil.

    This new, correct version of the sentence contains no pronouns. The original sentence is incorrect because *its* has no antecedent. *Oil* is an adjective in the expression *oil traders*, and therefore cannot be the antecedent of *its*.

5.  The players' <u>helmets</u> need to be repainted before they are used in Sunday's game.

    **CORRECT.** *Helmets* is the antecedent of *they*. You need not worry that *they* could refer to *players'*. Since *helmets* and *they* are the subjects of their respective clauses, there is a structural pointer that *they* refers to *helmets*. (This pointer is not required; it just helps to reinforce the connection.) *Helmets* is also a logical antecedent for *they*, so there is no ambiguity.

6.  A few Shakespearean scholars maintain that <u>Shakespeare</u> borrowed some of his most memorable lines from Christopher Marlowe.

    *Shakespeare* is the antecedent of *his*. The original sentence is incorrect because *he* has no antecedent. *Shakespearean* is an adjective that describes Shakespeare's works, so it cannot be the antecedent for *he*. One way to fix this sentence is to replace *he* with *Shakespeare*.

7.  The original sentence is far too ambiguous: Which family dislikes the other family's children? The antecedent of *they* is almost certainly not meant to be the same as the antecedent of *their*, a confusing state of affairs. To correct this sentence, you could get rid of the pronouns. One possible version: *The Smiths avoid the Browns because the Browns dislike the Smiths' children*. Another possible version: *The Smiths avoid the Browns because the Smiths dislike the Browns' children*. Without knowing the author's original intent, it's impossible to say which meaning is the correct one.

8.  <u>Samantha</u> took her laptop and her <u>books</u> with her on the airplane because she thought that she could use them to get some work done.

    *Samantha* is the antecedent of all three *her*'s and both *she*'s.

    *Her laptop and her book*s is the antecedent of *them*. (The original *these* is incorrect because *these* cannot be used as a stand-alone pronoun without a noun following.)

**7**

9. **(C):** The original sentence contains a meaning error: *Capable of surviving on land* is a noun modifier that describes the *tetrapods*. In answers (A) and (B), the sentence seems to say that the *lungs* themselves were capable of surviving on land. Instead, the noun modifier should be placed closer to the noun that it modifies (*tetrapods*). Eliminate choices (A) and (B) for this meaning error.

   Although choice (C) has two plural nouns (*tetrapods* and *lungs*) that seem like they could be the antecedent for the pronoun *they*, this sentence is not in fact ambiguous. First, *tetrapods* is the logical antecedent for *they*. Second, *tetrapods* and *they* are both the subjects of their respective clauses, so there is a structural pointer that reinforces the idea that *they* refers to *tetrapods*. (It is not required that both the noun and pronoun be subjects, but when they are, it reinforces the connection between the two.)

   Did the first half of the sentence in the previous set of parentheses sound awkward? It's a correct example of the subjunctive, a type of verb usage. You'll learn more about this in the next chapter.

10. **(B):** The original sentence intends to say that *the bite of the king cobra . . . can kill an Asian elephant*. However, the plural pronoun *they* can refer only to *neurotoxins*. While it is not illogical that *neurotoxins . . . can kill an Asian elephant*, the structure of the sentence indicates that the intent is to say that the *bite* does this. The idiom is as follows: *X (delivers) such Y that Z (occurs)*. The *Z* and *X* elements can be the same thing, but *Y* and *Z* cannot be the same thing. Eliminate choice (A) for faulty meaning based on the idiom structure.

   Answer choice (B) corrects this error. The singular pronoun *it* now clearly refers to the singular antecedent *bite*.

   Answer choice (C) changes the subject of the sentence to *neurotoxins*, shifting the meaning to indicate that the *neurotoxins . . . can kill an Asian elephant*. It also, however, changes the pronoun to *it*. In this construction, the singular pronoun *it* cannot correctly refer to plural *neurotoxins*. Eliminate choice (C) for the same error as (A).

11. **(A):** The GMAT often uses the awkward-sounding but grammatically correct construction *that in* in comparisons to throw the reader off the scent. Whenever you want to test a pronoun, grab the noun antecedent (in this case, *dialogue*) and put it in place of the pronoun; if that works, the pronoun is fine. The original sentence correctly conveys that Sorkin writes *dialogue that is wittier than* the dialogue *in most real-world interactions*.

   Choice (B) illogically compares *dialogue* to *interactions*. The intended comparison is between *dialogue* and *dialogue*. Eliminate this choice for a faulty comparison.

   Unlike choice (A), which uses the pronoun *that*, answer (C) uses the pronoun *it*. The word *that* can refer to a different "copy" of the same noun, but the word *it* must refer to the exact original copy. Thus, the meaning in answer (C) gets jumbled: *Aaron Sorkin is known for writing dialogue that is wittier than* the exact same dialogue *is in most real-world interactions*. However, dialogue written specifically for a TV script is, by definition, not actual real-world dialogue.

7

# CHAPTER 8

# Verbs

## In This Chapter:

**In this chapter, you will learn** the major verb tenses that are tested on the GMAT, as well as how to make the meaning clear and logical when a complex sentence talks about a sequence of several events.

# CHAPTER 8 **Verbs**

The **Verb Tense** of a working verb indicates *when* the action of the verb takes place. In addition, certain modifiers adopt the time frame of the main verb in the sentence.

In sentences with one action, verb tense is relatively easy. Knowing this, the GMAT tries to complicate sentences by incorporating more than one action. As a result, you will need to pay close attention to the *sequence* of actions in GMAT sentences. This sequence will be driven by meaning, so think about meaning as you work through this chapter.

The GMAT also sometimes tests something called **Voice** and something else called **Mood**, both of which you'll learn about in this chapter.

If you are a native speaker of American English, your ear may already be well-attuned to the right use of tense. Incorrect uses of tense (e.g., *He has gone to France last year*) will (correctly) sound funny to you; your instinctive correction (*He went to France last year*) will be correct. As you review this chapter, if you find that learning what these tenses are called interferes with your ability to recognize correct usage of the tense, feel free to ignore the names. You just need to know how to use the tenses on the test; you don't need to name them.

If you are not a native speaker of American English, however, you may need to learn these rules more consciously, in which case knowing the names can help you distinguish among the tenses. Patterns of verb tense vary drastically among languages, even those related to English. For example, *He is gone to France last year* is correct when translated word-for-word into French, German, and Italian, but it is never correct in English.

## Simple Tenses

The three simple tenses express three basic times:

    1. Simple present:       Sandy PLAYS well with her friends.

    2. Simple past:         Sandy PLAYED well with her friends yesterday.

    3. Simple future:        Sandy WILL PLAY well with her friends tomorrow.

The **Simple Present** tense is used to express both events happening now and "eternal" states or frequent events. In the simple present example, the sentence does not mean that Sandy is playing right now, but rather that, as a general rule, Sandy plays well with her friends.

The GMAT typically prefers the simple tenses, unless the sentence clearly requires one of the more complex tenses discussed later in this chapter. The more complex tenses each have particular circumstances in which they can be used; if those circumstances do not exist, then don't use a complex tense.

# Make Tenses Reflect Meaning

Sometimes, all the tenses in a sentence are the same, because all the actions take place in the same time frame:

Right: She WALKED to school in the morning and RAN home in the afternoon.

Right: She WALKS to school in the morning and RUNS home in the afternoon.

Right: She WILL WALK to school in the morning and RUN home in the afternoon.

In each sentence, the verbs are in the same tense: simple past in the first, simple present in the second, and simple future in the third. (Note that, in the third example, *run* is understood as *will run*; *will* is part of the root phrase and applies to both verbs.) In these examples, changing tense midstream would be confusing and incorrect.

However, in some sentences, the author clearly intends to discuss different time periods. The tense can and should change to reflect that intention:

Right: He IS thinner now because he WENT on a strict diet six months ago.

　　　　Simple Present　　　　Simple Past

The switch from present to past is logical given the clear indications of time (*now* and *six months ago*).

You could also switch the order of the sentence:

Right: Because he WENT on a strict diet six months ago, he IS thinner now.

Look what happens in this example:

Wrong: Because he IS STARTING a strict diet, he LOST weight.

This sentence can't be correct. Logically, if he LOST the weight in the past, then STARTING his diet in the present cannot be the cause of his weight loss.

The GMAT might add in distracting modifiers to hide this tense mismatch:

Wrong: Because he IS STARTING a strict diet and an exercise regimen that he BEGAN more than a year ago, he LOST weight.

Notice that the sentence does include another past tense verb, *began*. In addition to the existing meaning error, the introduction of *began* creates another. Logically, he can't currently be *starting . . . an exercise regimen that he began more than a year ago*. Either he's starting it now or he started it more than a year ago.

8

# The Perfect Tenses: An Introduction

The two most commonly tested complex tenses on the GMAT are the perfect tenses: past perfect and present perfect.

# Past Perfect: The Earlier Action

If two actions in a sentence occurred at *different* times in the past, you can use the **Past Perfect** tense for the earlier action and simple past for the later action. The past perfect is the "past of the past."

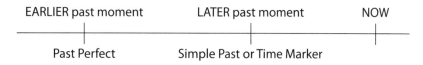

Here is an example:

Right:        The film HAD STARTED by the time we ARRIVED at the theater.

The past perfect tense is formed as follows:

**Past Perfect = HAD + Past Participle**

In order to use past perfect for one event, the sentence must contain a second event that occurred later than the first event, but still in the past. One way to do this is via a verb in the simple past tense:

Right:        The teacher THOUGHT that Jimmy HAD CHEATED on the exam.

The earlier past action, *had cheated*, pairs with a simple past action, *thought*: First, Jimmy took the exam (and possibly cheated on it!) and, later (but still in the past), the teacher began to suspect Jimmy.

Another option is to use a time marker. For example:

Right:        BY 1970, four astronauts HAD WALKED on the moon.

In this sentence, the four astronauts walked on the moon sometime prior to 1970 (a past time marker). Common time markers include *by*, *before*, *after*, *until*, and *since*.

Even when the circumstances allow past perfect to be used, the sentence is not necessarily required to employ this more complex tense. Some sentences still make sense even when you stick with simple tenses:

Right:        Laura LOCKED the deadbolt <u>before</u> she LEFT for work.

The word *before* indicates the sequence of events clearly; using past perfect is not necessary to convey the proper meaning. When the meaning of a sentence is already clear, the correct answer may or may not use past perfect to indicate an earlier action. In this case, do not cross off answers that use simple past. Instead, look for a different split to help you decide which answer to choose.

On hard questions, the GMAT may write a complicated sentence in which the past perfect verb is not the earliest action in the sentence—but it is still used correctly:

Right:        The band U2 WAS just one of many new groups on the rock music scene in the early 1980s, but less than 10 years later, U2 HAD fully ECLIPSED its early rivals in the pantheon of popular music.

The first independent clause uses simple past (*was*). The second independent clause (after the word *but*) contains a time marker (*10 years later*) and then mentions another action (*had eclipsed*) that occurs before that time marker. Even though *had eclipsed* is not the *earliest* action in the entire sentence, it is the earlier of the two actions in its independent clause. This complex construction is correct.

## Present Perfect: Bridging Past and Present

The **Present Perfect** tense is used for actions that started in the past but continue into the present or remain true. The present perfect tense effectively has one foot in the past and one foot in the present:

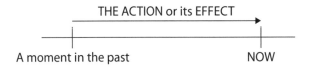

Consider this example:

Right:        The Millers HAVE LIVED in a hut for three days.

The Millers began living in the hut three days ago and they are still living in that hut. In comparison, a sentence in the simple past conveys a different meaning:

Right:        The Millers LIVED in a hut for three days.

At some point in the past, the Millers lived in a hut, but they no longer live in the hut now. How long ago did they live in the hut? The sentence doesn't tell you; it might have been a week ago or five years ago.

The present perfect tense is formed as follows:

**Present Perfect = HAVE/HAS + Past Participle**

For regular verbs such as *walk* or *live*, the past participle is the *–ed* form of the verb: *walked*, *lived*. Irregular verbs, such as *go* or *see*, have unique past participles (*gone*, *seen*). If you are a native English speaker, you likely already know the irregular forms. Otherwise, study the list of irregular past participles in the Glossary at the end of this guide.

**8**

Here are some examples of actions in the present perfect tense:

Right:      This country HAS ENFORCED strict immigration laws <u>for 30 years.</u>

Right:      They HAVE KNOWN each other <u>since 1987</u>.

Each example involves an action that began in the past and continues into the present. This country enforced strict immigration laws in the past and still enforces them today. They knew each other in the past and still know each other today. In each case, the idea of a continuing action is reinforced by a time phrase, such as *for 30 years* or *since 1987*, that states how long the action has been occurring (*enforced . . . for 30 years*) or for how long the information has been true (*have known . . . since 1987*).

Sometimes, the present perfect tense means that the action is definitely over, but its *effect* is still relevant to the present moment. For example:

Right:      The child HAS DRAWN a square in the sand.

In this example, the child is no longer in the act of drawing a square. However, the square is still there.

Right:      The child DREW a square in the sand, but the ocean ERASED it.

Right:      The child DREW a square in the sand, but the ocean HAS ERASED it.

Wrong:      The child HAS DRAWN a square in the sand, but the ocean HAS ERASED it.

The third example is incorrect because using the same tense for both actions implies that they took place at the same time. Logically, though, the ocean must have erased the square after it was drawn; the two events could not have happened simultaneously.

When using the word *since* as a time marker (since a certain time), use the present perfect to indicate an action or effect that continues to the present time:

Wrong:      <u>Since 1986</u>, no one BROKE that world record.

Wrong:      <u>Since 1986</u>, no one BREAKS that world record.

Right:      <u>Since 1986</u>, no one HAS BROKEN that world record.

(Note: The word *since* can also mean *because*—in that case, it doesn't have an effect on the verb tense used in the sentence.)

Like *since*, the constructions *within the past . . .* or *in the last . . .* (such as *within the past five minutes* or *in the last 10 days*) also cross into the present, so use the present perfect with these terms. In contrast, a time phrase that does *not* cross over into the present (*last month, in 2007*, etc.) should not be used with the present perfect. Use the simple past instead:

Wrong:      Veronica HAS TRAVELED all over the world <u>in 2007</u>.

Right:      Veronica TRAVELED all over the world <u>in 2007</u>.

8

You could also write *Veronica has traveled all over the world* and omit any specific time reference. In this case, you are saying that it is still true today that *Veronica has traveled all over the world.*

Finally, the present perfect can be used in certain circumstances to clarify an ambiguous sequence in time. For example, the word *when* can mean either "at the same time" or "after." The use of present perfect eliminates any ambiguity. Consider these examples:

> Right: The alarm WILL RING *when* the clock STRIKES 12. (no present perfect)
>
> = The alarm will ring <u>at the same time</u> that the clock strikes 12.

> Right: The company WILL REIMBURSE you *when* you HAVE SUBMITTED your expense report. (present perfect)
>
> = The company will reimburse you <u>after</u> you submit the report.

## *–ing* Modifiers: Follow the Main Verb

If you haven't already studied the Modifiers chapter or if your recall of *comma –ing* modifiers is a bit shaky, you may wish to review that material before proceeding here.

*Comma –ing* modifiers adopt the tense of the main working verb to which they are attached. For example:

> Right: <u>Peering</u> out of the window, Bran WATCHED his direwolf frolic on the lawn.

The main verb, *watched*, is in past tense. Bran is not currently *peering* out of the window; rather, he peered out of the window while he watched the direwolf. The modifier *peering* picks up the time frame of the main verb.

Here's another example:

> Right: The manager WILL SIGN the contract tomorrow, <u>barring</u> any unforeseen disruptions.

Again, the *–ing* word picks up the tense of the main verb. If any unforeseen disruptions occur *in the future*—between now and when the manager plans to sign the contract—then she might not sign after all.

## Present to Future or Past to Conditional

Have you learned about **Conditional** in the past but felt confused about this tense? It turns out that there are two different—but overlapping—things that are called *conditional* (and neither one is technically a tense!).

One of these is the **Conditional Mood**. One way it is used is to talk about the future from the past. First, consider this sentence that talks about the future from the present:

> Right: The scientist ANNOUNCES that the <u>supercollider WILL PROVIDE new insights</u> into the workings of the universe.

That example pairs present tense with future tense, a common construction. But what if the scientist made this announcement yesterday? Then, the sentence would look like this:

> Right:    The scientist ANNOUNCED that the <u>supercollider WOULD PROVIDE new insights</u> into the workings of the universe.

The scientist is talking about the future from the past. The conditional mood is formed by combining *would* with the base form of a verb: *would provide*. In the given sentence, the construction is used to express the future from the point of view of the past: At the point that the scientist made the announcement (in the past), new insights were expected to be provided at some time in the future.

The typical sequences for these types of sentences are either Present + Future or Past + Conditional:

> Right:    The scientist <u>BELIEVES</u> that the machine <u>WILL BE</u> wonderful.
>                        Present                    Future

> Wrong:    The scientist <u>BELIEVES</u> that the machine <u>WOULD BE</u> wonderful.
>                        Present                    Conditional

> Right:    The scientist <u>BELIEVED</u> that the machine <u>WOULD BE</u> wonderful.
>                        Past                    Conditional

> Wrong:    The scientist <u>BELIEVED</u> that the machine <u>WILL BE</u> wonderful.
>                        Past                    Future

The other usage you'll see for the term *conditional* is when writing conditional sentences, most commonly constructed in **If–Then** form: *If* you meet a certain condition, *then* some result will follow. For example, if you practice guitar chords daily, then you will become better at finger placement on the fretboard.

Some If–Then sentences will use the conditional mood in the sentence and some will not. This example uses the conditional: If you practiced guitar daily, you would be able to play the major chords by now.

You can learn more about both conditional sentences and conditional mood in the advanced materials located online in Atlas.

## Verbs and Parallelism

One more thing. Remember learning about parallelism a few chapters ago? Let's make the supercollider sentence even more complicated:

> The scientist ANNOUNCED that the <u>supercollider WAS ready</u>, that <u>it HAD not COST too much to build</u>, and that <u>it WOULD PROVIDE new insights</u> into the workings of the universe.

The sentence uses multiple tenses in its *X, Y, and Z* list:

The scientist announced that...

> ...*the supercollider WAS ready.* (simple past)
>
> ...*it HAD not COST too much to build.* (past perfect)
>
> ...*it WOULD PROVIDE new insights.* (conditional mood)

A sentence can make multiple different verb tenses parallel, as long as each verb tense is appropriate for the meaning of that part of the sentence. Also note that all of the tenses have to pair appropriately with the starting tense in the root phrase, *announced*. The cost was incurred before the scientist *announced* anything, so the past perfect *had (not) cost* is appropriate. The prediction that it *would provide new insights* is an instance of future from the past, so the conditional mood is the right pairing.

## Active and Passive Voice

Verbs are written in either **Active Voice** or **Passive Voice**. In the active voice, the subject of the sentence performs the action. In the passive voice, the subject of the sentence has an action performed on it by someone or something else. For example:

| | |
|---|---|
| Active: | The hungry students ATE the pizza. |
| Passive: | The pizza WAS EATEN by the hungry students. |

The passive voice is formed with a form of the verb *to be* (in this case, *was*), followed by the past participle (*eaten*).

Though passive voice has a reputation for sounding awkward, it is a valid construction:

| | |
|---|---|
| Passive: | It HAS BEEN DECIDED by Jason that he will not attend college. |
| Active: | Jason HAS DECIDED not to attend college. |

The active version may sound better to you than the passive one, but both are correct. People often think that the passive voice is inherently wrong, and the GMAT sometimes exploits this myth by making the awkward, passive answer *correct*. Meanwhile, the problem will also offer an answer in the active voice that sounds great but has a subtle error elsewhere. Consider the following example:

| | |
|---|---|
| Passive: | It HAS BEEN DECIDED by Jason that he will not attend college next fall. |
| Active: | Jason HAS DECIDED next fall not to attend college. |

The active voice example says that Jason *decided next fall*. This is illogical! He either already *decided* (in the past) or he *will decide next fall* (in the future). Meanwhile, the passive sentence is correct, even though it sounds awkward.

You could fix the active version this way: *Jason has decided not to attend college next fall.* But the GMAT might not offer you this option because it's too easy. The passive version shown earlier is a better trap— people will cross it off because it sounds clunkier than active voice, completely missing the error in the active version.

8

Don't be biased against the passive. Check what else is going on in the sentence. Sometimes, you're forced to have the sentence in passive voice simply due to the placement of the underline.

As a final note, you do not have to make active or passive voice parallel throughout a sentence. For example:

Right:        The shuttle launch <u>TOOK</u> place flawlessly and <u>WAS SEEN</u> on television.

Both parallel elements work with the root phrase of the sentence: *The shuttle launch took place* and *the shuttle launch was seen on television.*

# Problem Set

Problems 1–6 contain one or more underlined sections. If an underlined section contains no errors, mark it as CORRECT. Otherwise, write down a correct version of the underlined section. For extra credit, explain your decisions with respect to the tense, mood, and voice of the relevant verbs.

1.  Mozart, who died in 1791, <u>has lived</u> in Salzburg for most of his life.

    *lived*

2.  The local government <u>has built</u> the school that was destroyed by the earthquake.

    *Correct*

3.  The editor of our local newspaper, who has earned much acclaim in her long career, <u>has been awarded</u> a Pulitzer Prize yesterday.

    *Correct*

4.  She already <u>woke up</u> when the phone rang.

    *had woken*

5.  In the Fischer–Tropsch process, which <u>developed</u> in Germany by Franz Fischer and Hans Tropsch, coal <u>is converted</u> into a liquid fuel similar to petroleum.

    *that was*

    *has been*

6.  Last Monday, Mary realized that she <u>will have</u> to spend all of that night rewriting her application because she <u>did not back up</u> her files.

    *Correct*

Problems 7–9 are multiple choice with one correct answer. As on the real GMAT, answer (A) repeats the original sentence. Unlike the real GMAT, though, these problems have only three answer choices.

7. By the end of the Apollo program, 12 Americans had walked on the moon, but no one will have reached the moon's surface since then.

   (A) had walked on the moon, but no one will have

   (B) walked on the moon, and no one has

   (C) had walked on the moon, though no one has

8. Water freezes if it were cooled to zero degrees Celsius.

   (A) freezes if it were

   (B) would freeze if it was

   (C) freezes if

9. The art dealer, whose collection included works by a number of master painters, could not bring himself to part with his prized piece when he was asked to sell a painting by Picasso.

   (A) The art dealer, whose collection included works by a number of master painters, could not bring himself to part with his prized piece when he was asked to sell a painting by Picasso.

   (B) When the art dealer was asked to sell his favorite Picasso painting, a prized piece from his collection of works by a number of master painters, he could not bring himself to do so.

   (C) When the art dealer has been asked to sell his favorite Picasso painting, which was a prized piece from his collection of works by a number of master painters, he could not bring himself to do so.

# Solutions

1.  Mozart, who died in 1791, <u>has lived</u> in Salzburg for most of his life.

    *Has lived* (present perfect tense) should be *lived* (simple past tense) or possibly *had lived* (past perfect). One possible reason to use the present perfect (*has lived*) is to indicate that an action or state of affairs is still in progress. Mozart is dead, so this reason does not apply here.

    The other possible reason to use the present perfect is to indicate that an action, though completed in the past, still has some continuing effect on the subject of the verb. Since Mozart is dead, this reason does not apply either.

    Since neither reason for using the present perfect applies to this sentence, use the simple past. There is no real need to use the past perfect (*had lived*), because the sequence of past events (Mozart's life and death) is obvious. Moreover, the actions are not contrasted (e.g., if he *lived* one place but *died* somewhere else). That said, to emphasize the sequence of events, you could choose to use the past perfect in this sentence:

    |            |                                                                          |
    |------------|--------------------------------------------------------------------------|
    | Correction: | Mozart, who died in 1791, <u>lived</u> in Salzburg for most of his life. |
    | OR         | Mozart, who died in 1791, <u>had lived</u> in Salzburg for most of his life. |

2.  The local government <u>has built</u> the school that was destroyed by the earthquake.

    *Has built* (present perfect tense) should be *built* (simple past tense) OR *had built* (past perfect). Sometimes, the present perfect is used to indicate that an action or state of affairs is still in progress. However, the original process of building the school cannot be continuing now, because the school was destroyed by the earthquake. The government might be rebuilding the school now, but that is not the same as building the school. The other possible reason to use the present perfect is to indicate that an action, though completed in the past, still has some continuing effect on the subject and object of the verb. The effects of the action of building were essentially wiped out by the earthquake, because the earthquake destroyed the school. Since neither possible reason for using the present perfect applies to this sentence, you cannot use the present perfect.

    Either the simple past or the past perfect is possible. In the simple past version, the writer's mental time frame is concurrent with *built*. The following clause (*that was destroyed by the earthquake*) just serves to identify the school, and the writer might go on to discuss the building process. However, the past perfect emphasizes the sequence of events more than the simple past does. In the past perfect version, the writer's mental time frame is concurrent with *was destroyed*. The use of *had built* indicates that the writer is dipping back in time for only a moment to the building process. In fact, the writer might proceed to write more about the destruction (perhaps the consequences of shoddy construction methods). For example:

    |            |                                                                          |
    |------------|--------------------------------------------------------------------------|
    | Correction: | The local government <u>built</u> the school that was destroyed by the earthquake. |
    | OR         | The local government <u>had built</u> the school that was destroyed by the earthquake. |

8

3. The editor of our local newspaper, who has earned much acclaim in her long career, <u>has been awarded</u> a Pulitzer Prize yesterday.

   *Has been awarded* (present perfect tense) should be *was awarded* (simple past tense). The verb has to be in the simple past because you are told that the action occurred at a specific time in the past (*yesterday*):

   Correction: The editor of our local newspaper, who has earned much acclaim in her long career, <u>was awarded</u> a Pulitzer Prize yesterday.

4. She already <u>woke up</u> when the phone rang.

   *Already woke up* (simple past) should be *had already woken up* (past perfect). You need to use the past perfect here because the word *already* requires this use for a momentary action such as *wake up*, when placed prior to another past action. It would be fine to say *she was already awake when the phone rang*, because *was awake* is a state and thus takes up time. In that case, *already* would indicate that this state was in effect before the phone rang. However, when you use *already* with the simple past of a momentary action, you convey a present perfect meaning. As your spouse shakes you out of bed, you might say *I already woke up*, but in proper English, you should say *I HAVE already woken up*. In other words, the action is complete AND the effect (your wakefulness) continues to the present. In the sample sentence, since you want the subject's wakefulness to continue up through some point in the past (*when the phone rang*), you must use the past perfect of *wake up*:

   Correction: She <u>had</u> already <u>woken up</u> when the phone rang.

5. In the Fischer–Tropsch process, which <u>developed</u> in Germany by Franz Fischer and Hans Tropsch, coal <u>is converted</u> into a liquid fuel similar to petroleum.

   *Developed* (active voice) should be *was developed* (passive voice). The passive voice is required because the people who developed the process appear in the non-underlined phrase *by Franz Fischer and Hans Tropsch*.

   *Is converted* (passive voice) is correct. The passive voice is required because unnamed agent(s), rather than the coal itself, cause the conversion of the coal into a liquid fuel. Supposing that the whole sentence were underlined and that you were therefore free to rewrite it completely, should you change it into the active voice? No, because the passive voice is ideally suited to the purposes of this sentence. The author wants to tell you about the Fischer–Tropsch process, not to list the various parties who happen to use that process. It is therefore fitting for the words *Fischer–Tropsch process* to be in the subject position. To put *Fischer–Tropsch* in the subject position, the verb *to develop* must be in the passive voice:

   Correction: In the Fischer–Tropsch process, which <u>was developed</u> in Germany by Franz Fischer and Hans Tropsch, coal <u>is converted</u> into a liquid fuel similar to petroleum.

8

6.  Last Monday, Mary realized that she <u>will have</u> to spend all of that night rewriting her application because she <u>did not back up</u> her files.

    *Will have* (simple future tense) should be *would have* (conditional tense). Mary made her realization on Monday. At that time, her sleepless night spent rewriting the application was in the future. However, last Monday night is now in the past. An action that was in the future (relative to the time of the main verb, *realized*), but is now in the past, must be rendered in the conditional tense. This tense is formed by replacing *will* with *would*.

    *Did not back up* (simple past tense) should be *had not backed up* (past perfect tense). The past perfect tense is required here because Mary's failure to back up her files must logically have occurred *before* Mary became aware of (*realized*) this failure:

    Correction:     Last Monday, Mary realized that she <u>would have</u> to spend all of that night rewriting her application because she <u>had not backed</u> up her files.

7.  **(C):** The original sentence contains two time markers: *by the end* and *since then*. The time marker *by the end of the Apollo program* indicates that the action in the main clause (12 Americans walking on the moon) occurred in the past prior to *the end of the Apollo program*. Thus, the proper tense is the past perfect *had walked*. The original sentence is correct on this point, but the simple past tense *walked* in answer choice (B) is incorrect.

    The time marker *since then* indicates an action that started in the past but continues (or is still true) in the present. The proper tense for the last verb is the present perfect *has reached*. Choice (A) incorrectly uses *will have reached*.

    Finally, there is a choice of conjunction after the comma. The meaning of the sentence requires a contrast. Twelve Americans walked on the moon previously; however, no one has since then. *But* or *though* has the correct meaning; *and* is incorrect.

8.  **(C):** The original sentence is an if–then statement: If water becomes cold enough, then it *would freeze* (conditional) or *freezes* (present tense used to convey a general truth or a rule). Reordering the sequence of the verbs to an if–then order can help you check the verb sequence.

    Choice (A) says that if *it were cooled to zero degrees*, then *water freezes*. The hypothetical *were cooled* should be followed by the hypothetical *would freeze*, so the present tense *freezes* is incorrect.

    Choice (B) says that if *it was cooled to zero degrees*, then *water would freeze*. The past tense *was cooled* is factual, not hypothetical, so the logical outcome is that the *water froze* or the *water did freeze* in the simple past tense.

    Choice (C) says that if *cooled to zero degrees*, then *water freezes*. The first part implies the present tense (*if* it is *cooled* ), and the second part uses the present tense *freezes*, both of which imply a general truth—a physical property of water.

8

9.   **(B):** When the entire sentence is underlined, look for variations in meaning and sentence structure. The original sentence intends to say that the *art dealer . . . could not bring himself to part with his prized . . . painting by Picasso.*

However, *when he was asked to sell a painting by Picasso* could be interpreted as *Picasso asked the dealer to sell a painting.* This subtle ambiguity is difficult to spot; notice the split between *Picasso painting* in (B) and (C) and *by Picasso* in (A). Eliminate (A) for ambiguous meaning.

Compare answers (B) and (C) to spot the differences. They use different tenses for the first verb: *was asked* vs. *has been asked.* Either might be okay if that were the only clause, but only answer (B) works with the sequence of events in the rest of the sentence. Choice (C) says *When he has been asked to sell, . . . he could not bring himself to do so.* Since *has been asked* is in the present perfect, the second action (which takes place later in time) can't be in the past. For example, this would work: *When he has been asked to sell, . . . he has not been able to bring himself to do so.*

8

# Idioms

## In This Chapter:

- Spot–Extract–Replace
- Idiom List

**In this chapter, you'll learn** how to spot some of the more common idioms tested on the GMAT. You will also learn a technique to help you identify the correct idiom that should be used in the sentence.

# CHAPTER 9 Idioms

**Idioms** are expressions that have unique forms. There is no hard and fast rule for determining the form of an idiom; rather, it is just a form that you know or memorize. For example, *They tried to reach the summit and succeeded in doing so* is correct, but *They tried in reaching the summit and succeeded to do so* is not correct. The verb *to try* is followed by an infinitive, but the verb *to succeed* is followed by *in* and an *–ing* form of the verb. Why? There is no great reason. *Try to do* and *succeed in doing* are the accepted English idioms.

Many idioms are about meaning, at heart, so you can often use meaning to help you remember the proper form. It wouldn't make sense to say *both X or Y*, since the word *both* signals that you want to reference the two things together. It makes logical sense that the correct idiom is *both X and Y*.

If you are a native English speaker, most idiomatic expressions are already wired into your brain from years of hearing and speaking English. For non-native speakers, the task is more difficult. However, the GMAT does tend to focus on certain common idioms. Review the common idiom list in this chapter and memorize any that you do not know. If you want an especially high Verbal GMAT score, you can also spend some time learning some of the expressions listed in the Idioms appendix (Appendix A) of this guide (though there are enough that you may not want to try to memorize them all).

## Spot–Extract–Replace

Your ear is your most valuable weapon as you try to figure out the proper form of an idiom. Here's how to use your ear well:

- (A) Some historians attribute the eventual development of accurate methods for measuring longitude as the monetary prizes offered by various governments.
- (B) Some historians attribute the eventual development of accurate methods for measuring longitude to the monetary prizes offered by various governments.

1.  <u>SPOT the suspect idiomatic expression</u>. Compare answer choices to find the splits. In the choices above, the words that vary are *as* and *to*. What pairs with *as* or *to*? In this case, the idiom revolves around the use of the verb *attribute*.

2.  <u>EXTRACT the various forms of the idiom</u> and put them into simpler sentences that you can easily compare. You can delete words, such as extraneous modifiers, or you can make up brand-new sentences. Either way, strip the sentence to a simple example:

    - (A) Historians attribute the development AS the prizes.
    - (B) Historians attribute the development TO the prizes.

    If you know this idiom, then the correct version will sound better to your ear. *Attribute TO* is the correct idiom. If neither version sounds better, then ignore this split and go find something else (or guess and move on).

3. <u>REPLACE the corrected idiom in the sentence</u> and confirm that it works:

(B) Some historians <u>attribute</u> the eventual development of accurate methods for measuring longitude TO the monetary prizes offered by various governments.

The choice that your ear preferred should work in the entire GMAT sentence. If it does not work, either check your work or set aside this issue and move forward with something else.

## Idiom List

The English language includes thousands of idioms. You can't possibly memorize them all, so concentrate on those that are tested most frequently. You've already seen many of the most common idioms earlier in this guide, particularly in the Parallelism and Comparisons chapters. The following list contains the next most commonly tested idioms, as seen on official GMAT test questions. The Idioms appendix contains additional idioms that have appeared on real questions but that are less common than the ones in this chapter.

| Label | Definition |
| --- | --- |
| RIGHT: | Expressions that the GMAT considers correct |
| SUSPECT: | *Expressions that the GMAT seems to avoid if possible. These expressions are sometimes grammatically correct, but they may be wordy, controversial, or simply less preferred than other forms.* |
| WRONG: | *Expressions that the GMAT considers incorrect* |

**ABILITY**

| | |
| --- | --- |
| RIGHT: | I value my ABILITY TO SING. |
| WRONG: | *I value my ABILITY OF SINGING.* |
| | *I value my ABILITY FOR SINGING.* |
| | *I value the ABILITY FOR me TO SING.* |

**ALLOW**

| | |
| --- | --- |
| RIGHT: | The holiday ALLOWS Maria TO WATCH the movie today. (permits an action) |
| | Maria WAS ALLOWED TO WATCH the movie. |
| | The demolition of the old building ALLOWS FOR new construction. (permits the existence of) |
| WRONG: | *The holiday ALLOWED FOR Maria TO WATCH the movie.* |
| | *The holiday ALLOWED Maria the WATCHING OF the movie.* |
| | *The holiday ALLOWS THAT homework BE done (or CAN BE done).* |
| | *Homework is ALLOWED FOR DOING BY Maria.* |
| | *The ALLOWING OF shopping TO DO (or TO BE DONE).* |

9

**ALTHOUGH**     See BUT.

**AND**

RIGHT:     We are concerned about the forests AND the oceans.

We are concerned about the forests, the oceans, AND the mountains.

The company is profitable, AND the CEO is famous. (Note the comma before AND.)

.......................................................................................................

SUSPECT:     *We are concerned about the forests AND ALSO the oceans.*

.......................................................................................................

WRONG:     *We are concerned about the forests, ALSO the oceans.*

**AS**

RIGHT:     AS I walked, I became more nervous. (during)

AS I had already paid, I was unconcerned. (because, since)

AS we did last year, we will win this year. (in the same way)

JUST AS we did last year, we will win this year. (in the same way)

AS the president of the company, she works hard. (in the role of)

AS a child, I delivered newspapers. (in the stage of being)

My first job was an apprenticeship AS a sketch artist. (in the role of)

AS PART OF the arrangement, he received severance.

.......................................................................................................

SUSPECT:     *AS A PART OF the arrangement, he received severance.* (Don't include the word *A*.)

.......................................................................................................

WRONG:     *My first job was an apprenticeship OF a sketch artist.*

*The students worked AS a sketch artist.* (The nouns must agree in number.)

*WHILE BEING a child, I delivered newspapers.*

*AS BEING a child, I delivered newspapers.*

*WHILE IN childhood, I delivered newspapers.*

9

### AS...AS

RIGHT:

Cheese is AS great AS people say.

Cheese is NOT AS great AS people say.

We have AS MANY apples AS need to be cooked.

We have THREE TIMES AS MANY pears AS you.

We have AT LEAST AS MANY apples AS you.

We have 10 apples, ABOUT AS MANY AS we picked yesterday.

His knowledge springs AS MUCH from experience AS from schooling.

His knowledge springs NOT SO MUCH from experience AS from schooling.

He wins frequently, AS MUCH because he plays SO hard AS because he cheats.

......................................................................................................................

SUSPECT:

*We have AS MANY apples AS OR MORE apples THAN you.*

*We have AS MANY apples AS THERE need to be cooked.*

......................................................................................................................

WRONG:

*Cheese is SO great AS people say.*

*Cheese is NOT SO great AS people say.*

*Cheese is SO great THAT people say.*

*Cheese is AS great THAT people say.*

*We have AS MANY apples THAN you.*

*We have SO MANY apples AS you.*

*We have AS MANY OR MORE apples THAN you.*

*We have THREE TIMES AS MANY MORE pears AS you.*

*We have 10 apples, ABOUT EQUIVALENT TO what we picked yesterday.*

*His knowledge springs NOT from experience AS from schooling.*

### BECAUSE

RIGHT:

BECAUSE the sun shines, plants grow.

Plants grow BECAUSE the sun shines.

BECAUSE OF the sun, plants grow.

BY SHINING, the sun makes plants grow.

Plants grow, FOR the sun shines. (grammatically correct but very formal)

......................................................................................................................

SUSPECT:

*Plants grow BECAUSE OF the sun, which shines.*

*Plants are amazing IN THAT they grow in the sun.* (correct but wordy)

*The growth of plants IS EXPLAINED BY THE FACT THAT the sun shines.* (correct but wordy)

......................................................................................................................

9

WRONG: *Plants grow BECAUSE OF the sun SHINING.*

*Plants grow AS A RESULT OF the sun SHINING.*

*BECAUSE OF SHINING, the sun makes plants grow.*

*ON ACCOUNT OF SHINING or ITS SHINING, the sun makes plants grow.*

*BECAUSE the sun shines IS the REASON that plants grow.*

*The ABILITY OF plants TO grow IS BECAUSE the sun shines.*

*BEING THAT the sun shines, plants grow.*

*The growth of plants IS EXPLAINED BECAUSE OF the shining of the sun.*

*The growth of plants IS EXPLAINED BECAUSE the sun shines.*

## BEING

RIGHT: BEING infected does not make you sick.

The judges saw the horses BEING led to the stables.

................................................................................

SUSPECT: *BEING an advocate of reform, I would like to make a different proposal.*

Note: The word BEING is often wordy or awkward. However, having caught on to the "BEING is wrong" shortcut, the GMAT problem writers have created a few problems that force you to choose BEING. It's true that BEING appears in many more wrong answers than right ones; however, the word can be used correctly as a gerund or as a participle.

## BELIEVE

RIGHT: She BELIEVES THAT Gary IS right.

She BELIEVES Gary TO BE right.

IT IS BELIEVED THAT Gary IS right.

Gary IS BELIEVED TO BE right.

................................................................................

SUSPECT: *Gary IS BELIEVED BY her TO BE right.*

## BOTH...AND

RIGHT: She was interested BOTH in plants AND in animals.

She was interested in BOTH plants AND animals.

................................................................................

WRONG: *She was interested BOTH in plants AND animals.*

*She was interested BOTH in plants AS WELL AS in animals.*

*She was interested BOTH in plants BUT ALSO in animals.*

9

## BUT

RIGHT:       I STUDY hard BUT TAKE breaks.

I STUDY hard, BUT I TAKE breaks.

ALTHOUGH I TAKE frequent naps, I STUDY effectively.

DESPITE TAKING frequent naps, I STUDY effectively.

I TAKE frequent naps, YET I STUDY effectively.

..................................................................................................................

SUSPECT:    *DESPITE THE FACT THAT I TAKE frequent naps, I STUDY effectively.*

*ALTHOUGH a frequent napper, I STUDY effectively. (ALTHOUGH should generally be followed by a clause.)*

..................................................................................................................

WRONG:    *I STUDY effectively ALTHOUGH TAKING frequent naps.*

*ALTHOUGH I TAKE frequent naps, YET I STUDY effectively.*

*ALTHOUGH I TAKE frequent naps, AND I STUDY effectively.*

*DESPITE TAKING frequent naps, YET I STUDY effectively.*

## CAN

RIGHT:       The manager CAN RUN the plant.

The plant CAN CAUSE damage.

The manager IS CAPABLE OF RUNNING the plant.

..................................................................................................................

SUSPECT:    *It is POSSIBLE FOR the plant TO CAUSE damage.*

*The plant POSSIBLY CAUSES damage.*

..................................................................................................................

WRONG:    *The manager HAS THE CAPABILITY OF RUNNING the plant.*

*The manager HAS THE ABILITY OF RUNNING the plant.*

*The plant HAS THE POSSIBILITY OF CAUSING damage.*

..................................................................................................................

## CONSIDER

RIGHT:       I CONSIDER her a friend.

I CONSIDER her intelligent.

(Note: You can switch the order of the two objects; if one is long, place it second, as in the next example.)

I CONSIDER illegal the law passed last week by the new regime.

The law IS CONSIDERED illegal.

..................................................................................................................

| SUSPECT: | *The judge CONSIDERS the law TO BE illegal.* |
|---|---|

| WRONG: | *The judge CONSIDERS the law AS illegal* (or *AS BEING illegal*). |
|---|---|
| | *The judge CONSIDERS the law SHOULD BE illegal.* |
| | *The judge CONSIDERS the law AS IF IT WERE illegal.* |

## EITHER...OR

| RIGHT: | I will take EITHER the subway OR the bus. |
|---|---|

| WRONG: | *I will take EITHER the subway AND the bus.* |
|---|---|

## EXPECT

| RIGHT: | We EXPECT the price TO FALL. |
|---|---|
| | The price IS EXPECTED TO FALL. |
| | We EXPECT THAT the price WILL FALL. |
| | IT IS EXPECTED THAT the price WILL FALL. |
| | Inflation rose more than we EXPECTED. |
| | There IS an EXPECTATION THAT the price will fall. |

| SUSPECT: | *There IS an expectation the price WILL FALL.* |
|---|---|
| | *There IS an expectation OF the price FALLING.* |

| WRONG: | *The price IS EXPECTED FOR IT TO FALL.* |
|---|---|
| | *IT IS EXPECTED THAT the price SHOULD FALL.* |

| **FOR** (conjunction) | See BECAUSE. |
|---|---|

## FROM...TO

| RIGHT: | The price fell FROM 10 euros TO 3 euros. |
|---|---|
| | The price fell TO 3 euros FROM 10 euros. |

| WRONG: | *The price fell FROM 10 euros DOWN TO 3 euros.* |
|---|---|
| | *The price rose FROM 3 euros UP TO 10 euros.* |

9

## IN ORDER TO

RIGHT:    She drank coffee IN ORDER TO STAY awake.

She drank coffee TO STAY awake. (Infinitive TO STAY indicates purpose.)

.....................................................................................................................

SUSPECT:    *She drank coffee IN ORDER THAT (or SO THAT) she MIGHT STAY awake.*

*She drank coffee SO AS TO STAY awake.*

.....................................................................................................................

WRONG:    *She drank coffee FOR STAYING awake.*

*Coffee was drunk by her TO STAY awake (or IN ORDER TO STAY awake). (The subject COFFEE is not trying TO STAY awake.)*

## INDICATE

RIGHT:    A report INDICATES THAT unique bacteria LIVE on our skin.

.....................................................................................................................

SUSPECT:    *A report IS INDICATIVE OF the presence of unique bacteria on our skin.*

.....................................................................................................................

WRONG:    *A report INDICATES unique bacteria LIVE on our skin. (THAT is needed.)*

*A report IS INDICATIVE THAT unique bacteria LIVE on our skin.*

*A report INDICATES unique bacteria AS present on our skin.*

*A report INDICATES unique bacteria TO LIVE on our skin.*

**INSTEAD OF**    See RATHER THAN.

**LIKE**    See also SUCH AS.

RIGHT:    LIKE his sister, Matt drives fast cars. (Both drive fast cars.)

Matt drives fast cars LIKE his sister's.

(Both drive <u>similar</u> cars; or, less optimally, one of the cars he drives is his sister's.)

.....................................................................................................................

WRONG:    *Matt drives fast cars LIKE his sister does.*

*LIKE his sister, SO Matt drives fast cars.*

## NOT...BUT

RIGHT:    She DID NOT EAT mangoes BUT ATE other kinds of fruit.

She DID NOT EAT mangoes BUT LIKED other kinds of fruit AND later BEGAN to like kiwis, too.

A tomato is NOT a vegetable BUT a fruit.

A tomato is NOT a vegetable BUT RATHER a fruit.

.....................................................................................................................

WRONG:    *She DID NOT EAT mangoes BUT other kinds of fruit.*

9

## NOT ONLY...BUT ALSO

RIGHT:    We wore NOT ONLY boots BUT ALSO sandals.

We wore NOT ONLY boots, BUT ALSO sandals. (The comma is optional.)

We wore NOT JUST boots BUT ALSO sandals.

We wore NOT ONLY boots BUT sandals.

...................................................................................................................

SUSPECT:    *We wore NOT ONLY boots BUT sandals AS WELL.*

*We wore boots AND ALSO sandals.*

...................................................................................................................

WRONG:    *We wore NOT ONLY boots AND ALSO sandals.*

*We wore NOT ONLY boots BUT, AS WELL, sandals.*

## RATHER THAN

RIGHT:    He wrote with pencils RATHER THAN with pens.

...................................................................................................................

SUSPECT:    *He wrote with pencils, BUT NOT pens.*

...................................................................................................................

WRONG:    *He wrote with pencils INSTEAD OF with pens. (OF with is incorrect.)*

## SO...AS TO

SUSPECT:    *The sauce was SO hot AS TO burn my mouth.*

Note: The GMAT has an inconsistent position on this idiom. At least one official explanation claims that this idiom is "incorrect" but provides no further explanation as to why. However, at least one official problem uses this idiom in a correct answer choice. Other authorities consider this idiom correct, and we agree. Nevertheless, you should be wary of its use.

...................................................................................................................

WRONG:    *The sauce had SUCH heat AS TO burn my mouth.*

*The sauce had SO MUCH heat AS TO burn my mouth.*

## SO...THAT    See also ENOUGH in Idioms appendix.

RIGHT:    The book was SO SHORT THAT I could read it in one night.

The book was SHORT ENOUGH FOR me TO READ in one night.

Note: These two expressions have slightly different emphases, but it is unlikely that you will need to choose an answer solely on this basis.

...................................................................................................................

9

| | |
|---|---|
| SUSPECT: | *The book was SO SHORT I could read it.* (*THAT* is preferred.) |
| | *The book was OF SUCH SHORTNESS THAT I could read it.* |
| | *SUCH was the SHORTNESS of the book THAT I could read it.* |

....................................................................................................

| | |
|---|---|
| WRONG: | *The book had SO MUCH SHORTNESS THAT I could read it.* |
| | *The book was OF SUCH SHORTNESS, I could read it.* |
| | *The book was SHORT TO SUCH A DEGREE AS TO ALLOW me to read it.* |

### SO THAT

| | |
|---|---|
| RIGHT: | She gave money SO THAT the school could offer scholarships. (purpose) |

....................................................................................................

| | |
|---|---|
| SUSPECT: | *She gave money, SO the school was grateful.* (result) |

....................................................................................................

| | |
|---|---|
| WRONG: | *She gave money SO the school could offer scholarships.* |

### SUCH AS

| | |
|---|---|
| RIGHT: | Matt drives fast cars, SUCH AS Ferraris. (introducing examples) |
| | Matt enjoys driving SUCH cars AS Ferraris. |
| | Matt enjoys intense activities, SUCH AS DRIVING fast cars. |

....................................................................................................

| | |
|---|---|
| SUSPECT: | *Matt drives fast cars LIKE Ferraris.* (intended to be an example) |
| | Note: The GMAT has backed off from claiming that *like* cannot introduce examples, but it is probable that the GMAT will continue to avoid using *like* with examples, because *like* typically means *similar to*. |

....................................................................................................

| | |
|---|---|
| WRONG: | *Matt drives Ferraris AND THE LIKE.* |
| | *Matt drives Ferraris AND OTHER cars SUCH AS THESE.* |
| | *Matt trains in many ways SUCH AS BY DRIVING on racetracks.* |
| | *Matt enjoys intense activities, SUCH AS TO DRIVE fast cars.* |

### THAN

| | |
|---|---|
| RIGHT: | His books are MORE impressive THAN those of other writers. |
| | This paper is LESS impressive THAN that one. |
| | This paper is NO LESS impressive THAN that one. |
| | This newspaper cost 50 cents MORE THAN that one. |
| | MORE THAN 250 newspapers are published here. |
| | Sales are HIGHER this year THAN last year. |

....................................................................................................

| | |
|---|---|
| WRONG: | *His books are MORE impressive AS those of other writers.* |
| | *This paper is MORE impressive RATHER THAN that one.* |
| | *This paper is MORE impressive INSTEAD OF that one.* |
| | *This paper is NO LESS impressive AS that one.* |
| | *This paper is NONE THE LESS impressive THAN that one.* |
| | *This newspaper cost 50 cents AS MUCH AS that one.* |
| | *AS MANY AS OR MORE THAN 250 newspapers are published here.* |
| | *Sales are HIGHER this year OVER last year.* |

**<u>UNLIKE</u>**  See also CONTRAST in Idioms appendix.

RIGHT:  UNLIKE the spiny anteater, the aardvark is docile.

...........................................................................................................

WRONG:  *UNLIKE WITH the spiny anteater, the aardvark is docile.*

**<u>WHETHER</u>**

RIGHT:  I do not know WHETHER I will go.

...........................................................................................................

SUSPECT:  *I do not know WHETHER OR NOT I will go.*

...........................................................................................................

WRONG:  *I do not know IF I will go.* (IF requires a consequence.)

**<u>WHETHER...OR</u>**

RIGHT:  I decided to eat the food, WHETHER it was tasty OR NOT.

WHETHER trash OR treasure, the recyclables must be picked up.

...........................................................................................................

WRONG:  *WHETHER trash OR ALSO treasure, the recyclables must be picked up.*

*WHETHER THEY BE trash OR treasure, the recyclables must go.*

**<u>YET</u>**  See BUT.

9

# Problem Set

Problems 1–3 contain at least one idiom. Underline correct idioms and box incorrect idioms. For idioms that are split up, be sure to identify both parts. Evaluate each idiom using the Spot–Extract–Replace method.

1.   The ring-tailed squirrel is more adept at surviving harsh winter conditions as its cousin, the golden-mantled squirrel, so that the golden-mantled squirrel typically lives in warmer climates.

2.   It is expected that advances in the production of high-temperature superconductors should increase the viability of so-called "maglev" trains that float on magnetic fields.

3.   Faced with an increase of natural disasters, such as floods and wildfires, many state governments have imposed significant taxes on their citizens in order for raising funds in advance of the next calamity.

Problems 4–6 each contain a pair of correct sentences with slight variations in idioms that result in big changes in meaning. Describe the difference in meaning between the two sentences.

4.   The robber served a shortened prison sentence so that he could receive proper medical treatment.

   The robber served a shortened prison sentence, so he could receive proper medical treatment.

5.   In an attempt to reach a favorable plea deal, the defense attorney argued passionately with his client.

   In an attempt to reach a favorable plea deal, the defense attorney argued passionately for his client.

6.   The patient asked for the doctor when the patient arrived at the hospital.

   The patient asked about the doctor when the patient arrived at the hospital.

Problems 7–9 are multiple choice with one correct answer. As on the real GMAT, answer (A) repeats the original sentence. Unlike the real GMAT, though, these problems have only four answer choices.

7.  These results <u>indicate the health of the marsh's ecosystem has seriously declined</u>.

    (A)  indicate the health of the marsh's ecosystem has seriously declined

    (B)  indicate that the health of the marsh's ecosystem has seriously declined

    (C)  are indicative that the health of the marsh's ecosystem has seriously declined

    (D)  seriously indicate a decline in the health of the marsh's ecosystem

8.  The conflict started <u>both because of ethnic tensions as well as</u> because of economic dislocations.

    (A)  both because of ethnic tensions as well as

    (B)  because of both ethnic tensions and

    (C)  not because of ethnic tensions but also

    (D)  as a result of ethnic tensions and worsened

9.  <u>Unlike humans and guinea pigs, most mammals have the ability of synthesizing vitamin C from glucose, a simple sugar.</u>

    (A)  Unlike humans and guinea pigs, most mammals have the ability of synthesizing vitamin C from glucose, a simple sugar.

    (B)  Unlike humans and guinea pigs, most mammals have the ability for synthesis of vitamin C from glucose, a simple sugar.

    (C)  Most mammals, unlike humans and guinea pigs, have the ability to synthesize vitamin C from glucose, a simple sugar.

    (D)  Most mammals have the ability to synthesize vitamin C from glucose, a simple sugar, unlike humans and guinea pigs.

9

# Solutions

1. Two-part idioms are in bold to show which two parts are connected.

   The ring-tailed squirrel is |**more**| adept at surviving harsh winter conditions |**as**| its cousin, the golden-mantled squirrel, |so that| the golden-mantled squirrel typically <u>lives in</u> warmer climates.

   Corrected sentence: The ring-tailed squirrel is **more** adept at surviving harsh winter conditions **than** its cousin, the golden-mantled squirrel, <u>so</u> the golden-mantled squirrel typically lives in warmer climates.

   The sentence contains two separate idioms. The correct comparison idiom is *more…than*; *more…as* is incorrect.

   The idiom *so that* indicates purpose, similar to *in order to*. For example, *I lift weights so that I can gain muscle.* In the sentence above, *so* is used as a synonym for *therefore* to convey a conclusion; the word *that* should be removed.

2. It is |**expected that**| <u>advances</u> in the <u>production of</u> high-temperature superconductors |**should**| increase the viability of so-called "maglev" trains that float on magnetic fields.

   Corrected sentence: It is **expected that** advances in the production of high-temperature superconductors **will** increase the viability of so-called "maglev" trains that float on magnetic fields.

   *Expected that* indicates what might or will happen. *Should*, on the other hand, indicates what ought to happen. The proper idiom is *expected that…will*.

3. Faced with an |increase of| natural disasters, such as floods and wildfires, many state governments have **imposed** significant taxes **on** their citizens |in order for raising| funds <u>in advance of</u> the next calamity.

   Corrected sentence: Faced with an <u>increase in</u> natural disasters, such as floods and wildfires, many state governments have imposed significant taxes on their citizens <u>in order to raise</u> funds in advance of the next calamity.

   The proper idiom is *increase in*.

   *In order* must be followed by an infinitive verb (*to X*) at some point in the sentence: *in order to raise*. The verb need not follow immediately—consider the following sentence:

   *In order for students to succeed, they must study hard.*

   Thus, *in order* can be followed by *for*, but what follows *for* must be the subject for the subsequent infinitive verb. This sentence lacks an infinitive verb altogether.

4. In the first sentence, *so that* indicates purpose. *The robber served a shortened prison sentence* in order to *receive proper medical treatment*.

   In the second sentence, *so* preceded by a comma indicates a consequence: Because *the robber served a shortened prison sentence*, he was able to *receive proper medical treatment*. In this case, *the shortened sentence* enabled the robber to *receive proper medical treatment*, but he didn't serve a shortened sentence for that specific purpose.

5.  In the first sentence, the *defense attorney* argues *with his client*; the argument is taking place between these two people.

    The second sentence changes *with* to *for*. To argue *for* someone is to argue in that person's defense. Here, the *defense attorney* is arguing in support of his client, and that argument is taking place with someone else (perhaps the prosecutor or the judge).

6.  The phrase *asked for* means to request someone's presence. In the first sentence, *the patient* requested to be seen by the doctor.

    In contrast, the phrase *asked about* in the second sentence means that *the patient* wanted to know more information *about the doctor*.

7.  **(B):** The original sentence incorrectly connects two independent clauses without the word *that*. Eliminate answer (A) for faulty sentence structure.

    In answer choice (C), *are indicative* should be followed by *of*.

    Answer choice (D) incorrectly places the adverb *seriously*. It is intended to modify how much the *health of the marsh's ecosystem has declined*. Its placement in this sentence incorrectly modifies *indicate*.

    Answer choice (B) correctly uses the subject–verb–that–subject–verb sentence structure and properly places *seriously* to modify how much the *health of the marsh's ecosystem has declined*.

8.  **(D):** The original sentence contains an idiom error. *Both…as well as* is incorrect; the correct idiom is *both X and Y*.

    In answer choice (B), the idiom *both X and Y* requires the *X* and *Y* elements to be parallel. However, the noun *ethnic tensions* is not parallel to the conjunction *because*.

    Answer choice (C) fixes the parallelism issue in answer choice (B), but the comparison idiom is incorrect. The proper idiom is either *not only X but also Y* or *not only X but Y*.

    Answer choice (D) removes the idiom errors in previous answers and contains two verb structures that are properly parallel to each other: 1) *started as a result of ethnic tensions* and 2) *worsened because of economic dislocations*.

9.  **(C):** The answer choices have a split around the preposition that follows the word *ability*: *of*, *for*, or *to*. *Ability for* is never correct; eliminate answer choice (B).

    *Ability of* and *ability to* can both be correct idioms, but they mean different things. *Ability of* refers to someone's ability, as in this example: *The sprinting ability of the cheetah is unmatched*. On the other hand, *ability to* introduces the ability that is being discussed: *The ability to sprint fast is vital to the cheetah's survival*. The original sentence uses *ability of* when it should use *ability to*. Eliminate answer choice (A).

    Answers (C) and (D) both correctly use *ability to*. However, choice (D) has a comparison error. The placement of *unlike humans and guinea pigs* after *a simple sugar* seems to say that *humans and guinea pigs* are not like *sugar*. The intended comparison is between *humans and guinea pigs* and *most mammals*. Correct answer (C) places *humans and guinea pigs* next to *most mammals*.

# UNIT TWO

# Reading Comprehension

In this unit, you will learn a process for reading passages effectively without getting too bogged down in the details and for keeping the information organized and accessible as you answer questions. You will also learn how to recognize the different Reading Comprehension (RC) question types, what steps to take to identify the correct answer, and how to avoid trap answers.

## In This Unit:

# The Foundation

## In This Chapter:

- How Reading Comprehension Works
- Find the Simple Story
- 4 Steps to the Simple Story
- Answer the Question

**In this chapter, you will learn** how to read passages efficiently in order to extract the main points you need without getting stuck in unnecessary detail.

# CHAPTER 10 The Foundation

Picture this:

> You've just received an email from your boss, asking you to review the Summary of Acme Company's annual report before the two of you go into a conference call with Acme's CEO. The Summary is six pages long and the phone call starts in five minutes.
>
> The pressure is on! What do you do?
>
> (A) Speed-read your way through the entire thing. You won't actually remember or understand what you're reading, but hey, you did technically "read" it.
>
> (B) Start reading carefully, even though you won't be able to finish before the conference call starts.
>
> (C) Hand in your resignation.
>
> (D) Read the first paragraph carefully to get oriented, then start picking up the pace. Slow down for the big ideas, but speed up on the details.

The correct answer is (D), of course! You can't possibly read everything carefully in the allotted time, so you prioritize, looking for main ideas while minimizing the details for now. If the conversation does turn to a detail about one of those main ideas, then you'll have a rough idea where to look and can glance quickly through the summary to find the information. In fact, this whole exercise probably sounds a lot like decisions you make every day at work.

Reading Comprehension (RC) on the GMAT is a test of your real-world executive reasoning skills, even though it often feels like a school test. You typically won't have enough time to read everything thoroughly and carefully—the test literally doesn't give you enough time to do that—so you're going to need to prioritize. This unit will teach you how.

## How Reading Comprehension Works

On the GMAT, you will probably see a total of four Reading Comprehension passages, most commonly accompanied by three questions, though occasionally you may be given four questions. (It's possible for these details to change slightly, but this is the most common configuration.)

The passage will always be on the left side of the screen and one question at a time will appear on the right, as depicted here:

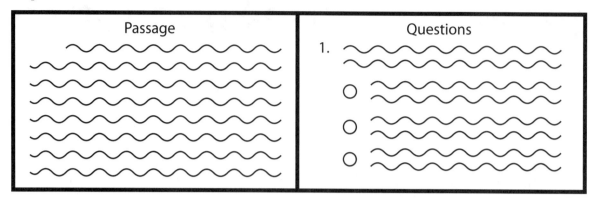

When you answer the first question, a new one will appear in its place. The passage will remain on the left-hand side of the screen. The GMAT will not tell you how many questions you're going to get; you'll know that you're done with the passage when the passage goes away and an entirely new question appears on the screen.

You'll want to spend about 2 to 3 minutes reading the passage (more on this later) and then an average of about 1.5 minutes per question. (You'll learn more about RC time management in Atlas, your online learning platform.)

The passages range from about 200 words up to about 350 words and from one to four paragraphs. Most people will see three shorter passages and one longer one, though this mix can change. The topics are fairly academic, covering areas in hard science, social science, history, and business.

You may see some topics that you enjoy, but you're also likely to see at least one that you don't like much. Try to resist the temptation to dismiss any of the passages as "boring" or "not my topic." If you can convince yourself that the passage is interesting, you'll fare much better on the questions. (Don't worry: This guide will help you to develop this active reading stance!) In the meantime, keep in mind that you're not expected to bring any outside knowledge to the task—whether the passage is about municipal bonds or polypeptide chains, you'll be provided with all of the information you need to answer the questions.

When you start to work through RC problems from *The Official Guide for GMAT Review*, you will see that the passages show line numbers on the left side of the paragraphs, and some questions will make direct reference to a line number. The actual GMAT exam does *not* number the lines in each passage. Instead, when the exam wants to draw your attention to a particular term or phrase in the passage, you will suddenly see that text highlighted in yellow when the relevant question pops up on the screen.

## Find the Simple Story

Think back to the annual report challenge. You can't read everything carefully before the meeting. On the other hand, you don't want to just skim over the whole thing or you won't learn anything useful for the meeting.

The goal in situations like this is to find the **Simple Story**: the main points that you would use to summarize that annual report in just a few sentences for your boss. In order to do this, you really do need to read the text, but you do so selectively, paying attention to the main ideas while setting aside the details for now. Later, if you do need a detail, you can look it up; the report will be right in front of you for the whole meeting.

Try to find the simple story in the passage below. This is a shorter passage, so give yourself approximately 2 minutes to read through the passage. At the end, you'll need to answer a question about the main idea of the passage, so keep that in mind as you read; you want the big picture, not the details.

Take any notes that you like (or none at all—it's up to you), but resist the temptation to write on this page. Since the GMAT is administered on a computer, get used to taking notes on a separate piece of scratch paper and looking back and forth between the two.

Bacteria

> Recent research into antibiotic-resistant bacterial strains suggests the need for a reexamination of the frequency with which doctors prescribe antibacterial therapy. One study demonstrated, for example, that most minor bacterial infections will resolve without treatment within 5 to 14 days of onset of symptoms; a course of antibiotics might reduce that time frame by only 1 to 2 days. A second study indicated that the incidence of "superbugs," which have resistance to a wide variety of antibacterial agents, is increasing significantly and that these bugs are more likely to spread among those who have been treated with antibiotics within the past 5 years. In particular, researchers have become alarmed by NDM-1 (New Delhi metallo-beta-lactamase), which is not a single bacterial species, but a multiple-antibiotic-resistant enzyme capable of infecting other strains of bacteria.
>
> It is true that the proliferation of superbugs likely owes a great deal to the mistaken prescription of antibacterial treatment for viral infections, against which such treatment is ineffective, and to the routine addition of antibiotics to livestock feed in order to increase meat yields. Additionally, it is possible that ongoing research into the means by which resistance spreads among bacterial communities may lead to a new generation of antibiotics to which bacteria are unable to develop resistance. Yet these factors do not change the need for individual physicians to be more circumspect about drug therapy when treating cases of true bacterial infection.

Did you stick to the 2-minute time frame given? You have a little leeway (30 seconds or so extra), but resist the urge to spend much more time; the real test punishes those who don't manage their time well, and you'll build bad habits if you don't learn to work in the way that the GMAT requires.

If you feel a little panicky about the thought of having to read that fast, take a deep breath and remind yourself that you don't need to understand the annoying details—at least, not right now. You just need to get the big picture straight before the "meeting with your boss" starts.

Can you summarize, in one sentence, the overall idea of this passage? Go ahead and do so.

If you're struggling to do that, you may have gotten distracted by the details. If you took notes, glance at them. Do you have NDM-1 written down?

If so, then you probably got too pulled into the detail; that's very common at this stage. Now you know that you're going to need to retrain yourself to read at a higher level and actually let a lot of detail go (on your first read through).

Now, give yourself about a minute to try the following question:

The passage is primarily concerned with

(A) discussing research into the common symptoms associated with a particular medical condition

(B) explaining the frequency with which a certain medical condition is diagnosed

(C) contrasting the views of doctors and medical researchers with respect to the diagnosis of a particular medical condition

(D) questioning the current standard of treatment for a particular medical condition

(E) contending that physicians need to be more careful about distinguishing between two different, but related, medical conditions

Before reviewing the problem, let's talk about how to read the passage and find the simple story in the first place.

The first one to three sentences of a passage lay the groundwork for the entire passage, so at first, read carefully. Pay the most attention to the easier words that really tell you what's going on—not the technical ones that are just there to distract you.

Here's how a very strong test-taker might read the first paragraph. (The bold font represents text the reader pays close attention to.)

| Passage Text | Reader's Thoughts |
|---|---|
| **Recent research** into antibiotic-resistant bacterial strains **suggests the need for a reexamination of the frequency with which doctors prescribe** antibacterial therapy. | *Hmm. I don't know much about* antibacterial therapy, *but I know that* suggests the need for a reexamination of the frequency *means something's not quite right about how often doctors are using it. Presumably the passage is about to tell me why.* |
| **One study** demonstrated, **for example**, that **most minor** bacterial infections will **resolve without treatment** within 5 to 14 days of onset of symptoms; | *Wait, so at least some of the time, you'd get better without even taking drugs?* |
| a course of antibiotics might reduce that time frame by only 1 to 2 days. | *If you do take drugs, they might not really have a huge impact. Interesting. Okay, so this whole example supports the idea that doctors use antibiotics too much.* |
| A **second study indicated** that the incidence of **"superbugs,"** which have **resistance** to a wide variety of antibacterial agents, **is increasing significantly** | *I've read stuff before about antibiotic resistance; I'm pretty sure it's not a good thing. And* superbug *definitely doesn't sound good.* |
| and that **these bugs are more likely to spread among those who have been treated with antibiotics within the past 5 years**. | *Yay, no weird words here. So these superbug things are definitely bad for people who've been taking antibiotics.* |
| In particular, researchers have become alarmed by NDM-1 (New Delhi metallo-beta-lactamase), which is not a single bacterial species but a multiple-antibiotic-resistant enzyme capable of infecting other strains of bacteria. | *Uhh. Most of this makes no sense to me, but I get that NDM-1 is bad. It's also a detail, so I really don't care right now. Moving on!* |

Right now, you may be thinking: Wait a second—what if I get a question about that detail?

The GMAT test writers might create as many as eight or nine questions for a passage, but you will be given only three or four of those questions. The passage will contain some details that you aren't asked about—and that might be the case for the NDM-1 detail. Do you want to learn about it just because you're very diligent and think it's the right thing to do, even if you never get asked about it?

10

Of course not! Don't waste time learning details that you might never need, especially when time is so tight. Rather, set the details aside for now. If you do get a question about NDM-1 later, you can return to this text and spend a little time working to understand it.

On to the second paragraph:

| Passage Text | Reader's Thoughts |
|---|---|
| **It is true that the proliferation of superbugs likely owes a great deal to the mistaken prescription** of antibacterial treatment for viral infections, **against which such treatment is ineffective**, | It is true that—*you use that kind of language when you want to acknowledge some detail that doesn't fit with your overall point.*<br><br>*The previous paragraph was about* bacterial *infections. Now, it's saying that there are also* mistaken prescriptions *for* viral *infections. And it's saying that this stuff doesn't even work against viruses anyway.* |
| and to the routine **addition of antibiotics to livestock feed** in order to increase meat yields. | *And a second reason there are superbugs…this is just another detail, so I can speed up a bit. I've got the big idea: It is true that there are other reasons for the proliferation of superbugs besides those given in the first paragraph.* |
| **Additionally**, it is possible that **ongoing research** into the means by which resistance spreads among bacterial communities **may lead to a new generation of antibiotics to which bacteria are unable to develop resistance**. | *An additional example…so this is more of the same? Research might solve the problem longer term.* |
| **Yet** these factors **do not change the need for individual physicians to be more circumspect about drug therapy** when treating cases of true bacterial infection. | Yet! *This is going against the ideas just presented. I'm not sure what* circumspect *means, but it looks like the author is coming back to the earlier point— doctors have to be more careful or thoughtful about prescribing these drugs so much.* |

Here's the reader's simple story:

> *Something's not quite right about how often doctors are prescribing antibiotics for infections. Two studies support this idea: First, in some cases, the drugs don't help much, and second, something about superbugs.*
>
> *There are some other potential causes of these superbugs—prescribing antibiotics for infections isn't the only problem—but it's still the case that doctors have to be more careful about using these drugs even for legitimate reasons.*

Notice how much that simple story leaves out. There isn't even a mention of NDM-1, let alone what it is or how it works. That's perfectly fine—if you get a question about it, you can go back to find the relevant text and read in more detail. (Or you could decide that you disliked that detail enough that you would rather guess and move on.)

# 4 Steps to the Simple Story

Here's the basic process to find your simple story:

**Step 1: Get oriented.** Read the first sentence or two pretty carefully:

- Understand the topic under discussion and keep an eye out for any main ideas.
- Know the main idea of a paragraph by the time you're done reading that paragraph. You may want to jot down a note. (You'll learn more about taking notes in a later chapter.)
- Read the first paragraph of the passage more carefully than any of the others (when there is more than one paragraph in the passage).

**Step 2: Find the main idea of each paragraph.** When you start a new paragraph, pay close attention to (at least) the first sentence. Find the main idea of that paragraph—why was it included in the passage?

**Step 3: Set aside the details.** When you get to examples or other very specific details, focus on *why* the information is present. How does this example fit the overall story? Pay less attention to all of the nitpicky little details.

**Step 4: Articulate the simple story.** When you're done, pause for a moment to articulate the simple story to yourself. If you had to give someone a 10-second summary of the passage, what would you say?

In subsequent chapters, you'll learn techniques to help you develop the simple story and set yourself up to answer both general and specific detail questions. For now, take a look at how this approach can make the process of answering certain questions easier.

# Answer the Question

Now that you have a better idea of how to find the simple story, feel free to try the problem again before you continue reading. Here it is:

The passage is primarily concerned with

(A)  discussing research into the common symptoms associated with a particular medical condition

(B)  explaining the frequency with which a certain medical condition is diagnosed

(C)  contrasting the views of doctors and medical researchers with respect to the diagnosis of a particular medical condition

(D)  questioning the current standard of treatment for a particular medical condition

(E)  contending that physicians need to be more careful about distinguishing between two different, but related, medical conditions

This is a primary purpose question; you'll learn about this question type in more detail in the General Questions chapter. The correct answer will convey the overall point or main idea of the simple story. Before reading the answers, remind yourself of that story. Then, eliminate answers that go too far beyond the story, that focus too much on certain details without conveying the main idea, or that actually contradict the passage in some way.

The passage is primarily concerned with

(A)   discussing research into the common symptoms associated with a particular medical condition

**Incorrect.** The passage mentions only that symptoms can resolve without treatment; the symptoms themselves are not discussed.

(B)   explaining the frequency with which a certain medical condition is diagnosed

**Incorrect.** The first sentence does suggest that the frequency with which antibiotics are prescribed may need to change, but this is not the same as the frequency with which the medical condition is diagnosed in the first place.

(C)   contrasting the views of doctors and medical researchers with respect to the diagnosis of a particular medical condition

**Incorrect.** The first paragraph does present information that might seem to imply a difference of opinion between doctors and researchers as to whether or how frequently antibiotics should be prescribed—but this is a difference in opinion about treatment. The passage doesn't indicate that the doctors and researchers might disagree about how to diagnose the condition.

(D)   questioning the current standard of treatment for a particular medical condition

**CORRECT.** The first and last sentences of the passage together indicate that the author believes that doctors may be overprescribing antibiotics—in other words, that the current standard of treatment might not be appropriate. This fits the simple story: The first paragraph presents research to support this opinion, and the second acknowledges other causes of the "superbug" problem before reiterating that the frequency with which antibiotics are used for bacterial infections is still an issue.

(E)   contending that physicians need to be more careful about distinguishing between two different, but related, medical conditions

**Incorrect.** This is tempting. The passage does mention two types of infections: viral and bacterial. However, the passage doesn't say that doctors are mistakenly diagnosing a bacterial infection when a patient actually has a viral infection. The passage says only that patients with viral infections are sometimes mistakenly treated with antibiotics; it could be that such patients are diagnosed correctly but given an inappropriate treatment.

The only answer that fits with the simple story is answer (D). Take a moment to review and summarize each answer:

(A) Symptoms? Not discussed.

(B) Passage is about frequency of the *treatment*, not frequency of the condition itself.

(C) The *treatment* is the issue, not the diagnosis.

(D) Correct!

(E) The *treatment* is the issue, not the diagnosis.

Note that answers (C) and (E) are incorrect for the same underlying reason, and answer (B) is incorrect for a very similar reason. If you can learn to "abstract" out the trap answers to this level on both Reading Comprehension and Critical Reasoning, you can get quite good at these two question types.

622

# Breaking Down the Passage

## In This Chapter:

- Engage with the Passage

- Passage Components

- Language Clues

- Optional Strategy: Breaking Down Complex Sentences

**In this chapter, you will learn** how to break down the different parts of a passage in order to distill the simple story. You will also learn how to separate the big picture from the details and how to handle especially complex sentences.

# CHAPTER 11 Breaking Down the Passage

Sometimes, you hit a passage that just speaks to you. You like the topic, the language doesn't seem as challenging, and you might even be somewhat familiar with the technical examples given. When this happens, go with it! Read the passage as though you're reading for pleasure and don't worry as much about building an explicit simple story. (Just be careful not to bring in outside knowledge.)

More often, though, you're not going to get that lucky. Remember the last time you started to read a passage and you wanted to groan aloud because you found the topic boring? Yet you still had to get through the passage and answer questions about it. What to do?

## Engage with the Passage

The first step may seem minor, but it will be a real help. Think of someone you know who actually does like the topic. Pretend that you're going to tell her about it later: "Oh, Robyn would like this. I want to remember enough to tell her about the main gist of it." Who knows—you might actually discover that the topic isn't as boring as you thought.

What do you want to remember to tell Robyn? Certainly not some very specific detail four sentences into the second paragraph. Rather, you want to tell her the simple story. Having Robyn in mind will keep you focused on that task. Lean forward a bit in your seat, smile, and do your best to convince yourself that you are reading this passage by choice and not just because you have to.

## Passage Components

Do you remember what a thesis statement is? When you were writing academic papers in school, you had to include a thesis statement and provide support for that thesis. You were expected to have an introduction and a conclusion. In many cases, you were even expected to raise questions or acknowledge contrasting points of view, while ultimately showing that your thesis still held.

GMAT passages are, for the most part, excerpts of academic papers. They are much shorter, of course, so they don't contain all of the expected components of an academic work, but certain components will be present.

You do not need to memorize the different components, nor do you need to explicitly label every sentence that you read. If you know what to look for, though, then you'll be better equipped to find the simple story.

### The Point

**The Point** is the thesis statement: It is the single most important message of the passage and the heart of your simple story. The author has written the passage in order to convey the point, even if nothing else gets through to the reader.

Take a look back at the *Bacteria* passage from the last chapter. Where does the author express the point?

> Recent research into antibiotic-resistant bacterial strains suggests the need for a reexamination of the frequency with which doctors prescribe antibacterial therapy. One study demonstrated, for example, that most minor bacterial infections will resolve without treatment within 5 to 14 days of onset of symptoms; a course of antibiotics might reduce that time frame by only 1 to 2 days. A second study indicated that the incidence of "superbugs," which have resistance to a wide variety of antibacterial agents, is increasing significantly and that these bugs are more likely to spread among those who have been treated with antibiotics within the past 5 years. In particular, researchers have become alarmed by NDM-1 (New Delhi metallo-beta-lactamase), which is not a single bacterial species, but a multiple-antibiotic-resistant enzyme capable of infecting other strains of bacteria.
>
> It is true that the proliferation of superbugs likely owes a great deal to the mistaken prescription of antibacterial treatment for viral infections, against which such treatment is ineffective, and to the routine addition of antibiotics to livestock feed in order to increase meat yields. Additionally, it is possible that ongoing research into the means by which resistance spreads among bacterial communities may lead to a new generation of antibiotics to which bacteria are unable to develop resistance. Yet these factors do not change the need for individual physicians to be more circumspect about drug therapy when treating cases of true bacterial infection.

The point is encapsulated in the first and last sentences:

> Recent research into antibiotic-resistant bacterial strains suggests the need for a reexamination of the frequency with which doctors prescribe antibacterial therapy.

> Yet these factors do not change the need for individual physicians to be more circumspect about drug therapy when treating cases of true bacterial infection.

The basic idea is this: *The frequency with which doctors prescribe antibiotics is problematic and doctors have to be more careful.*

This is the single most important idea that the author was trying to convey in writing the passage. If you can't articulate the point, or if you think something else is the point, you are probably going to miss at least some of the questions associated with the passage.

Your simple story will always contain the point. The point can be anywhere in the passage, but it is most often found in the first paragraph or the beginning of the second paragraph. Most of the time, the point will be contained in a single sentence, but occasionally you'll have to combine two or three sentences to get it.

What about the rest of the information in the simple story? Read on.

## Support and Background

Some amount of the information in any passage will serve to **Support** the author's point. This support is part of the story.

You may also think of some information as **Background**: It doesn't strongly support the point, but it sets the context for information presented in the passage. Although this information does not strictly support the point, you don't need to distinguish background information from support—you can group it all together. Certainly, you wouldn't want to brush past a whole paragraph without understanding it simply because it looks like background. You need to understand enough of the supporting and background information to build your simple story, but you do not have to thoroughly comprehend or memorize how these details work.

Looking back at the passage, where do you see information that supports the author's point?

The supporting information is contained in the second part of the first paragraph: Two studies support the point. In the simple story, these studies were compressed down to one sentence:

*Two studies support this idea: First, in some cases, the drugs don't help much, and second, something about superbugs.*

The sentences in the passage contain a whole lot more detail than that, but it is enough to know that these examples support the point. If you are asked a question about any particular supporting detail, you'll know to go back to the latter part of the first paragraph.

## Counterpoints, Acknowledgments, and Implications

Some passages will contain **Counterpoints**, information that goes against the author's point (or at least appears to). Passages might also **Acknowledge** a certain point or piece of evidence that does not support the point but that doesn't go against it either.

As with support and background, your goal is to know how the high-level information fits into the simple story, while leaving specific details for later.

Take a look at the passage one more time. Does it contain any counterpoints or acknowledgments?

The second paragraph of the passage begins by acknowledging that there are other possible factors (aside from the treatment of bacterial infections) that are contributing to the superbug problem.

Nevertheless, the author eventually concludes that the original point holds: Doctors have to be more careful about prescribing antibiotics even for legitimate purposes.

Whether you thought of these other factors as counterpoints or as acknowledgments is not all that important. It is important just to recognize that they did not ultimately support the author's point.

Occasionally, passages will contain **Implications** for the future, answering the question, "So what might happen from here or what should we do about the situation?" The *Bacteria* passage does not contain implications, but you could imagine that the author might have discussed a need to fund additional research to establish that the over-prescription of antibiotics for bacterial infections is contributing to resistant bacteria. Alternatively, the author might have proposed a government panel to study how to influence doctors to reduce the number of antibiotic prescriptions. Both of those would be implications.

Use all of these components to help you find your simple story.

**Step 1: Get oriented.** Read the first sentence or two pretty carefully.

- Understand the topic under discussion and keep an eye out for any main ideas.
- Know the main idea of a paragraph by the time you're done reading that paragraph.
- Read the first paragraph of the passage more carefully than any of the others (when there is more than one paragraph in the passage).

**Step 2: Find the main idea of each paragraph.** When you start a new paragraph, pay close attention to (at least) the first sentence. Find the main idea of that paragraph—why was it included in the passage?

**Step 3: Set aside the details.** When you get to examples or other very specific details, focus on *why* the information is present. How does this example fit the overall story? Pay less attention to all of the nitpicky little details.

**Step 4: Articulate the simple story.** When you're done, pause for a moment to articulate the simple story to yourself. If you had to give someone a 10-second summary of the passage, what would you say?

# Language Clues

Sometimes, specific language in the passage will signal important categories of information that will help you to build your simple story. Keep an eye out for clues about four big categories:

1. Big Picture
2. Foreshadowing
3. Changes of Direction
4. Detail

## Big Picture

**Big-Picture** language introduces or summarizes some kind of main idea. When you see words like these in a sentence, they should almost jump off the page. Don't get distracted by New Delhi metallo-beta-whatever. Pay attention to the big picture!

In the table below are some common language clues that signal a main idea:

| Signal | Implication |
|---|---|
| In general; To a great extent; Broadly speaking; In conclusion; In sum; In brief; Therefore; Thus; So; Hence; As a result; Overall | A generalization or conclusion follows. |
| First, Second, etc.; To begin with; Next; Finally; Again | Two or more important points or examples are outlined. Pay attention to the overall purpose; *why* is the author mentioning these points or examples? |
| *X* argues that; *X* contends that; theory; hypothesis | A named person or group holds a specific theory or opinion. |

## Foreshadowing

When you watch a movie or television show, you don't just passively gaze at the screen. You are actively engaging with the story, anticipating what might be coming: Uh oh, the lawyer got distracted by the guy with the gun just as she was piecing together key arguments for the legal case—I bet she's going to make a mistake and mess up in court! Showing this distraction is a way for the director to foreshadow upcoming events.

**Foreshadowing** works the same way in writing: The author can drop a clue about something that he plans to say later in the passage. When you spot foreshadowing, you can use it to anticipate the point or other important ideas in the passage.

Given the following as the first sentence of an RC passage, where might you anticipate the passage could go next?

> Given recent company stumbles, it is important to ask: Is the potential return on investment worth the risk?

When an author asks a question in the beginning of a passage, she is almost certainly going to address that question in her passage. She may discuss how a company should weigh the risks and rewards of a potential investment; alternatively, she may provide examples of things that a company should *not* consider. She will probably provide at least one example of how a specific company messed this up or got this right.

How about this opener?

> For some time, government officials disagreed as to where to store high-level radioactive waste.

There are many possibilities for what immediately follows: Perhaps the author will describe the opinions held by different government officials, or perhaps he will explain what caused the disagreement in the first place. However, it seems certain that by the end of the passage the officials will have come to an agreement. The language *for some time*, coupled with the past tense verb *disagreed*, indicates that the problem existed in the past but no longer exists today. At some point, the passage will likely tell you that the officials came to an agreement and determined where to store that nuclear waste.

Here are some examples of common foreshadowing signals:

| Signal | Implication |
| --- | --- |
| Traditionally; For some time; It was once believed; It had been assumed | Contrast coming up soon; now, things are different |
| Some (people) claim (believe, define, attribute, etc.); It is true that | Acknowledge a valid opposing point |
| Statement of a problem or question | Possible fix for problem or answer to question (or statement that it can't be fixed or answered, or more research needs to be done) |
| Current theory; conventional wisdom | New or different theory or idea coming up soon |

The list above is meant to help you to start thinking about foreshadowing, but there are many possible language clues; don't just stick to that list. As you read the first paragraph, look for foreshadowing language to help you anticipate where the passage might be going. The sooner you start to have an idea of the big picture and the point, the better.

## Changes of Direction

**Change-of-Direction** language can signal some kind of twist—a contrast or a qualification that could make for a good test question. In addition, twists can signal a counterpoint or a return to the main point.

In the *Bacteria* passage, the final sentence contains a change-of-direction signal:

> Yet these factors do not change the need for individual physicians to be more circumspect about drug therapy when treating cases of true bacterial infection.

The beginning of that same paragraph acknowledged some information that doesn't actually support the overall point. The appearance of the word *yet* signals that the author is about to change direction and jump back to that point.

**11**

Here are some common change-of-direction signals:

| Signal | Implication |
|---|---|
| However; Yet; On one hand/On the other hand; While; Rather; Instead; In contrast; Alternatively | Indicate contrasting ideas |
| Granted; It is true that; Certainly; Admittedly; Despite; Although | Concede a point (author acknowledges or reluctantly agrees) |
| Actually; In fact; Indeed; Surprisingly | Indicate an unexpected result or phenomenon |
| Nevertheless; Nonetheless; That said; Even so | Assert a position after conceding a point |
| Supposedly; It was once thought; Seemingly; For some time | Something appeared to be a certain way, but it really wasn't that way at all |

## Detail

Certain clues will signal that you should pay less attention on your first read through. When you see these words, still run your eyes over the information, but change your goal: Understand why the information is there, but don't try to understand or remember every last detail given.

| Signal | Implication |
|---|---|
| For example; As an example; In particular; For instance | Provide an example |
| Furthermore; Moreover; In addition; As well as; Also; Likewise; Too | Add to something that was already said |
| Likewise; In the same way | Provide a new example or detail that goes along with a previous one |
| In other words; That is; Namely; So to speak; a semicolon (;) | Restate something that was already said (in this case, you can use whichever set of words is easier for you to interpret!) |

# Optional Strategy: Breaking Down Complex Sentences

It is not unusual for a GMAT test-taker to read a sentence, pause for a moment, and think, "Huh? I have no idea what that means." The test writers are masters of the complex sentence, so it might be worth your while to take a few pages to practice in-depth reading on a sentence-by-sentence level.

You may or may not need this section. If you are a strong reader who often reads complex material for pleasure or for work, then you have likely already developed your own techniques for breaking down complex sentences into simpler thoughts so that you can digest the full meaning. If that is the case, don't feel that you have to change what already works for you.

If, on the other hand, you can think of at least one "Huh?" moment while reading RC passages, then read on.

What does this sentence mean?

> In a diachronic investigation of possible behavioral changes resulting from accidental exposure in early childhood to environmental lead dust, two sample groups were tracked over decades.

At this point, you may be distracted by the word *diachronic*. If you don't happen to know the meaning of that word, you have plenty of company! Believe it or not, you can ignore those kinds of words. When the test writers toss jargon words at you—scientific terms and the like—one of two things will happen. If you need to know what the word means, then the passage will give you a definition or a contrasting word that lets you figure out the weird word from context. If not, then the passage will just move on, and you should, too. Don't let one unfamiliar word prevent you from processing the rest of the material.

One way to move past such words is to turn them into single letters for ease of reading:

*In a D investigation of possible behavioral changes...*

Here's how a reader might go about stripping that first sentence down to more manageable parts:

| Passage Text | Reader's Thoughts |
|---|---|
| In a diachronic investigation of possible behavioral changes | *Someone was investigating behavior changes.* |
| resulting from accidental exposure in early childhood to environmental lead dust, | *I don't know what* environmental lead dust *is, specifically, but I've heard that lead is supposed to be bad for kids. Okay, this makes sense: Some kids were accidentally exposed to lead and someone then investigated some consequences.* |
| two sample groups were tracked over decades. | *Specifically, they investigated two groups of kids for a long time.* |
| | *Put it all together: Kids were accidentally exposed to lead, and somebody investigated two groups of these kids to see whether their behavior changed over time.* *Hmm, I wonder whether the lead did affect the kids? Presumably, the passage will get into that.* |

Here are the steps that the reader took:

| Steps | Example |
|---|---|
| 1. **Break the sentence down into smaller ideas; ignore technical jargon.** | The reader above read just one idea, then she stopped to understand that one part before continuing to read and add new information. She also ignored the word *diachronic*. |
| 2. **Make connections to things you already know; simplify complex language.** | The reader didn't get flustered by *environmental lead dust*. Instead, she made a connection to something she already knew: Lead is bad for kids. This knowledge went along with what the sentence was saying, helping her to wrap her head around the second part of the sentence. |
| 3. **Link to previous information.** | As the reader understood each new idea, she linked it back to what she'd already read. At the end, she made sure that she had a handle on the entire sentence. |
| 4. **Anticipate.** | Finally, the reader speculated about where the passage might be going. Such anticipation can help keep you actively engaged with the passage—even when the topic isn't your favorite! |

As you might guess, breaking down sentences takes time. You won't be able to do this for every sentence in the passage.

Fortunately, you won't need to. First of all, you will actually understand many of the sentences just by reading them once. Second of all, think back to your overall goal: Find the simple story. You don't need to understand every sentence. You only need to understand the sentences that present the big ideas—the ideas that will help you to find the story. When you get to complex sentences about examples or other details, you can just read right over them and keep going.

Try another:

> While *Don Giovanni* is today widely considered Wolfgang Amadeus Mozart's greatest achievement, eighteenth-century audiences in Vienna—Mozart's own city—and the rest of Europe differed greatly in their opinion of a new work unexpectedly mixing traditions of moralism with those of comedy.

| Passage Text | Reader's Thoughts |
|---|---|
| While *Don Giovanni* is today widely considered Wolfgang Amadeus Mozart's greatest achievement, | *While is a huge clue: contrast! I'm guessing that* today *is another important word: The contrast seems to be that DG is considered M's best work* today, *but maybe it wasn't in the past…?* |
| eighteenth-century audiences in Vienna—Mozart's own city—and the rest of Europe | *There are some details about location, but the important thing is that this part talks about 18th-century audiences. As I suspected, it's talking about the past now, specifically about people who were there when* Don Giovanni *was written.* |
| differed greatly in their opinion of a new work | *They didn't agree—did they all think it was bad? No, it says they* differed greatly *among each other: Some liked it and some didn't. Wait, so what's the contrast?*<br><br>*Oh, I see. Today, it's widely considered his greatest achievement. Back then, some people liked it and some didn't.* |
| unexpectedly mixing traditions of moralism with those of comedy. | *This feels like detail. If I get questions about why some people liked it and some didn't, I'll come back here.* |
| | *The basic message: Today, people think DG is M's greatest achievement. In the 18th century, though, the opinion was mixed.* |

# Problem Set

For each of the four passages below, take 2 to 3 minutes to read the passage and tell yourself the simple story. Then, compare to the version in the solution. There are certainly many ways to convey the same content; just make sure that your version covers all of the big ideas of the passage.

## Passage A: Animal Treatment

Over the course of the eighteenth and early nineteenth centuries, educated Britons came to embrace the notion that animals must be treated humanely. By 1822, Parliament
5 had outlawed certain forms of cruelty to domestic animals, and by 1824 reformers had founded the Society for the Prevention of Cruelty to Animals.

This growth in humane feelings was part of
10 a broader embrace of compassionate ideals. One of the great movements of the age was abolitionism, but there were many other such causes. In 1785, a Society for the Relief of Persons Imprisoned for Small Sums persuaded
15 Parliament to limit that archaic punishment. The Society for Bettering the Condition of the Poor was founded in 1796 and a Philanthropic Society founded in 1788 provided for abandoned children. Charity schools, schools
20 of midwifery, and hospitals for the poor were being endowed. This growth in concern for human suffering encouraged reformers to reject animal suffering as well.

Industrialization and the growth of towns
25 also contributed to the increase in concern for animals. The people who protested against cruelty to animals tended to be city folk who thought of animals as pets rather than as live stock. It was not just animals, but all of
30 nature, that came to be seen differently as Britain industrialized. Nature was no longer a menacing force that had to be subdued, for society's "victory" over wilderness was conspicuous everywhere. A new sensibility,
35 which viewed animals and wild nature as things to be respected and preserved, replaced the old adversarial relationship. Indeed, animals were to some extent romanticized as emblems of a bucolic,
40 pre-industrial age.

## Passage B: Higher Education

Critics of our higher education system point out the often striking difference between the skills students develop in university courses and the skills desired by employers. Students
5 generally enter university with the expectation that a degree will improve their job prospects, the argument goes, so why not give employers more direct control over the education process? Some commentators have even
10 gone so far as to suggest that traditional postsecondary courses be replaced with short, standardized skills-training workshops.

However, the provision of vocational training is not the goal of most university programs.
15 Rather, universities seek to provide students with experience in a particular field of inquiry, as well as exposure to a wide range of disciplines and worldviews. University students learn to situate themselves not only within the
20 adult world of work and responsibility, but also within the broader streams of historical, social, and physical development that shape and are shaped by their actions and experiences.

It is certainly reasonable to ask whether this
25 vision of education serves the interests of the roughly 2/3 of United States high school graduates who enroll immediately in 2- or 4-year programs after high school. Might some of these students' needs be better met by more narrowly
30 focused vocational programs? Current research suggests that, rather than serving as a reliable engine of social mobility, the United States system of postsecondary education can actually reinforce existing inequalities. However, it is not
35 at all clear that a more employer-oriented system, in which immediate economic need might deter many students from entering academically oriented degree programs, would be any more effective at producing opportunity
40 for traditionally disadvantaged student populations. Further, it is worth considering that the kind of education traditionally provided by universities may confer benefits to society that are not as easily measured as an immediate
45 boost in individual earnings. Before we make any sweeping changes on utilitarian grounds, we ought to consider the utility of the existing order.

11

## Passage C: Rock Flour

Although organic agriculture may seem to be the wave of the future, some experts believe that the next stage in agricultural development requires the widespread adoption of
5   something very inorganic: fertilizer made from powdered rocks, also known as "rock flour." The biochemical processes of life depend not only on elements commonly associated with living organisms, such as oxygen, hydrogen,
10  and carbon, but also on many other elements in the periodic table. Specifically, plants need the so-called "big six" nutrients: nitrogen, phosphorus, potassium, calcium, sulfur, and magnesium. In modern industrial agriculture,
15  these nutrients are commonly supplied by traditional chemical fertilizers.

However, these fertilizers omit trace elements, such as iron, that are components of essential plant enzymes and
20  pigments. For instance, the green pigment chlorophyll, which turns sunlight into energy that plants can use, requires iron. As crops are harvested, the necessary trace elements are not replaced and become depleted in the
25  soil. Eventually, crop yields diminish, despite the application or even over-application of traditional fertilizers. Rock flour, produced in abundance by quarry and mining operations, may be able to replenish trace elements
30  cheaply and increase crop yields dramatically.

Not all rock flour would be suitable for use as fertilizer. Certain chemical elements, such as lead and cadmium, are poisonous to humans; thus, applying rock flour containing
35  significant amounts of such elements to farmland would be inappropriate, even if the crops themselves do not accumulate the poisons, because human contact could result directly or indirectly (e.g., via soil
40  runoff into water supplies). However, most rock flour produced by quarries seems safe for use. After all, glaciers have been creating natural rock flour for thousands of years as they advance and retreat, grinding
45  up the ground underneath. Glacial runoff carries this rock flour into rivers and, downstream, the resulting alluvial deposits are extremely fertile. If the use of man-made rock flour is incorporated into
50  agricultural practices, it may be possible to make open plains as rich as alluvial soils.

## Passage D: Pro-Drop Languages

In many so-called "pro-drop" or "pronoun-drop" languages, verbs inflect for number and person. In other words, by adding a prefix or suffix or by changing in some other way,
5   the verb itself indicates whether the subject is singular or plural, as well as whether the subject is first person (*I* or *we*), second person (*you*), or third person (*he, she, it,* or *they*). For example, in Portuguese, which is at least
10  partially a pro-drop language, the verb *falo* means "I speak": the –o at the end of the word indicates first person, singular subject (as well as present tense). As a result, the subject pronoun *eu*, which means "I" in Portuguese,
15  does not need to be used with *falo* except to emphasize who is doing the speaking.

It should be noted that not every language that drops its pronouns inflects its verbs. Neither Chinese nor Japanese verbs,
20  for instance, change form at all to indicate number or person; however, personal pronouns are regularly omitted in both speech and writing, leaving the proper meaning to be inferred from contextual clues. Moreover, not every language
25  that inflects its verbs drops subject pronouns in all non-emphatic contexts. Linguists argue about the pro-drop status of the Russian language, but there is no doubt that, although the Russian present-tense verb *govoryu* ("I speak")
30  unambiguously indicates a first person, singular subject, it is common for Russian speakers to express "I speak" as *ya govoryu*, in which *ya* means "I," without indicating either emphasis or contrast.

35  Nevertheless, Russian speakers do frequently drop subject and object pronouns; one study of adult and child speech indicated a pro-drop rate of 40–80 percent. Moreover, personal pronouns must in fact be dropped in
40  some Russian sentences in order to convey particular meanings. It seems safe to conjecture that languages whose verbs inflect unambiguously for person and number permit pronoun dropping, if only
45  under certain circumstances, in order to accelerate communication without loss of meaning. After all, in these languages, both the subject pronoun and the verb inflection convey the same information, so there is no
50  real need both to include the subject pronoun and to inflect the verb.

# Solutions

## Passage A: Animal Treatment

In the 18th and 19th centuries, people in Britain grew concerned about the humane treatment of animals. This was part of a general movement toward more compassionate treatment of others. Industrialization also shifted people's views: In the new industrialized world, nature no longer seemed like a threat.

## Passage B: Higher Education

University education doesn't always fit with what employers want, so some people think schools should focus on more job-oriented skills. In the U.S., universities want to teach more than that, but what would be best for students? Maybe the current system doesn't help everyone, but the author thinks the new idea is not necessarily better and wants to be cautious about making changes.

## Passage C: Rock Flour

Rock flour, a type of fertilizer made from powdered rocks, could provide a cheap source of nutrients for plants, significantly improving crop yields. While some rock flour might be dangerous, most of it should be safe to use.

## Passage D: Pro-Drop Languages

In "pro-drop" languages, the speaker often drops pronouns (*I*, *you*, etc.) because the verb form makes the subject clear. However, these two things don't always go together: Some languages drop pronouns even though the verb doesn't indicate the subject, and some languages keep the pronoun even though the verb also makes the subject clear. The author thinks that some languages allow the speaker to drop the subject pronoun to accelerate communication.

# Mapping the Passage

## In This Chapter:

- Why Use a Passage Map?
- Making the Passage Map
- Common Notations

**In this chapter, you will learn** how to make a passage map, a particular way of taking notes that makes you articulate the main points of the passage and prepares you to quickly find the information needed to answer the questions.

# CHAPTER 12 Mapping the Passage

You have one more skill to develop before diving into the questions. These passages are complex; even the simple story is several sentences long. You wouldn't want to take the time to write the story out, but it is very useful to jot down certain things. So, you're going to create a **Passage Map**.

A caveat: Your goal is absolutely *not* to take notes the way that you took notes in school. You aren't going to be studying this same passage again weeks from now; once you're done with the passage, you can forget about it forever.

Instead, your goal is to jot down just a few words that will help you to develop and remember your simple story (including the point) and to remember where in the passage to look when you need support to answer a question.

## Why Use a Passage Map?

You're going to have to answer two types of questions: general and specific. The passage map will help you to accomplish two important goals:

1.  Predict the answers to general questions
2.  Know where in the passage to find the details you'll need to answer specific questions

The two goals above will indicate whether you're creating an effective map. If you can't answer general questions based on the information in your map, then you didn't learn enough about the big picture on the first read through. You'll need to practice picking up on the main ideas and major changes in direction.

On specific questions, though, you actually do *not* want to be able to find the answers on your map. If you can, then you likely spent too much time diving into the detail on your read through. The GMAT will always include more detail in the passage than you will need to answer the questions; if you pay careful attention to all of that detail, you may run out of time on the test. You'll actually need to practice minimizing the attention you pay to details, possibly to the point of skimming some information.

Avoid relying too heavily on your memory when answering the detail questions. Remember, this is an "open book" test, and it is full of traps for those who are pretty confident that they remember the details. Check the passage! If you form good habits and apply a consistent and efficient process even on the easier-for-you questions, you'll have a better chance to answer the difficult questions correctly.

## Making the Passage Map

Your passage map reflects the simple story, but it will be heavily abbreviated. Your map should include the following information (and not much more):

- The point
- The purpose of each paragraph
- Any other information you would include in the simple story, organized by paragraph

Every reader's map will be different. You have the flexibility to organize in a way that makes sense for you. Of course, this makes creating an answer key to passage mapping a little difficult, but this unit will model the process in a way that provides guidance while leaving your own passage map style up to you.

Try creating a map of the *Bacteria* passage that you saw earlier in this unit. Use any format you like as long as it reflects your simple story.

12

> Recent research into antibiotic-resistant bacterial strains suggests the need for a reexamination of the frequency with which doctors prescribe antibacterial therapy. One study demonstrated, for example, that most minor bacterial infections will resolve without treatment within 5 to 14 days of onset of symptoms; a course of antibiotics might reduce that time frame by only 1 to 2 days. A second study indicated that the incidence of "superbugs," which have resistance to a wide variety of antibacterial agents, is increasing significantly and that these bugs are more likely to spread among those who have been treated with antibiotics within the past 5 years. In particular, researchers have become alarmed by NDM-1 (New Delhi metallo-beta-lactamase), which is not a single bacterial species, but a multiple-antibiotic-resistant enzyme capable of infecting other strains of bacteria.
>
> It is true that the proliferation of superbugs likely owes a great deal to the mistaken prescription of antibacterial treatment for viral infections, against which such treatment is ineffective, and to the routine addition of antibiotics to livestock feed in order to increase meat yields. Additionally, it is possible that ongoing research into the means by which resistance spreads among bacterial communities may lead to a new generation of antibiotics to which bacteria are unable to develop resistance. Yet these factors do not change the need for individual physicians to be more circumspect about drug therapy when treating cases of true bacterial infection.

Here is the simple story:

*Something's not quite right about how often doctors are prescribing antibiotics for infections. Two studies support this idea: First, in some cases, the drugs don't help much, and second, something about superbugs.*

*There are some other potential causes of these superbugs—prescribing antibiotics for infections isn't the only problem—but it's still the case that doctors have to be more careful about using these drugs even for legitimate reasons.*

Here's one potential passage map for this story:

① Problem: Drs prescribe antiB a lot—too much?

    1.   Sometimes antiB don't help!

    2.   Superbugs ↑ = bad

② Other things cause superbugs, too

    BUT Drs still have to be careful about using antiB Ⓟ

The map reflects the major elements of the story. It clearly delineates the point Ⓟ. It shows what information is in paragraph 1 versus paragraph 2. It mentions the support and the acknowledgment.

This map wouldn't take long to produce, but you can certainly abbreviate more heavily, depending on how strong your short-term memory is.

Here's a more abbreviated version:

① Prob: Drs use antiB a lot—too?

    1.   May not help!

    2.   Superbug ☹

② Other → superbugs

    STILL Drs must be careful re: antiB Ⓟ

Someone with a great short-term memory and strong RC skills in general might abbreviate to the point that the map resembles hieroglyphics; only she or he would be able to read it. Here's an example:

① Prob: Drs AB too much

    1.  ≠ help

    2.  SB

② Other → SB

    Drs must take care w/AB Ⓟ

Now, give yourself about 1.5 minutes to try this problem.

> The research cited in the first paragraph suggests which of the following about antibacterial therapy?
>
> (A) It frequently leads to infection with NDM-1.
> (B) It is not generally used to treat minor bacterial infections.
> (C) It may help to reduce the incidence of superbugs that are especially hard to treat.
> (D) Reducing the rate at which such therapy is used would cause fewer bacteria to develop resistance to antibiotics.
> (E) Its short-term benefits, if they exist, may not outweigh the potential harm to the broader population.

This question asks about the studies in the first paragraph. Some of the answers are very detailed, but it's certainly okay to make a quick pass to look for an answer that matches the simple story. If nothing turns up, then go back and analyze the details.

> The studies cited in the first paragraph suggest which of the following about antibacterial therapy?
>
> (A) It frequently leads to infection with NDM-1.
>
> *I don't know! I skimmed the info about NDM-1. Come back later.*
>
> (B) It is not generally used to treat minor bacterial infections.
>
> *They said it is used to treat minor infections—it only reduces treatment time by a couple of days. This one's wrong.*
>
> (C) It may help to reduce the incidence of superbugs that are especially hard to treat.
>
> *I don't know. Come back later.*
>
> (D) Reducing the rate at which such therapy is used would cause fewer bacteria to develop resistance to antibiotics.
>
> *I don't know. Come back later.*
>
> (E) Its short-term benefits, if they exist, may not outweigh the potential harm to the broader population.
>
> **CORRECT.** *The paragraph does mention that such therapy might reduce the illness by one to two days. This could be a short-term benefit, but the author minimizes this benefit and goes on to discuss a much worse drawback (the superbug). That all fits with the simple story and the first paragraph.*

It's sometimes possible to find the right answer even if you don't yet know why some of the wrong ones are wrong. On the real test, pick (E) and move on. When you're studying, go back afterwards to learn why answers (A), (C), and (D) are wrong.

(A) It frequently leads to infection with NDM-1.

> **Incorrect.** The passage does say that patients who have used antibiotics within the past five years are more likely to pick up superbugs, but it doesn't indicate how often this happens, especially in the case of NDM-1 in particular. Perhaps this bug is still very rare.

(C) It may help to reduce the incidence of superbugs that are especially hard to treat.

> **Incorrect.** This paragraph mentions nothing about what causes the incidence of superbugs to decrease. In fact, the story hinges on the idea that these superbugs are *increasing*, so this answer contradicts the story.

(D) Reducing the rate at which such therapy is used would cause fewer bacteria to develop resistance to antibiotics.

> **Incorrect.** This is tempting! The question points you specifically to the first paragraph, though, and the first paragraph does not discuss what causes bacteria to become antibiotic-resistant. (The second paragraph does touch on this a bit, but it does not discuss how *antibacterial therapy* might contribute to this phenomenon—read the question carefully!)

In this case, the wrong answers weren't necessarily easy to eliminate, but the right answer was definitely connected to the simple story.

If the correct answer didn't match your take on the passage, you may not have read carefully enough. This typically happens for one of two reasons:

1.  You read so quickly that you aren't really taking in what you're reading. Have you ever read something and then realized that you have no idea what you just read and you have to read it again? You'll need to learn to read actively on RC; purposefully looking for the simple story will help.

2.  You get distracted by the technical words, the examples, and the minutiae; you're paying so much attention to those details that you forget to tell yourself the simple story. In this case, you're going to have to learn how to strip out the details and concentrate on the big picture.

As this unit progresses, you'll learn techniques to help you overcome these (and other) problems by actively reading for the big picture and using that understanding to simplify the process of answering the questions.

# Common Notations

You don't have much time to read the passage and make your passage map. The good news is that you'll only need your map for the few minutes it takes you to answer the questions. In fact, you may find that once your map has done its job and helped you to understand the passage, you don't end up looking back at it at all. With this in mind, don't try to create the kind of clear document you might study from in school; you're not really going to be using this map for very long.

Given that, you can abbreviate heavily in your map. Consider the following notations:

| Tactic | Passage Language | Abbreviation |
|---|---|---|
| Abbreviate technical words or hard-to-pronounce names with a single letter, an acronym, or a much shorter version of the word. | serotonin<br><br>Mihaly Csikszentmihalyi | S or sero<br><br>C or MC |
| Use an arrow to show cause–effect or change over time. | Instability in interest rates can cause investors to avoid bonds. | IR unstable → ppl avoid bonds |
| Use a colon (:) to attribute an opinion or point of view to a specific person or group. | Many historians believe that economic interests can prolong a war. | H: $$ issues → longer war |
| Mark examples with parentheses or *eg*. | A classic example is the behavior of the female sphex wasp. | e.g., ♀ S wasp |
| Use up and down arrows to indicate increases or decreases. | An increasing number of businesses are expected to reduce benefits for part-time employees. | ↑ biz: ↓ ben part-time |
| Use math and science symbols that you already know. | greater than (or much greater than) | > (>>) |
|  | less than (or much less than) | < (<<) |
|  | change | Δ |
|  | therefore | ∴ |

# Problem Set

For each of the four passages below, take 2 to 3 minutes to read and map the passage and articulate the simple story.

The solutions present one version of a passage map, but your version will vary; this is fine! The solutions also include simple stories, but you don't need to write these down when you are working a passage—the passage map should be enough to allow you to put together the simple story.

## Passage E: Redlining

In the 1960s, Northwestern University sociologist John McKnight coined the term redlining, the practice of denying or severely limiting service to customers in
5   particular geographic areas, areas often determined by the racial composition of the neighborhood. The term came from the practice of banks outlining certain areas in red on a map; within the red outline, banks
10   refused to invest. With no access to mortgages, residents within the red line suffered low property values and landlord abandonment; buildings abandoned by landlords were then more likely to become
15   centers of drug dealing and other crime, thus further lowering property values.

Redlining in mortgage lending was made illegal by the Fair Housing Act of 1968, which prohibited such discrimination based
20   on race, religion, gender, familial status, disability, or ethnic origin, and by community reinvestment legislation in the 1970s. However, redlining has sometimes continued in less explicit ways and can also
25   take place in the context of constrained access to health care, jobs, insurance, and more. Even today, some credit card companies send different offers to homes in different neighborhoods, and some auto
30   insurance companies offer different rates based on zip code.

Redlining can lead to reverse redlining, which occurs when predatory businesses specifically target minority or low-income
35   consumers for the purpose of charging them more than would typically be charged for a particular service. When mainstream retailers refuse to serve a certain area, people in that area can fall prey to opportunistic smaller
40   retailers who sell inferior goods at higher prices.

## Passage F: Tokugawa

The Tokugawa period in Japan (1603–1867) serves as a laboratory for organizational behavior historians for the same reason that Iceland is an ideal location for geneticists—
5   isolation removes extraneous variables. The Tokugawa shoguns brought peace to a land of warring feudal lords. To preserve that tranquility, the Tokugawa shogunate forbade contact with the outside world, allowing only
10   a few Dutch trading ships to dock at one restricted port. Domestically, in pursuit of the same goal, the social order was fixed; there were four classes—warriors [samurai], artisans, merchants, and farmers or
15   peasants—and social mobility was prohibited. The ensuing stability and peace brought a commercial prosperity that lasted nearly two hundred years.

However, as psychologists and social
20   historians have observed, in varying ways, humans often fail to anticipate unintended consequences. In the Tokugawa period, the fixed social hierarchy placed the samurai on top; they and the government were essentially
25   supported by levies on the peasantry, as the other two classes were demographically and economically inconsequential. However, prosperity brought riches to the commercial classes and their numbers burgeoned.
30   Eventually, their economic power dwarfed that of their supposed superiors, the samurai, but the social structure was so ingrained that it was unthinkable to change. By the early nineteenth century, this imbalance between
35   social structure and economic reality eroded the stability of the society. This condition was one of the primary factors that led to the eventual collapse of the shogunate in 1867. In short, the success of the self-imposed order
40   led to its undoing through consequences that were beyond the ken of the founders.

## Passage G: Prescription Errors

In Europe, medical prescriptions were historically written in Latin. A prescription for eye drops written in Amsterdam could be filled in Paris, because the abbreviation *OS*
5   meant "left eye" in both places. With the disappearance of Latin as a lingua franca, however, abbreviations such as *OS* can easily be confused with *AS* (left ear) or *per os* (by mouth), even by trained professionals.
10  Misinterpretations of medical instructions can be fatal. In the early 1990s, two infants died in separate but identical tragedies: They were each administered 5 milligrams of morphine, rather than 0.5 milligrams, as the dosage was
15  written without an initial zero. The naked decimal (.5) was subsequently misread.

The personal and economic costs of misinterpreted medical prescriptions and instructions are hard to quantify. However,
20  anecdotal evidence suggests that misinterpretations are prevalent. While mistakes will always happen in any human endeavor, medical professionals, hospital administrators, and policymakers should
25  continually work to drive the prescription error rate to zero, taking simple corrective steps and also pushing for additional investments.

Certain measures are widely agreed upon
30  but may be difficult to enforce, given the decentralization of the healthcare system in the United States. For instance, professional organizations have publicly advocated against the use of Latin abbreviations and other relics
35  of historical pharmacology. As a result, incidents in which *qd* (every day) and *qid* (four times a day) have been mixed up seem to be on the decline. Other measures have been taken by regulators. For instance, the Federal
40  Drug Administration asked a manufacturer to change the name of Losec, an antacid, to Prilosec, so that confusion with Lasix, a diuretic, would be reduced. Unfortunately, there have been at least a dozen reports of
45  accidental switches between Prilosec and Prozac, an antidepressant. As more drugs reach the market, drug-name "traffic control" will only become more complicated.

Other measures are controversial or
50  require significant investment. For instance, putting the patient's condition on the prescription would allow double-checking but also compromise patient privacy. Computerized prescriber order entry (CPOE)
55  systems seem to fix the infamous problem of illegible handwriting, but many CPOE systems permit naked decimals and other dangerous practices. Moreover, since fallible humans must still enter and retrieve the data, any
60  technological fixes must be accompanied by substantial training. Ultimately, a multi-pronged approach is needed to address the issue.

## Passage H: Ether's Existence

In 1887, an ingenious experiment performed by Albert Michelson and Edward Morley severely undermined classical physics by failing to confirm the existence of "ether," a
5  ghostly massless medium that was thought to permeate the universe. This finding had profound results, ultimately paving the way for acceptance of Einstein's special theory of relativity.

10  Prior to the Michelson–Morley experiment, nineteenth-century physics conceived of light as a wave propagated at constant speed through the ether. The existence of ether was hypothesized in part to explain the
15  transmission of light, which was believed to be impossible through "empty" space. Physical objects, such as planets, were also thought to glide frictionlessly through the unmoving ether.

20  The Michelson–Morley experiment relied on the fact that the Earth, which orbits the Sun, would have to be in motion relative to a fixed ether. Just as a person on a motorcycle experiences a "wind" caused by her own
25  motion relative to the air, the Earth would experience an "ethereal wind" caused by its motion through the ether. Such a wind would affect our measurements of the speed of light. If the speed of light is fixed with respect
30  to the ether, but the Earth is moving through the ether, then to an observer on Earth light must appear to move faster in a "downwind" direction than in an "upwind" direction.

35  In 1887, there were no clocks sufficiently precise to detect the speed differences that would result from an ethereal wind. Michelson and Morley surmounted this problem by using the wavelike properties of light itself to test for such speed differences. In their apparatus,
40  known as an "interferometer," a single beam of light is split in half. Mirrors guide each half of the beam along a separate trajectory before ultimately reuniting the two half-beams into a single beam. If one half-beam
45  has moved more slowly than the other, the reunited beams will be out of phase with each other. In other words, peaks of the first half-beam will not coincide exactly with peaks of the second half-beam, resulting in an
50  interference pattern in the reunited beam. Michelson and Morley detected only a tiny degree of interference in the reunited light beam—far less than what was expected based on the motion of the Earth.

Solutions on next page. ▶ ▶ ▶

# Solutions

## Passage E: Redlining

Passage map:

① Redlining: deny/limit svc to minorities

② Now illegal, but still happens

③ Leads to reverse redL: charging more than typical

Simple story:

Redlining is denying or limiting services to minority customers. It's been illegal since the late '60s, but some businesses still do it. It can also lead to reverse redlining, where businesses do offer service to minority communities, but at a higher price than they would typically charge.

## Passage F: Tokugawa

Passage map:

① T isolated; fixed social order; peace/stable.

② BUT merchants → wealthy, messed up social order, system collapsed. Fixed soc. order was once good, later bad.

Simple story:

The T period in Japan is good to study because it was isolated. The social order was fixed and it was a really stable era. Later, a "lower" group became wealthy, but the rigid social system stayed. So what helped make things stable at first eventually caused the system to collapse.

## Passage G: Prescription Errors

Passage map:

① Eur. Rx in Latin, but now errors, dangerous

② DK how much error, but maybe lots. Try to ↓

③ Pop. measures: no Latin, no similar names

④ Other measures controv.: listing condition, computers

Simple story:

There are many ways to misinterpret medical prescriptions, and this can be dangerous. Some measures—such as eliminating the use of Latin and making names unambiguous—are agreed upon, but others are more controversial.

## Passage H: Ether's Existence

Passage map:

① 1887, M&M—no ether; made way for Einstein

② Old: ether explained how light moved

③ Basis for exp: Earth "wind"

④ DTL: How M&M showed lack of ether

DTL is an abbreviation for the word *detail*.

Simple story:

Prior to 1887, scientists thought that space was not "empty," but filled with a substance called ether. In 1887, Michelson and Morley conducted an experiment that involved splitting a beam of light. There was less interference than there should have been if ether existed, so the experiment showed that ether might not actually exist.

## In This Chapter:

**In this chapter, you will learn** how to handle general questions. These big-picture questions ask about the primary purpose or main point of the entire passage or of one paragraph in the passage.

# CHAPTER 13 General Questions

Reading Comprehension questions can be grouped into two major categories:

1. **General** questions, such as Primary Purpose, Paragraph

2. **Specific** questions, such as Detail, Inference, Specific Purpose

This chapter will cover general questions, which may ask you about the overall purpose of the passage or about the purpose of a specific paragraph. The next chapter will cover specific question types.

You typically won't see more than one general question per passage; in fact, on some passages you won't see any. On average, expect to spend 30–60 seconds on each general question.

## 4 Steps to the Answer

In this chapter, you'll learn how to answer **Primary Purpose** and **Paragraph** questions using a standard 4-step process that you'll use for all RC questions.

**Step 1: Identify the question.** This chapter will tell you how to recognize that you have a Primary Purpose or a Paragraph question.

**Step 2: Find the support.** Your initial read of the passage and any map you make will give you a strong idea of the overall point and the purpose of each paragraph. At this stage, you may take a look at your passage map to remind yourself of the big picture, or you may feel comfortable not even doing that. (Note: On specific questions, you *will* have to go back to reread some part of the passage—more on this in the next chapter.)

**Step 3: Predict an answer.** Take a look at the question again and, using your map or memory, try to formulate a rough answer in your own words. You're not trying to match the correct answer exactly; rather, you're just trying to articulate the *kind* of information you would expect to find in the correct answer.

**Step 4: Eliminate and find a match**. Evaluate each answer, while keeping in mind your predicted answer. Eliminate any that definitely don't match. When you find a potential match, leave it in and continue to evaluate the remaining answers:

- If you eliminate four answers, great! Pick the remaining one and move on.

- If you still have two or three answers left, compare the answers to the relevant information in your map. If the answers are very similar, you may also compare them to each other.

- If you still have four or five answers left, make sure you are answering the right question! After that, it's probably best to cut your losses: Guess and move on.

Finally, one last word of advice. This might seem obvious, but *every single word* in the answer choice must be supported in order for that choice to be correct. Make sure that you are reading methodically. Don't rush just because you're stressed; saving 10 seconds is not worth the risk of missing a question due to a careless mistake.

# Practice Passage: Insect Behavior

Give yourself approximately 4 minutes to read the passage below and answer the questions that follow.

At times, insect behavior appears to be explicable in terms of unconscious stimulus-response mechanisms; when scrutinized, it often reveals a stereotyped, inflexible quality.
5 A classic series of experiments were performed on the female sphex wasp. The mother leaves her egg sealed in a burrow alongside a paralyzed grasshopper or other insect, which her larva can eat when it hatches.
10 Typically, before she deposits the grasshopper in the burrow, she leaves it at the entrance and goes inside to inspect the burrow. If the inspection reveals no problems, she drags the grasshopper inside by its antennae. Once the
15 larvae hatch, they feed on the paralyzed insects until ready to spin a cocoon and undergo metamorphosis.

Entomologist Jean-Henri Fabre discovered that if the grasshopper's antennae are
20 removed while the wasp is inside inspecting the nest, the wasp will not drag it into the burrow, even though the legs or ovipositor could serve the same function as the antennae. Later Fabre found more evidence
25 of the wasp's dependence on predetermined routine. While a wasp was performing her inspection of a burrow, he moved the grasshopper a few centimeters away from the burrow's mouth. The wasp brought the
30 grasshopper back to the edge of the burrow, then began a whole new inspection. When Fabre took this opportunity to move the food again, the wasp repeated her routine. Fabre performed his disruptive maneuver
35 forty times, and the wasp's response never changed.

1. The primary purpose of the passage is to

   (A) demonstrate, based on examples, that insects lack awareness of their surroundings

   (B) argue that insects are unique in their dependence on rigid routines

   (C) analyze the maternal behavior of wasps

   (D) contrast typical wasp behavior with unconscious behavior

   (E) contend that insect behavior can rely on rigid routines that appear to be unconscious

2. Which of the following best describes the purpose of the second paragraph of the passage?

   (A) To provide experimental evidence for the thesis articulated in the first paragraph

   (B) To introduce a hypothesis about insect behavior

   (C) To illustrate the ways in which grasshoppers are unsuitable for the wasp's purposes

   (D) To explore the significance of the wasp's varied reactions to certain stimuli

   (E) To acknowledge experimental evidence that does not support the author's thesis

Here's one example of a simple story, with the point noted:

| The point | → | *Insect behavior is sometimes inflexible or unconscious. Normally, a wasp inspects the burrow and then brings the grasshopper inside. Later, the larvae feed on the grasshopper.* |

> *Fabre discovered that the wasp will* only *drag a grasshopper by the antennae. He also found that, if the grasshopper is moved during the inspection phase, then the wasp will put the grasshopper back and inspect the burrow again, over and over.*

> *Hmm. That sounds pretty inflexible—it's as though it can't think or adapt.*

That last line is not stated in the passage, but a reader might summarize the simple story in this way.

Here's one example of a passage map:

① Insects: behavior inflex, unconsc
Typ: wasp inspect burrow, bring GH, larvae eat

② F: ONLY drag by antennae
If GH moves, wasp re-inspects, every time

Here's a much more abbreviated version:

① Insect: inflex
Normal behav

② F: weird behav

The second map is so abbreviated that it serves only as a quick reminder of things that the reader already remembers: The normal behavior is described in the first paragraph and the second paragraph has the weird behavior. If your short-term memory is strong, then feel free to use a hyper-abbreviated map like this one. (You might not even write anything at all, but only follow that path if you can maintain a strong mental sense of the passage throughout the process of reading and answering the questions. Don't avoid writing anything simply because you think it will save you time.)

## Primary Purpose Questions

Step 1 on any question is to **identify the question type**:

1. The primary purpose of the passage is to

This is a **Primary Purpose** question—the test writers are asking for the point of the whole passage. These are also known as **Main Idea** questions.

Most of the time, these questions will ask you to identify the *primary purpose* of the passage or what the author is *primarily concerned with*. The correct answer should fit with the point that you have articulated to yourself.

Steps 2 and 3 merge for Primary Purpose questions: **Find the support** and **predict an answer**. For Primary Purpose questions, you don't need to go back to the passage. You will already have identified the point—if not, briefly review your map. In this passage, the point is that some insect behaviors seem to be inflexible; the insects can't adapt to changing situations.

Once you have that set in your head, it's time for step 4: **Eliminate and find a match**. For Primary Purpose questions, eliminate any choice that doesn't match the point. For example:

13

| | |
|---|---|
| (A) demonstrate, based on examples, that insects lack awareness of their surroundings | *The insect is aware—she sees that the grasshopper has moved and she goes and gets it. The point is about insects' unconscious behavior, not their general awareness.* |
| (B) argue that insects are unique in their dependence on rigid routines | *The author does argue that insects are dependent on rigid routines but never claims that they are* unique *in this way. No other types of animals are mentioned.* |
| (C) analyze the maternal behavior of wasps | *The author uses a couple of examples of wasp behavior to make a more general point about insect behavior; the main point is not that these wasps are making a nest for their offspring.* |
| (D) contrast typical wasp behavior with unconscious behavior | *The author does not present* typical behavior *and* unconscious behavior *as different things. Rather, the typical behavior never changes, even when a disruption of the routine would seem to warrant changing a behavior.* |
| (E) contend that insect behavior can rely on rigid routines that appear to be unconscious | ***CORRECT***. *The author claims that, at times, insect behavior is inflexible, or rigid, and the insect may not always be capable of responding to an unexpected or changed situation.* |

Several types of trap answers appeared in this question.

| | |
|---|---|
| **One word off:** | These trap answers mostly look good, but one word isn't supported by the passage, taking the answer choice out of contention. Answer (B) was one word off (*unique*). (Note: This can stretch to a couple of words off!) |
| **Extreme:** | These trap answers contain an extreme word, such as *all* or *never*, that is not supported by the passage. It is certainly possible for extreme words to appear in a correct answer, but only if the passage provides direct support for such extreme language. Answer (B) contained an extreme word (*unique*) that was not supported by the passage (sometimes, a wrong answer can fit multiple trap categories!). |
| **Out of scope:** | These trap answers will typically touch on aspects of the passage, but will go further than what the passage actually discusses. Sometimes, these answers are just a bit too broad; other times, they are way off. Answer (A) talks about *awareness of their surroundings*, which isn't discussed in the passage. |
| **True but not right:** | These answers will typically reflect things that are true according to the passage, but they do not answer the specific question asked. Answer (C) falls into this category. The examples used in the passage *are* about maternal wasp behavior, but the overall point is about a broader topic: the inflexible nature of insect behavior in general. |
| **Direct contradiction:** | Answer (D) is an example of a direct contradiction: The passage says the opposite of what this answer choice conveys. |

# Paragraph Questions

In order to answer **Paragraph** questions correctly, you will need to have a strong grasp of the point of the passage as well as the purpose of each paragraph.

Most of the time, Paragraph questions will ask you for one of two things: 1) the purpose of a particular paragraph in the context of the whole passage or 2) the purpose of a particular paragraph in relation to another particular paragraph.

First, identify the question:

2. Which of the following best describes the purpose of the second paragraph of the passage?

In this case, the question asks for the purpose of the second paragraph in the context of the entire passage.

Second, find the support. Locate paragraph 2 in your map:

① Insects: behavior inflex, unconsc
Typ: wasp inspect burrow, bring GH, larvae eat

② F: ONLY drag by antennae
If GH moves, wasp re-inspects burrow, every time

Third, predict an answer. The second paragraph provides examples that support the overall point that insect behavior is inflexible.

Once you have that set in your head, eliminate and find a match. For Paragraph questions, try to disprove each answer. If the answer contains something that wasn't part of the passage, or was restricted to a different paragraph, cross it off.

Before you look at the explanations below, try to label some of the wrong answers using the trap categories you learned on the last problem.

(A) To provide experimental evidence for the thesis articulated in the first paragraph

*CORRECT. The second paragraph does talk about experiments, and those experiments do support what the author claimed in the first paragraph.*

(B) To introduce a hypothesis about insect behavior

*The passage does introduce such a hypothesis, but it does so in the* first *paragraph, not the second one. This is the overall point of the passage, but the question asks about only the second paragraph. (True but not right)*

(C) To illustrate the ways in which grasshoppers are unsuitable for the wasp's purposes

*The passage doesn't say that the grasshoppers are unsuitable. This trap might be set for someone who is reading very quickly or superficially and draws an erroneous conclusion about the experiments with grasshoppers. (Out of scope)*

(D) To explore the significance of the wasp's varied reactions to certain stimuli

*The point of the passage is that the wasp does* not *change her behavior even when the circumstances of her situation change; her reactions do not vary. (Direct contradiction)*

(E) To acknowledge experimental evidence that does not support the author's thesis

*The evidence in the second paragraph does support the author's thesis. (Direct contradiction)*

All of the traps here were discussed earlier in the chapter; flip back if you want a refresher on any of the categories.

If a question asks about the entire passage, then you have a Primary Purpose question. Remind yourself of the overall point, using your map as needed.

If the question asks specifically about one paragraph in the context of the whole, then use your map to remind yourself what that one paragraph is about and how it fits into the overall story of the passage.

Try to come up with your own answer to the question before you look at the answers. Then, dive into those answers and start eliminating anything that is too far from what you articulated. Do check all five answers, even after you think you've found the right one. Finally, verify that your final answer matches both the question asked and the answer you articulated to yourself up front.

Don't forget to keep an eye out for the common traps (summarized in your Cheat Sheet on the next page).

**13**

## Primary Purpose Cheat Sheet

**Identify** the Question

| | |
|---|---|
| **Primary Purpose:** | The primary purpose (or function) of the passage is to . . . |
| | The author of the passage is primarily concerned with . . . |
| | Which of the following most accurately states the purpose of the passage? |
| | Which of the following titles best summarizes the passage? |
| | With which of the following would the author be most likely to agree? |
| **Paragraph:** | What is the purpose of the second paragraph? |
| | Which of the following best describes the relationship of the third paragraph to the passage as a whole? |

**Find the** Support

Use map or overall understanding of the passage.

**Predict** an Answer

Articulate the point or the purpose of the paragraph *before* looking at the answer choices.

**Eliminate**

Check all of the answers! Common traps:

| Trap | Characteristics |
|---|---|
| Direct contradiction | The passage says the opposite |
| Extreme | Extreme word *without support* in the passage |
| One word off | Looks very tempting but one or two words are wrong |
| Out of scope | Goes beyond what the passage says |
| True but not right | The passage does say this, but it does not answer the question asked |

Flash card the information on this page for future review. Don't copy down the exact language; put it in your own words and you'll remember it better.

# Problem Set

The three passages in this problem set appear in both the General and Specific chapters, but different questions are presented in each chapter.

Give yourself 2 to 3 minutes to read each passage and up to 60 seconds to answer each question. After you're done, review your point and passage map before you check the solutions, thinking about ways to improve your process next time. If you come up with ways to improve your map, actually rewrite it to reinforce what you want to do differently next time. Then, check your work against the solution key.

## Passage I: Japanese Swords

Historians have long recognized the Japanese sword, or *nihonto*, as one of the finest cutting weapons ever produced. But to regard the sword that is synonymous
5   with the samurai as merely a weapon is to ignore what makes it so special. The Japanese sword has always been considered a splendid weapon and even a spiritual entity. The traditional Japanese adage "the sword is the
10  soul of the samurai" reflects not only the sword's importance to its wielder but also its permanent connection to its creator, the master smith.

Master smiths may not have been
15  considered artists in the classical sense, but each smith exerted great care in the process of creating swords, no two of which were ever forged in exactly the same way. Over hundreds of hours, two types of steel were
20  repeatedly heated, hammered, and folded together into thousands of very thin layers, producing a sword with an extremely sharp and durable cutting edge and a flexible, shock-absorbing blade. It was common,
25  though optional, for a master smith to place a physical signature on a blade; moreover, each smith's secret forging techniques left an idiosyncratic structural signature on his blades. Each master smith brought a high
30  level of devotion, skill, and attention to detail to the sword-making process, and the sword itself was a reflection of his personal honor and ability. This effort made each blade as distinctive as the samurai who wielded it, such
35  that today the Japanese sword is recognized as much for its artistic merit as for its historical significance.

1.  The primary purpose of the passage is to

(A)  challenge the observation that the Japanese sword is highly admired by historians

(B)  introduce new information about the forging of Japanese swords

(C)  discuss an obsolete weapon of great historical significance

(D)  argue that Japanese sword makers were motivated by honor

(E)  explain the value attributed to the Japanese sword

2.  Which of the following is the primary function of the second paragraph?

(A)  To present an explanation for a change in perception

(B)  To determine the historical significance of Japanese swords

(C)  To discuss the artistic aspects associated with creating Japanese swords

(D)  To compare Japanese master smiths to classical artists

(E)  To review the complete process of making a Japanese sword

13

## Passage J: Polygamy

Polygamy in Africa has been a popular topic for social research over the past half-century; it has been analyzed by many distinguished minds and in various well-publicized works. In
5 1961, when Remi Clignet published his book *Many Wives, Many Powers*, he was not alone in his view that in Africa co-wives may be perceived as direct and indirect sources of increased income and prestige.
10 By the 1970s, such arguments had become crystallized and popular. Many other African scholars who wrote on the subject became the new champions of this philosophy. For example, in 1983, John Mbiti proclaimed that
15 polygamy is an accepted and respectable institution serving many useful social purposes. Similarly, G.K. Nukunya, in his paper "Polygamy as a Symbol of Status," reiterated Mbiti's idea that a plurality of wives is a
20 legitimate sign of affluence and power in the African society.

The colonial missionary voice, however, provided consistent opposition to polygamy. Invoking the authority of the Bible,
25 missionaries argued that the practice was unethical and destructive of family life, and they propagated the view that Africans had to be coerced into abiding by the monogamous view of marriage favored by Western
30 culture. In some instances, missionaries even dictated immediate divorce for newly converted men who had already entered into polygamous marriages. Unfortunately, neither the missionary voice nor the scholarly
35 voice considered the views of African women important. Although there was some awareness that women regarded polygamy as both a curse and a blessing, the distanced, albeit scientific, perspective of an outside
40 observer predominated both at the pulpit and in scholarly writings.

Contemporary research in the social sciences has begun to focus on the protagonist's voice in the study of culture,
45 recognizing that the views and experiences of those who take part in a given reality ought to receive close examination. This privileging of the protagonist seems appropriate, particularly given that women in Africa have
50 often used literary productions to comment on marriage, family, and gender relations.

1. Which of the following best describes the primary purpose of the passage?

   (A) To discuss scholarly works that view polygamy as a sign of prestige, respect, and affluence in the African society

   (B) To trace the origins of the missionary opposition to African polygamy

   (C) To argue for imposing restrictions on polygamy in African society

   (D) To explore the reasons for women's acceptance of polygamy

   (E) To discuss multiple perspectives on African polygamy and contrast them with contemporary research

2. The third paragraph of the passage plays which of the following roles?

   (A) It discusses the rationale for viewing polygamy as an indication of prestige and affluence in African society.

   (B) It supports the author's view that polygamy is unethical and destructive of family life.

   (C) It contrasts the views of the colonial missionaries with the position of the most recent contemporary research.

   (D) It describes the views on polygamy held by the colonial missionaries and indicates a flaw in this vision.

   (E) It demonstrates that the colonial missionaries were ignorant of the scholarly research on polygamy.

13

**13**

## Passage K: Sweet Spot

Most tennis players strive to strike the ball on the racket's vibration node, more commonly known as the "sweet spot." However, many players are unaware of the
5  existence of a second, lesser-known location on the racket face—the center of percussion—that will also greatly diminish the strain on a player's arm when the ball is struck.

In order to understand the physics of this
10  second sweet spot, it is helpful to consider what would happen to a tennis racket if the player's hand were to vanish at the moment of impact with the ball. The impact of the ball would cause the racket to bounce backwards,
15  resulting in a translational motion away from the ball. The tendency of this motion would be to jerk all parts of the racket, including the end of its handle, backward, or away from the ball. Unless the ball happened to hit precisely
20  at the racket's center of mass, the racket would additionally experience a rotational motion around its center of mass—much as a penny that has been struck near its edge will start to spin. Whenever the ball hits the racket
25  face, the effect of this rotational motion is to jerk the end of the handle forward, towards the ball. Depending on where the ball strikes the racket face, one or the other of these motions will predominate.

30  However, there is one point of impact, known as the center of percussion, which causes neither motion to predominate; if a ball strikes this point, the impact does not impart any motion to the end of the handle.
35  The reason for this lack of motion is that the force on the upper part of the hand would be equal and opposite to the force on the lower part of the hand, resulting in no net force on the tennis player's hand or forearm.
40  The center of percussion constitutes a second sweet spot because a tennis player's wrist is typically placed next to the end of the racket's handle. When the player strikes the ball at the center of percussion, her wrist is
45  jerked neither forward nor backward, and she experiences greatly reduced vibration in the arm.

The manner in which a tennis player can detect the center of percussion on a given
50  tennis racket follows from the nature of this second sweet spot. The center of percussion can be located via simple trial and error by holding the end of a tennis racket between the finger and thumb and throwing a ball onto the
55  strings. If the handle jumps out of the player's hand, then the ball has missed the center of percussion.

1. What is the primary message the author is trying to convey?

(A) A proposal for an improvement to the design of tennis rackets

(B) An examination of the differences between the two types of sweet spot

(C) A definition of the translational and rotational forces acting on a tennis racket

(D) A description of the ideal area in which to strike every ball

(E) An explanation of a lesser-known area on a tennis racket that reduces unwanted vibration

2. What is the primary function served by the second paragraph in the context of the entire passage?

(A) To establish the main idea of the passage

(B) To provide an explanation of the mechanics of the phenomenon discussed in the passage

(C) To introduce a counterargument that elucidates the main idea of the passage

(D) To explain the physics of tennis

(E) To explain why the main idea of the passage would be useful for tennis players

# Solutions

## Passage I: Japanese Swords

Historians have long recognized the Japanese sword, or *nihonto*, as one of the finest cutting weapons ever produced. But to regard the sword that is synonymous
5 with the samurai as merely a weapon is to ignore what makes it so special. The Japanese sword has always been considered a splendid weapon and even a spiritual entity. The traditional Japanese adage "the sword is the
10 soul of the samurai" reflects not only the sword's importance to its wielder but also its permanent connection to its creator, the master smith.

Master smiths may not have been
15 considered artists in the classical sense, but each smith exerted great care in the process of creating swords, no two of which were ever forged in exactly the same way. Over hundreds of hours, two types of steel were
20 repeatedly heated, hammered, and folded together into thousands of very thin layers, producing a sword with an extremely sharp and durable cutting edge and a flexible, shock-absorbing blade. It was common,
25 though optional, for a master smith to place a physical signature on a blade; moreover, each smith's secret forging techniques left an idiosyncratic structural signature on his blades. Each master smith brought a high
30 level of devotion, skill, and attention to detail to the sword-making process, and the sword itself was a reflection of his personal honor and ability. This effort made each blade as distinctive as the samurai who wielded it, such
35 that today the Japanese sword is recognized as much for its artistic merit as for its historical significance.

Sample passage map (yours will likely differ):

① J sword: not just weapon, spirit

② Master smith: skilled
  how to make
  artistic merit + history

The point (articulate to yourself; don't write): Japanese sword is a weapon *and* a work of art, important to both samurai and smith. The smiths were basically artists.

1. First, identify the question type:

*The primary purpose of the passage is to*

The wording here indicates that this is a Primary Purpose, or Main Idea, question. Glance at your map (find the support) and remind yourself of the point (predict the answer). Finally, go to the answers to find a match.

(A) *challenge the observation that the Japanese sword is highly admired by historians*

The passage does not challenge the idea that historians admired the swords; the entire passage reflects great admiration for the swords and their makers. (Direct contradiction)

(B) *introduce new information about the forging of Japanese swords*

The second paragraph does talk about how swords are forged, but does not present this information as *new*. Moreover, information about the forging process is only one part of the passage; it is not the overall point of the passage. (One word off)

(C) *discuss an obsolete weapon of great historical significance*

An *obsolete* weapon would no longer exist today; the passage does not indicate that Japanese swords are no longer used or no longer produced. (One word off)

(D) *argue that Japanese sword makers were motivated by honor*

The passage does indicate that the swords were a reflection of the master smith's personal honor, but this is a narrow detail; it is not the point of the entire passage. (True but not right)

(E) *explain the value attributed to the Japanese sword*

**CORRECT.** The passage does explain the value of the sword to the samurai (in the first paragraph—"*the sword is the soul of the samurai*" [lines 9–10]) and to the master smith (in the second paragraph).

13

2. First, identify the question type:

   *Which of the following is the primary function of the second paragraph?*

This is a Paragraph question. Next, find the support (second paragraph of your map) and predict an answer. The master smith was an artist; the swords were effectively the smith's artwork. Sometimes, they even signed the swords!

Finally, check the answers to find a match.

(A) *To present an explanation for a change in perception*

The passage does not indicate that a general *change* in perception has occurred. Rather, the author is putting forth his own idea that smiths might be considered artists. (Out of scope)

(B) *To determine the historical significance of Japanese swords*

The last sentence of the paragraph does mention the historical significance, but the rest of the paragraph focuses on the forging process and the *artistic merit*. The paragraph does not discuss the historical significance. (Out of scope)

(C) *To discuss the artistic aspects associated with creating Japanese swords*

**CORRECT.** The paragraph begins by indicating that the smiths *may not have been considered artists in the classical sense* (lines 14–15), but goes on to underscore the uniqueness of the finished products (no two were forged the same way, the swords were often signed, the finished product was a reflection of the smith's personal honor and ability). The last sentence indicates that the swords are highly regarded for their *artistic merit* (line 36).

(D) *To compare Japanese master smiths to classical artists*

While the passage does imply that the smiths might be considered artists, there is no mention of actual classical artists, nor is any comparison made. (Out of scope)

(E) *To review the complete process of making a Japanese sword*

The passage does provide some details of the sword-making process, but it does not review the *complete* process. (Extreme)

13

## Passage J: Polygamy

Polygamy in Africa has been a popular topic for social research over the past half-century; it has been analyzed by many distinguished minds and in various well-publicized works. In
5 1961, when Remi Clignet published his book *Many Wives, Many Powers*, he was not alone in his view that in Africa co-wives may be perceived as direct and indirect sources of increased income and prestige.
10 By the 1970s, such arguments had become crystallized and popular. Many other African scholars who wrote on the subject became the new champions of this philosophy. For example, in 1983, John Mbiti proclaimed that
15 polygamy is an accepted and respectable institution serving many useful social purposes. Similarly, G.K. Nukunya, in his paper "Polygamy as a Symbol of Status," reiterated Mbiti's idea that a plurality of wives is a
20 legitimate sign of affluence and power in the African society.

The colonial missionary voice, however, provided consistent opposition to polygamy. Invoking the authority of the Bible,
25 missionaries argued that the practice was unethical and destructive of family life, and they propagated the view that Africans had to be coerced into abiding by the monogamous view of marriage favored by Western
30 culture. In some instances, missionaries even dictated immediate divorce for newly converted men who had already entered into polygamous marriages. Unfortunately, neither the missionary voice nor the scholarly
35 voice considered the views of African women important. Although there was some awareness that women regarded polygamy as both a curse and a blessing, the distanced, albeit scientific, perspective of an outside
40 observer predominated both at the pulpit and in scholarly writings.

Contemporary research in the social sciences has begun to focus on the protagonist's voice in the study of culture,
45 recognizing that the views and experiences of those who take part in a given reality ought to receive close examination. This privileging of the protagonist seems appropriate, particularly given that women in Africa have
50 often used literary productions to comment on marriage, family, and gender relations.

Sample passage map (yours will likely differ):

① Polyg Afr
  '61 Clignet: P = income, prestige

② 70s, 80s: positive dtls

③ Missionary: against
  no one listened to W

④ Now listen to W

The point (articulate to yourself; don't write):
Some scholars thought polygamy was a good thing. Missionaries were against it. Now, people are actually paying attention to what the women think.

1. First, identify the question type:

*Which of the following best describes the primary purpose of the passage?*

This is a Primary Purpose, or Main Idea, question. Check your passage map (or your memory!) to predict the kind of information the answer should include.

Finally, look for a match in the answers.

(A) *To discuss scholarly works that view polygamy as a sign of prestige, respect, and affluence in the African society*

The first two paragraphs do talk about works that portray polygamy positively, but the rest of the passage explores different viewpoints. This is one side of the story, not the overall point. (True but not right)

(B) *To trace the origins of the missionary opposition to African polygamy*

The passage does discuss missionary opposition to polygamy, but does not detail its origins; in addition, the missionary point of view is just one side of the story. (Out of scope)

(C) *To argue for imposing restrictions on polygamy in African society*

While it might be possible that the author would support a restriction on polygamy, the passage does not make such an argument. In fact, the passage never directly supports a particular position on polygamy—rather, it explores different perspectives on the topic. (Out of scope)

(D) *To explore the reasons for women's acceptance of polygamy*

The passage does indicate that women found polygamy *a curse and a blessing* (line 38), but it does not explore their reasons for thinking that polygamy might sometimes be a blessing. (Out of scope)

(E) *To discuss multiple perspectives on African polygamy and contrast them with contemporary research*

**CORRECT.** The first few paragraphs look at different past perspectives (scholars, missionaries). Then, the passage ends by indicating that contemporary researchers are paying attention to what women think (something the earlier groups didn't do).

2.  First, identify the question type:

*The third paragraph of the passage plays which of the following roles?*

This is a Paragraph question. Glance at your map and articulate the purpose of the third paragraph to yourself before you look for a match in the answers.

The third paragraph begins by discussing the missionary view of polygamy (against) and goes on to say that both the missionaries and the scholars mentioned earlier failed to take into account the point of view of the women involved in these polygamous marriages.

(A) *It discusses the rationale for viewing polygamy as an indication of prestige and affluence in African society.*

This occurs in the first two paragraphs, not the third. (True but not right)

(B) *It supports the author's view that polygamy is unethical and destructive of family life.*

The author does not present a personal viewpoint in the passage. (Out of scope)

(C) *It contrasts the views of the colonial missionaries with the position of the most recent contemporary research.*

The third paragraph does discuss the missionary viewpoint, but contemporary research is discussed in the *fourth* paragraph, not the third. (True but not right and one word off)

(D) *It describes the views on polygamy held by the colonial missionaries and indicates a flaw in this vision.*

**CORRECT.** The paragraph does talk about the missionary view of polygamy. It also indicates a flaw in this thinking: that the missionaries failed to consider the views of women in polygamous marriages.

(E) *It demonstrates that the colonial missionaries were ignorant of the scholarly research on polygamy.*

The passage presents the missionary view separately from the views of the scholars mentioned earlier in the passage; it does not indicate whether the missionaries were familiar with the scholarly position. (Out of scope)

13

## Passage K: Sweet Spot

Most tennis players strive to strike the ball on the racket's vibration node, more commonly known as the "sweet spot." However, many players are unaware of the
5 existence of a second, lesser-known location on the racket face—the center of percussion— that will also greatly diminish the strain on a player's arm when the ball is struck.

In order to understand the physics of this
10 second sweet spot, it is helpful to consider what would happen to a tennis racket if the player's hand were to vanish at the moment of impact with the ball. The impact of the ball would cause the racket to bounce backwards,
15 resulting in a translational motion away from the ball. The tendency of this motion would be to jerk all parts of the racket, including the end of its handle, backward, or away from the ball. Unless the ball happened to hit precisely
20 at the racket's center of mass, the racket would additionally experience a rotational motion around its center of mass—much as a penny that has been struck near its edge will start to spin. Whenever the ball hits the racket
25 face, the effect of this rotational motion is to jerk the end of the handle forward, towards the ball. Depending on where the ball strikes the racket face, one or the other of these motions will predominate.
30 However, there is one point of impact, known as the center of percussion, which causes neither motion to predominate; if a ball strikes this point, the impact does not impart any motion to the end of the handle.
35 The reason for this lack of motion is that the force on the upper part of the hand would be equal and opposite to the force on the lower part of the hand, resulting in no net force on the tennis player's hand or forearm.
40 The center of percussion constitutes a second sweet spot because a tennis player's wrist is typically placed next to the end of the racket's handle. When the player strikes the ball at the center of percussion, her wrist is
45 jerked neither forward nor backward, and she experiences greatly reduced vibration in the arm.

The manner in which a tennis player can detect the center of percussion on a given
50 tennis racket follows from the nature of this second sweet spot. The center of percussion can be located via simple trial and error by holding the end of a tennis racket between the finger and thumb and throwing a ball onto the
55 strings. If the handle jumps out of the player's hand, then the ball has missed the center of percussion.

Sample passage map (yours will likely differ):

① 2 SS (↓ strain), one less known

② if hand disappear?

③ center perc = no motion, ↓↓ vibration

④ find center perc

The point (articulate to yourself; don't write): People usually know about one sweet spot but not the other. Both reduce vibration in the arm. (Plus lots of technical details—ignore for now!)

1. First, identify the question type:

*What is the primary message the author is trying to convey?*

This is a Primary Purpose, or Main Idea, question. Glance at your map to remind yourself of the point before you go to the answers.

(A) *A proposal for an improvement to the design of tennis rackets*

The passage doesn't talk about this at all. (Out of scope)

(B) *An examination of the differences between the two types of sweet spot*

It does talk about two different types of sweet spot. Leave this in for now.

(C)   *A definition of the translational and rotational forces acting on a tennis racket*

One paragraph did mention these forces, but that was only one paragraph. This is not the point of the whole thing. (True but not right)

(D)   *A description of the ideal area in which to strike every ball*

The passage does say that striking the ball at a sweet spot can reduce vibration, but it never says that spot is the ideal area in which to strike *every* ball. (Extreme)

(E)   *An explanation of a lesser-known area on a tennis racket that reduces unwanted vibration*

It does talk about this. Leave this in.

Compare answers (B) and (E) to the support in the passage. The first paragraph mentions both sweet spots. After that, though, the passage focuses just on the lesser-known one; it doesn't go back-and-forth contrasting the two. Answer (E) is more appropriate than answer (B).

The correct answer is **(E)**.

2.   First, identify the question type:

*What is the primary function served by the second paragraph in the context of the entire passage?*

This is a Paragraph question. Glance at your map and articulate the purpose of the second paragraph to yourself before you check the answers.

The second paragraph begins with the text *In order to understand the physics of this second sweet spot.* It then goes into lots of detail about what would happen if the player's hand vanished and various forces and... wait! Don't get sucked into the detail. The first sentence is probably enough: This is how the second sweet spot works. Check the answers.

(A)   *To establish the main idea of the passage*

The first paragraph establishes the main idea. The second paragraph provides detail about how the second sweet spot works. (Out of scope)

(B)   *To provide an explanation of the mechanics of the phenomenon discussed in the passage*

**CORRECT.** The second paragraph does explain the physics, or the *mechanics*, of the phenomenon (the second sweet spot) mentioned in the first paragraph.

(C)   *To introduce a counterargument that eluci- dates the main idea of the passage*

The second paragraph does elucidate (or explain) the main idea, but it is not a counterargument to anything.
(One word off)

(D)   *To explain the physics of tennis*

The paragraph does discuss the physical forces relevant to the sweet spot, but it does not explain all of the physics behind the game of tennis. That would be a very long paragraph! (Out of scope)

(E)   *To explain why the main idea of the passage would be useful for tennis players*

The first and third paragraphs explain why the main idea is useful: to reduce vibration in the arm. The second paragraph does not do this. (True but not right)

# Specific Questions

## In This Chapter:

**In this chapter, you will learn** how to handle the most commonly asked specific questions on the GMAT. You'll learn how to use your passage map to efficiently find relevant details, what analysis each type of question requires, and how to identify the correct answer and avoid trap answers.

# CHAPTER 14 Specific Questions

Most of the questions you will see on the GMAT will ask you about specific details in the passage. On average, expect to spend about 1.5 minutes on each specific question.

Here are the three most common types of specific questions:

1. **Detail questions.** These questions ask you to find a specific detail explicitly stated in the passage.

2. **Inference questions.** On these, the correct answer will *not* be stated explicitly in the passage, but it can be proven true using information stated in the passage.

3. **Specific Purpose questions.** These questions ask you *why* the author mentions a specific piece of information or employs a particular example.

You may occasionally see another type, such as a Strengthen or Weaken question. These are more commonly given on Critical Reasoning questions; if you do see one on Reading Comprehension, you can use the same strategies that you use for CR.

## 4 Steps to the Answer

You'll use the same process you learned for general questions in order to answer specific questions:

**Step 1: Identify the question.** This chapter will tell you the common language to expect for the different question types.

**Step 2: Find the support.** Expect to go back into the passage for all specific questions. Use your map to quickly figure out where to go, then read the relevant one to three sentences. Do not skip this step! Many specific questions have trap answers designed specifically to catch people who don't look back at the passage.

**Step 3: Predict an answer.** Take a look at the question again and, using the relevant passage text, try to formulate a rough answer in your own words. But there's a caveat: This won't work 100 percent of the time. This chapter will explain what to do when you can't predict the answer.

**Step 4: Eliminate and find a match.** Do a first pass through the answers, crossing off anything that is definitely wrong. Leave in any potential matches for your predicted answer as well as any for which you're not sure (whether you think they might be right or wrong). Don't spend time debating an answer choice (yet). When you're done with your first pass, see what you have left:

- If you have eliminated four answers, great! Pick the remaining one and move on.

- If you still have two or three answers left, compare the answers to the relevant information in the passage. If the answers are very similar, you may also compare them to each other. Use this to narrow down to the best answer of the remaining options.

- If you still have four or five answers left, make sure you didn't misread the question! After that, it may be best to cut your losses: Guess and move on.

# Practice Passage: Electroconvulsive Therapy

Give yourself approximately 8 minutes to read the passage below and answer the four questions that follow. Mimic real test conditions. Answer the questions in the order given; pick an answer before you move to the next one, and don't return to a question you've already answered.

Electroconvulsive therapy (ECT) is a controversial psychiatric treatment involving the induction of a seizure in a patient by passing electricity through the brain. While
5 beneficial effects of electrically induced seizures are evident and predictable in most patients, a unified mechanism of action has not yet been established and remains the subject of numerous investigations. ECT is extremely
10 effective against severe depression, some acute psychotic states, and mania, though, like many medical procedures, it has its risks.

Since the inception of ECT in 1938, the public has held a strongly negative conception
15 of the procedure. Initially, doctors employed unmodified ECT. Patients were rendered instantly unconscious by the electrical current, but the strength of the muscle contractions from uncontrolled motor seizures often led to
20 compression fractures of the spine or damage to the teeth. In addition to the effect this physical trauma had on public sentiment, graphic examples of abuse documented in books and movies, such as Ken Kesey's *One*
25 *Flew Over the Cuckoo's Nest*, portrayed ECT as punitive, cruel, overused, and violative of patients' legal rights.

Modern ECT is virtually unrecognizable from its earlier days. The treatment is
30 modified by the muscle relaxant succinylcholine, which renders muscle contractions practically nonexistent. Additionally, patients are given a general anesthetic. Thus, the patient is asleep and
35 fully unaware during the procedure, and the only outward sign of a seizure may be the rhythmic movement of the patient's hand or foot. ECT is generally used in severely depressed patients for whom psychotherapy
40 and medication prove ineffective. It may also

be considered when there is an imminent risk of suicide, since antidepressants often take several weeks to work effectively. Exactly how ECT exerts its effects is not known, but
45 repeated applications affect several neurotransmitters in the brain, including serotonin, norepinephrine, and dopamine.

ECT has proven effective, but it is not without controversy. Though decades-old
50 studies showing brain cell death have been refuted in recent research, many patients do report loss of memory for events that occurred in the days, weeks, or months surrounding the ECT. Some patients have also
55 reported that their short-term memories continue to be affected for months after ECT, though some doctors argue that this memory malfunction may reflect the type of amnesia that sometimes results from severe
60 depression.

1. According to the passage, why has ECT been viewed negatively by the public?

(A) Though ECT is effective in many cases, the medical community is not certain exactly how it works.

(B) Early incarnations of ECT often resulted in physical trauma to the patient.

(C) Effective use of ECT requires exposure to concerning medications, such as muscle relaxants and anesthesia.

(D) ECT does not benefit individuals with anxiety disorders.

(E) ECT cannot be performed without subsequent loss of memory in the patient.

2. Which of the following can be inferred about the way in which the modern form of ECT works?

   (A) Greater amounts of the neurotransmitters serotonin, norepinephrine, and dopamine seem to reduce symptoms of depression.

   (B) ECT cannot be used prior to attempting psychotherapy or medication.

   (C) Succinylcholine completely immobilizes the patient's body.

   (D) ECT often works faster than antidepressants.

   (E) One ECT treatment is often sufficient to reduce symptoms of depression significantly.

3. The author mentions amnesia as a possible side effect of severe depression in order to

   (A) acknowledge one of the possible negative side effects associated with ECT

   (B) emphasize the seriousness of severe depression as a debilitating disease

   (C) introduce a possible alternative cause for short-term memory loss reported by some patients

   (D) draw a connection between brain cell death and short-term memory loss

   (E) refute claims that ECT is responsible for any form of amnesia in patients

4. Each of the following is cited in the passage as a current or historical criticism of electroconvulsive therapy EXCEPT

   (A) ECT may cause the death of brain cells and memory loss

   (B) in certain cases, ECT was portrayed as a means to punish individuals

   (C) ECT had the potential to be used in inappropriate situations

   (D) early forms of ECT did not adequately protect patients from secondary harm brought on by the treatment

   (E) repeated applications of ECT affect several neurotransmitters in the brain

14

The questions above represent four distinct question types. The following sections will each cover one type and provide an explanation of the relevant question. First, here's what a reader might be thinking while reading the passage and jotting down a map:

*ECT (electricity → seizure) has positives and negatives. Don't know how it works, but it is effective against depression and some other things.*

*Public doesn't like ECT. Early forms caused serious bodily trauma. Books and movies depicted it as cruel and abusive.*

*Modern ECT is much better. No trauma. Still don't know how it works but it helps really depressed people who can't get help in other ways.*

*It still has drawbacks, though, primarily around memory loss.*

| | ECT + / − | |
|---|---|---|
| | + | − |
| ① | treats depression | how work? |
| ② | | public percep trauma |
| ③ | Modern = no trauma helps v. depr. ppl | cruel, etc. how work? |
| ④ | | memory loss |

Here's a simple story for the passage:

*ECT was pretty bad at first but it's much better now. They don't really know how it works, but it does work for severe depression. Even though ECT is better now, it still has some drawbacks.*

## Detail Questions

**Detail questions** typically include the language *according to the passage* (or something very similar). If you see this language, then you are being asked to find a particular piece of information, explicitly stated somewhere in the passage, that answers that particular question. The first question is a Detail question:

1. According to the passage, why has ECT been viewed negatively by the public?

Most of the time, the question stem will provide enough information to tell you where in the passage to look for the answer. Where does this particular question stem signal that you should look?

The question stem specifically references the public's negative view of ECT. This concept is the topic sentence of the second paragraph, so your passage map would likely contain some reference to this idea.

Your map, then, tells you where to go for step 2 of the process (find the support). Return to paragraph 2 and read as far as you need to in order to get an idea of why people disliked ECT:

Since the inception of ECT in 1938, the public has held a strongly negative conception of the procedure. Initially, doctors employed unmodified ECT. Patients were rendered instantly unconscious by the electrical current, but the strength of the muscle contractions from uncontrolled motor seizures often led to compression fractures of the spine or damage to the teeth. In addition to the effect this physical trauma had on public sentiment, graphic examples of abuse documented in books and movies, such as Ken Kesey's *One Flew Over the Cuckoo's Nest*, portrayed ECT as punitive, cruel, overused, and violative of patients' legal rights.

Use this information to try to predict the answer (step 3 of the process). First, people experienced some serious types of physical trauma (spinal fractures, damage to the teeth). Second, books and movies portrayed ECT as abusive and cruel. The correct answer should address one or both of those two topics.

Time for step 4: Eliminate and find a match! Try to identify any trap answer types that you have already learned.

| | |
|---|---|
| (A) Though ECT is effective in many cases, the medical community is not certain exactly how it works. | *The passage does say this, but it does not say that this is why people dislike ECT. (True but not right)* |
| (B) Early incarnations of ECT often resulted in physical trauma to the patient. | ***CORRECT.** This matches the first of the two reasons given in paragraph 2: Initially, people often experienced serious physical injuries when undergoing ECT treatment.* |
| (C) Effective use of ECT requires exposure to concerning medications, such as muscle relaxants and anesthesia. | *The passage does state that ECT now uses muscle relaxants and anesthesia, but the passage does not call these medications concerning. If anything, the passage seems to consider these advances positive because they allow the patient to be asleep and fully unaware. (Could be considered either One word off or True but not right)* |
| (D) ECT does not benefit individuals with anxiety disorders. | *The passage does not mention individuals with anxiety disorders. (Out of scope)* |
| (E) ECT cannot be performed without subsequent loss of memory in the patient. | *The last paragraph does mention that ECT can result in memory loss, but does not say that this side effect is always present. (Nor does the passage mention public perception with respect to memory loss.) (Extreme)* |

As you work through the answers, your thought process might be something along these lines:

(A)  *Not one of the two reasons I stated before.*

(B)  *Yes, this was one of the reasons I stated. Leave in.*

(C)  *Not one of the two reasons I stated before.*

(D)  *Not one of the two reasons I stated before.*

(E)  *Not one of the two reasons I stated before. I do remember the passage saying something about this though, and memory loss is obviously not good. Leave in for now.*

    *Hmm, (B) vs. (E). Answer (B) is an exact match for what I said, so I'm going to go for it. If I didn't have such a good match, I'd go and check the part that talked about memory loss.*

If you do want to check the passage for the memory loss information, use the same process. Check your map; where was that info?

Paragraph 4. Reread the relevant text: *Many patients do report loss of memory for events that occurred in the days, weeks, or months surrounding the ECT. Some patients have also reported that their short-term memories continue to be affected for months after ECT.*

Check that against the choice. First, this text says *many*, not *all*, patients experience memory loss, so this is an *extreme* trap. Second, this paragraph is not where the passage discussed why the public has such a negative view of ECT.

The wrong answers represent several common traps, all of which were first presented in the General Questions chapter. For a quick review, reference your Cheat Sheet at the end of that chapter.

If you see a question that begins *According to the passage*, you almost certainly have a detail question. Use your map to figure out what paragraph you'll need; in this case, the concept of negative public perception was a good clue to look in the second paragraph.

Whenever possible, try to formulate an answer to the question before you look at the answer choices. Note that there may be more than one possibility. In this case, the correct answer could have talked about the bodily trauma or about the depictions in books and movies.

At times, you may struggle to understand certain parts of a passage, in which case you may not be able to predict an answer. In this case, do one of two things. If you think you understand the main points in the relevant text, use that to try to eliminate some answers before you guess. (Sometimes, you might be able to eliminate all four wrong answers!)

If you don't understand the text well enough to pick up the main points, then guess and move on. (Don't be stubborn and waste valuable time that you could use elsewhere; when you don't get it, admit that to yourself and move on right away.)

## Inference Questions

**Inference questions** ask you to find an answer that must be true based on information presented in the passage—but the information in the correct answer will *not* be explicitly given to you in the passage.

For example, if your boss tells you that Acme Co is your company's most important client, what can you infer?

You might imagine that Acme Co is responsible for a larger chunk of the company's revenue than is any other client. This is a reasonable inference in the real world, but it will lead you to a wrong answer on the GMAT. Why? Because it doesn't *have* to be true. Perhaps Acme is the company's most prestigious client. Perhaps your boss is good friends with Acme's CEO.

In fact, you have no idea *why* Acme Co is the most important client. The boss just stated a fact and didn't give you any insight into the reason for that fact.

The GMAT is never asking you to come up with reasonable real-world inferences. Rather, it is asking you to deduce what *must be true* given the available evidence.

So if Acme Co is the company's most important client, what else has to be true?

For starters, your company has to have at least one other client. If Acme were the only client, then your boss couldn't call it the *most important* client.

If one of the company's other clients is Widget Inc, you could also correctly infer that Widget Inc is not the company's most important client—that spot is already taken by Acme!

Which problem in the *Electroconvulsive Therapy* set was the Inference problem? The wording of the question stem will tell you:

> 2.    Which of the following can be inferred about the way in which the modern form of ECT works?

In this case, the word *inferred* is in the question stem. When you see any form of the words *infer, imply,* or *suggest,* you have an Inference question.

Now, find the support (step 2). *Modern ECT* is first mentioned in the third paragraph, so look there to find and reread the relevant text. Step 3 (predict an answer), however, is pretty tough: The paragraph is all about how ECT works. In this case, it would be tough for anyone to try to predict an answer in advance.

Instead, return to the third paragraph to remind yourself of the type of information it contains, then start to check the answers, crossing off anything you cannot prove to be true based on information from that paragraph. Here's the third paragraph:

> Modern ECT is virtually unrecognizable from its earlier days. The treatment is modified by the muscle relaxant succinylcholine, which renders muscle contractions practically nonexistent. Additionally, patients are given a general anesthetic. Thus, the patient is asleep and fully unaware during the procedure, and the only outward sign of a seizure may be the rhythmic movement of the patient's hand or foot. ECT is generally used in severely depressed patients for whom psychotherapy and medication prove ineffective. It may also be considered when there is an imminent risk of suicide, since antidepressants often take several weeks to work effectively. Exactly how ECT exerts its effects is not known, but repeated applications affect several neurotransmitters in the brain, including serotonin, norepinephrine, and dopamine.

Think big picture; don't get too caught up in the details. The modern form of ECT is much safer for patients—they're asleep and won't have the same issues that caused injuries before. Modern ECT can be very effective for depression and risk of suicide. Move to the answers and check them against the paragraph:

| | |
|---|---|
| (A) Greater amounts of the neurotransmitters serotonin, norepinephrine, and dopamine seem to reduce symptoms of depression. | *The third paragraph does mention these neurotransmitters and that ECT is effective for depression. The technical detail is annoying, so leave this in for now; if you still have more than one choice left at the end, then you can examine this more closely.* |
| (B) ECT cannot be used prior to attempting psychotherapy or medication. | *Whenever you see an extreme word, check whether the passage justifies the usage. In this case, the third paragraph does not justify the use of the word* cannot; *it says only that those other therapies are tried first at least some of the time. (Extreme)* |
| (C) Succinylcholine completely immobilizes the patient's body. | *Another extreme word! Check it. The second sentence states that succinylcholine* renders muscle contractions practically nonexistent. *The qualifier* practically *means the muscle contractions are* almost *gone, but* not *entirely. The word* completely *is too extreme. (Extreme)* |
| (D) ECT often works faster than antidepressants. | *The third paragraph does mention antidepressants; leave this in for now.* |
| (E) One ECT treatment is often sufficient to reduce symptoms of depression significantly. | *The passage does not discuss the number of treatments necessary to reduce symptoms significantly. At one point, it does mention* repeated *applications, so, if anything, it appears that more than one treatment might be typical. (Out of scope)* |

Compare (A) and (D)

(A) *Scan for these words; they appear in the last sentence. What's the message? Nobody really knows how ECT works, just that it affects these neurotransmitters—but it doesn't say that ECT results in* greater *amounts of these things, just that they are* affected. *The word* greater *in the answer choice isn't supported. (One word off)*

(D) **CORRECT**. *The third paragraph states that ECT* may also be considered when there is an imminent risk of suicide, since antidepressants often take several weeks to work effectively. *If ECT is used as an emergency intervention for suicide, because antidepressants take a while to work, then it must be true that ECT often works more quickly than antidepressants.*

If you see a question that contains some form of the words *infer*, *imply*, or *suggest*, then you know you have an Inference question. In most cases, the question stem will also contain some specific info that will help you to determine which paragraph you'll need. In this problem, a key term in the question stem (*modern ECT*) is mentioned for the first time at the beginning of the third paragraph.

If you can, try to formulate an answer to the question before you look at the answer choices. Note that, sometimes, the question stem will be too vague to predict a solid answer in advance (this can happen on any type of specific question). When this happens, remind yourself of the main points in any relevant paragraph(s) or sentences and then start to test the answers. (If you know that you don't understand the question well enough to formulate an answer for that reason, consider guessing and moving on.)

If you find yourself struggling with RC Inference questions, you may want to consider cross-training in Critical Reasoning. CR Inference questions work the same way, so you may find that you learn this more easily for CR and can then come back and apply your skills to RC.

On either question type, it can be helpful to analyze your work by comparing each answer choice carefully to the supporting text (after you have finished solving the problem). This will help you learn to distinguish a valid inference from an answer choice that goes too far.

## Specific Purpose Questions

**Specific Purpose questions** are not as common as either Detail or Inference questions, but you can expect to see at least one on the Verbal section of the GMAT. These questions ask you for what purpose, or why, the author mentions a specific piece of information—so they are often called **Why** questions for short.

As with Inference questions, you can't just repeat back what the passage explicitly states. Instead, you have to do a little bit of processing. For example, consider this information:

> Silicon chip manufacturers struggle to maintain profit margins due to the exorbitantly high overhead costs associated with building semiconductor factories. Such factories typically cost a minimum of two billion dollars to build and may be obsolete within three to five years. As such, the manufacturers seek out customers who need very high volumes of products, allowing the overhead costs to be spread out over a large number of units.

Here's the question:

> The author states that semiconductor factories may become obsolete within three to five years of being built in order to

*Why* does the author talk about this particular detail? In the prior sentence, the author asserts that *chip manufacturers struggle to maintain profit margins* because these factories have *exorbitantly high overhead costs*, so she is providing information to support her contention that these costs really are so high as to impact profit significantly. The correct answer might say something like:

> emphasize the unusually high costs associated with manufacturing silicon chips

Here's the Specific Purpose question from the ECT passage:

> 3.   The author mentions amnesia as a possible side effect of severe depression in order to

What similarities can you spot between the semiconductor question stem and the one above? Both talk about the *author*. Both finish with *in order to*. Specific Purpose questions are typically structured to say *the author* (mentions some specific detail) *in order to*, and then you have to fill in the blank with the answer that explains *why* the author mentioned that particular detail.

So, where did the author of the ECT passage talk about amnesia and severe depression?

You may not have noted this very specific detail about amnesia in your map, so you may have to go on a hunt. The passage mentions *severe depression* in three out of the four paragraphs, so don't scan for those key words. Instead, scan for the word *amnesia*. One more clue: Amnesia is a type of memory loss. You might have noted or you may remember that the last paragraph talks about memory loss. Here's the relevant text from the fourth paragraph:

> Some patients have also reported that their short-term memories continue to be affected for months after ECT, though some doctors argue that this memory malfunction may reflect the type of amnesia that sometimes results from severe depression.

On to step 3: Formulate your own answer to the question. *Why* does the author bring up amnesia in the context of severe depression?

Some people appear to attribute short-term memory problems to ECT; this is consistent with much of the rest of the passage, which discusses negative side effects and risks associated with ECT. The second half of the quoted text, however, indicates that some doctors think that these symptoms might actually be caused by the depression itself. In other words, it's possible that this particular side effect is not actually a result of ECT.

The author, then, is pointing out that not every possible negative effect is definitely due to ECT. What answer choice goes along with this idea? (Also, try to identify any wrong answer traps that you have already learned.)

| | |
|---|---|
| (A) acknowledge one of the possible negative side effects associated with ECT | *The passage does talk about many negative side effects associated with ECT, but the reference to amnesia is intended to introduce the idea that certain side effects actually might not be due to ECT. (Direct contradiction)* |
| (B) emphasize the seriousness of severe depression as a debilitating disease | *This choice sounds very tempting; in the real world, amnesia is a very serious issue and severe depression is a debilitating disease. However, depression is mentioned only as a possible alternative cause; the passage does not state that the amnesia is definitely a result of the depression. (True but not right)* |
| (C) introduce a possible alternative cause for short-term memory loss reported by some patients | ***CORRECT.** The first half of the sentence brings up patient reports of memory loss due to ECT. The second half indicates a different potential cause: Some doctors think this memory loss might actually be due to amnesia from depression.* |
| (D) draw a connection between brain cell death and short-term memory loss | *The fourth paragraph mentions both brain cell death and short-term memory loss. The passage does not connect the two ideas, however. In fact, it says that reports of brain cell death have been refuted, though memory loss is still in evidence. (Mix-up)* |
| (E) refute claims that ECT is responsible for any form of amnesia in patients | *The sentence does offer a possible alternative cause, but ECT is not definitively ruled out as one possible cause. (Extreme)* |

The wrong answers represent several common traps, one of which hasn't shown up in earlier problems. A **Mix-Up** is a tricky trap in which the test writers use wording straight from the passage to convey a different meaning than what is presented in the passage. They are expecting you to think it sounds familiar and jump on the choice without giving it too much thought, and in fact that's exactly what many test-takers do.

In answer (D) above, the keywords used are all straight from the passage. The meaning of the answer, however, does not fit with the author's reason for mentioning amnesia. In fact, the answer does not even convey what the passage really said.

*In order to* is the most common clue that you are facing a Specific Purpose question; if the question says the author brought up some detail *in order to* do something, then you're trying to figure out why the author brought up that detail.

As for all specific questions, use your map to figure out what paragraph you'll need; in this case, the words *amnesia* and *severe depression* indicated the fourth paragraph.

Whenever possible, try to formulate an answer to the question before you look at the answer choices. If you can't, remind yourself of the main points in any relevant sentences or paragraph(s) and then start to test the answers.

## EXCEPT Questions

Any question type can also be written as an **EXCEPT question**; most of the time, when you see an EXCEPT question, you'll be dealing with a Detail question or an Inference question.

Here is the fourth question from the ECT passage. What question type is it?

4.  Each of the following is cited in the passage as a current or historical criticism of electroconvulsive therapy EXCEPT

The language *each of the following is cited* indicates that this is a Detail question. The information in four of the answers is explicitly stated in the passage. The fifth answer, the one *not* cited in the passage, will be the correct answer.

Follow the same process you would normally use for a Detail question, with one twist.

It would be inefficient to try to find all of the criticisms of ECT in the passage first and only then go check the answers to find the matches. Instead, go straight to the answers and work backwards: Use the keywords to try to find the information in the passage. If you've spent more than about 20 seconds on an answer and still haven't found it in the passage, leave it and move to the next answer.

As you work, label the answers either True or False on your scrap paper. On this problem, true (or T) means that the answer is indeed cited in the passage as a criticism of ECT. False (or F) means that it is not. Cross off the four T answers and pick the odd one out, the lone F answer.

Also, note one important thing about the question: It asks for *current or historical criticism*, so something that was once criticized but is no longer considered problematic today would still count as a criticism of ECT.

(A) ECT may cause the death of brain cells and memory loss.

*T. The fourth paragraph mentions that very old research showed brain cell death (even though that research has been refuted today) and that memory loss is an ongoing concern.*

(B) In certain cases, ECT was portrayed as a means to punish individuals.

*T. Line 26 indicates that ECT was portrayed as* punitive.

(C) ECT had the potential to be used in inappropriate situations.

*T. Tricky! Line 26 indicates that ECT was portrayed as* over-used. *If a treatment is overused, then at least some of those uses shouldn't be happening, or are inappropriate.*

(D) Early forms of ECT did not adequately protect patients from secondary harm brought on by the treatment.

*T. Lines 19–21 indicate that early forms of ECT* often led to compression fractures of the spine or damage to the teeth.

(E) Repeated applications of ECT affect several neurotransmitters in the brain.

***CORRECT***. *F. Lines 45–47 do mention that ECT affects neurotransmitters, but this information is not presented as a criticism of ECT. Rather, it is presented as a partial means of understanding how ECT works.*

The standard wrong answer trap categories don't necessarily apply to EXCEPT questions. The four wrong answers are "right" in the sense that they were truly in the passage. The one correct answer on an EXCEPT question (the false one) can fall into one of the standard trap categories. Which trap does answer (E), above, represent?

According to the passage, it is true that ECT affects neurotransmitters, but it is false that this was *cited in the passage as a current or historical criticism* of ECT. So answer (E) is a variation of a true but not right trap answer.

EXCEPT questions are not a separate type of question; any of the main question types could be presented as an EXCEPT question. Use your usual clues to identify the question type. Then, work backwards: Go straight to the answers and try to find them in the passage. You're going to cross off the four true answers (for which you will find support in the passage) and select the one false answer.

## Specific Question Cheat Sheet

**Identify**
the Question

| Detail: | Most common: *Accoring to the passage. . .* |
| | *indicates explicitly . . .* |
| | *mentions (or proposes) which of the following . . .* |
| Inference: | Most common: *infer, imply, suggest, provides support for. . .* |
| | *author would be most likely to describe* (or *predict*) X |
| Specific Purpose: | Most common clue: *in order to* |
| | *The author's reference* (to X) *serves primarily to . . .* |
| EXCEPT: | Any can also be EXCEPT questions. Use keywords from the answers to find the support in the passage. |

**Find the**
Support

Use your map to find specific paragraph of sentences needed. If you can't, go to answers to try to work backwards. If this doesn't work, guess and move on.

**Predict**
an Answer

Try to formulate an answer in your own words. If you can't, go to anwers to try to work backwards. If this doesn't work, guess and move on.

**Eliminate**

Check all of the answers! Common traps include the following:

| Trap | Characteristics |
|------|-----------------|
| Direct contradiction | The passage says the opposite. |
| Extreme | Extreme word *without support* in the passage. |
| One word off | Looks very tempting but one or two words are wrong. |
| Out of scope | Goes beyond what the passage says. |
| Mix-up | Uses words directly from the passage, but the meaning is not what the passage says. |
| True but not right | The passage says this (or it's true in the real word), but it does not answer the question asked. |

Flash card the information on this page for future review. Don't copy down the exact language; put it in your own words and you'll remember it better.

# Problem Set

The three passages in this problem set appear in both the General and Specific chapters, but different questions are presented in each chapter.

Give yourself 2 to 3 minutes to read each passage and up to 60 seconds to answer each question. After you're done, review your point and passage map before you check the solutions, thinking about ways to improve your process next time. If you come up with ways to improve your map, actually rewrite it to reinforce what you want to do differently next time. Then, check your work against the solution key.

## Passage I: Japanese Swords

Historians have long recognized the Japanese sword, or *nihonto*, as one of the finest cutting weapons ever produced. But to regard the sword that is synonymous with the
5  samurai as merely a weapon is to ignore what makes it so special. The Japanese sword has always been considered a splendid weapon and even a spiritual entity. The traditional Japanese adage "the sword is the soul of the
10  samurai" reflects not only the sword's importance to its wielder but also its permanent connection to its creator, the master smith.

Master smiths may not have been
15  considered artists in the classical sense, but each smith exerted great care in the process of creating swords, no two of which were ever forged in exactly the same way. Over hundreds of hours, two types of steel were
20  repeatedly heated, hammered, and folded together into thousands of very thin layers, producing a sword with an extremely sharp and durable cutting edge and a flexible, shock-absorbing blade. It was common, though
25  optional, for a master smith to place a physical signature on a blade; moreover, each smith's secret forging techniques left an idiosyncratic structural signature on his blades. Each master smith brought a high level
30  of devotion, skill, and attention to detail to the sword-making process, and the sword itself was a reflection of his personal honor and ability. This effort made each blade as distinctive as the samurai who wielded it such
35  that today the Japanese sword is recognized as much for its artistic merit as for its historical significance.

1. Which of the following can be inferred about the structural signature of a Japanese sword?

   (A) It is an inscription that the smith places on the blade during the forging process.

   (B) It refers to the particular characteristics of a blade created by a smith's unique forging process.

   (C) It suggests that each blade can be traced back to a known master smith.

   (D) It reflects the soul of the samurai who wielded the sword.

   (E) It refers to the actual curved shape of the blade.

2. Each of the following is mentioned in the passage EXCEPT

   (A) Every Japanese sword has a unique structure that can be traced back to a special forging process.

   (B) Master smiths kept their forging techniques secret.

   (C) The Japanese sword was considered by some to have a spiritual quality.

   (D) Master smiths are now considered artists by most major historians.

   (E) The Japanese sword is considered both a work of art and a historical artifact.

3.  The author explains the way in which swords were made in order to

    (A) establish that the Japanese sword is the most important handheld weapon in history

    (B) claim that the skill of the samurai is what made each Japanese sword unique

    (C) support the contention that the master smiths might be considered artists as well as craftsmen

    (D) illustrate that master smiths were more concerned with the artistic merit of their blades than with the blades' practical qualities

    (E) demonstrate that the Japanese sword has more historical importance than artistic importance

## Passage J: Polygamy

Polygamy in Africa has been a popular topic for social research over the past half-century; it has been analyzed by many distinguished minds and in various well-publicized works. In
5 1961, when Remi Clignet published his book *Many Wives, Many Powers*, he was not alone in his view that in Africa co-wives may be perceived as direct and indirect sources of increased income and prestige.
10 By the 1970s, such arguments had become crystallized and popular. Many other African scholars who wrote on the subject became the new champions of this philosophy. For example, in 1983, John Mbiti proclaimed that
15 polygamy is an accepted and respectable institution serving many useful social purposes. Similarly, G.K. Nukunya, in his paper "Polygamy as a Symbol of Status," reiterated Mbiti's idea that a plurality of wives is a
20 legitimate sign of affluence and power in the African society.

The colonial missionary voice, however, provided consistent opposition to polygamy. Invoking the authority of the Bible,
25 missionaries argued that the practice was unethical and destructive of family life, and they propagated the view that Africans had to be coerced into abiding by the monogamous view of marriage favored by Western culture.
30 In some instances, missionaries even dictated immediate divorce for newly converted men who had already entered into polygamous marriages. Unfortunately, neither the missionary voice nor the scholarly voice
35 considered the views of African women important. Although there was some awareness that women regarded polygamy as both a curse and a blessing, the distanced, albeit scientific, perspective of an outside
40 observer predominated both at the pulpit and in scholarly writings.

Contemporary research in the social sciences has begun to focus on the protagonist's voice in the study of culture,
45 recognizing that the views and experiences of those who take part in a given reality ought to receive close examination. This privileging of the protagonist seems appropriate, particularly given that women in Africa have
50 often used literary productions to comment on marriage, family, and gender relations.

1. According to the passage, colonial missionaries and popular scholars shared which of the following traits in their approach to the issue of polygamy?

(A) Both considered polygamy a sign of social status and success.

(B) Neither accounted for the views of local women.

(C) Both attempted to limit the prevalence of polygamy.

(D) Both pointed out polygamy's destructive effects on family life.

(E) Both exhibited a somewhat negative attitude toward polygamy.

2. The author implies which of the following about Nukunya and Mbiti's works?

(A) From their point of view, a man who lacks wealth and influence is less likely to have many wives.

(B) They adjusted their initial views on polygamy, recognizing that the experiences of African women should receive closer attention.

(C) Their arguments represented a significant departure from those of Remi Clignet.

(D) Their analyses may have been tainted by the fact that both men practiced polygamy themselves.

(E) Their views reflected the majority opinion of the African population.

3. The passage mentions each of the following, EXCEPT

(A) the year of publication of Remi Clignet's book *Many Wives, Many Powers*

(B) the year in which John Mbiti made a claim that polygamy is an accepted institution

(C) examples of African women's literary productions devoted to family relations

(D) reasons for missionary opposition to polygamy

(E) current-day perspectives with respect to studying polygamy

14

## Passage K: Sweet Spot

Most tennis players strive to strike the ball on the racket's vibration node, more commonly known as the "sweet spot." However, many players are unaware of the
5 existence of a second, lesser-known location on the racket face—the center of percussion—that will also greatly diminish the strain on a player's arm when the ball is struck.

In order to understand the physics of this
10 second sweet spot, it is helpful to consider what would happen to a tennis racket if the player's hand were to vanish at the moment of impact with the ball. The impact of the ball would cause the racket to bounce backwards,
15 resulting in a translational motion away from the ball. The tendency of this motion would be to jerk all parts of the racket, including the end of its handle, backward, or away from the ball. Unless the ball happened to hit precisely
20 at the racket's center of mass, the racket would additionally experience a rotational motion around its center of mass—much as a penny that has been struck near its edge will start to spin. Whenever the ball hits the racket
25 face, the effect of this rotational motion is to jerk the end of the handle forward, towards the ball. Depending on where the ball strikes the racket face, one or the other of these motions will predominate.

30 However, there is one point of impact, known as the center of percussion, which causes neither motion to predominate; if a ball strikes this point, the impact does not impart any motion to the end of the handle. The
35 reason for this lack of motion is that the force on the upper part of the hand would be equal and opposite to the force on the lower part of the hand, resulting in no net force on the tennis player's hand or forearm. The center of
40 percussion constitutes a second sweet spot because a tennis player's wrist is typically placed next to the end of the racket's handle. When the player strikes the ball at the center of percussion, her wrist is jerked neither
45 forward nor backward, and she experiences greatly reduced vibration in the arm.

The manner in which a tennis player can detect the center of percussion on a given tennis racket follows from the nature of this
50 second sweet spot. The center of percussion can be located via simple trial and error by holding the end of a tennis racket between the finger and thumb and throwing a ball onto the strings. If the handle jumps out of the
55 player's hand, then the ball has missed the center of percussion.

1. The author mentions a penny that has been struck near its edge in order to

   (A) illustrate what happens at the lesser-known center of percussion

   (B) argue that a penny spins in the exact way that a tennis racket spins

   (C) illustrate the difference between two types of motion

   (D) draw an analogy to help explain a type of motion

   (E) demonstrate that pennies and tennis rackets do not spin in the same way

2. According to the passage, which of the following occurs when a ball strikes the racket strings on a sweet spot?

   (A) The jolt that accompanies most strokes will be more pronounced.

   (B) The racket experiences rotational motion but not translational motion.

   (C) The racket experiences translational motion but not rotational motion.

   (D) The player experiences less vibration in the arm holding the racket.

   (E) The center of mass and the center of percussion coincide.

3.  Which of the following can be inferred about the forces acting on the racket handle?

    (A)  A player whose grip is anywhere other than at the end of the racket's handle will experience a jolting sensation when striking the ball.

    (B)  Striking a ball at the well-known sweet spot will result in fewer vibrations than striking it at the lesser-known sweet spot.

    (C)  Striking a ball on the vibration node will impart some amount of motion to the handle of the racket.

    (D)  Depending on where the ball strikes, the handle will experience either translational or rotational motion.

    (E)  If the player's hand could disappear at the moment of impact, the racket would drop straight to the ground.

14

# Solutions

The solutions show a sample passage map and the point, as well as explanations for each answer choice. No simple story is provided, but do try to develop that level of understanding of the passage when creating your map. Where appropriate, wrong answers have been labeled by wrong answer category.

## Passage I: Japanese Swords

Historians have long recognized the Japanese sword, or *nihonto*, as one of the finest cutting weapons ever produced. But to regard the sword that is synonymous with the
5 samurai as merely a weapon is to ignore what makes it so special. The Japanese sword has always been considered a splendid weapon and even a spiritual entity. The traditional Japanese adage "the sword is the soul of the
10 samurai" reflects not only the sword's importance to its wielder but also its permanent connection to its creator, the master smith.

Master smiths may not have been
15 considered artists in the classical sense, but each smith exerted great care in the process of creating swords, no two of which were ever forged in exactly the same way. Over hundreds of hours, two types of steel were
20 repeatedly heated, hammered, and folded together into thousands of very thin layers, producing a sword with an extremely sharp and durable cutting edge and a flexible, shock-absorbing blade. It was common, though
25 optional, for a master smith to place a physical signature on a blade; moreover, each smith's secret forging techniques left an idiosyncratic structural signature on his blades. Each master smith brought a high level
30 of devotion, skill, and attention to detail to the sword-making process, and the sword itself was a reflection of his personal honor and ability. This effort made each blade as distinctive as the samurai who wielded it such
35 that today the Japanese sword is recognized as much for its artistic merit as for its historical significance.

Sample passage map (yours will likely differ):

① J sword: not just weapon, spirit

② Master smith: skilled
how to make
artistic merit + history

The point (articulate to yourself; don't write): Japanese sword is a weapon *and* a work of art, important to both samurai and smith. The smiths were basically artists.

1. First, identify the question type:

   *Which of the following can be inferred about the structural signature of a Japanese sword?*

The wording *can be inferred* indicates that this is an Inference question. Next, the question asks about the *structural signature* of a sword. Look at your map; in which paragraph would that information likely be found? The second paragraph talked about how the smiths forged the swords, so go to that paragraph and scan for the phrase *structural signature*.

The relevant sentence says:

   It was common, though optional, for a master smith to place a physical signature on a blade; moreover, each smith's secret forging techniques left an idiosyncratic structural signature on his blades. (lines 24–29)

The sentence references both a *physical signature* and a *structural signature*, so the structural signature must not be a literal signature. Further, the sentence indicates that each smith's structural signature is distinctive to the individual (*idiosyncratic*), a result of that smith's *secret forging techniques*.

(A) *It is an inscription that the smith places on the blade during the forging process.*

   This refers to the physical signature, not the structural signature. (True but not right)

(B) *It refers to the particular characteristics of a blade created by a smith's unique forging process.*

   **CORRECT.** This matches the information articulated in step 3 (predict an answer). Each smith's process resulted in a structural signature unique to that smith.

14

(C) *It suggests that each blade can be traced back to a known master smith.*

Tricky! The passage does say that a structural signature is unique to one smith, but it does not say that records survive indicating specifically who that smith was. A historian might be able to tell that three blades came from the same smith, but she may not be able to tell who that smith was. (Out of scope)

(D) *It reflects the soul of the samurai who wielded the sword.*

The first paragraph does include a quote about the soul of the samurai, but this information is not presented in relation to the information about the structural signature. (Mix-up)

(E) *It refers to the actual curved shape of the blade.*

Careful: If you have ever seen a samurai sword, then you may remember that it is curved—but the passage doesn't say so! In any case, since the signature is individual to the smith, something that all swords had in common wouldn't be helpful here. (Out of scope)

2. First, identify the question type:

*Each of the following is mentioned in the passage EXCEPT*

The question indicates that four of the answers *are* mentioned in the passage, so this is a Detail EXCEPT question. The question is too vague to formulate an answer in advance, so work backwards: Go straight to the first answer choice and try to find it in the passage.

(A) *Every Japanese sword has a unique structure that can be traced back to a special forging process.*

True. This is mentioned in the second paragraph (lines 26–29): *each smith's secret forging techniques left an idiosyncratic structural signature on his blades.*

(B) *Master smiths kept their forging techniques secret.*

True. This is mentioned in the second paragraph (lines 26–27): *each smith's secret forging techniques.*

(C) *The Japanese sword was considered by some to have a spiritual quality.*

True. This is mentioned in the first paragraph (lines 6–8): the *sword has always been considered a splendid weapon and even a spiritual entity.*

(D) *Master smiths are now considered artists by most major historians.*

**CORRECT.** False. The passage does not say this. Some people may recognize the smiths as artists (see answer [E] below), but there is no indication that this view is held by *most major historians.* (Extreme)

(E) *The Japanese sword is considered both a work of art and a historical artifact.*

True. This is mentioned in the last sentence of the second paragraph (lines 35–37): the *sword is recognized as much for its artistic merit as for its historical significance.*

3. First, identify the question type:

*The author explains the way in which swords were made in order to*

The *in order to* language indicates that this is a Specific Purpose (Why) question. Paragraph 2 explains how the swords were made; why did the author include this information?

The beginning and end of the paragraph provide clues. First, the author says that smiths may not have been considered artists *in the classical sense*, foreshadowing the idea that perhaps they could still be considered artists. The end of the passage indicates that the forging process resulted in such a distinctive blade that the sword is now recognized for its artistic merit as well as its historical significance.

(A)  *establish that the Japanese sword is the most important handheld weapon in history*

The passage does call the Japanese sword *one of the finest cutting weapons ever produced* (lines 2–3), but this is not quite as strong as calling it the most important handheld weapon in history. In any case, this is not the author's purpose in describing how the sword was made. (Extreme)

(B)  *claim that the skill of the samurai is what made each Japanese sword unique*

The passage claims that the smith's secret forging techniques, not the skill of the samurai, made a blade unique. (Direct contradiction)

(C)  *support the contention that the master smiths might be considered artists as well as craftsmen*

**CORRECT.** The default definition for the smiths is craftsmen, but the detailed information about the forging process, as well as the opening and closing sentences, indicate that the smiths might be considered artists as well.

(D)  *illustrate that master smiths were more concerned with the artistic merit of their blades than with the blades' practical qualities*

The passage discusses both the artistic merits and the practical qualities of the swords, but the passage does not indicate whether the smiths thought one was more important than the other. (Out of scope)

(E)  *demonstrate that the Japanese sword has more historical importance than artistic importance*

The last sentence does talk about both of these concepts, but it does not indicate that one is more important than the other. (Out of scope)

## Passage J: Polygamy

Polygamy in Africa has been a popular topic for social research over the past half-century; it has been analyzed by many distinguished minds and in various well-publicized works. In
5 1961, when Remi Clignet published his book *Many Wives, Many Powers*, he was not alone in his view that in Africa co-wives may be perceived as direct and indirect sources of increased income and prestige.

10 By the 1970s, such arguments had become crystallized and popular. Many other African scholars who wrote on the subject became the new champions of this philosophy. For example, in 1983, John Mbiti proclaimed that
15 polygamy is an accepted and respectable institution serving many useful social purposes. Similarly, G.K. Nukunya, in his paper "Polygamy as a Symbol of Status," reiterated Mbiti's idea that a plurality of wives is a
20 legitimate sign of affluence and power in the African society.

The colonial missionary voice, however, provided consistent opposition to polygamy. Invoking the authority of the Bible,
25 missionaries argued that the practice was unethical and destructive of family life, and they propagated the view that Africans had to be coerced into abiding by the monogamous view of marriage favored by Western culture.
30 In some instances, missionaries even dictated immediate divorce for newly converted men who had already entered into polygamous marriages. Unfortunately, neither the missionary voice nor the scholarly voice
35 considered the views of African women important. Although there was some awareness that women regarded polygamy as both a curse and a blessing, the distanced, albeit scientific, perspective of an outside
40 observer predominated both at the pulpit and in scholarly writings.

Contemporary research in the social sciences has begun to focus on the protagonist's voice in the study of culture,
45 recognizing that the views and experiences of those who take part in a given reality ought to receive close examination. This privileging of the protagonist seems appropriate, particularly given that women in Africa have
50 often used literary productions to comment on marriage, family, and gender relations.

Sample passage map (yours will likely differ):

① Polyg Afr '61 Clignet: P = income, prestige

② 70s, 80s: positive dtls

③ Missionary: against no one listened to W

④ Now listen to W

The point (articulate to yourself; don't write): Some scholars thought polygamy was a good thing. Missionaries were against it. Now, people are actually paying attention to what the women think.

1. What type of question is this?

*According to the passage, colonial missionaries and popular scholars shared which of the following traits in their approach to the issue of polygamy?*

The language *according to the passage* indicates that this is a Detail question. In general, the scholars' view was positive while the missionaries' view was negative, so these two groups would not appear to have many traits in common. The missionary viewpoint is not mentioned until the third paragraph, so begin searching there.

Halfway through the third paragraph, the author states that *neither the missionary voice nor the scholarly voice considered the views of African women important* (lines 33–36).

(A) *Both considered polygamy a sign of social status and success.*

This represents the position of the scholars, but not the missionaries. (Direct contradiction)

(B) *Neither accounted for the views of local women.*
**CORRECT.** This choice matches the relevant sentence from the passage.

(C) *Both attempted to limit the prevalence of polygamy.*

(D) *Both pointed out polygamy's destructive effects on family life.*

Choices (C) and (D) describe things that the missionaries did. The passage provides no information on this topic with respect to the scholars; since the scholars had a positive view of polygamy, they probably did not do these things. (Out of scope)

(E)   *Both exhibited a somewhat negative attitude toward polygamy.*

The scholars cited had a positive attitude toward polygamy. (Direct contradiction)

2.   First, identify the question type:

*The author implies which of the following about Nukunya and Mbiti's works?*

The word *implies* indicates that this is an Inference question. The two scholars were discussed in the second paragraph.

Both had positive views of polygamy. The question asks about both Mbiti and Nukunya's views, and only one view is attributed to both: Nukunya agreed with Mbiti's idea that polygamy is a *sign of affluence and power in the African society* (lines 20–21). The correct answer will be something that follows from that information.

(A)   *From their point of view, a man who lacks wealth and influence is less likely to have many wives.*

**CORRECT.** If polygamy leads to affluence and power, then someone who does not have those two things is less likely to be practicing polygamy.

(B)   *They adjusted their initial views on polygamy, recognizing that the experiences of African women should receive closer attention.*

The passage does not indicate that they adjusted their views. In fact, the third paragraph says that the *scholarly voice* did not consider women's views important. (Direct contradiction)

(C)   *Their arguments represented a significant departure from those of Remi Clignet.*

Clignet was pro-polygamy, as were Mbiti and Nukunya; their views were not different from Clignet's. (Direct contradiction)

(D)   *Their analyses may have been tainted by the fact that both men practiced polygamy themselves.*

The passage does not indicate whether the two men practiced polygamy themselves. (Out of scope)

(E)   *Their views reflected the majority opinion of the African population.*

The passage indicates only that polygamy in Africa has been a popular research topic. The passage does not indicate whether a majority of Africans supported polygamy or considered it in a positive light. (Out of scope)

3.   This is a Detail EXCEPT question.

*The passage mentions each of the following, EXCEPT*

Work backwards from the answers.

(A)   *the year of publication of Remi Clignet's book Many Wives, Many Powers*

True. Clignet's book was published in 1961 (line 5).

(B)   *the year in which John Mbiti made a claim that polygamy is an accepted institution*

True. Mbiti made this claim in 1983 (lines 14–16).

(C)   *examples of African women's literary productions devoted to family relations*

**CORRECT.** False. Though the passage does mention that African women used literary productions in certain ways, it is false that the passage gives any examples of this.

(D)   *reasons for missionary opposition to polygamy*

True. The second sentence of paragraph 3 provides specific reasons that the missionaries opposed polygamy.

(E)   *current-day perspectives with respect to studying polygamy*

True. The final paragraph indicates that contemporary research has finally begun to recognize that it is important to focus on the voices of those who are actually in polygamous marriages, including women.

14

## Passage K: Sweet Spot

Most tennis players strive to strike the ball on the racket's vibration node, more commonly known as the "sweet spot." However, many players are unaware of the
5 existence of a second, lesser-known location on the racket face—the center of percussion— that will also greatly diminish the strain on a player's arm when the ball is struck.

In order to understand the physics of this
10 second sweet spot, it is helpful to consider what would happen to a tennis racket if the player's hand were to vanish at the moment of impact with the ball. The impact of the ball would cause the racket to bounce backwards,
15 resulting in a translational motion away from the ball. The tendency of this motion would be to jerk all parts of the racket, including the end of its handle, backward, or away from the ball. Unless the ball happened to hit precisely
20 at the racket's center of mass, the racket would additionally experience a rotational motion around its center of mass—much as a penny that has been struck near its edge will start to spin. Whenever the ball hits the racket
25 face, the effect of this rotational motion is to jerk the end of the handle forward, towards the ball. Depending on where the ball strikes the racket face, one or the other of these motions will predominate.

30 However, there is one point of impact, known as the center of percussion, which causes neither motion to predominate; if a ball strikes this point, the impact does not impart any motion to the end of the handle. The
35 reason for this lack of motion is that the force on the upper part of the hand would be equal and opposite to the force on the lower part of the hand, resulting in no net force on the tennis player's hand or forearm. The center of
40 percussion constitutes a second sweet spot because a tennis player's wrist is typically placed next to the end of the racket's handle. When the player strikes the ball at the center of percussion, her wrist is jerked neither
45 forward nor backward, and she experiences greatly reduced vibration in the arm.

The manner in which a tennis player can detect the center of percussion on a given tennis racket follows from the nature of this
50 second sweet spot. The center of percussion

can be located via simple trial and error by holding the end of a tennis racket between the finger and thumb and throwing a ball onto the strings. If the handle jumps out of the
55 player's hand, then the ball has missed the center of percussion.

Sample passage map (yours will likely differ):

① 2 SS (↓ strain), one less known

② if hand disappear?

③ center perc = no motion, ↓↓ vibration

④ find center perc

The point (articulate to yourself; don't write): People usually know about one sweet spot but not the other. Both reduce vibration in the arm. (Plus lots of technical details—ignore for now!)

1. First, identify the question type:

   *The author mentions a penny that has been struck near its edge in order to*

The *in order to* language indicates that this is a Specific Purpose (Why) question. Paragraph 2 mentions the penny; why did the author include this information?

Here's the relevant text (lines 19–24):

   Unless the ball happened to hit precisely at the racket's center of mass, the racket would additionally experience a rotational motion around its center of mass—much as a penny that has been struck near its edge will start to spin.

The first part of the sentence talks about a certain motion that the tennis racket experiences—don't worry too much about exactly what it means. After the dash, the *much as a penny* language indicates that this example is an analogy: The racket is spinning in the same way that the penny would spin. The author uses this analogy to help the reader understand what is happening to the racket.

(A) *illustrate what happens at the lesser-known center of percussion*

This choice is tricky. The beginning of the third paragraph indicates that the motion described at the end of the second paragraph is *not* what happens at the center of percussion; if you spot that, you can eliminate this choice, but that's a pretty specific detail. Even if you miss that, though, it's enough to find another answer choice that does match your pre-stated idea—so keep looking. (Direct contradiction)

(B) *argue that a penny spins in the exact way that a tennis racket spins*

The author is trying to draw a parallel between the two but does not say that they spin in the *exact* same way. (Extreme)

(C) *illustrate the difference between two types of motion*

The paragraph does talk about two types of motion, but the penny example applies just to one of them. (True but not right)

(D) *draw an analogy to help explain a type of motion*

**CORRECT.** The penny analogy explains how the tennis racket spins.

(E) *demonstrate that pennies and tennis rackets do not spin in the same way*

The analogy indicates that they spin in a similar way. (Direct contradiction)

2. What type of question is this?

*According to the passage, which of the following occurs when a ball strikes the racket strings on a sweet spot?*

The language *according to the passage* indicates that this is a Detail question. A large portion of the passage talks about what happens when a ball strikes a racket on a sweet spot. Where should you look?

When the question is this broad, find the first mention of the topic. This first mention will give you the main idea and you can eliminate some answers. If you cannot eliminate all four, then you can go to the next

mention of the topic and use that to eliminate until you get down to one answer (or you can decide that you'd rather guess and move on).

The first paragraph indicates that there are two sweet spots and that striking a ball there will *greatly diminish the strain on a player's arm.*

(A) *The jolt that accompanies most strokes will be more pronounced.*

This goes against the basic idea that the strain will *diminish.* (Direct contradiction)

(B) *The racket experiences rotational motion but not translational motion.*

(C) *The racket experiences translational motion but not rotational motion.*

Answers (B) and (C) talk about the same two forces, so deal with them together. The second paragraph does talk about these forces, but the details are pretty technical. Check the remaining answers first to see whether one matches your predicted answer; if so, you never have to check the technical detail.

(D) *The player experiences less vibration in the arm holding the racket.*

**CORRECT.** This is the basic benefit of the sweet spot: When a player hits a ball there, the strain, or vibration, felt in the arm is lessened.

(E) *The center of mass and the center of percussion coincide.*

Because answer (D) already works, dismiss this answer.

In the case of answers (B), (C), and (E), the test writer is trying to slow you down. You aren't required to assess each answer choice in order; when you hit something that requires a deeper dive, check the other answer choices first.

Striking the ball at a sweet spot can result in both translational and rotational motion, so answers (B) and (C) are both wrong. The passage never indicates a time when the center of mass and center of percussion would be in the same location, so answer (E) is also wrong.

14

3. First, identify the question type.

*Which of the following can be inferred about the forces acting on the racket handle?*

The word *inferred* indicates that this is an Inference question. The forces acting on the racket handle are first discussed in paragraph 2.

Warning: This passage is a hard one and this question is seriously challenging. If you like the topic, feel free to delve into the technical details. If you don't, summarize only the high-level points, or just guess right now and move on. (And on the real test, be a little pleased—yes, pleased!—that you earned such a hard question.)

The question asks specifically about the *racket handle*. Scan the second paragraph for mentions of the handle. Translational motion moves the racket handle backward. Rotational motion jerks the handle forward.

The third paragraph adds that if a ball strikes the center of percussion, there will be *no* motion at the end of the handle.

(A) *A player whose grip is anywhere other than at the end of the racket's handle will experience a jolting sensation when striking the ball.*

The passage does not address what would happen if the player gripped the racket somewhere other than the end of the handle. The "sweet spot" describes where the ball strikes the strings, not where the player holds the racket. (Out of scope)

(B) *Striking a ball at the well-known sweet spot will result in fewer vibrations than striking it at the lesser-known sweet spot.*

The passage does not address which sweet spot might result in fewer vibrations. (Out of scope)

(C) *Striking a ball on the vibration node will impart some amount of motion to the handle of the racket.*

**CORRECT.** This is a very tricky answer! The third paragraph indicates that striking the ball at the center of percussion will result in no motion—and the author further specifies that this lack of motion occurs only when the ball is struck at this one location. If the ball strikes any *other* point on the racket, then the handle will experience some motion. The vibration node is the well-known sweet spot (see the first paragraph), so it qualifies as a spot other than the center of percussion.

(D) *Depending on where the ball strikes, the handle will experience either translational or rotational motion.*

If the ball is struck at the center of percussion, it will experience neither type of motion. If the ball is struck elsewhere, it will experience both types of motion. (Direct contradiction)

(E) *If the player's hand could disappear at the moment of impact, the racket would drop straight to the ground.*

The second paragraph states that, if the player's hand somehow disappeared, then the racket would bounce backward, among other motions. (Direct contradiction)

This last problem was incredibly hard. Even if you didn't find the support for (C), congratulate yourself if you were able to eliminate some of the incorrect answers. Also, notice that the second question in the set, while also a Detail question, was easier to answer because it did not require as much technical understanding of the passage. If you are having trouble following a very technical passage, you may get lucky and be offered a specific question that you can answer with only a high-level understanding. However, it's likely that at least one question will require enough technical understanding that the best choice may be to guess quickly and move on.

# Extra Problem Set

## In This Chapter:

- Extra Problem Set

**In this chapter, you will gain** additional practice on all aspects of Reading Comprehension problems: reading and mapping the passage and answering questions of all types.

# CHAPTER 15 Extra Problem Set

Time to put it all together! This chapter contains four passages with either four or five accompanying questions each. (Note: The real test will give you either three or four questions per passage.)

Each title is followed by a suggested length of time to give yourself to complete the passage and all questions. You can, of course, choose to spend extra time—but on the real test, that time will have to come from other questions. (If you receive extended time on the test, adjust accordingly.)

# Problem Set

## Passage L: The Invention of TV (8 minutes)

In the early years of television, Vladimir Zworykin was considered the device's inventor, at least publicly. His loudest champion was his boss, David Sarnoff, then president of RCA and
5 a man regarded even today as "the father of television." Current historians agree, however, that Philo Farnsworth, a self-educated prodigy who was the first to transmit live images, was television's technical inventor.

10     In his own time, Farnsworth's contributions went largely unnoticed, in large part because he was excluded from the process of introducing the invention to a national audience. Sarnoff put televisions into living
15 rooms, and Sarnoff was responsible for a dominant paradigm of the television industry that continues to be relevant today: advertisers pay for the programming so that they can have a receptive audience for their
20 products. Sarnoff had already utilized this construct to develop the radio industry, and it had, within ten years, become ubiquitous. Farnsworth thought the television should be used as an educational tool, but he had little
25 understanding of the business world, and was never able to implement his ideas.

    Some argue that Sarnoff simply adapted the business model for radio and television from the newspaper industry, replacing the
30 revenue from subscriptions and newsstand purchases with that of television set sales, but Sarnoff promoted himself as nothing less than a visionary. Some television critics argue that the construct Sarnoff implemented has played
35 a negative role in determining the content of the programs themselves, while others contend that it merely created a democratic platform from which the audience can determine the types of programming it
40 desires.

**15**

1. The primary purpose of the passage is to

   (A) correct public misconceptions about Farnsworth's role in developing early television programs

   (B) debate the influence of television on popular culture

   (C) challenge the current public perception of Vladimir Zworykin

   (D) chronicle the events that led from the development of radio to the invention of the television

   (E) describe both Sarnoff's influence on the public perception of television's inception and the debate around the impact of Sarnoff's paradigm

2. Which of the following best illustrates the relationship between the second and third paragraphs?

   (A) The second paragraph dissects the evolution of a contemporary controversy; the third paragraph presents differing viewpoints on that controversy.

   (B) The second paragraph explores the antithetical intentions of two men involved in the infancy of an industry; the third paragraph details the eventual deterioration of that industry.

   (C) The second paragraph presents differing views of a historical event; the third paragraph represents the author's personal opinion about that event.

   (D) The second paragraph provides details that are necessary to support the author's opinion, which is presented in the third paragraph.

   (E) The second paragraph presents divergent visions about the implementation of a technology; the third paragraph further explores one of those perspectives.

3.  According to the passage, the television industry, at its inception, earned revenue from

    (A) advertising only
    (B) advertising and the sale of television sets
    (C) advertising and subscriptions
    (D) subscriptions and the sale of television sets
    (E) advertising, subscriptions, and the sale of television sets

4.  The passage suggests that Farnsworth might have earned greater public notoriety for his invention if

    (A) Vladimir Zworykin had been less vocal about his own contributions to the television
    (B) Farnsworth had been able to develop and air his own educational programs
    (C) Farnsworth had involved Sarnoff in his plans to develop, manufacture, or distribute the television
    (D) Sarnoff had involved Farnsworth in his plans to develop, manufacture, or distribute the television
    (E) Farnsworth had conducted research into the type of programming the audience most wanted to watch

## Passage M: Life on Mars (7 minutes)

     Because of the proximity and likeness of Mars to Earth, scientists have long speculated about the possibility of life on Mars. As early as the mid-seventeenth century, astronomers

5  observed polar ice caps on Mars, and by the mid-nineteenth century, scientists discovered other similarities to Earth, including the length of day and axial tilt. But in 1965, photos taken by the Mariner 4 probe revealed a

10  Mars without rivers, oceans, or signs of life. Moreover, in the 1990s, it was discovered that Mars, unlike Earth, no longer possessed a substantial global magnetic field, allowing celestial radiation to reach the planet's surface

15  and solar wind to eliminate much of Mars's atmosphere over the course of several billion years.

     More recent probes have investigated whether there was once liquid water on Mars.

20  Some scientists believe that this question is definitively answered in the affirmative by the presence of certain geological landforms. Others posit that alternative explanations, such as wind erosion or carbon dioxide oceans,

25  may be responsible for these formations. Mars rovers *Opportunity* and *Spirit*, which began exploring the surface of Mars in 2004, have both discovered geological evidence of past water activity. In 2013, the rover *Curiosity*

30  found evidence that the soil on the surface of Mars is approximately 2 percent water by weight. These findings substantially bolster claims that there was once life on Mars.

1.   The passage is primarily concerned with which of the following?

   (A)  Disproving a widely accepted theory

   (B)  Initiating a debate about an unproven theory

   (C)  Presenting evidence in support of a recently formulated claim

   (D)  Describing various discoveries made concerning the possibility of life on Mars

   (E)  Detailing the findings of the Mars rovers *Opportunity*, *Spirit*, and *Curiosity*

2.   Each of the following discoveries is mentioned in the passage EXCEPT

   (A)  Wind erosion and carbon dioxide oceans are responsible for certain geological landforms on Mars.

   (B)  Mars does not have a substantial global magnetic field.

   (C)  Mars had water activity at some point in the past.

   (D)  The length of a day on Mars is similar to that on Earth.

   (E)  The axial tilt of Mars is similar to that of Earth.

3.   The passage suggests which of the following about polar ice caps?

   (A)  Until recently, the ones on Mars were thought to consist largely of carbon dioxide.

   (B)  By 1965, the ones on Mars had disappeared.

   (C)  They are also found on Earth.

   (D)  Their formation is tied to length of day and axial tilt.

   (E)  They indicate that conditions on the planet Mars were once very different than they are at present.

15

4.  Which of the following pieces of evidence, if found on Mars, would most support the claim that Mars once held life?

    (A) Carbon dioxide oceans

    (B) Celestial radiation and solar wind

    (C) High daily level of sunlight reaching the planet's surface

    (D) Volcanic eruptions

    (E) A significant global magnetic field

## Passage N: Fossils (8.5 minutes)

In archaeology, as in the physical sciences, new discoveries frequently undermine accepted findings and give rise to new theories. This trend can be seen in the
5 reaction to the recent discovery of a set of 3.3-million-year-old fossils in Ethiopia, the remains of the earliest well-preserved child ever found. The fossilized child was estimated to be about 3 years old at death,
10 female, and a member of the *Australopithecus afarensis* species. The *afarensis* species, a major human ancestor, lived in Africa from earlier than 3.7 million to 3 million years ago. "Her completeness, antiquity, and age at
15 death make this find unprecedented in the history of paleoanthropology," said Zeresenay Alemseged, a noted paleoanthropologist. Other scientists said that the discovery could reconfigure conceptions about the lives and
20 capacities of these early humans.

Prior to this discovery, it had been thought that the *afarensis* species had abandoned the arboreal habitat of its ape cousins. However, while the lower limbs of this fossil supported
25 findings that *afarensis* walked upright, its gorilla-like arms and shoulders suggested that it retained the ability to swing through trees. This has initiated a reexamination of many accepted theories of early human
30 development. Also, the presence of a hyoid bone, a rarely preserved bone in the larynx that supports muscles of the throat, has had a tremendous impact on theories about the origins of speech. The fossil bone is primitive
35 and more similar to that of apes than to that of humans, but it is the first hyoid found in such an early human-related species.

1. The primary purpose of the passage is to

   (A) discuss a controversial scientific discovery
   (B) contrast varying theories of human development
   (C) support a general contention with a specific example
   (D) argue for the importance of a particular field of study
   (E) refute a widely believed myth

2. The passage quotes Zeresenay Alemseged in order to

   (A) qualify the main idea of the first paragraph
   (B) provide contrast to the claims of other scientists
   (C) support the theory regarding the linguistic abilities of the *afarensis* species
   (D) support the stated significance of the discovery
   (E) provide a subjective opinion that is refuted in the second paragraph

3. It can be inferred from the passage's description of the discovery of the fossil hyoid bone that

   (A) *Australopithecus afarensis* was capable of speech
   (B) the discovered hyoid bone is less primitive than the hyoid bone of apes
   (C) the hyoid bone is necessary for speech
   (D) the discovery of the hyoid bone necessitated the reexamination of prior theories about speech
   (E) the hyoid bone was the most important fossil found at the site

15

4.  Each of the following is cited as a reason that the fossils discovered in Ethiopia were important EXCEPT

    (A) the fact that the remains were those of a child

    (B) the age of the fossils

    (C) the location of the discovery

    (D) the presence of a bone not usually discovered

    (E) the intact nature of the fossils

5.  The impact of the discovery of the hyoid bone in the field of archaeology is most closely analogous to which of the following situations?

    (A) The discovery and analysis of cosmic rays lend support to a widely accepted theory of the origin of the universe.

    (B) The original manuscript of a deceased nineteenth-century author confirms ideas about the development of an important work of literature.

    (C) The continued prosperity of a state-run economy stirs debate in the discipline of macroeconomics.

    (D) Newly revealed journal entries by a prominent Civil War–era politician lead to a questioning of certain accepted historical interpretations about the conflict.

    (E) Research into the mapping of the human genome gives rise to nascent applications of individually tailored medicines.

### Passage O: Chaos Theory (8.5 minutes)

Around 1960, mathematician Edward Lorenz found unexpected behavior in apparently simple equations representing atmospheric air flows. Whenever he reran his model with
5 the same inputs, different outputs resulted, although the model lacked any random elements. Lorenz realized that tiny rounding errors in the initial data mushroomed over time, leading to erratic results. His findings
10 marked a seminal moment in the development of chaos theory, which, despite its name, has little to do with randomness.

Lorenz's experiment was one of the first to demonstrate conclusively that unpredictability
15 can arise from deterministic equations, which do not involve chance outcomes. In order to understand this phenomenon, first consider the non-chaotic system of two poppy seeds placed in a round bowl. As the seeds roll to
20 the bowl's center, a position known as a point attractor, the distance between the seeds shrinks. If, instead, the bowl is flipped over, two seeds placed on top will roll away from each other. Such a system, while still not
25 technically chaotic, enlarges initial differences in position.

Chaotic systems, such as a machine mixing bread dough, are characterized by both attraction and repulsion. As the dough is
30 stretched, folded, and pressed back together, any poppy seeds sprinkled in are intermixed seemingly at random. But this randomness is illusory. In fact, the poppy seeds are captured by "strange attractors," staggeringly complex
35 pathways whose tangles appear accidental but are in fact determined by the system's fundamental equations.

During the dough-kneading process, two poppy seeds positioned next to each
40 other eventually go their separate ways. Any early divergence or measurement error is repeatedly amplified by the mixing until the position of any seed becomes effectively unpredictable. It is this "sensitive dependence
45 on initial conditions" and not true randomness that generates unpredictability in chaotic systems, of which one example may be the Earth's weather. According to the popular interpretation of the "Butterfly Effect," a
50 butterfly flapping its wings causes hurricanes. A better understanding is that the butterfly

causes uncertainty about the precise state of the air. This microscopic uncertainty grows until it encompasses even hurricanes. Few
55 meteorologists believe that we will ever be able to predict rain or shine for a particular day years in the future.

1. The primary purpose of this passage is to

(A) explain how non-random systems can produce unpredictable results

(B) trace the historical development of a scientific theory

(C) distinguish one theory from its opposite

(D) describe the spread of a technical model from one field of study to others

(E) contrast possible causes of weather phenomena

2. According to the passage, what is true about poppy seeds in bread dough, once the dough has been thoroughly mixed?

(A) They have been individually stretched and folded over, like miniature versions of the entire dough.

(B) They are scattered in random clumps throughout the dough.

(C) They are accidentally caught in tangled objects called strange attractors.

(D) They are bound to regularly dispersed patterns of point attractors.

(E) They are in positions dictated by the underlying equations that govern the mixing process.

15

3. According to the passage, the small rounding errors in Lorenz's model

   (A) rendered the results unusable for the purposes of scientific research

   (B) were deliberately included to represent tiny fluctuations in atmospheric air currents

   (C) had a surprisingly large impact over time

   (D) were at least partially expected, given the complexity of the actual atmosphere

   (E) shrank to insignificant levels during each trial of the model

4. The passage mentions each of the following as an example or potential example of a chaotic or non-chaotic system EXCEPT

   (A) a dough-mixing machine

   (B) atmospheric weather patterns

   (C) poppy seeds placed on top of an upside-down bowl

   (D) poppy seeds placed in a right-side-up bowl

   (E) fluctuating butterfly flight patterns

15

# Solutions

The solutions show a sample passage map and the point, as well as explanations for each answer choice. No simple story is provided, but do try to develop that level of understanding of the passage when creating your map. Where appropriate, wrong answers have been labeled by wrong answer category.

## Passage L: The Invention of TV

In the early years of television, Vladimir Zworykin was considered the device's inventor, at least publicly. His loudest champion was his boss, David Sarnoff, then president of RCA and
5  a man regarded even today as "the father of television." Current historians agree, however, that Philo Farnsworth, a self-educated prodigy who was the first to transmit live images, was television's technical inventor.
10  In his own time, Farnsworth's contributions went largely unnoticed, in large part because he was excluded from the process of introducing the invention to a national audience. Sarnoff put televisions into living
15  rooms, and Sarnoff was responsible for a dominant paradigm of the television industry that continues to be relevant today: advertisers pay for the programming so that they can have a receptive audience for their
20  products. Sarnoff had already utilized this construct to develop the radio industry, and it had, within ten years, become ubiquitous. Farnsworth thought the television should be used as an educational tool, but he had little
25  understanding of the business world, and was never able to implement his ideas.
Some argue that Sarnoff simply adapted the business model for radio and television from the newspaper industry, replacing the
30  revenue from subscriptions and newsstand purchases with that of television set sales, but Sarnoff promoted himself as nothing less than a visionary. Some television critics argue that the construct Sarnoff implemented has played
35  a negative role in determining the content of the programs themselves, while others contend that it merely created a democratic platform from which the audience can determine the types of programming it
40  desires.

Sample passage map (yours will likely differ):

① VZ = inventor
S = father of TV
really F

② F not part of process, focus edu
S made comm (same as radio)

③ S just adapt? or visionary?
Some see S neg, some pos

The point (articulate to yourself; don't write): Farnsworth really invented TV, but he didn't know how to turn it into a business. Sarnoff used the radio model to make television big business. People have differing feelings about his role.

1.  First, identify the question type:

    *The primary purpose of the passage is to*

The wording indicates that this is a Primary Purpose question. Glance at your map and remind yourself of the point before you go to the answers.

(A)  *correct public misconceptions about Farnsworth's role in developing early television programs*

The passage does correct the misconceptions about Farnsworth's role. This is only a detail of the passage, however; most of the passage talks about Sarnoff's development of the business model for television. (True but not right)

(B)  *debate the influence of television on popular culture*

The passage does not delve into popular culture. (Out of scope)

15

(C) *challenge the current public perception of Vladimir Zworykin*

Zworykin is not the focus of the passage, nor does the passage say anything about *current* public perception of Zworykin; it only indicates that he was once considered the inventor of the technology. (Out of scope)

(D) *chronicle the events that led from the development of radio to the invention of the television*

The passage is not about the events that led to the invention of television, nor is it about radio. Radio is only mentioned because Sarnoff used a similar business model to launch the business of television. (Out of scope)

(E) *describe both Sarnoff's influence on the public perception of television's inception and the debate around the impact of Sarnoff's paradigm*

**CORRECT.** The passage does describe how Sarnoff made television popular; some critics think that his role was positive while others think that it was negative. Notice that this is the only answer choice that mentions Sarnoff. He is featured prominently in every paragraph, so any answer choice representing the point of the passage should not mention other people while ignoring him.

2.   First, identify the question type:

*Which of the following best illustrates the relationship between the second and third paragraphs?*

This is a paragraph question. Glance at your map and articulate to yourself the relationship between the second and third paragraphs before you check the answers.

The second paragraph explains how Sarnoff made television a commercial success and why Farnsworth was not able to do so. The third paragraph expands on Sarnoff's work, indicating both positive and negative views.

(A) *The second paragraph dissects the evolution of a contemporary controversy; the third paragraph presents differing viewpoints on that controversy.*

Perhaps the fact that the wrong man was initially credited with television's invention could be considered a controversy, but that controversy is not contemporary, nor is it the purpose of the second or third paragraphs. (Out of scope)

(B) *The second paragraph explores the antithetical intentions of two men involved in the infancy of an industry; the third paragraph details the eventual deterioration of that industry.*

The second paragraph might be described in this way, but the third paragraph does not talk about the deterioration of television. Rather, the industry was (and is!) a success. Perhaps it didn't live up to Farnsworth's hopes, but the passage doesn't describe any decline—in fact, Farnsworth's vision didn't get off the ground. (Direct contradiction)

(C) *The second paragraph presents differing views of a historical event; the third paragraph represents the author's personal opinion about that event.*

The second paragraph provides historical details of the launch of television, not different views of the launch. The third paragraph does not present the author's personal opinion. (Out of scope)

(D) *The second paragraph provides details that are necessary to support the author's opinion, which is presented in the third paragraph.*

The author does not provide his own opinion; rather, he conveys the opinions of others (*some argue; some television critics argue*). (Out of scope)

(E) *The second paragraph presents divergent visions about a new technology; the third paragraph further explores one of those perspectives.*

**CORRECT.** The second paragraph does present the two different visions held by Farnsworth and Sarnoff. The third paragraph does provide additional information about Sarnoff's particular vision.

3. First, identify the question type:

   *According to the passage, the television industry, at its inception, earned revenue from*

The language *according to the passage* indicates that this is a Detail question. The passage discusses television revenues in the second and third paragraphs. Search for the information.

Paragraph 2 (line 18): *advertisers pay for the programming*

Paragraph 3 (lines 29–31): *replacing the revenue from subscriptions and newsstand purchases with that of television set sales*

   (A) *advertising only*

   Revenue was also earned from the sale of TV sets. (True but not right)

   (B) *advertising and the sale of television sets*

   **CORRECT.** Revenue was earned from advertisers and the sale of TV sets.

   (C) *advertising and subscriptions*

   (D) *subscriptions and the sale of television sets*

   (E) *advertising, subscriptions, and the sale of television sets*

   Choices (C), (D), and (E) mention subscriptions. Subscriptions were used in the newspaper industry, not the television industry. (Mix-up)

4. First, identify the question type:

   *The passage suggests that Farnsworth might have earned greater public notoriety for his invention if*

The word *suggests* signals that this is an Inference question, so you will need to go back to the passage. Farnsworth's contributions are discussed in the second paragraph:

   [Farnsworth] was excluded from the process of introducing the invention to a national audience . . . Farnsworth thought the television should be used as an educational tool, but he had little understanding of the business world, and was never able to implement his ideas. (lines 12–26)

If Farnsworth hadn't been excluded, maybe he would have earned more acclaim. Alternatively, if he had understood business better, then he might have earned more acclaim. Look for an answer with a similar meaning.

   (A) *Vladimir Zworykin had been less vocal about his own contributions to the television*

   The passage says that Sarnoff, not Zworykin himself, was vocal about Zworykin's contributions. (Mix-up)

   (B) *Farnsworth had been able to develop and air his own educational programs*

   It's possible that if Farnsworth had been able to follow through on his goal of using television for education, he would have earned public acclaim, but the passage says nothing to indicate this. Because he had little understanding of business, his programs might not have been great successes even if he had been able to produce them. (Out of scope)

   (C) *Farnsworth had involved Sarnoff in his plans to develop, manufacture, or distribute the television*

   There is no indication that Farnsworth had any such plans. Rather, it would have helped Farnsworth to be involved with Sarnoff's plans. (Mix-up)

15

(D) *Sarnoff had involved Farnsworth in his plans to develop, manufacture, or distribute the television*

**CORRECT.** If Farnsworth hadn't been excluded, then he might have garnered acclaim as Sarnoff and Zworykin did.

(E) *Farnsworth had conducted research into the type of programming the audience most wanted to watch*

The passage indicates that Farnsworth had little understanding of the business world; even if he knew what audiences wanted to watch, he wouldn't necessarily have known how to build a successful business model. (Out of scope)

## Passage M: Life on Mars

Because of the proximity and likeness of Mars to Earth, scientists have long speculated about the possibility of life on Mars. As early as the mid-seventeenth century, astronomers
5 observed polar ice caps on Mars, and by the mid-nineteenth century, scientists discovered other similarities to Earth, including the length of day and axial tilt. But in 1965, photos taken by the Mariner 4 probe revealed a
10 Mars without rivers, oceans, or signs of life. Moreover, in the 1990s, it was discovered that Mars, unlike Earth, no longer possessed a substantial global magnetic field, allowing celestial radiation to reach the planet's surface
15 and solar wind to eliminate much of Mars's atmosphere over the course of several billion years.
More recent probes have investigated whether there was once liquid water on Mars.
20 Some scientists believe that this question is definitively answered in the affirmative by the presence of certain geological landforms. Others posit that alternative explanations, such as wind erosion or carbon dioxide oceans,
25 may be responsible for these formations. Mars rovers *Opportunity* and *Spirit*, which began exploring the surface of Mars in 2004, have both discovered geological evidence of past water activity. In 2013, the rover *Curiosity*
30 found evidence that the soil on the surface

of Mars is approximately 2 percent water by weight. These findings substantially bolster claims that there was once life on Mars.

Sample passage map (yours will likely differ):

① Life on M?
+ sim to E
− diff too

② Water? debate
recent: yes, water

The point (articulate to yourself; don't write): Debate about life on Mars. Positives and negatives, but the big deal was the discovery of water, increasing the chance that there was life on Mars.

1. First, identify the question type:

*The passage is primarily concerned with which of the following?*

This is a Primary Purpose question. Glance at your map and remind yourself of the point before you go to the answers.

(A) *Disproving a widely accepted theory*

There is no widely accepted theory, just speculation. Plus, that speculation is more positive than negative! (Out of scope)

(B) *Initiating a debate about an unproven theory*

The passage does discuss a potential theory (that there may once have been life on Mars), but the passage itself does not initiate any debate. Rather, it reports on various findings and opinions of others. (Out of scope)

(C) *Presenting evidence in support of a recently formulated claim*

The earliest mentioned interest in Mars was in the mid-seventeenth century; this is not recent. (One word off)

(D) *Describing various discoveries made concerning the possibility of life on Mars*

**CORRECT.** The passage does describe various discoveries made in the mid-seventeenth and mid-nineteenth centuries, as well as, more recently, discoveries that concern the possibility of life on Mars.

(E) *Detailing the findings of the Mars rovers* Opportunity, Spirit, *and* Curiosity

The passage does discuss this, but the rovers are details; they are not the overall point of the passage. (True but not right)

2. First, identify the question type:

*Each of the following discoveries is mentioned in the passage EXCEPT*

The question indicates that four of the answers *are* mentioned in the passage, so this is a Detail EXCEPT question. The entire passage is about discoveries, so go straight to the first answer choice and try to find it in the passage.

(A) *wind erosion and carbon dioxide oceans are responsible for certain geological landforms on Mars*

**CORRECT.** False. The passage says only that wind erosion or carbon dioxide *may* be responsible for certain geological landforms, not that they *are*. This is an unusual form of an Extreme answer: Though the word *are* is not an extreme word itself, it is more extreme than *may*. (Extreme)

(B) *Mars does not have a substantial global magnetic field*

True. The first paragraph says that Mars *no longer possessed a substantial global magnetic field* (lines 12–13).

(C) *Mars had water activity at some point in the past*

True. The second paragraph says that *Mars rovers* Opportunity *and* Spirit...*discovered geological evidence of past water activity* (lines 25–29).

(D) *the length of a day on Mars is similar to that on Earth*

True. The first paragraph discusses Mars's *similarities to Earth, including the length of day* (lines 7–8).

(E) *the axial tilt of Mars is similar to that of Earth*

True. The first paragraph discusses Mars's *similarities to Earth, including the...axial tilt* (lines 7–8).

3. First, identify the question type:

*The passage suggests which of the following about polar ice caps?*

The word *suggests* points to an inference question. The passage mentions polar ice caps in the first paragraph:

As early as the mid-seventeenth century, astronomers observed polar ice caps on Mars, and by the mid-nineteenth century, scientists discovered other similarities to Earth, including the length of day and axial tilt. (lines 3–8)

The second half of the sentence states that scientists discovered *other* similarities to Earth, implying that polar ice caps are also a similarity between the two planets.

(A) *Until recently, the ones on Mars were thought to consist largely of carbon dioxide.*

The passage does mention carbon dioxide, but not in the context of polar ice caps. (Mix-up)

(B) *By 1965, the ones on Mars had disappeared.*

The passage does mention that photos taken in 1965 showed that Mars was *without rivers, oceans, or signs of life* (line 10), but this sentence makes no reference to the polar ice caps. (Mix-up)

(C) *They are also found on Earth.*

**CORRECT.** The sentence says that scientists discovered *other* similarities to Earth, implying that the earlier discovery (polar ice caps) is also similar to what is found on Earth.

15

(D) *Their formation is tied to length of day and axial tilt.*

The passage mentions length of day and axial tilt as examples of other similarities to Earth, but it does not indicate that those had anything to do with the formation of polar ice caps. (Out of scope)

(E) *They indicate that conditions on the planet Mars were once very different than they are at present.*

It's possible that conditions were once very different, but the passage does not provide any information to indicate that this is the case. (Out of scope)

4.  First, identify the question type:

*Which of the following pieces of evidence, if found on Mars, would most support the claim that Mars once held life?*

The words *most support the claim* indicate that this is a Strengthen question. Both paragraphs discuss characteristics that indicate the possibility of life. Because there are so many possible indicators, work backwards from the answers and try to find them in the passage. First, though, remind yourself that the passage also discusses characteristics that are incompatible with life. Read carefully!

(A) *Carbon dioxide oceans*

The second paragraph mentions that carbon dioxide oceans, rather than water, might be responsible for certain landforms, and the passage makes clear that water is an important indicator of possible life. Carbon dioxide oceans, then, would weaken the evidence for water presence and thus *decrease* the chances of life. (Weaken)

(B) *Celestial radiation and solar wind*

The first paragraph mentions celestial radiation and solar wind in the context of a scenario in which there is *not* life. (Weaken)

(C) *High daily level of sunlight reaching the planet's surface*

You might posit that abundant sunlight would improve the odds of life, but the passage does not provide any information about this. (Out of scope)

(D) *Volcanic eruptions*

The passage does not provide any information about volcanic eruptions. (Out of scope)

(E) *A significant global magnetic field*

**CORRECT.** The first paragraph says that scientists posited that life could exist on Mars due to the similarities between Earth and Mars. However, Mars, unlike Earth, does *not* have a substantial global magnetic field, and this difference between Mars and Earth is presented as a negative in the debate about life on Mars. The implication, then, is that a global magnetic field would be positive evidence in favor of life on Mars.

## Passage N: Fossils

In archaeology, as in the physical sciences, new discoveries frequently undermine accepted findings and give rise to new theories. This trend can be seen in the
5   reaction to the recent discovery of a set of 3.3-million-year-old fossils in Ethiopia, the remains of the earliest well-preserved child ever found. The fossilized child was estimated to be about 3 years old at death,
10   female, and a member of the *Australopithecus afarensis* species. The *afarensis* species, a major human ancestor, lived in Africa from earlier than 3.7 million to 3 million years ago. "Her completeness, antiquity, and age at
15   death make this find unprecedented in the history of paleoanthropology," said Zeresenay Alemseged, a noted paleoanthropologist. Other scientists said that the discovery could reconfigure conceptions about the lives and
20   capacities of these early humans.

Prior to this discovery, it had been thought that the *afarensis* species had abandoned the arboreal habitat of its ape cousins. However, while the lower limbs of this fossil supported
25  findings that *afarensis* walked upright, its gorilla-like arms and shoulders suggested that it retained the ability to swing through trees. This has initiated a reexamination of many accepted theories of early human
30  development. Also, the presence of a hyoid bone, a rarely preserved bone in the larynx that supports muscles of the throat, has had a tremendous impact on theories about the origins of speech. The fossil bone is primitive
35  and more similar to that of apes than to that of humans, but it is the first hyoid found in such an early human-related species.

Sample passage map (yours will likely differ):

①  new disc → undermine old
    new theories eg child fossil

②  2 things changed w/child
    walking / limbs
    speech / hyoid

The point (articulate to yourself; don't write): New discoveries change old ideas and give rise to new theories. A detailed archaeological example illustrates this overall point. The discovery of a particular skeleton led researchers to reexamine theories about early human life.

1.  First, identify the question type:

    *The primary purpose of the passage is to*

This is a Primary Purpose question. Glance at your map and remind yourself of the point before you go to the answers.

(A)  *discuss a controversial scientific discovery*

    The passage does not indicate that the discovery was in any way controversial. (Out of scope)

(B)  *contrast varying theories of human development*

    The passage does discuss how certain theories about early human development have changed over time, but it does not contrast different theories. (Out of scope)

(C)  *support a general contention with a specific example*

    **CORRECT.** The first sentence of the passage makes a general contention (*In archaeology . . . new discoveries frequently undermine accepted findings* [lines 1–3]). The rest of the passage provides a specific example (the Ethiopian fossils) that supports that contention.

(D)  *argue for the importance of a particular field of study*

    The author does not make a case about the *importance* of archaeology (or any other field) specifically. (Out of scope)

(E)  *refute a widely believed myth*

    A *myth* is something that people erroneously believe to be true, typically without any credible evidence. A *myth* is not what the passage describes: new evidence that led researchers to revise an existing theory. (Out of scope)

2.  First, identify the question type:

    *The passage quotes Zeresenay Alemseged in order to*

The *in order to* language indicates that this is a Specific Purpose (Why) question. Return to the passage and articulate in your own words why the author quoted Alemseged in paragraph 1.

"Her completeness, antiquity, and age at death make this find unprecedented in the history of paleoanthropology," said Zeresenay Alemseged, a noted paleoanthropologist. Other scientists said that the discovery could reconfigure conceptions about the lives and capacities of these early humans. (lines 14–20)

The author is trying to use this example to support the point that discoveries can give rise to new theories. Alemseged's quote reinforces the idea that the discovery of this set of fossils is extremely significant (*unprecedented*), as does the fact that other scientists agree with Alemseged in this respect.

15

(A) *qualify the main idea of the first paragraph*

To qualify a piece of information is to limit or diminish it. Alemseged's quote does the opposite: It reinforces the point. (Direct contradiction)

(B) *provide contrast to the claims of other scientists*

Alemseged's quote emphasizes the importance of the discovery. The other scientists mentioned share this perspective. (Direct contradiction)

(C) *support the theory regarding the linguistic abilities of the* afarensis *species*

Linguistic abilities are mentioned at the end of the second paragraph, but Alemseged's quote is about the general significance of the find and it doesn't provide any support for a particular theory. (Mix-up)

(D) *support the stated significance of the discovery*

**CORRECT.** This choice matches the answer predicted above.

(E) *provide a subjective opinion that is refuted in the second paragraph*

Alemseged's opinion is reinforced, not refuted, by the second paragraph, which delves into the important consequences of the discovery. (Direct contradiction)

3.  First, identify the question type:

*It can be inferred from the passage's description of the discovery of the fossil hyoid bone that*

This is an inference question. The hyoid bone was mentioned in the second paragraph:

> This has initiated a reexamination of many accepted theories of early human development. Also, the presence of a hyoid bone, a rarely preserved bone in the larynx that supports muscles of the throat, has had a tremendous impact on theories about the origins of speech. The fossil bone is primitive and more similar to that of apes than to that of humans, but it is the first hyoid found in such an early human-related species. (lines 28–37)

The first sentence sets up the idea that the hyoid discovery was an example of the need to reexamine some earlier theory. Specifically, it had a *tremendeous impact on theories about the origins of speech* (lines 33–34). Since it was the earliest hyoid bone found in a human-related species, perhaps it indicates that speech may have arisen earlier than previously thought.

(A) Australopithecus afarensis *was capable of speech*

This is tempting but goes too far. The passage relates the hyoid to speech but does not provide information as to whether *afarensis* could actually speak. (Out of scope)

(B) *the discovered hyoid bone is less primitive than the hyoid bone of apes*

Check the last sentence of the paragraph. Tricky! The sentence calls the bone primitive and similar to that of apes, but does not say that it is less primitive than the ones found in apes. (Out of scope)

(C) *the hyoid bone is necessary for speech*

The passage does connect the hyoid bone to speech, but does not provide information that would imply that the bone is *necessary*. (Extreme)

(D) *the discovery of the hyoid bone necessitated the reexamination of prior theories about speech*

**CORRECT.** Leading into the hyoid example, the passage talks about discoveries leading to a reexamination of many accepted theories. The passage then says that the hyoid discovery has had a *tremendous impact* (line 33) on prior theories. The implication is that the hyoid discovery has also resulted in a reexamination of those prior theories.

(E) *the hyoid bone was the most important fossil found at the site*

The discovery of the hyoid was certainly important, but the passage provides no information about which discovery was the most important. (Extreme)

15

4. First, identify the question type:

*Each of the following is cited as a reason that the fossils discovered in Ethiopia were important EXCEPT*

The question indicates that four of the answers *are* mentioned in the passage, so this is a Detail EXCEPT question. Most of the passage discusses fossil discoveries, so go straight to the first answer choice and try to find it in the passage.

(A) *the fact that the remains were those of a child*

True. Alemseged's quote indicates that the *age at death* was important (lines 14–16).

(B) *the age of the fossils*

True. Alemseged's quote indicates that the *antiquity* of the bones was important (line 14).

(C) *the location of the discovery*

**CORRECT.** False. While the geographic location of the discovery is given in the passage, the location was not cited as a reason that the fossils were important.

(D) *the presence of a bone not usually discovered*

True. The hyoid example indicates that the bone is *rarely preserved* (line 31) and that it was the *first hyoid found in such an early human-related species* (lines 36–37). The passage says that the discovery of the hyoid bone had a *tremendous impact* (line 33).

(E) *the intact nature of the fossils*

True. Alemseged's quote indicates that the *completeness* of the bones was important (line 14).

5. First, identify the question type:

*The impact of the discovery of the hyoid bone in the field of archaeology is most closely analogous to which of the following situations?*

This is an unusual question that does not fall into one of the common categories; it's more like a Critical Reasoning question. It is asking you to make an analogy to the situation presented in the passage. You may or may not see an RC question like this on the test.

The hyoid is mentioned in the second paragraph, so read the appropriate text and ask yourself what the *impact of the discovery* was. Then, examine the answers to find a match.

The bone was the first hyoid found for this species, and it had a *tremendous impact on theories about the origins of speech* (lines 33–34). Find a similar situation in the answers.

(A) *The discovery and analysis of cosmic rays lend support to a widely accepted theory of the origin of the universe.*

The hyoid discovery led to a reexamination of an existing theory. In this answer, the new evidence supported the existing theory.

(B) *The original manuscript of a deceased nineteenth-century author confirms ideas about the development of an important work of literature.*

The hyoid discovery led to a reexamination of an existing theory. In this answer, the new evidence confirmed the existing theory.

(C) *The continued prosperity of a state-run economy stirs debate in the discipline of macroeconomics.*

The hyoid discovery inserted an important new piece of information into the conversation; this choice does not mention anything about new information or evidence.

(D) *Newly revealed journal entries by a prominent Civil War–era politician lead to a questioning of certain accepted historical interpretations about the conflict.*

**CORRECT.** The hyoid discovery, like the newly revealed journal entries in this choice, led to a questioning of certain interpretations or theories.

(E) *Research into the mapping of the human genome gives rise to nascent applications of individually tailored medicines.*

The hyoid discovery had an impact on previously formulated theories. This choice does not address previous applications or theories.

## Passage O: Chaos Theory

Around 1960, mathematician Edward Lorenz found unexpected behavior in apparently simple equations representing atmospheric air flows. Whenever he reran his model with
5 the same inputs, different outputs resulted, although the model lacked any random elements. Lorenz realized that tiny rounding errors in the initial data mushroomed over time, leading to erratic results. His findings
10 marked a seminal moment in the development of chaos theory, which, despite its name, has little to do with randomness.

Lorenz's experiment was one of the first to demonstrate conclusively that unpredictability
15 can arise from deterministic equations, which do not involve chance outcomes. In order to understand this phenomenon, first consider the non-chaotic system of two poppy seeds placed in a round bowl. As the seeds roll to
20 the bowl's center, a position known as a point attractor, the distance between the seeds shrinks. If, instead, the bowl is flipped over, two seeds placed on top will roll away from each other. Such a system, while still not
25 technically chaotic, enlarges initial differences in position.

Chaotic systems, such as a machine mixing bread dough, are characterized by both attraction and repulsion. As the dough is
30 stretched, folded, and pressed back together, any poppy seeds sprinkled in are intermixed seemingly at random. But this randomness is illusory. In fact, the poppy seeds are captured by "strange attractors," staggeringly complex
35 pathways whose tangles appear accidental but are in fact determined by the system's fundamental equations.

During the dough-kneading process, two poppy seeds positioned next to each
40 other eventually go their separate ways. Any early divergence or measurement error is repeatedly amplified by the mixing until the position of any seed becomes effectively unpredictable. It is this "sensitive dependence
45 on initial conditions" and not true randomness that generates unpredictability in chaotic systems, of which one example may be the Earth's weather. According to the popular interpretation of the "Butterfly Effect," a
50 butterfly flapping its wings causes hurricanes. A better understanding is that the butterfly causes uncertainty about the precise state of the air. This microscopic uncertainty grows until it encompasses even hurricanes. Few
55 meteorologists believe that we will ever be able to predict rain or shine for a particular day years in the future.

Sample passage map (yours will likely differ):

① L: diff results from rounding errors chaos theory (not random)

② not chaos: bowl + poppy seeds

③ chaos: bowl + dough attract, repulse

④ not random, depends on start cond butterfly

The point (articulate to yourself; don't write): Lorenz discovered something about chaos theory (which is not really about randomness). Non-chaotic systems are predictable. Chaotic systems increase initial differences, so even though they are not actually random, they are hard to predict.

1. First, identify the question type:

*The primary purpose of this passage is to*

This is a Primary Purpose question. Glance at your map and remind yourself of the point before you go to the answers.

(A) *explain how non-random systems can produce unpredictable results*

**CORRECT.** The passage does explain how chaotic (*non-random*) systems aren't actually predictable. The passage gives the example of poppy seeds kneaded into bread dough until their position *becomes effectively unpredictable* (lines 43–44).

(B) *trace the historical development of a scientific theory*

The passage does discuss some of Lorenz's contributions to chaos theory, but the passage does not trace the entire historical development of the theory. (Out of scope)

(C) *distinguish one theory from its opposite*

Only one theory (chaos theory) is mentioned in the passage. The passage does contrast two systems (non-chaotic and chaotic), but these are not both theories, nor is the overall point to contrast these two systems. (Out of scope)

(D) *describe the spread of a technical model from one field of study to others*

The passage does not discuss multiple fields of study. (Out of scope)

(E) *contrast possible causes of weather phenomena*

The end of the passage does mention the weather, but there is no mention of different possible causes of weather phenomena. Even if there were, this would be detail, not the point. (Out of scope)

2. First, identify the question type:

*According to the passage, what is true about poppy seeds in bread dough, once the dough has been thoroughly mixed?*

The language *according to the passage* indicates that this is a Detail question. The bread dough concept is introduced in the third paragraph and continued in the fourth paragraph. Start with the third paragraph:

As the dough is stretched, folded, and pressed back together, any poppy seeds sprinkled in are intermixed seemingly at random. But this randomness is illusory. In fact, the poppy seeds are captured by "strange attractors," staggeringly complex pathways whose tangles appear accidental but are in fact determined by the system's fundamental equations. (lines 29–37)

After the dough is mixed, then, the seeds have separated based on some equations, but it's not possible to predict how. See whether there's a match in the answers; if not, try the fourth paragraph.

(A) *They have been individually stretched and folded over, like miniature versions of the entire dough.*

The paragraph indicates that the dough is stretched and folded over, not the seeds. (Mix-up)

(B) *They are scattered in random clumps throughout the dough.*

The paragraph specifically indicates that the movement is *not* random. (Direct contradiction)

(C) *They are accidentally caught in tangled objects called strange attractors.*

"Strange attractor" is a technical name for a complex, tangled pathway. There are no tangled objects. Moreover, there is nothing accidental about the movement. (Mix-up)

(D) *They are bound to regularly dispersed patterns of point attractors.*

The seeds are not in regularly dispersed patterns; the patterns are so complex that the outcome is *seemingly at random* (line 32). Later, in the fourth paragraph, the passage makes clear that the final positions are not predictable (and therefore not regularly dispersed) even though they are actually governed by equations. (Out of scope)

(E) *They are in positions dictated by the underlying equations that govern the mixing process.*

**CORRECT.** The final sentence of the third paragraph indicates that the system's fundamental equations determine the final position of the poppy seeds.

3. First, identify the question type:

*According to the passage, the rounding errors in Lorenz's model*

The language *according to the passage* indicates that this is a Detail question. The first paragraph introduces Lorenz's model and the rounding errors:

Edward Lorenz found unexpected behavior in apparently simple equations representing atmospheric air flows. Whenever he reran his

15

model with the same inputs, different outputs resulted—although the model lacked any random elements. Lorenz realized that tiny rounding errors in his analog computer mushroomed over time, leading to erratic results. (lines 1–9)

The rounding errors were tiny at first but mushroomed (got much larger) over time, such that the final results of seemingly similar starting points could be quite different.

Since the question stem contains the first half of a sentence that the answer choices finish, remind yourself of the text before reading the answers: *The rounding errors in Lorenz's model . . .*

(A) *rendered the results unusable for the purposes of scientific research*

The passage does not indicate whether Lorenz was still able to use the results for his purposes. If anything, the errors led to a positive, not negative, result: The erratic results led to *a seminal moment in the development of chaos theory* (lines 10–11). (Out of scope)

(B) *were deliberately included to represent tiny fluctuations in atmospheric air currents*

Lorenz did not deliberately include the rounding errors. At first, he did not realize that they were present and couldn't understand why he kept getting different results. (Direct contradiction)

(C) *had a surprisingly large impact over time*

**CORRECT.** The rounding errors were so tiny that Lorenz did not notice them immediately, but they *mushroomed over time* until they produced different results even with seemingly the same inputs. The passage describes this behavior as *unexpected*.

(D) *were at least partially expected, given the complexity of the actual atmosphere*

The rounding errors were simply computer errors; the passage does not indicate that they resulted from the complexity of the atmosphere. (Mix-up)

(E) *shrank to insignificant levels during each trial of the model*

On the contrary, the rounding errors grew a great deal, or *mushroomed*, over time. (Direct contradiction)

4. First, identify the question type:

*The passage mentions each of the following as an example or potential example of a chaotic or non-chaotic system EXCEPT*

The question indicates that four of the answers *are* mentioned in the passage, so this is a Detail EXCEPT question. The entire passage talks about both chaotic and non-chaotic systems, so it's not possible to formulate an answer in advance. Go straight to the first answer choice and try to find it in the passage.

(A) *a dough-mixing machine*

True. The first sentence of the third paragraph indicates that a *machine mixing bread dough* (lines 27–28) is an example of a chaotic system.

(B) *atmospheric weather patterns*

True. The fourth paragraph mentions one possible example of a chaotic system as *Earth's weather* (lines 48–50).

(C) *poppy seeds placed on top of an upside-down bowl*

(D) *poppy seeds placed in a right-side-up bowl*

Answers (C) and (D) discuss the poppy seed examples. True. The second paragraph describes both examples as non-chaotic systems (lines 18–19).

(E) *fluctuating butterfly flight patterns*

**CORRECT.** False. While it is true that the passage discusses a *butterfly flapping its wings* (line 50), the passage does not mention anything about butterfly flight patterns.

# Critical Reasoning

In this unit, you will learn a process for deconstructing arguments in order to understand how the information fits together logically. You will also learn how to recognize the different Critical Reasoning question types, what kind of analysis to do for each specific type, and how to avoid trap answers.

## In This Unit:

# Argument Structure

## In This Chapter:

**In this chapter, you will learn** how to deconstruct arguments into their core components, or building blocks. You'll also learn how to recognize certain common types of arguments that will be discussed throughout the rest of this unit.

# CHAPTER 16 **Argument Structure**

Here is an example of a typical GMAT argument in a Critical Reasoning (CR) problem:

> The expansion of the runways at the Bay City Airport will allow larger planes to use the airport. These new planes will create a lot of noise, a nuisance for residents who live near the airport. However, many of the residents in this neighborhood work in construction, and the contract to expand the runways has been awarded to a local construction company. Thus, the expansion of the runways will lead to an increased quality of life for the residents of this neighborhood.

In order to solve CR problems effectively and efficiently, you need to pay close attention to the specific information given for that problem, while keeping in mind how to reason through a problem of that type.

For every question, begin by understanding what you are *given*:

What is this author actually arguing?

What are the pieces of this argument?

How do they fit together?

Think about these questions in relation to the argument above before you keep reading.

On the GMAT:

1.  All arguments contain at least one **Premise**. A premise is information used by the author to support some claim or conclusion. That information may be a fact or an opinion. In the example above, sentence 3 is a premise because it helps to support the author's conclusion.

2.  Most (though not all) arguments contain a **Conclusion**, the primary claim the author is trying to prove or the outcome of a plan that someone is proposing. In the runway expansion example, sentence 4 is a conclusion.

3.  Many arguments (though not all) contain **Background** information, which provides context to allow you to understand the basic situation. The information is true but does not either support or go against the conclusion. In the runway argument, sentence 1 provides background.

4.  Some arguments contain a **Counterpoint** or **Counterpremise**—a piece of information that goes against the author's conclusion. In the example above, sentence 2 represents a counterpoint because it goes against the author's conclusion.

5.  Many arguments rely on one or more **Assumptions**—something that is not stated in the argument but that the author *must believe to be true* in order to draw the given conclusion. Without the assumption, the argument fails. By definition, you will not be able to identify an assumption in the text of the argument because it is unstated. In the runway expansion argument, one assumption is that the construction jobs are more important to quality of life than the nuisance and noise of the increase in flights.

Collectively, these categories represent the **Building Blocks** of an argument. How do you know which sentences fall into which categories? Try to articulate your own thought process for the argument above, then take a look at the decision process of this fictional student:

| Argument | Reader's Thoughts |
|---|---|
| The expansion of the runways at the Bay City Airport will allow larger planes to use the airport. | *Hmm. This is a fact. It could be a **premise** or it could just be background. I'm not sure yet.* |
| These new planes will create a lot of noise, a nuisance for residents who live near the airport. | *Now they're moving into claim territory. Something negative will come from this project. Why are they telling me this? I can't figure that out until I know the conclusion.* |
| However, many of the residents in this neighborhood work in construction, and the contract to expand the runways has been awarded to a local construction company. | *The word* however *indicates a contrast between sentences 2 and 3. What's the contrast? The noise is a negative consequence of the expansion, while winning a work contract is a positive consequence. Looks like I've got a **premise** and a **counterpoint** in these two sentences, but I don't know which one is which yet.* |
| Thus, the expansion of the runways will lead to an increased quality of life for the residents of this neighborhood. | *The word* thus *usually indicates a **conclusion**. Yes, this does seem like a conclusion—this project will have a certain outcome (better quality of life in this neighborhood), and I can now see how the previous two sentences fit into this conclusion. Sentence 3 is a **premise** because it provides one way in which the quality of life might be better for these people (they might make more money), and sentence 2 is a **counterpremise** because it tells me a negative consequence.* |
| After reading the argument: What is the author assuming? | *The author presents a cost of the plan (noise) and a benefit (construction jobs). In order for the expansion to increase quality of life, the author **assumes** that the benefit outweighs the cost.* |

Notice how many times the reader thought, "I'm not sure yet" (or something along those lines). That will happen frequently while reading an argument. You're gathering information and trying to understand what each piece might be, but you won't really know how everything fits together until you know what the conclusion is—and that might not be until the end of the argument. Here's the argument again, with each sentence labeled:

# The Core

The premise (or premises) and conclusion represent the **Core** of the argument. Remember that not all arguments will have a conclusion, but all will have at least one premise, so you will always have at least a partial core. The core represents what the author is trying to tell you or prove to you.

In this problem, the core consists of these two pieces:

However, many of the residents in this neighborhood work in construction, and the contract to expand the runways has been awarded to a local construction company.  Thus, the expansion of the runways will lead to an increased quality of life for the residents of this neighborhood.

Premise: provides one piece of evidence toward the conclusion

Conclusion: the claim supported by the given evidence

The argument is not airtight. For example, do you know for sure that residents of the neighborhood work for the local construction company that won the contract? If they don't, then perhaps residents won't benefit after all. As you'll see later in this book, that kind of reasoning will help when you get to the question-answering stage.

# Building Blocks of an Argument

Here are the **building blocks** discussed so far:

### Premise

- Is part of the **core** of the argument; present in every argument.
- Supports the author's conclusion.
- Can be a fact or an opinion; can be a description, historical information, data, or a comparison of things.
- Is often signaled by words or phrases such as *because of, since, due to,* or *as a result of.*

### Conclusion

- Is part of the **core** of an argument; present in most arguments.
- Represents the author's main opinion or claim; can be in the form of a prediction, a judgment of quality or merit, a statement of causality, or the outcome of a plan.
- Is supported by at least one **premise**.
- Is often signaled by words such as *therefore, thus, so,* or *consequently* (although harder arguments might use such a word elsewhere in the argument in an attempt to confuse you).

### Background

- Is not part of the **core**; not always present.
- Provides context to help understand the **core**; similar to premises but less important to the argument itself.
- Is almost always fact-based; can be in almost any form: historical information, data, descriptions of plans or ideas, definitions of words or concepts, and so on.

## Counterpoint or Counterpremise

- Is not part of the **core**; only present occasionally.

- Opposes or goes against the author's **conclusion** in some way.

- Introduces multiple opportunities for traps: believing that the **conclusion** is the opposite of what it is, mistakenly thinking that a **counterpoint** is a **premise** (and vice versa), and so on.

- Is often signaled by a transition word such as *although, though, however, yet*, and *but* (recognize, though, that the counterpoint may come before such words).

## Assumption

- Is not part of the **core**; is not written down in the argument.

- Is something that the author must believe is true in order to draw the given **conclusion**.

## Argument Structure

The argument above used all four of the building blocks in this order:

**Background–Counterpoint–Premise–Conclusion**

The GMAT can vary the types of building blocks used in a particular argument, and it can also vary the order of those building blocks. Most arguments on the GMAT will contain at least one premise and one conclusion; you will see some arguments later on that contain only premises. If you can categorize the building blocks given in any particular argument, you're one step closer to answering the question correctly.

## Pop Quiz

It's time to test your skills. You have three tasks. First, read the argument and try to identify the role of each sentence or major piece of information (note that one sentence could contain two different pieces of information). Use that information to jot down the premise(s) and conclusion. Second, try to articulate in your own words *how* the premise(s) support the conclusion. Third, identify any assumptions that must be true to draw the given conclusion.

1. Budget Fitness will grow its membership base by 10 percent in the next six months. Budget Fitness has recently crafted a clever ad campaign that it plans to air on several local radio stations.

2. Last year, the Hudson Family Farm was not profitable. However, the farm will be profitable this year. The farm operators have planted cotton, rather than corn, in several fields. Because cotton prices are expected to rise dramatically this year, the farm can expect larger revenues from cotton sales than it previously earned from corn.

Answers can be found on page 275.

# Signal Words

Certain words can provide valuable clues as to whether you've got a conclusion, a premise, or a counterpoint. If an argument says, "Adnan will earn a high test score because he has studied hard," the word *because* signals a cause–effect relationship. One thing (he has studied hard) is supposed to lead to another (he will earn a high score on the test). The premise here is the cause that follows the *because*, and the conclusion is the claimed result.

Finish the following exchange:

> Sam: Can I borrow your car?
>
> Marie: Even though you don't have a driver's license . . .

What is Marie likely to say next? She has acknowledged a reason that she should *not* let Sam borrow her car, but her sentence implies that she's about to let him borrow it anyway. (Not very wise, Marie!)

What if the conversation had gone this way?

> Sam: Can I borrow your car?
>
> Marie: I like you, Sam. However, you don't have a driver's license, so . . .

This time, Marie's not falling for Sam's charming smile! She's about to deny him access to her car.

What's the difference? How do you know that, in the first case, Marie seems willing to lend Sam her car, while, in the second case, she isn't going to do so?

Signal words! The term *even though* signals an acknowledgment of or a concession to an opposing point of view. Even though it's true that Sam doesn't have a driver's license, Marie will still let him borrow her car. The contrast word *however*, on the other hand, flips a switch: Marie may like Sam, but she's not about to let him use her car when he doesn't even have a driver's license.

You can use these kinds of language clues to help you classify information in arguments:

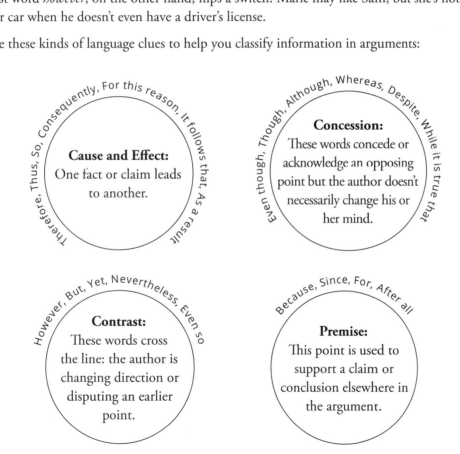

**Cause and Effect:** One fact or claim leads to another.
*Therefore, Thus, So, Consequently, For this reason, It follows that, As a result*

**Concession:** These words concede or acknowledge an opposing point but the author doesn't necessarily change his or her mind.
*Even though, Though, Although, Whereas, Despite, While it is true that*

**Contrast:** These words cross the line: the author is changing direction or disputing an earlier point.
*However, But, Yet, Nevertheless, Even so*

**Premise:** This point is used to support a claim or conclusion elsewhere in the argument.
*Because, Since, For, After all*

You likely know most or all of these words already, but you might not have consciously considered why they're used in certain contexts. Start paying attention! These signal words will make your job easier during the test.

# Intermediate Conclusions and the Therefore Test

You have one more building block to learn in this chapter. Read and deconstruct the argument below:

> The owner of a small publishing company plans to lease a new office space that has floor-to-ceiling windows and no internal walls, arguing that the new space will enhance worker productivity. The owner cites a recent study showing that workers exposed to natural light throughout the day tended to report, on average, a higher level of job satisfaction than did those who worked in office spaces that used fluorescent lighting. Thus, the owner concluded, exposure to natural light has a positive effect on workers' job satisfaction.

| | |
|---|---|
| The owner of a small publishing company plans to lease a new office space that has floor-to-ceiling windows and no internal walls, | *This is likely to be background information because it introduces a plan to do something but no actual claim (yet). The argument is probably about the plan, or a result of the plan.* |
| arguing that the new space will enhance worker productivity. | *This might be the conclusion because it describes the predicted future benefit of the company's plan.* |
| The owner cites a recent study showing that workers exposed to natural light throughout the day tended to report, on average, a higher level of job satisfaction than did those who worked in office spaces that used fluorescent lighting. | *This seems to be a premise in support of that conclusion. The workers will be more productive because the new space will provide exposure to natural light through the floor-to-ceiling windows.* |
| Thus, the owner concluded, exposure to natural light has a positive effect on workers' job satisfaction. | *Hmm, this is strange. This appears to be the conclusion as well. It uses the word* thus, *it represents an explanation for the study's results, and it even says that* the owner concluded *this!* |

This is a tough one! In this case, you have *two* claims that could be conclusions. Now what?

This brings you to another building block, the **Intermediate Conclusion** (also known as the secondary conclusion). What is an intermediate conclusion? Look at this simpler example:

> The burglar is clumsy and often makes a lot of noise while robbing homes. As a result, he is likely to get caught. Thus, in the near future, he will probably end up in jail.

The first sentence is a basic premise: It indicates some factual information about the robber. The second sentence is a claim made based upon that premise: *Because* he makes noise, he is likely to get caught. This is a conclusion—but, wait, there's a third sentence! That third sentence also contains a claim, and this claim follows from the previous claim: *Because* he is likely to get caught, there is a good chance he will end up in jail.

Essentially, a premise supports a conclusion, and that conclusion then supports a further conclusion. If you place the events in logical order, then the first conclusion can be called the **intermediate conclusion**. The second conclusion can be called the final conclusion to distinguish it from the intermediate conclusion. Alternatively, you might reserve the word *conclusion* for the final conclusion and call the intermediate conclusion another premise—just recognize that it's a claim that is supported by other premises, and that in turn supports the (final) conclusion.

**16**

Either way, how do you figure out which is which? Use the **Therefore Test**. Call the two claims A (he's likely to get caught) and B (he will probably end up in jail). Plug the two claims into two sentences using *because* and *therefore*, and ask yourself which one is true:

BECAUSE A (he's likely to get caught), THEREFORE B (he will probably end up in jail).

OR

BECAUSE B (he will probably end up in jail), THEREFORE A (he's likely to get caught).

(Using both *because* and *therefore* may seem like overkill, but it ensures that you keep the roles straight!) Which sentence makes more sense to you? The first scenario makes sense, but the second one doesn't. The fact that he will probably end up in jail should follow the *therefore*, so it is the final, real conclusion. The fact that he's likely to get caught follows the *because*, so it is only an intermediate conclusion.

In the burglar passage above, the three pieces were presented in logical progression: **premise–intermediate conclusion–final conclusion**. Arguments won't always follow this logical order, however; they might mix up the order and toss in additional information.

Try the Therefore Test with the job satisfaction argument. You have two possible conclusions:

1.  (A)…arguing that the new space will enhance worker productivity.

2.  (B) Thus, the owner concluded, exposure to natural light has a positive effect on workers' job satisfaction.

Which scenario makes more sense?

BECAUSE the new space will enhance worker productivity, THEREFORE exposure to natural light has a positive effect on workers' job satisfaction.

OR

BECAUSE exposure to natural light has a positive effect on workers' job satisfaction, THEREFORE the new space will enhance worker productivity.

The second scenario makes more sense, so B is the intermediate conclusion and A is the final conclusion.

As is typical of arguments with an intermediate conclusion, the premise supports the intermediate conclusion, which then supports the final conclusion:

A study found a correlation between natural lighting and job satisfaction.  The owner concludes that exposure to natural light causes better job satisfaction.  The owner then concludes that the new, light-filled space will enhance productivity.

Here's the original argument again:

The owner of a small publishing company plans to lease a new office space that has floor-to-ceiling windows and no internal walls, arguing that the new space will enhance worker productivity. The owner cites a recent study showing that workers exposed to natural light throughout the day tended to report, on average, a higher level of job satisfaction than did those who worked in office spaces that used fluorescent lighting. Thus, the owner concluded, exposure to natural light has a positive effect on workers' job satisfaction.

The argument begins with **background** information, then goes straight into the final **conclusion**. Next, you're given a **premise** followed by an **intermediate conclusion**.

As the argument above demonstrates, the logical structure of a GMAT argument can get a little complicated. If there is more than one logical step, make sure that your understanding is firm before you attempt to answer the question.

# Common Argument Types

GMAT arguments cover a variety of topics from business to biology to traffic patterns of cities. Although the topics are varied, many arguments feature similar logic. Some of the most common argument types are presented in this section.

Approach all arguments on the GMAT as a skeptical reader. As you read, consider the "what if" questions you would want to ask the author when evaluating whether you believe the author's conclusion. In the discussion of argument types below, some of the issues and questions that are most relevant for each type are provided.

### Causation

In causation arguments, circumstances are presented. The conclusion proposes a particular cause for that set of circumstances.

> In October, a local news station completed a redesign of its website. In November, the number of articles read on the website increased by 50 percent. Thus, the redesigned website clearly attracted more users or encouraged users to read more articles per visit.

For causation arguments, correct answer choices often relate to potential other causes for the observed result. In this case, the conclusion states that the redesign is responsible for the increase in articles read; you would want to consider what else might have caused the increase. For example, what if the news station provided extensive coverage of an important local election taking place in November?

### Plan

A plan proposes a course of action to achieve a specific goal. In a plan, the conclusion is the goal of the plan. The words *in order to* or simply *to* frequently precede the goal of the plan.

> Metropolis has experienced an increase in the amount of trash in its city parks. In order to reduce the amount of litter in the parks, Metropolis plans to double the number of trash cans in each city park.

A plan must work as expected to achieve its aim. A plan may fail if the steps of the plan don't work as anticipated or there are unexpected costs or hindrances not discussed in the original argument. In this case, the plan seeks to limit people from littering in the park by making trash cans more accessible. What if the litter in the park is actually blowing into the park from the surrounding streets and sidewalks?

### Prediction

Sometimes arguments conclude with a prediction of a future event.

> Rainfall totals were higher this year than they were last year in Eastown. Since wheat farmers rely on rain to irrigate their fields, yields of wheat per acre in Eastown will be higher than last year's yields.

16

In order for a prediction to come true, no other circumstances can intervene that might work against the prediction. In this case, the argument discusses only precipitation. How have temperatures this year affected wheat growth?

## Profit

When arguments discuss profit, the conclusion often states that profits will increase or decrease—in other words, profit arguments are frequently a sub-category of predictions. You are expected to know that Profit = Revenue − Cost. Often, arguments will discuss only one element of profit (either revenues or costs), whereas the answer choice will focus on the other component.

Not every argument will fit into one of these categories, and sometimes the lines between categories get blurry. You might read an argument that seems like a plan to increase profit. Don't stress if you are not sure how to classify an argument; instead, think of the classification as another tool that can help you understand the argument and lead you toward the right answer. In subsequent chapters, you will learn what to expect in answer choices for each type of argument for different question types.

# Answers to Pop Quiz

| 1. | Budget Fitness will grow its membership base by 10 percent in the next six months. | *This is a prediction about the future, so it is a claim, not a fact. This is a good candidate to be the conclusion.* |
|----|-----------------------------------------------------------------------------------|----------------------------------------------------------------------------------------------------------------------|
|    | Budget Fitness has recently crafted a clever ad campaign that it plans to air on several local radio stations. | *Budget Fitness already crafted the campaign—this is a fact. It is also a fact that the company currently "plans" to air the campaign (though whether it will actually air is uncertain, since that is a future event). This information supports the claim in the first sentence, so it is a premise.* |

(Task 1) The order of the parts is **conclusion–premise**. If you rewrite it as premise → conclusion, then you have something like this:

> BF has ad to air on radio → BF will grow members 10 percent in 6 mos

(Task 2) The author claims that the gym *will* increase its membership in the future *because* the company will launch an ad campaign. Presumably, the company thinks that this campaign will help attract new customers.

(Task 3) The argument assumes that the ad campaign will be effective in attracting new customers. (Note: There are often many assumptions contained in a given argument and many ways to word similar assumptions. The answer provided is just one example.)

16

| 2. | Last year, the Hudson Family Farm was not profitable. | *This is a fact; it already occurred in the past. This may be background info, a premise, or a counterpoint.* |
|---|---|---|
| | However, the farm will be profitable this year. | *The word* however *indicates a change in direction. This prediction is the opposite of what happened last year. This future prediction is a good candidate to be the conclusion, in which case the previous sentence would be a counterpoint.* |
| | The farm operators have planted cotton, rather than corn, in several fields. | *This is a fact. Hmm, why does it matter which crop the farm is planting?* |
| | Because cotton prices are expected to rise dramatically this year, the farm can expect larger revenues from cotton sales than it previously earned from corn. | *Okay, planting cotton will lead to more revenue than was earned last year. The author is using this information to support his conclusion in sentence 2.* |

(Task 1) The order of the parts is **counterpoint–conclusion–premise–premise**. Reordering as premises →
conclusion, you get this:

Cotton prices will be higher and the farm is planting cotton. → The farm will be profitable this year.

You might have been unsure about the third sentence. Does it really support the conclusion (**premise**)
or does it just describe the situation (**background**)? Don't worry too much about this distinction. There
are frequently sentences that could be classified either way. Your classification of this type of information is unlikely to influence your ability to answer the question correctly as long as you correctly
identify the conclusion.

(Task 2) The argument predicts that an unprofitable farm *will* become profitable *because* a change in
crops will result in higher revenues.

(Task 3) What about costs? The premise states that revenues will be higher, but revenues and profits are
not the same thing. The author assumes the costs associated with cotton are not high enough to cancel
out the increased revenues.

16

## Argument Structure Cheat Sheet

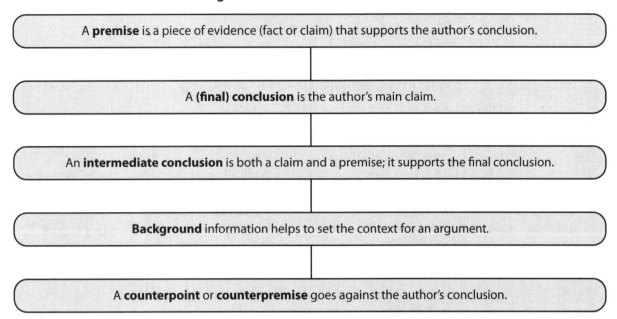

A **premise** is a piece of evidence (fact or claim) that supports the author's conclusion.

A **(final) conclusion** is the author's main claim.

An **intermediate conclusion** is both a claim and a premise; it supports the final conclusion.

**Background** information helps to set the context for an argument.

A **counterpoint** or **counterpremise** goes against the author's conclusion.

These building blocks will help you to understand the structure of an argument and answer the question.

When there is more than one conclusion or claim, use the **Therefore Test** to find the final conclusion. One of these two scenarios will work: either "*Because A is true, therefore B is true*" or "*Because B is true, therefore A is true.*" The claim that follows the *therefore* in the working scenario is the final, real conclusion.

# Problem Set

Identify the role of each sentence or major piece of information.

1. The school library currently depends heavily on donated books, which are often out of date or in poor condition. In order to encourage more students to use the library, the school administration has designated $10,000 of next year's budget to be used solely for the purchase of new books.

2. A program instituted by a state government to raise money allows homeowners to prepay their future property taxes at the current rate. Even if the government were to raise the tax rate in a subsequent year, any prepaid taxes would allow the homeowner to maintain taxes at the lower rate, lowering the overall property tax burden over time. For this reason, homeowners should participate in the program.

3. Tay-Sachs disease, a usually fatal genetic condition caused by the buildup of gangliocides in nerve cells, occurs more frequently among Ashkenazi Jews than among the general population. The age of onset is typically six months and generally results in death by the age of four.

4. The average level of physical fitness among students at North High School is likely to decline over the next few years. Due to recent changes in the way that the school calculates students' grades, earning a high grade in a physical education class will no longer improve a student's grade point average. Therefore, students who would otherwise have taken optional gym classes will be more likely to choose other electives in which earning a high grade is worth more points.

16

Determine whether each sentence or major piece of information is **part of the main argument** (a conclusion or premise) or **part of a counterargument** (a counterpoint). Then, determine what role the information plays in the main argument or counterargument: Is it a **conclusion** or a **premise**?

5.  Some critics have argued that the price of food and drink at Ultralux, a restaurant, is too high for the quality offered. However, Ultralux features a beautiful interior and comfortable seating. Research has shown that consumers actually perceive food and drink as being of higher quality when they are consumed in such a setting. Thus, the food and drink at Ultralux are reasonably priced.

6.  When compared to non-exercisers, people who exercise regularly also spend more time sitting or lying down in each 24-hour period. Because the risk of cancer and heart disease is higher among people who are more sedentary, doctors often recommend that their patients engage in regular physical exercise. However, since people who exercise are in fact often more sedentary than those who do not, this recommendation is counterproductive.

## Solutions

1.

| | |
|---|---|
| The school library currently depends heavily on donated books, which are often out of date or in poor condition. | **Background.** *This is a statement of fact. It doesn't directly support the conclusion, which is that more students will use the library in the future. Instead, it helps to explain why a particular plan was chosen (rather than supporting the conclusion that the plan will work).* |
| In order to encourage more students to use the library, | **Conclusion.** *This argument describes a plan. When an argument describes a plan, the outcome of the plan is the conclusion of the argument.* |
| the school administration has designated $10,000 of next year's budget to be used solely for the purchase of new books. | **Premise.** *This statement explains why more students will use the library. Any statement that helps explain why the conclusion is true is a premise, since it supports the conclusion.* |

2.

| | |
|---|---|
| A program instituted by a state government to raise money allows homeowners to prepay their future property taxes at the current rate. | **Background.** *This is a statement of fact. It isn't a premise, because it doesn't support the idea that homeowners should participate in the program—it just tells you what the program is.* |
| Even if the government were to raise the tax rate in a subsequent year, | **Counterpoint.** *In this part of the argument, the author is bringing up a potential problem with the argument: The government might raise taxes. Since this is something that might pose a problem for the argument, it's a counterpoint.* |
| any prepaid taxes would allow the homeowner to maintain taxes at the lower rate, lowering the overall property tax burden over time. | **Premise.** *The author now argues against the counterpoint. By showing that the counterpoint isn't actually a major issue, the author supports the main argument.* |
| For this reason, homeowners should participate in the program. | **Conclusion.** *This is what the author wants to convince you of. Notice that it has a* because … therefore *relationship with the rest of the argument: Because homeowners would have a lower tax burden, they should therefore participate in the program.* |

3.

| | |
|---|---|
| Tay-Sachs disease, a usually fatal genetic condition caused by the buildup of gangliocides in nerve cells, occurs more frequently among Ashkenazi Jews than among the general population. | **Premise (or Background).** *This is a tricky one. There actually isn't a conclusion in this argument! Normally, the key to spotting premises is to find statements that support the conclusion. But if there isn't a conclusion, that won't work. You'd probably see this "argument" in an Inference problem, which we'll look at later. For now, if you see an argument that doesn't have a conclusion, treat all of the statements in it like premises.* |
| The age of onset is typically six months and generally results in death by the age of four. | **Premise (or Background).** *Like the sentence above, this is a statement of fact, so it can't be a conclusion. This "argument" just consists of two facts and doesn't draw a conclusion from either of them. You'd only see this in an Inference problem, which we'll learn about later on. For now, think of both of these sentences as premises.* |

16

| 4. | The average level of physical fitness among students at North High School is likely to decline over the next few years. | *Conclusion.* *When you first read this, it may not be obvious that it's the main conclusion. You can't necessarily spot the conclusion until you've read the entire argument. This is the main conclusion because everything else in the argument supports it. For instance, the fact that students will take fewer gym classes supports the belief that students will become less physically fit.* |
| --- | --- | --- |
| | Due to recent changes in the way that the school calculates students' grades, earning a high grade in a physical education class will no longer improve a student's grade point average. | *Premise.* *This is a statement of fact, so it can't be a conclusion. It supports the intermediate conclusion (in the next sentence), by explaining why students will take fewer gym classes.* |
| | Therefore, students who would otherwise have taken optional gym classes will be more likely to choose other electives in which earning a high grade is worth more points. | *Intermediate conclusion.* *This sentence starts with* therefore, *and it's supported by the premise in the previous sentence. Don't be fooled! It isn't the main conclusion, because it supports the conclusion in the first sentence. If a statement is supported by part of the argument, but supports another part of the argument, it's an intermediate conclusion.* |

| 5. | Some critics have argued that the price of food and drink at Ultralux, a restaurant, is too high for the quality offered. | *Counterargument.* *This is the conclusion drawn by the critics, who the author of the argument disagrees with.* |
| --- | --- | --- |
| | However, Ultralux features a beautiful interior and comfortable seating. | *Main argument.* *This is one of the author's premises. It supports the point the author is making, which is that Ultralux actually isn't overpriced.* |
| | Research has shown that consumers actually perceive food and drink as being of higher quality when they are consumed in such a setting. | *Main argument.* *This is another one of the author's premises. It helps to explain why the author believes that Ultralux has fair prices.* |
| | Thus, the food and drink at Ultralux are reasonably priced. | *Main argument.* *This is the author's conclusion: It's the main point that the author's evidence supports.* |

16

| 6. | When compared to non-exercisers, people who exercise regularly also spend more time sitting or lying down in each 24-hour period. | ***Main argument.*** *It isn't obvious right away that this is part of the main argument. It's a fact, not an opinion, so it won't be the conclusion. Keep reading until you find the author's conclusion, which states that recommending exercise is counterproductive. Since this statement supports that conclusion, this is one of the author's premises.* |
|---|---|---|
| | Because the risk of cancer and heart disease is higher among people who are more sedentary, | ***Counterargument.*** *This is the reasoning used by doctors, who the author disagrees with. It supports the doctors' conclusion, so it's being used as a premise.* |
| | doctors often recommend that their patients engage in regular physical exercise. | ***Counterargument.*** *This is the doctors' recommendation. If an argument offers a recommendation and supports that recommendation with evidence, the recommendation itself is the conclusion. The author disagrees with this conclusion, so in this argument, this is a counterpoint.* |
| | However, since people who exercise are in fact often more sedentary than those who do not, | ***Main argument.*** *This is basically the same thing that the author said in the first sentence! It's just restated to make it clear that sitting or lying down equates to being sedentary. Just like the first sentence, this is a premise belonging to the author.* |
| | this recommendation is counterproductive. | ***Main argument.*** *This is what the author wants to convince you of! It's her conclusion. She disagrees with the doctors; her two premises explain why she disagrees.* |

16

# Methodology

## In This Chapter:

**In this chapter, you will learn** a 4-step process for use on all Critical Reasoning questions. The process will help you to identify the different question types, do the analysis required to reach the correct answer, and avoid trap answers.

# CHAPTER 17 **Methodology**

In the previous chapter, you learned about argument building blocks and examined how to *deconstruct* an argument in order to understand how the pieces of information are related. These tasks represent the first two steps of the overall 4-step approach for any Critical Reasoning problem.

Before diving into the 4-step process, let's discuss what you *don't* want to do. While you have a lot of flexibility in how you work your way through the problem, there are some approaches that are downright bad, such as this one:

1. Read the argument pretty quickly, don't write anything down, don't understand the big picture.

2. Read the question.

3. Realize you need to read the argument again in order to answer; reread the argument.

4. Reread the question.

5. Examine the answers, eliminating one or several.

6. Read the argument for the third time.

7. Eliminate another answer.

8. Start checking each remaining answer against the argument and rereading the argument.

9. Repeat until one answer is left.

What's the problem? That's incredibly inefficient! If you've ever taken any standardized test before, you know that these tests have serious time pressure. The GMAT is no exception. In fact, you need to average about 2 minutes per CR question. So what do you do instead?

Use Manhattan Prep's 4-step approach for all CR questions:

Step 1: Identify the question.

Step 2: Deconstruct the argument.

Step 3: State the goal.

Step 4: Work from wrong to right.

## Step 1: Identify the Question

Most arguments are followed by a question (you'll learn about one exception later). The wording of the question stem allows you to identify which type of question you're about to answer. You will need to employ different kinds of reasoning for different types of questions, so you want to know, right from the start, what kind of question you have.

There are three broad categories of Critical Reasoning questions: the **Structure-Based Family**, the **Assumption-Based Family**, and the **Evidence-Based Family**. Each of these families contains a few distinct question types. In later chapters, you'll learn how to identify all of the question types.

## The Structure-Based Family

These questions ask you to determine something based upon the building blocks of the argument. What pieces are included in the argument and how do they fit together?

| Question Type | Sample Question Phrasing | Goal |
|---|---|---|
| *Describe the Role* | In the argument given, the two boldface portions play which of the following roles? | Identify the roles (building blocks) of the boldface portions of the argument. |
| *Describe the Argument* | In the passage, the mayor challenges the council member's argument by doing which of the following? | Describe how a certain piece of information affects the argument. |

## The Assumption-Based Family

These questions all depend upon an understanding of the **assumptions** made by the author to reach a certain conclusion. As discussed in the last chapter, an assumption is something that the author *does not state* in the argument, but something that the author *must believe to be true* in order to draw the given conclusion. Without the assumption, the argument fails.

You'll learn much more about assumptions in future chapters; for now, take a look at this short example:

> Pedro received a higher score than Dan did on a recent algebra test. Therefore, Pedro is better at math than Dan.

You may have identified one or more logical jumps that the author had to make to get from the premise (higher score on an algebra test) to the conclusion (better at math). Assumptions fill these gaps in logic; they are what must be true for the conclusion to hold. Below are a couple examples of assumptions in this argument:

> Assumption: Scores on the algebra test are representative of overall math ability.

> Assumption: Dan and Pedro took the test under similar conditions (e.g., they were given the same amount of time).

If you were to insert an assumption into the argument, it would make the argument better:

> Pedro received a higher score than Dan did on a recent algebra test. Scores on the algebra test are representative of overall math ability. Therefore, Pedro is better at math than Dan.

An assumption should plug a hole in the argument. Most arguments on the GMAT rely on multiple assumptions, so inserting one assumption doesn't make the argument airtight. The assumption will be necessary to the argument; that is, if the assumption *isn't* true, the argument breaks down.

There are five types of Assumption Family questions, as shown below, which will be covered further in subsequent chapters:

| Question Type | Sample Question Phrasing | Goal |
| --- | --- | --- |
| *Find the Assumption* | The argument depends on which of the following assumptions? | Identify an unstated assumption. |
| *Strengthen the Argument* | Which of the following, if true, provides the most support for the argument above? | Identify a new piece of information that strengthens the author's argument. |
| *Weaken the Argument* | Which of the following, if true, most seriously weakens the argument? | Identify a new piece of information that weakens the author's argument. |
| *Evaluate the Argument* | Which of the following must be studied in order to evaluate the argument above? | Identify a piece of information that would help to determine the soundness of the argument. |
| *Find the Flaw* | Which of the following indicates a flaw in the reasoning above? | Identify something illogical in the argument. |

## The Evidence-Based Family

These arguments all lack conclusions; they consist entirely of premises. They also won't include any assumptions. You're asked to find something that *must be true* or something that *resolves a discrepancy* in order to answer the question. You'll learn more about both of these question types later in the book.

| Question Type | Sample Question Phrasing | Goal |
| --- | --- | --- |
| *Inference* | Which of the following can be logically concluded from the passage above? | Identify something that must be true based on the given information. |
| *Explain a Discrepancy* | Which of the following, if true, most helps to explain the surprising finding? | Identify a new piece of information that resolves some apparent paradox in the argument. |

This book also discusses a variation called Complete the Argument. This variation is not a different question type; rather, it's a different way of presenting one of the other question types.

As you go through each of the families and their question types, you will learn what kind of language signals specific question types—and so you'll know how to identify the question, the first step in the process.

# Step 2: Deconstruct the Argument

Now that you've identified the family and question type, you can use that information to deconstruct the argument. You began to learn how to do this in the prior chapter when you labeled arguments using the building block components.

At this stage, many people take a few light notes. If Critical Reasoning is already a strength for you and you don't write anything, then you may not need to start. If, on the other hand, you want to improve CR significantly, then making an argument map will likely be one of your necessary strategies.

Revisit the first argument from last chapter. As you deconstruct the argument, jot down an abbreviated map of the argument.

> The expansion of the runways at the Bay City Airport will allow larger planes to use the airport. These new planes will create a lot of noise, a nuisance for residents who live near the airport. However, many of the residents in this neighborhood work in construction, and the contract to expand the runways has been awarded to a local construction company. Thus, the expansion of the runways will lead to an increased quality of life for the residents of this neighborhood.

Here's one method of note-taking, idea by idea:

BC ↑ rnwy → ↑ P → > noise

BUT res work in constr [so work for them?]

© plan → better life for res

This map may seem cryptic by itself, but remember, you will always have access to the argument on your screen. You do not have to answer the question using only your notes. In fact, if you are taking too many notes, it can be helpful to imagine that you cannot use those notes to answer the question. The process of creating them is what matters.

Avoid writing down full sentences. Try to abbreviate dramatically, even reducing whole words to single letters on the fly, as was done above:

BC = Bay City Airport

↑ = expansion, larger

rnwy = runway

→ = therefore

> = more

P = planes

res = residents

constr = construction

If these abbreviations are too cryptic for you, of course, make them longer. But if you practice, you'll be amazed by how much you can abbreviate. Some of your abbreviations will be one-off creations; others you'll use all the time (e.g., a right arrow to mean *therefore*). The goal as you create these notes is not to re-create every detail of the argument, but rather to help your brain understand the argument in real time. An effective map will summarize the core of the argument, including the premises and the conclusion. Now that you've delineated the parts of the argument for yourself, you'll be in a better position to answer the question.

Here are a few tips for effective note-taking on the fly. First, most people would probably write down only the information from the first sentence first:

BC ↑ rnwy → ↑ P

Then, as you continue reading, you might realize that the second sentence follows from the first: Those bigger planes then cause more noise. As a result, you might choose to continue writing on the same line, even though the additional information is given in a separate sentence. In this fashion, you are linking together the parts of the argument.

Second, did you note the question in the brackets: *[so work for them?]* Why is that there? The argument says that many residents work in construction. It also says a local company was awarded the contract to do the work. Did you notice anything missing? The argument never actually said that the residents of this neighborhood work for the local construction company. That might be something to think about as you try to answer the question. Feel free to jot down any thoughts you have about the argument, in particular its holes, as you go. Just be sure to bracket those thoughts, so that you don't ever think they're part of the argument itself.

Not everyone writes this much; some people don't write anything at all. Throughout the examples in this book, you will see samples of sentence-by-sentence notes for a variety of arguments. Practice to determine what works best for you. At first, you might write down too much and get bogged down. Keep practicing for at least a few weeks; as you gain skill, you'll discover how quickly you can take useful, highly abbreviated notes.

## Step 3: State the Goal

This is a crucial step: What exactly are you trying to do when you answer this question? What's your goal? At this stage, you know what kind of question you have, you (hopefully) understand the argument and how it fits together, and you know the conclusion (if there is one). What's next?

In stating your goal, consider how the question type applies to the specific argument. Each question type requires a certain kind of reasoning and demands certain characteristics from the correct answer. For example, imagine that the question for the Bay City Airport argument asked:

Which of the following most strengthens the argument?

This is a **Strengthen the Argument** question; on these questions, you are looking for a new piece of information that makes the conclusion more likely to be true. You'll learn what to look for in correct answers for each question type as you work through this guide. What do you think of the following goal statements for the Bay City Airport argument?

- Which answer makes the conclusion more likely?
- Which answer makes it more likely that the runway expansion will improve quality of life in the neighborhood?

The first statement is too general; all it does is reiterate the general goal on Strengthen the Argument questions, and it provides no information about the conclusion you are trying to strengthen. The second, on the other hand, brings together the general goal with the specific conclusion of the argument. A more specific goal statement makes it easier to differentiate between answers that are related to the conclusion versus those that are not.

After you have stated your goal, spend a little time thinking about any issues you see in the argument. Are there any logical flaws? Are there other factors that are important to the conclusion but that the author has not mentioned? You may not identify issues on all arguments, but a little brainstorming can help as you move on to step 4.

# Step 4: Work from Wrong to Right

Finally, the answer choices! On GMAT Verbal in general, you're asked to find the "best" answer. You're going to use a 2-step process to do so:

1.  First, look through all five answers and eliminate as many "definitely wrong" answers as you can. Do *not* try to decide which is the *right* answer right now. Instead, concentrate on eliminating *wrong* answers.

2.  If you have only one answer left after this first pass, great; you're done. If you have two or more answers left, then compare those remaining answers.

Why do you want to attack the answers this way, "working from wrong to right"? By definition, finding the *best* answer is a comparison; if you spot a tempting wrong answer, you might not be able to spot what is wrong with it until you've read the right answer. It's most efficient to dump all of the "No way!" answers as fast as you can, and then directly compare the remaining, more tempting answers. Of course, there will always be only one right answer, but your final choice will be made easier if you have already eliminated the bad wrong answers.

Finally, remember one last tip for Verbal questions: When you've narrowed it down to two answers, compare those two answers just once more. Then pick and move on. Going back and forth multiple times is a waste of time—either you know it after comparing the first time or you don't.

When you work from wrong to right, it's critical to keep track of your thinking on your scrap paper. You need to decide how to write down ABCDE and how to notate your thoughts.

### Decision 1: How do I write down ABCDE?

| Option 1 | Pros | Cons |
| --- | --- | --- |
| Write ABCDE for each question. | Can write on/cross off each letter; can keep letters right next to map about argument. | Have to write 36 separate times as you proceed through the Verbal section. |

This option might look like this, if the first question is Weaken the Argument (noted with a W) and the second question is Strengthen the Argument (noted with an S):

W    A ~~B~~ C ~~D~~ E

notes
notes


S    A B ~~C~~ D E

notes
notes

| Option 2 | Pros | Cons |
|---|---|---|
| Write ABCDE at the top of the page, then move to a new line for each question. | Only have to write once for each page (several times for entire test). | Have to keep track "below" each letter; map might not be right next to answer tracking row. |

This option might look like the diagram below, in which the first question is Weaken and the second question is Strengthen. The scrap pad you'll be given is graph paper, so there will already be lines built in to separate the five answer choices.

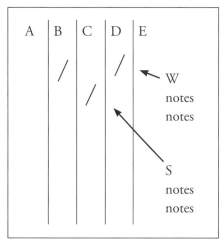

### Decision 2: What symbols will I use to keep track of my thoughts?

You need four symbols. You can use any symbols you prefer as long as you consistently use the same symbols:

    X or /    Definitely wrong

    ~    Maybe

    ?    I have no idea.

    ○    This is it!

Try using the this 4-step process on an actual problem:

> Many companies use automated telephone services: Callers hear a machine-generated voice and are able to select options using the numbers on the telephone keypad. Research shows that callers are more patient when the machine-generated voice is that of a woman. Thus, smaller companies that cannot afford an automated service should consider hiring women, rather than men, to interact with customers by phone.
>
> Which of the following, if true, would be most damaging to the conclusion above?
>
> (A) Automated telephone services are becoming cheaper and cheaper every year.
> (B) Patient customers tend to order more products and return fewer products than impatient customers.
> (C) A separate study indicated that the extra patience exhibited by callers is limited to interactions with an automated system.
> (D) Some customers prefer automated systems to talking with a live person.
> (E) On average, callers are only slightly more patient when interacting with a female voice, rather than a male voice, in an automated telephone system.

How did you do with each step? Did you identify the question type? Do you feel comfortable with your map, and did you identify the conclusion (if there is one)? Did you remember to state the goal (briefly) before looking at the answers? Did you use the 2-step process to assess the answer choices, working from wrong to right?

Here's how someone might work through the problem above, step-by-step. The table displays text from the problem, the student's thoughts, and the relevant notes on scrap paper:

### Step 1: Identify the Question

| Argument | Thoughts | Paper |
| --- | --- | --- |
| Which of the following, if true, would be most damaging to the conclusion above? | Most damaging to the conclusion *means this is a Weaken. I need to find the conclusion, and I need to think about what flaws or gaps might exist in the argument.* | W <br><br> A <br> B <br> C <br> D <br> E |

### Step 2: Deconstruct the Argument

| Argument | Thoughts | Paper |
| --- | --- | --- |
| Many companies use automated telephone services: | *Sounds like background, but I'll jot down a note anyway.* | auto phone |
| Callers hear a machine-generated voice and are able to select options using the numbers on the telephone keypad. | *This is describing what an automated phone system is; I probably don't need to write that down.* | |
| Research shows that callers are more patient when the machine-generated voice is that of a woman. | *This is a fact, not a claim, so it has to be either a premise or counter-premise. It's probably a premise, since there's only one sentence left.* | Res: female = ↑ patience |
| Thus, smaller companies that cannot afford an automated service should consider hiring women, rather than men, to interact with customers by phone. | *This is the only claim, so it's the conclusion. Now I can go back and add a Ⓒ to the conclusion in my map and a + to the premise.* | Small co's → use women phone |

The final map might look something like this:

W      A B C D E

auto phone

+ Res: female = ↑ patience

© Small co's → use women phone

Your map might look very different from the map above. That's perfectly fine as long as your map conveys to you the basic flow of information clearly and concisely as you put it together. Remember, the map is most useful as you make it, not as you look at it later.

## Step 3: State the Goal

The question is a Weaken question, so briefly restate the main reasoning and conclusion of the argument. Once you have stated your specific goal, do a little brainstorming about any concerns you have with the argument.

> *Small companies should hire women to answer the phones, because callers are more patient when hearing automated female voices.*
>
> *How would I weaken this specific argument? What would make it less likely that companies should hire women to answer phones?*
>
> *Hmm. The evidence is about automated female voices, while the conclusion is about real women. Is there any kind of disconnect there?*

## Step 4: Work from Wrong to Right

Now, attack the answers!

| Argument | Thoughts | Paper |
|---|---|---|
| (A) Automated telephone services are becoming cheaper and cheaper every year. | *The conclusion discusses what companies should do when they can't afford automated services. This choice addresses those who can buy the service, so it's irrelevant to the argument.* | A̶ |
| (B) Patient customers tend to order more products and return fewer products than impatient customers. | *This is a good reason for the company to do whatever it can to keep its customers in a patient mood. If anything, that would strengthen the argument.* | B̶ |
| (C) A separate study indicated that the extra patience exhibited by callers is limited to interactions with an automated system. | *Hmm. This highlights a distinction between automated and live voices... Does that distinction have anything to do with the argument? Well, the conclusion only talks about hiring actual people, but it looks like all of the evidence is about automated systems. That could be a problem for the argument. Keep this one in.* | C ~ |
| (D) Some customers prefer automated systems to talking with a live person. | *This argument is about only those companies that can't afford the system and are using real people. Nope, this isn't it.* | D̶ |
| (E) On average, callers are only slightly more patient when interacting with a female voice, rather than a male voice, in an automated telephone system. | *This one seems to be telling me there isn't a huge difference between hearing male and female voices—but there is still a small positive effect for female voices. If anything, this strengthens the argument; after all, as a small business owner, I'll take any necessary steps that will get me more business! I've crossed off four answers, so (C) is the correct answer.* | E̶ |

At the end, the answer choice letters on your paper would look like this:

A̶  B̶  Ⓒ  D̶  E̶

# Exercise: Identify the Question

Warm up by matching each Critical Reasoning question stem to the type of question it's asking:

1. Which of the following indicates a vulnerability of the argument above?  G

2. Which of the following, if true, most strongly suggests that the plan will fail to achieve its desired outcome?  E

3. In the argument given, the boldfaced portion plays which of the following roles?  A

4. In the passage above, the biologist responds to the journalist's claim by doing which of the following?  B

5. Which of the following, if true, would best explain the garden snail's paradoxical behavior?  I

6. Which of the following conclusions is most strongly supported by the statements given?  H

7. Which of the following would be most useful to research in order to assess the likelihood that the teacher's claim is correct?  F

8. Which of the following, if true, would provide the strongest justification for the mayor's conclusion?  D

9. Which of the following is an assumption on which the school board's argument depends?  C

| (A) Describe the Role | (D) Strengthen the Argument | (G) Find the Flaw |
| (B) Describe the Argument | (E) Weaken the Argument | (H) Inference |
| (C) Find the Assumption | (F) Evaluate the Argument | (I) Explain a Discrepancy |

17

Ready? Here are the answers to the exercise:

1. **(G):** The right answer to a Find the Flaw problem will point out, in general terms, a vulnerability or logical problem with the argument.

2. **(E):** If an argument describes a plan, the outcome of the plan is the conclusion of the argument. Weakening the argument means showing that the plan might fail.

3. **(A):** Describe the Role problems are the only problems in which parts of the argument appear in bold.

4. **(B):** A Describe the Argument problem asks you to describe the logic of someone's argument in more general terms.

5. **(I):** Explain a Discrepancy problems often refer to a surprise, paradox, or unusual finding in the question stem. Your task is to explain why it occurred.

6. **(H):** This question stem implies that the conclusion will be in the answer choices, not in the argument itself. This makes it an Inference problem. Be careful not to confuse this with a Strengthen the Argument question, which might also use the word *support!*

7. **(F):** Evaluate the Argument questions ask you to find the most useful question to ask or topic to research.

8. **(D):** Providing a justification for an argument is the same as strengthening that argument.

9. **(C):** Find the Assumption questions will ask you to find an assumption made by the author or something upon which the argument relies.

**Methodology Cheat Sheet**

| | |
|---|---|
| **Identify**<br>the Question | You'll learn how to do this in later chapters.<br><br>The question type indicates what kind of information you can expect to find in the argument and what kind of reasoning will help to answer the question. |
| **Deconstruct**<br>the Argument | Break the argument down into its building blocks.<br><br>Make a very abbreviated map showing both the details and the "flow" of the information. |
| State the **Goal** | Very briefly articulate your goal based upon this question type (again, you'll learn the goals for each type in later chapters). |
| Work from<br>**Wrong** to **Right** | Plan to go through the answers twice.<br><br>On the first pass, focus on eliminating anything that is definitely wrong; leave everything else in.<br><br>On the second pass, compare any choices that remain, then pick. |

Know how you're going to keep track of your answers on your scrap paper. First, decide whether to have a separate ABCDE grid for each problem or whether to use the "write once per page" method described earlier in the chapter. Second, make sure you have four consistent symbols for these four labels:

1. Definitely wrong
2. Maybe
3. I have no idea.
4. This is it!

**17**

# Problem Set

Map each argument on your paper, identifying the conclusion (if one exists) and the premise(s).

1. The overwhelming majority of advertisers prefer not to have their products associated with *premise* controversial content. In order to increase its advertising revenue, a large blogging platform plans to stop placing advertisements on blogs that deal with controversial topics, thus attracting *premise* advertisers who would otherwise be reluctant to advertise on the platform. *conclusion*

2. A series of research studies has reported that flaxseed oil can have a beneficial effect in reducing *premise* tumor growth in mice, particularly the kind of tumor found in human postmenopausal breast cancer. Thus, flaxseed oil should be recommended as an addition to the diets of all postmenopausal women. *conclusion*

3. During the past 30 years, the percentage of the population that smokes cigarettes has consistently *premise* declined. During the same time period, however, the number of lung cancer deaths attributed to smoking cigarettes has increased. *counter*

4. The Chinese white dolphin is a territorial animal that rarely strays far from its habitat in the Pearl *premise* River Delta. In recent years, increasing industrial and agricultural runoff to the delta's waters has *premise* caused many white dolphins to perish before they reach breeding age. Unless legislation is enacted to ensure there is no further decline in the delta's water quality, the Chinese white dolphin will become extinct. *conclusion*

5. Most doctors recommend consuming alcohol only in moderation, since the excessive intake of *premise* alcohol has been linked to several diseases of the liver. Drinking alcohol is no more dangerous for the liver, however, than abstaining from alcohol entirely. Last year, more nondrinkers than drinkers were diagnosed with liver failure. *counter* *counter*

6. To increase the productivity of the country's workforce, the government should introduce new *premise* *conclusion* food guidelines that recommend a vegetarian diet. A study of thousands of men and women *premise* revealed that those who stick to a vegetarian diet have IQs that are approximately five points higher than those who regularly eat meat. The vegetarians were also more likely to have earned advanced degrees and hold high-paying jobs. *premise*

# Solutions

Note: The sample maps shown below represent one style of map. Just make sure that your map is legible and concise and that it conveys the main points in a way that makes sense to you.

1.

| Argument | Thoughts | Paper |
|---|---|---|
| The overwhelming majority of advertisers prefer not to have their products associated with controversial content. | *This is a fact. It could be background. Or, if it supports the conclusion, it's a premise.* | Adv: controv = bad |
| In order to increase its advertising revenue, | *Somebody is trying to increase revenue. That sounds like a goal. When the argument describes a plan, I can think of the goal of that plan as the conclusion.* | Ⓒ Adv rev ↑ |
| a large blogging platform plans to stop placing advertisements on blogs that deal with controversial topics, | *This is a premise describing how the goal will be achieved.* | Plan: no ads on controv blogs |
| thus attracting advertisers who would otherwise be reluctant to advertise on the platform. | *This is the result of the previous premise, and it supports the conclusion. This is an intermediate conclusion.* | Plan: no ads on controv blogs → more adv |

The structure of this argument is **premise–conclusion–premise–intermediate conclusion**.

2.

| Argument | Thoughts | Paper |
|---|---|---|
| A series of research studies has reported that flaxseed oil can have a beneficial effect in reducing tumor growth in mice, particularly the kind of tumor found in human postmenopausal breast cancer. | *This is a fact. It's either background or a premise.* | Res: flax helps ↓ tumor mice esp postmen b-cancer |
| Thus, flaxseed oil should be recommended as an addition to the diets of all postmenopausal women. | *Definitely the conclusion.* | Ⓒ Postmen women shd take flax |

The structure of this argument is **premise–conclusion**.

3.

| Argument | Thoughts | Paper |
|---|---|---|
| During the past 30 years, the percentage of the population that smokes cigarettes has consistently declined. | *This is a fact. It's either background or a premise.* | 30y: percent pop smoke cig ↓ steady |
| During the same time period, however, the number of lung cancer deaths attributed to smoking cigarettes has increased. | *Another fact, so another premise. There isn't a conclusion.* | Same time: lung canc dead from cig ↑ |

The structure of this argument is **premise–premise**. Remember, not all GMAT arguments contain conclusions.

**17**

4.

| Argument | Thoughts | Paper |
|---|---|---|
| The Chinese white dolphin is a territorial animal that rarely strays far from its habitat in the Pearl River Delta. | *This is a fact. It's either background or a premise.* | Dolphin stays in delta |
| In recent years, increasing industrial and agricultural runoff to the delta's waters has caused many white dolphins to perish before they reach breeding age. | *This is also a fact—either background or premise.* | Recent: ind + ag in delta → dolphin dies b4 breed |
| Unless legislation is enacted to ensure there is no further decline in the delta's water quality, the Chinese white dolphin will become extinct. | *And here's the conclusion. [Note: H2O here is an abbreviation for water, based on the chemical formula $H_2O$.]* | IF govt doesn't fix H2O → dolphin extinct |

The structure of this argument is **premise–premise–conclusion**.

5.

| Argument | Thoughts | Paper |
|---|---|---|
| Most doctors recommend consuming alcohol only in moderation, since the excessive intake of alcohol has been linked to several diseases of the liver. | *This is a fact. It's either background or a premise.* | Drs rec ↓ alc bc ↑ alc → liver dis |
| Drinking alcohol is no more dangerous for the liver, however, than abstaining from alcohol entirely. | *Oh, this has the word however! The last sentence was a counterpremise, and this one sounds like the conclusion.* | © Drink not worse than abstain |
| Last year, more nondrinkers than drinkers were diagnosed with liver failure. | *This supports the previous sentence; it's a premise. (It also seems pretty flawed. What **percentage** of nondrinkers vs. drinkers had liver disease?)* | Last yr: more nondrink had liv dis |

The structure of this argument is **counterpremise–conclusion–premise**.

6.

| Argument | Thoughts | Paper |
|---|---|---|
| To increase the productivity of the country's workforce, the government should introduce new food guidelines that recommend a vegetarian diet. | *This is definitely a claim. It sounds like a conclusion, though I don't know for sure yet.* | Govt shd rec veg to ↑ wrkr prod |
| A study of thousands of men and women revealed that those who stick to a vegetarian diet have IQs that are approximately five points higher than those who regularly eat meat. | *This is a fact—the results of a study. It also supports the claim above, so it's a premise.* | Study: veg ↑ IQ than non-veg |
| The vegetarians were also more likely to have earned advanced degrees and hold high-paying jobs. | *This is another premise supporting the first sentence.* | Veg > better schl + high pay |

The structure of this argument is **conclusion–premise–premise**.

**Tip:** When first learning this method, many people write too much. As part of your review, ask yourself, "Did I write this down in the most effective way? Did my map make sense? Did I write down something that I could have skipped, or did I use too many words when I could have abbreviated more?" If you were really off the mark, write out the map again in a more ideal way—and articulate to yourself why this new way is better than the old way.

17

# Structure-Based Family

## In This Chapter:

- Describe the Role

- Describe the Argument

- Exercise: Understanding Answer Choices

- Describe the Role Cheat Sheet

- Describe the Argument Cheat Sheet

**In this chapter, you will learn** how to answer Critical Reasoning question types testing your ability to deconstruct arguments and to identify the role played by specific information or the logic underlying the argument.

# CHAPTER 18 Structure-Based Family

In the first two chapters of this unit, you examined the building blocks of arguments and learned the 4-step approach for tackling any Critical Reasoning question:

Step 1: Identify the question.

Step 2: Deconstruct the argument.

Step 3: State the goal.

Step 4: Work from wrong to right.

Now, you're going to begin tackling the first of the three main Critical Reasoning families: the Structure-Based questions. As the name implies, these questions require you to understand the structure of the argument. What kinds of building blocks are present in the argument? What role does each building block play?

There are two main Structure question types: **Describe the Role** and **Describe the Argument**.

## Describe the Role

Of the two types, Describe the Role is more common. These problems present a standard argument, with one or two portions in **boldface** font. You are asked to describe the *role* that each portion of boldface font plays.

**Role** is just another term for concepts you already know. A bolded portion could be a premise, a conclusion, a counterpremise, an intermediate conclusion, or background information. It could also be a counterconclusion or opposing conclusion, which goes against the author's main conclusion. You might think of this as the final claim of the *other* side of the argument.

These question types are easy to identify, because one or (usually) two statements will be presented in boldface font and the question stem will include the word *boldface*.

You're going to learn two methods to determine the role of each boldface statement. The Primary Method will always work, but it may be a little more complicated and time-consuming to use. The Secondary Method will allow you to narrow down the answer choices more easily but may not get you all the way to one answer—that is, you may have to guess from a narrowed set of answers. Regardless of the method you use, do still read and deconstruct the argument before moving on to classifying the boldface statements.

| Primary Method |
| --- |
| Classify each statement in boldface as one of the following three things: |
| 1. (C) The author's **conclusion** |
| 2. (P) A **premise** (it supports the author's conclusion) |
| 3. (X) **Something else** (maybe a counterpremise, background information, acknowledgment of a weakness in the argument...) |

In your notes, you'll classify each statement using the labels C, P, or X, as described above. When you evaluate the answer choices, you'll look for language that matches your labels.

Try this example:

> CEO: Now that Apex Corporation has begun to compete in our market, investors are expecting us to cut our prices to maintain market share. I don't believe this is necessary, however, because the market is growing rapidly and **a certain percentage of customers will always pay more for high-quality products**.
>
> In the argument above, the portion in boldface plays which of the following roles?

How does this argument work? First, the CEO states that investors are expecting a certain action, but she disagrees. She then provides two pieces of evidence intended to support her opinion: The market is growing and some number of customers are willing to pay higher prices. The boldface portion, then, is a premise: It supports the CEO's conclusion that the company does not need to cut prices in order to maintain market share.

Next, look for a P among the answer choices. The answer choices tend to be written in a difficult, abstract style. For example, some answers might read:

(A) The statement is evidence that has been used to weaken a claim made by the argument.

(B) The statement has been used to support a claim made by the argument.

(C) The statement is the primary claim made in the argument.

Start with the most basic piece: a building block. The word *claim* is typically a synonym for the conclusion. The first answer says that the statement weakens the conclusion. Something used to weaken the conclusion is a counterpremise; such a statement would be labeled X, not P. Choice (A) is not the correct answer.

The second answer talks about something that *supports a claim*. Since the claim is the conclusion, this answer choice does indeed describe a P, or premise, supporting the conclusion. This is probably the correct answer, but check choice (C) just to make sure.

The third answer describes the conclusion itself, not a premise supporting the conclusion. This choice is incorrect, so choice (B) is the correct answer.

You may have noticed that all the answer choices refer to how the statement relates to *the argument*. On the GMAT, when an answer choice refers to *the argument*, it refers to the perspective of the person making the argument. For instance, this argument is made by the CEO, even though it also describes the perspective of investors. If an answer choice says that a sentence *supports the argument*, it must support the perspective of the CEO, not the investors. Describe the Role questions often feature multiple perspectives; be careful to keep the different perspectives straight.

**18**

If you can use this method accurately, you will be able to eliminate the four wrong answers and get to the right answer. You might take too much time to do so, though, because of the strange format of the answers (and don't forget that the official questions typically have two boldface statements, not just one). The Secondary Method may allow you to get rid of some answers more quickly. Find the conclusion first, then ask yourself these three questions:

| Secondary Method |
| --- |
| 1. Is the statement a *fact* or an *opinion*? |
| 2. Is the statement *for* or *against* the conclusion? |
| 3. If there are two statements, are they on the *same* side of the fence or *opposite* sides? |

> **Strategy Tip:** You can use the same side/opposite side trick with the Primary Method, too: C's and P's are on one side, while X's are on the other.

As with the Primary Method, you then look in the answer choices for matching language. How would this method work on the problem from above? The boldface statement is an *opinion* (she hasn't cited actual evidence from customers to support the claim). In addition, the statement is *for* the conclusion. The problem had only one statement, so the third question doesn't apply.

Next, check the answer choices. The word *evidence* typically indicates a fact, not an opinion, so answer (A) is likely incorrect. Answers (B) and (C) both describe claims, or opinions, and both are for the conclusion, so the Secondary Method wouldn't necessarily allow you to choose between the two. (In this case, you might notice the distinction between a conclusion and a premise and be able to choose the correct answer. This problem, though, is on the easier side.)

## Common Trap Answers

The most tempting trap answers on Role questions tend to be "off" by just one word, often at the end of the sentence. For example, imagine that you've decided the first boldface is a premise in support of the author's conclusion. A tempting wrong answer might read:

> (A) The first **[boldface statement]** provides evidence in support of the position that the argument seeks to reject.

Every word of that answer matches what you want to find with the exception of the very last word, *reject*. In fact, if you changed that one word, the answer would be correct:

> (A) The first **[boldface statement]** provides evidence in support of the position that the argument seeks to establish.

The first version of the answer choice says that the first boldface is a premise in support of some *counter*conclusion. That's not the kind of premise you want! Read every word carefully, all the way to the end of each answer choice.

18

## Putting It All Together

Try a full example:

> Mathematician: Recently, Zubin Ghosh made headlines when he was recognized to have solved the Hilbert Conjecture. Ghosh posted his work on the internet, rather than submitting it to established journals. In fact, **he has no job, let alone a university position**; he lives alone and has refused all acclaim. In reporting on Ghosh, the press unfortunately has reinforced the popular view that mathematicians are antisocial loners. But **mathematicians clearly form a tightly knit community**, frequently collaborating on important efforts; indeed, teams of researchers are working together to extend Ghosh's findings.

> In the argument above, the two portions in boldface play which of the following roles?

> (A) The first is an observation the author makes to illustrate a social pattern; the second is a generalization of that pattern.

> (B) The first is evidence in favor of the popular view expressed in the argument; the second is a brief restatement of that view.

> (C) The first is a specific example of a generalization that the author contradicts; the second is a reiteration of that generalization.

> (D) The first is a specific counterexample to a generalization that the author asserts; the second is that generalization.

> (E) The first is a judgment that counters the primary assertion expressed in the argument; the second is a circumstance on which that judgment is based.

### Step 1: Identify the Question

| In the argument above, the two portions in boldface play which of the following roles? | *This is a Role question. The argument contains bold font, and the question stem contains the words* boldface *and* role. | R <br><br> A <br> B <br> C <br> D <br> E |
| --- | --- | --- |

### Step 2: Deconstruct the Argument

| Mathematician: Recently, Zubin Ghosh made headlines when he was recognized to have solved the Hilbert Conjecture. | *A past fact—this is likely background. Still, jot down a note.* | M: Ghosh solved conjecture |
| --- | --- | --- |
| Ghosh simply posted his work on the internet, rather than submitting it to established journals. | *Sounds like more background.* | posted on int |
| In fact, **he has no job, let alone a university position**; he lives alone and has refused all acclaim. | *Here's the first boldface. He's not a mathematician; that's surprising. Still, I don't know what the conclusion is, so I don't know what role this sentence is playing.* | No job |

| | | |
|---|---|---|
| In reporting on Ghosh, the press unfortunately has reinforced the popular view that mathematicians are antisocial loners. | *So the first boldface is evidence of* the popular view *that mathematicians are loners… but the sentence also uses the word* unfortunately, *so it sounds like the author doesn't agree…* | Press: math = loners |
| But **mathematicians clearly form a tightly knit community**, frequently collaborating on important efforts; indeed, teams of researchers are working together to extend Ghosh's findings. | *I was right; the author disagrees. The author's conclusion is this second boldface statement, so I can label it with a* Ⓒ. | Ⓒ BUT math = commun, collab |
| | *Now, what about that first boldface statement? It's not the conclusion, and it doesn't support the conclusion, so it must be an X: something else.* | R<br>A<br>B<br>C<br>D<br>E<br><br>Ghosh solved conjecture posted on int Ⓧ No job Press: math = loners Ⓒ BUT math = commun, collab |

## Step 3: State the Goal

The first boldface statement is an X; that is, it is neither the conclusion nor a premise. In this case, it supports the alternate point of view, so call it a counterpremise. It goes against the conclusion. The second boldface statement is a C; it is the author's conclusion.

Remind yourself:

> *In the right answer, the first statement will be consistent with an X label and the second statement will be consistent with a C label. I'm looking for an XC combo, and those two labels are on opposite sides.*

### Step 4: Work from Wrong to Right

| | | |
|---|---|---|
| (A) The first is an observation the author makes to illustrate a social pattern; the second is a generalization of that pattern. | *Hmm. I'm not 100 percent sure what they mean by* illustrate a social pattern, *but the description of the two statements here makes them sound like they're on the same "side"—the first illustrates something, and the second generalizes that same thing. I want an "opposite sides" answer.* | ~~A~~ |
| (B) The first is evidence in favor of the popular view expressed in the argument; the second is a brief restatement of that view. | *The first supports a popular view … okay, maybe. You could call the press view the popular view. Oh, but then it says that the second restates that same view. These two are on the same side again, and I want an opposite sides answer.* | ~~B~~ |
| (C) The first is a specific example of a generalization that the author contradicts; the second is a reiteration of that generalization. | *"The first is a [something] that the author contradicts." The [something] part confuses me, but I agree that the author contradicts the first one; this is a good description of a "label X" statement. Hmm. The second repeats that generalization—the same one mentioned in the first statement? No, I'm looking for opposite sides, not a repetition.* | ~~C~~ |
| (D) The first is a specific counterexample to a generalization that the author asserts; the second is that generalization. | *The first is a counterexample to something the author says? Yes, that accurately describes a "label X." The second is that generalization. I crossed off the last one for this same language. But wait … which generalization is this referring to this time? Oh, a generalization that the author asserts; that's the conclusion, which is a "label C." Leave this answer in.* | D $\sim$ |
| (E) The first is a judgment that counters the primary assertion expressed in the argument; the second is a circumstance on which that judgment is based. | *Counters language—yes, the first statement does counter the conclusion, which is consistent with the label X. That judgment = the first boldface. The second is not something on which the first one is based—that would be same side, and I want opposite sides.* | ~~E~~ |

$$\text{~~A~~} \quad \text{~~B~~} \quad \text{~~C~~} \quad \text{(D)} \quad \text{~~E~~}$$

The correct answer is (D).

## Common Trap Answers

### Half Right

The test writers try to set some traps for you on incorrect Describe the Role answers. For example, one of the descriptions might match one of the boldface statements, but the other one won't match. Several of the wrong answers in the last problem were **Half Right** in this way.

### One Word Off

In addition, a very tricky trap answer might be wrong by just one word; we call this the **One Word Off** trap. For example, you might be looking for a premise that supports the conclusion. The answer choice might say, "The first boldface supports a claim that the argument as a whole argues against."

What does that really mean? This choice says that the boldface supports a counterconclusion, not the author's conclusion—but you wouldn't know until you read the very last word of the sentence. In fact, if you changed the word *against* to the word *for*, then the choice would be describing a premise in support of the conclusion!

# Describe the Argument

Describe the Argument questions can be similar to Role questions: Both often offer "abstract" answer choices based on the *structure* of the argument, perhaps referring to the various building blocks (conclusions, premises, and so on). The majority of these Argument questions will offer two competing points of view in a dialogue format. Then, you might be asked how the second person responds to the first person's argument.

Important note: Other question types can also be presented in this "two people speaking" format—the mere existence of two speakers does not make the problem a Describe the Argument problem. *Always identify the question type using the question stem.*

A minority of these questions will offer just one point of view and ask you how the author of that argument develops his or her point of view.

Common question formulations include:

> Baram responds to Sadie's argument by . . .
>
> Baram challenges Sadie's argument by . . .
>
> The author develops the argument by doing which of the following?

These all indicate that you have a Describe the Argument question.

Your task is to determine how a particular part of the text was constructed. When the text is a dialogue between two people, read and deconstruct the first person's complete argument just as you would do for any other GMAT argument. Next, examine the response and figure out which piece of the argument the response attacks.

Try an example:

> Baram: I need to learn the names of 100 muscles for the anatomy exam in two hours. I've just memorized 5 of them in 5 minutes, so I only need 95 more minutes to study. Therefore, I'll have plenty of time to memorize everything and get a perfect score on the test.
>
> Sadie: Are you sure? Perhaps the more you memorize, the harder it gets.
>
> Sadie responds to Baram by

What is Baram's argument? What is his conclusion and how does he support it?

> must learn 100 names in 2h
>
> mem 5 in 5m, so need 95m
>
> © will get 100 percent

Which part does Sadie attack? Does she attack the conclusion directly? No, but her words certainly cast doubt on Baram's eventual conclusion. She attacks Baram's assumption that he can maintain the same rate of learning, 1 name every minute, for all 100 names. He doesn't explicitly state that he can maintain that rate, but he clearly believes it to be true. The correct answer might be something like:

> Sadie calls into question an assumption Baram makes about the efficacy of his plan.

This answer addresses the appropriate part of the argument—an assumption that Baram makes about his plan. An incorrect answer might look something like:

> Sadie introduces new evidence that contradicts one of Baram's premises.

Sadie does say something new, but does it rise to the level of evidence? She only suggests that his memorization rate might not be constant; she doesn't prove that it is not. While you might be able to argue that the word *evidence* is okay, the word *contradicts* clearly takes things too far. Sadie does not definitively contradict Baram's premise that he will need only 95 more minutes; rather, she raises a question as to *whether* he can memorize the words in only 95 minutes.

Ultimately, the attack is designed to find fault with the conclusion, but don't assume that the second person is attacking the conclusion directly. Tearing down any piece of the argument would ultimately undermine the conclusion, so find the piece that the second person most directly attacks.

You probably won't be able to anticipate the exact wording of the correct answer, but if you can identify the part of the argument addressed, then you are in a much better position to identify the appropriate "matching" language in the correct answer.

Try a full example:

> Mayor: The recycling program costs us nearly $1 million to operate every year, and our budget shortfall this year is projected to be $5 million. Cutting the recycling program will help balance the budget.
>
> Consumer Advocate: It costs the city more to throw something out than to recycle it.
>
> The consumer advocate responds to the mayor by

(A)  establishing that the mayor's figures were incorrectly calculated

(B)  accepting the mayor's conclusion but questioning the legality of the plan

(C)  interpreting the mayor's evidence in a way that reduces the validity of the mayor's claim

(D)  introducing a new piece of information that calls into question the validity of the mayor's conclusion

(E)  pointing out that the mayor has not adequately considered the potential causes and effects of the budget shortfall

### Step 1: Identify the Question

| The consumer advocate responds to the mayor by | *This is a Describe the Argument question. Two people are talking, and I have to explain how one responds to the other.* | DA<br>A<br>B<br>C<br>D<br>E |
| --- | --- | --- |

### Step 2: Deconstruct the Argument

| Mayor: The recycling program costs us nearly $1 million to operate every year, and our budget shortfall this year is projected to be $5 million. | *The mayor is stating a couple of facts—recycling costs $1m and they're going to miss their budget by $5m.* | M: Recyc cost $1m; this yr $5m short |
| --- | --- | --- |

| | | |
|---|---|---|
| Cutting the recycling program will help balance the budget. | *So the mayor suggests that they cut the R program in order to help balance the budget.* | → Cut R → bal budg © |
| Consumer Advocate: It costs the city more to throw something out than to recycle it. | *That's interesting. The advocate says that it costs even more to throw something out. Why does this matter? If you can't recycle something, what are you going to do with it instead? Probably throw it out.* | Advoc: Throw away costs > R |

## Step 3: State the Goal

For Describe the Argument questions, you have to address how some part of the argument is made: in this case, how the consumer advocate responds to the mayor. First, it sounds as if the advocate thinks that the mayor's plan isn't going to work since the advocate says that throwing stuff out is more costly than recycling it. If that's true, then the plan to cut the recycling program just got a bit worse—it might not actually achieve the ultimate goal, which is to save money and balance the budget.

State your goal briefly to yourself before going to the answers:

*The answer I find should indicate that the consumer advocate disagrees with the mayor, specifically questioning whether the suggested action (cutting the recycling program) will result in the desired outcome (saving money, helping to balance the budget).*

## Step 4: Work from Wrong to Right

| | | |
|---|---|---|
| (A) establishing that the mayor's figures were incorrectly calculated | *The consumer advocate doesn't say anything about the mayor's figures— in fact, the advocate doesn't dispute the mayor's evidence at all. Rather, the advocate attacks the mayor's assumption that cutting the program will lead to balancing the budget.* | ~~A~~ |
| (B) accepting the mayor's conclusion but questioning the legality of the plan | *The advocate doesn't accept the conclusion, nor does the advocate say anything about legality. Rather, the advocate questions whether the plan will really lead to saving money.* | ~~B~~ |
| (C) interpreting the mayor's evidence in a way that reduces the validity of the mayor's claim | *Hmm. Maybe. The advocate does reduce the validity of the mayor's claim. I'm not 100 percent sure what* interpreting the evidence *means. I'll leave this in for now.* | C ~ |
| (D) introducing a new piece of information that calls into question the validity of the mayor's conclusion | *The advocate does call the mayor's conclusion into question, yes. Oh, I see—this one is better than answer (C) because the advocate does introduce a new piece of info (that it costs more to throw something away).* | D ~ |
| (E) pointing out that the mayor has not adequately considered the potential causes and effects of the budget shortfall | *This one is tricky. It's true that the mayor hasn't fully considered the potential effects of the plan to cut the recycling program—but that's not what this choice says. It talks about the causes and effects of the budget shortfall.* | ~~E~~ |

18

On the first pass, choices (C) and (D) were left in, but a direct comparison showed that choice (D) was better than (C). The correct answer is (D).

## Common Trap Answers

### One Word Off

The most tempting trap answers on Describe the Argument questions are similar to those on Role questions: Most of the answer is fine, but one or two words will throw the answer off.

In addition, because most of these arguments will consist of a second person objecting to something the first person says, it will always be tempting to choose an answer that indicates that, for example, the consumer advocate rejects the mayor's conclusion. The advocate's comment does weaken the mayor's conclusion, but it may not directly attack the conclusion—and the question asks you to articulate what the advocate directly attacks.

18

# Exercise: Understanding Answer Choices

One of the toughest things about Describe the Role problems is understanding the language in the answer choices. Before you do a full problem set, warm up by translating some answer choices for practice.

Each question gives you sample answer choice text from a Describe the Role problem. Your job is to determine what part of an argument that answer choice is actually referring to.

1.  A claim upon which the author's argument depends

    (A)  Author's premise
    (B)  Author's conclusion
    (C)  Premise of a counterargument
    (D)  Conclusion of a counterargument

2.  A conclusion that the author believes has been incorrectly drawn

    (A)  Author's premise
    (B)  Author's conclusion
    (C)  Premise of a counterargument
    (D)  Conclusion of a counterargument

3.  Reasoning that has been used to support the claim made by the opposing scientists

    (A)  Author's premise
    (B)  Author's conclusion
    (C)  Premise of a counterargument
    (D)  Conclusion of a counterargument

4.  A prediction supported by the author's interpretation of existing evidence

    (A)  Author's premise
    (B)  Author's conclusion
    (C)  Premise of a counterargument
    (D)  Conclusion of a counterargument

5.  The desired outcome of a plan, which the author believes will be more successful than the previous approach

    (A)  Author's premise
    (B)  Author's conclusion
    (C)  Premise of a counterargument
    (D)  Conclusion of a counterargument

## Answers to Exercise

1.  **(A) Author's premise:** *Claim* usually refers to the conclusion of an argument. However, the author's argument *depends* on this claim. Something that an argument depends on is a premise: Conclusions always depend on premises.

2.  **(D) Conclusion of a counterargument:** Since the author believes that this conclusion has been *incorrectly drawn*, it must be part of a counterargument that the author disagrees with.

3.  **(C) Premise of a counterargument:** Something that *supports a claim* is a premise. Since this claim belongs to the *opposing scientists*, it's one that the author disagrees with, so it's part of a counterargument.

4.  **(B) Author's conclusion:** A prediction is often a conclusion, and this one is *supported*: The rest of an argument always supports its conclusion. Since it's supported by the author's interpretation, it's part of the author's argument.

5.  **(B) Author's conclusion:** When an argument discusses a plan, the desired outcome of that plan—even if it's just that the plan will succeed—is the conclusion of the argument.

18

**Describe the Role Cheat Sheet**

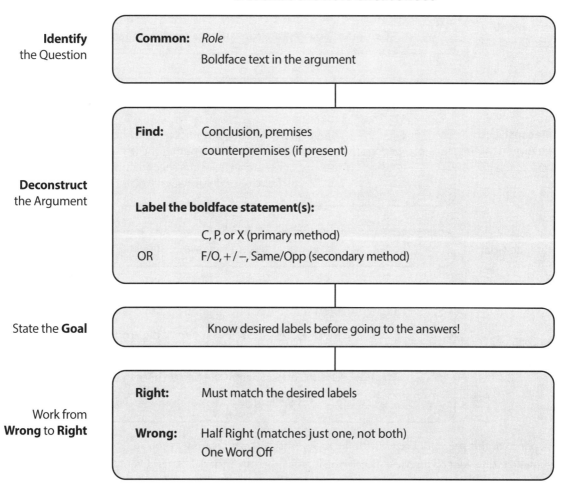

Take a photo of this page and keep it with the review sheets you're creating as you study. Better yet, use this page as a guide to create your own review sheet—you'll remember the material better if you write it down yourself.

## Describe the Argument Cheat Sheet

| | |
|---|---|
| **Identify**<br>the Question | **Common:** How one person *responds* or *objects* to something. |
| **Deconstruct**<br>the Argument | **Find:** Conclusion, premises<br><br>Does the second person flat-out contradict what the first one says? Or does the second person question whether the first's conclusion is relevant or accurate? Does the second person introduce new information? |
| State the **Goal** | What was attacked? How was it attacked? |
| Work from **Wrong** to **Right** | **Right:** Must match what the second person did<br>Must address the relevant part of the argument<br><br>**Wrong:** Doesn't address what the person directly attacks<br>One Word Off |

Take a photo of this page and keep it with the review sheets you're creating as you study. Better yet, use this page as a guide to create your own review sheet—you'll remember the material better if you write it down yourself.

# Problem Set

Answer each question using the 4-step Critical Reasoning process.

1. **Identify the question:** Is this a Describe the Role question or a Describe the Argument question?

2. **Deconstruct the argument:** Find the conclusion and map the argument on your paper.

3. **State the goal:** What will the right answer need to do?

4. **Work from wrong to right:** Eliminate four wrong answers. Watch out for common wrong answer types.

**1.** *Ad Revenues*

Media Critic: Network executives allege that television viewership is decreasing due to the availability of television programs on other platforms, such as the internet and mobile devices. These executives claim that **declining viewership will cause advertising revenue to fall and networks will thus be unable to spend the large sums necessary to produce high-quality programming**. That development, in turn, will lead to a dearth of programming for the very devices that cannibalized television's audience. However, research shows that users of alternative platforms are exposed to new programs and, **as a result, actually increase the number of hours per week that they watch television**. This demonstrates that alternative platforms will not prevent networks from increasing advertising revenue.

The portions in boldface play which of the following roles in the media critic's argument?

(A) The first is a trend that weighs against the critic's claim; the second is that claim.

(B) The first is a prediction that is challenged by the argument; the second is a finding upon which the argument depends.

(C) The first clarifies the reasoning behind the critic's claim; the second demonstrates why that claim is flawed.

(D) The first acknowledges a position that the network executives accept as true; the second is a consequence of that position.

(E) The first opposes the critic's claim through an analogy; the second outlines a scenario in which that claim will not hold.

2.  *Renaissance Masters*

Many people praise High Renaissance painting for creating very realistic images from observation, but **scholars have documented that some High Renaissance painters used pinhole cameras to project the likeness of their subjects onto the canvas and painted from there**. Thus, people who credit High Renaissance painters with superior artistic skills are misguided. **Painting from a projected image requires only an insignificant amount of additional skill beyond that needed to copy a picture outright**.

In the argument given, the two boldfaced portions play which of the following roles?

 (A)  The first is a finding that has been used to support a conclusion that the argument rejects; the second is a claim that supports that conclusion.

 (B)  The first is a finding that has been used to support a conclusion that the argument rejects; the second is that conclusion.

 (C)  The first is a claim put forth to support a conclusion that the argument rejects; the second is a consideration that is introduced to counter the force of that evidence.

 (D)  The first is evidence that forms the basis for the position that the argument seeks to establish; the second is a claim presented to solidify that position.

 (E)  The first is evidence that forms the basis for the position that the argument seeks to establish; the second is that position.

3.  *Democracy*

As the United States demonstrated during its early development, it is not enough for citizens simply to have rights; the successful functioning of a democracy requires that they also know how to exercise those rights. Access to formal education was one necessary component that helped the U.S. citizenry learn how to exercise its rights. Therefore, in order for a democracy to function successfully, its citizens must have access to a formal education.

The author develops the argument by

 (A)  using an analogy to establish a precedent for a planned future event

(B)  illustrating differences in the requirements for the functioning of a democracy depending upon the democracy in question

(C)  introducing an example that illustrates a common principle

(D)  forming a hypothesis that explains apparently contradictory pieces of evidence

(E)  supplying an alternate explanation for a known phenomenon

18

4.  *Malaria*

    In an attempt to explain the cause of malaria, a deadly infectious disease, early European settlers in Hong Kong attributed the malady to poisonous gases supposedly emanating from low-lying swampland. In the 1880s, however, doctors determined that Anopheles mosquitoes were responsible for transmitting the disease to humans after observing that **the female of the species can carry a parasitic protozoan that is passed on to unsuspecting humans when a mosquito feasts on a person's blood.**

    What function does the statement in boldface fulfill with respect to the argument presented above?

    (A) It provides support for the explanation of a particular phenomenon.

    (B) It presents evidence that contradicts an established fact.

    (C) It offers confirmation of a contested assumption.

    (D) It identifies the cause of an erroneous conclusion.

    (E) It proposes a new conclusion in place of an earlier conjecture.

5.  *Digital Marketing*

    Sania: The newest workers in the workforce are the most effective digital marketing employees because they are more likely to use social networking websites and tools themselves.

    Carlos: But effective digital marketing also requires very technical expertise, such as search engine optimization, that is best learned on the job via prolonged exposure and instruction.

    Carlos responds to Sania by

    (A) demonstrating that Sania's conclusion is based upon evidence that is not relevant to the given situation

    (B) questioning the accuracy of the evidence presented by Sania in support of her conclusion

    (C) reinforcing Sania's argument by contributing an additional piece of evidence in support of her conclusion

    (D) pointing out differences in the qualifications desired by different employers seeking digital marketing employees

    (E) providing an additional piece of evidence that undermines a portion of Sania's claim

18

6. *Innovative Design*

Products with innovative and appealing designs relative to competing products can often command substantially higher prices in the marketplace. **Because design innovations are quickly copied by other manufacturers**, many consumer technology companies charge as much as possible for their new designs to extract as much value as possible from them. But large profits generated by the innovative designs give competitors stronger incentives to copy the designs. Therefore, **the best strategy to maximize overall profit from an innovative new design is to charge less than the greatest possible price**.

In the argument above, the two portions in boldface play which of the following roles?

(A) The first is an assumption that supports a described course of action; the second provides a consideration to support a preferred course of action.

(B) The first is a consideration that helps explain the appeal of a certain strategy; the second presents an alternative strategy endorsed by the argument.

(C) The first is a phenomenon that makes a specific strategy unlikely to be successful; the second is that strategy.

(D) The first is a consideration that demonstrates why a particular approach is flawed; the second describes a way to amend that approach.

(E) The first is a factor used to rationalize a particular strategy; the second is a factor against that strategy.

7. *Gray Wolf Population*

Government representative: Between 1996 and 2005, the gray wolf population in Minnesota grew nearly 50 percent; the gray wolf population in Montana increased by only 13 percent during the same period. Clearly, the Minnesota gray wolf population is more likely to survive and thrive long term.

Environmentalist: But the gray wolf population in Montana is nearly 8 times the population in Minnesota; above a certain critical breeding number, the population is stable and does not require growth in order to survive.

The environmentalist challenges the government representative's argument by doing which of the following?

(A) Introducing additional evidence that undermines an assumption made by the representative

(B) Challenging the representative's definition of a critical breeding number

(C) Demonstrating that the critical breeding number of the two wolf populations differs significantly

(D) Implying that the two populations of wolves could be combined in order to preserve the species

(E) Suggesting that the Montana wolf population grew at a faster rate than stated in the representative's argument

# Solutions

1.  Ad Revenues: The correct answer is **(B)**.

    Step 1: Identify the Question

    | The portions in boldface play which of the following roles in the media critic's argument? | *This is a Role question. The question contains the word* boldface, *and I'm asked to find the* role *of each bold statement.* | R A B C D E |
    |---|---|---|

    Step 2: Deconstruct the Argument

    | Media Critic: Network executives allege that television viewership is decreasing due to the availability of television programs on other platforms, such as the internet and mobile devices. | *The word* allege *tells me this is a claim. Also, the critic is talking about what other people claim, so I'm guessing the critic is going to contradict what they claim—so this is probably a counter-premise.* | Critic: Execs say TV ↓ b/c use other plats |
    |---|---|---|
    | These executives claim that **declining viewership will cause advertising revenue to fall and networks will thus be unable to spend the large sums necessary to produce high-quality programming**. | *More from the execs. More claims about bad things happening. Is the last thing the execs' conclusion? This is the 1st boldface. If the critic contradicts the execs later, then this first boldface will be labeled an X.* | Execs: TV ↓ → ad ↓ → no \$ for qual prog |
    | That development, in turn, will lead to a dearth of programming for the very devices that cannibalized television's audience. | *Ah, I see. Ironic. The fact that people are watching on other platforms will eventually lead to not having enough programming for those other platforms. Conclusion of the execs.* | → No prog for other plats |
    | However, research shows that users of alternative platforms are exposed to new programs and, **as a result, actually increase the number of hours per week that they watch television**. | *Here's the contradiction! I'll wait till I find the conclusion for sure, but the first boldface is probably an X, which would make this one a premise (P).* | BUT users of alt plats watch MORE TV |
    | This demonstrates that alternative platforms will not prevent networks from increasing advertising revenue. | *Okay, the critic is concluding the opposite: that ad rates will go up. And if that's my conclusion, then the first boldface is indeed an X and the second one supports the critic's conclusion, so it's a P.* | © Ad rates Want: X P |

18

Step 3: State the Goal

*The question asks me to find the role of two boldface statements. The critic's conclusion is in the last line, and the second boldface, right before it, supports that conclusion. The second boldface is a premise (P). The first boldface is part of the executives' argument, which is the opposite of the critic's argument, so the first boldface is an X. I want to find the combo X P (in that order) in an answer choice.*

Step 4: Work from Wrong to Right

| | | |
|---|---|---|
| (A) The first is a trend that weighs against the critic's claim; the second is that claim. | Weighs against the critic's claim—*yes, that's consistent with an X label. The second is that claim, meaning the critic's claim. No. The second one is a P, not a C.* | ~~A~~ |
| (B) The first is a prediction that is challenged by the argument; the second is a finding upon which the argument depends. | *That's true, the critic does challenge the first one. That's an X. And the second one is a P, so this could be something upon which the critic's argument depends. I'll keep it in.* | B ~ |
| (C) The first clarifies the reasoning behind the critic's claim; the second demonstrates why that claim is flawed. | *Clarifies the critic's claim? No. The first one is something the execs claim. I don't even need to read the second half of the answer.* | ~~C~~ |
| (D) The first acknowledges a position that the network executives accept as true; the second is a consequence of that position. | *Yes, the execs do accept the first boldface as true—it's their premise. And they're on the opposite side of the critic, so something they think is an X. Okay, that's fine. The second is a consequence of that position. What position? Oh, they use* position *in the first half of the sentence . . . the execs' position. The second isn't something about the execs' position. It goes against the execs' position. No.* | ~~D~~ |
| (E) The first opposes the critic's claim through an analogy; the second outlines a scenario in which that claim will not hold. | *The first one does oppose what the critic concludes. I'm not quite sure whether it does so through an analogy. What about the second half? A scenario in which the critic's claim won't hold—meaning something that's on the opposite side of what the critic says. No! The second one outlines a scenario in which the execs' claim, not the critic's claim, won't hold.* | ~~E~~ |

2. Renaissance Masters: The correct answer is (**D**).

Step 1: Identify the Question

| In the argument given, the two boldfaced portions play which of the following roles? | *The word* boldfaced, *along with the boldface font in the argument, indicates that this is a Role question.* | R<br>A<br>B<br>C<br>D<br>E |
|---|---|---|

Step 2: Deconstruct the Argument

| Many people praise High Renaissance painting for creating very realistic images from observation, | *The many people* intro *feels like there's a contrast coming…and there is! Okay, just get this piece down first.* | Many like Hi Ren pics b/c realistic |
|---|---|---|
| but **scholars have documented that some High Renaissance painters used pinhole cameras to project the likeness of their subjects onto the canvas and painted from there**. | *People think the High Renaissance painters could paint realistically just by observing, but actually some were just projecting the images onto a canvas and sort of tracing the image.* | BUT some painters just projected + traced |
| Thus, people who credit High Renaissance painters with superior artistic skills are misguided. | *The word* thus *might mean this is the conclusion. The previous sentence only said that* some *painters did the tracing thing, not all of them. But this sentence seems to be condemning all of them.* | People who like Hi Ren = misguided |
| **Painting from a projected image requires only an insignificant amount of additional skill beyond that needed to copy a picture outright.** | *Okay, the last sentence was definitely the conclusion. This sentence is supporting the conclusion. If this is true, then yes, painters who use this technique aren't that great.* | project = low skill |
| | *I'm not 100 percent sure how to label the first boldface, but I did notice that the first one was a fact and the second one was an opinion. I could use the Secondary Method to solve.* | |

18

Step 3: State the Goal

*I need to identify the role of the two boldfaced statements as they relate to the conclusion—which was that people who think High Renaissance painters are really skilled are misguided. The first one is a fact, and the second one is an opinion. The first one is FOR the conclusion. So is the second one.*

Step 4: Work from Wrong to Right

| | | |
|---|---|---|
| (A) The first is a finding that has been used to support a conclusion that the argument rejects; the second is a claim that supports that conclusion. | *A* finding *could be a fact, and a claim is an opinion, so this one is okay so far.* | A ~ |
| (B) The first is a finding that has been used to support a conclusion that the argument rejects; the second is that conclusion. | *A* finding *could be a fact, and the conclusion is technically an opinion. But the boldface opinion is FOR the conclusion; it's not actually the conclusion itself.* | B̶ |
| (C) The first is a claim put forth to support a conclusion that the argument rejects; the second is a consideration that is introduced to counter the force of that evidence. | *A* claim *is not a fact. I can eliminate this one.* | C̶ |
| (D) The first is evidence that forms the basis for the position that the argument seeks to establish; the second is a claim presented to solidify that position. | *Evidence* can be a fact, and a claim is an opinion. This one has to stay in, too. | D ~ |
| (E) The first is evidence that forms the basis for the position that the argument seeks to establish; the second is that position. | *Evidence* can be a fact, but the second boldface is an opinion supporting the conclusion, while this choice says that the second boldface is the position, or conclusion. I can eliminate this one.* | E̶ |
| Compare (A) and (D) | *Based on the fact/opinion technique, I can't get any further; I just have to guess between (A) and (D).* <br><br> *The main technique can distinguish between (A) and (D): Both boldfaces are premises used to support the author's conclusion. Answer (A) says that the first boldface is used "to support a conclusion that the argument rejects." Eliminate answer (A).* | A̶ ~ and D ~ |

   Ⓓ E̶

18

3. Democracy: The correct answer is (**C**).

Step 1: Identify the Question

| | | |
|---|---|---|
| The author develops the argument by | *The wording is similar to a Describe the Argument question, though it doesn't have the "two people talking" feature. This might be one of the rare variants that doesn't have two people talking. A quick glance at the abstract wording of the answer choices confirms: This is a Describe Arg question.* | DA<br>A<br>B<br>C<br>D<br>E |

Step 2: Deconstruct the Argument

| | | |
|---|---|---|
| As the United States demonstrated during its early development, it is not enough for citizens simply to have rights; the successful functioning of a democracy requires that they also know how to exercise those rights. | *Okay, specific example of a principle: the U.S. showed that citizens need to have rights AND need to know how to exercise those rights.* | US: not just have rights but know how to exercise → success democ |
| Access to formal education was one necessary component that helped the U.S. citizenry learn how to exercise its rights. | *More detail on the U.S. example. Access to formal education was needed to know how to exercise those rights.* | Need access to formal educ → |
| Therefore, in order for a democracy to function successfully, its citizens must have access to a formal education. | *Conclusion. The author's just sort of putting together the two "end" pieces of the argument here.* | © Need formal edu for success democ |

Step 3: State the Goal

*The author concludes that formal education is necessary in general for a democracy to be successful. The evidence: It happened this way in one country (the U.S.).*

Step 4: Work from Wrong to Right

| (A) using an analogy to establish a precedent for a planned future event | *The argument used an example. Is that the same thing as an analogy? Maybe. Oh, but what's the planned future event? There isn't anything; rather, the author concluded with a general statement, not a discussion of an event.* | ~~A~~ |
|---|---|---|
| (B) illustrating differences in the requirements for the functioning of a democracy depending upon the democracy in question | *I can imagine that it would be true that there are different requirements for different governments… but that's not what this argument says. The author only mentions the U.S. and then concludes something in general about that.* | ~~B~~ |
| (C) introducing an example that illustrates a common principle | *This looks decent. The argument did introduce an example and then used that to conclude a general principle.* | C ~ |
| (D) forming a hypothesis that explains apparently contradictory pieces of evidence | *It would be reasonable to describe the conclusion as a hypothesis… but there aren't any contradictory things in the argument. Rather, the example given does illustrate the conclusion.* | ~~D~~ |
| (E) supplying an alternate explanation for a known phenomenon | *The author doesn't supply an* alternate *explanation; he isn't arguing against anyone. He just concludes something from the U.S. example.* | ~~E~~ |

~~A~~     ~~B~~     Ⓒ      ~~D~~     ~~E~~

18

Ⓜ

4.  Malaria: The correct answer is (**A**).

Step 1: Identify the Question

| What function does the statement in boldface fulfill with respect to the argument presented above? | *This is a Role question. The question contains the word* boldface, *and I'm asked to find the* function *of each bold statement.* | R A B C D E |
| --- | --- | --- |

Step 2: Deconstruct the Argument

| In an attempt to explain the cause of malaria, a deadly infectious disease, early European settlers in Hong Kong attributed the malady to poisonous gases supposedly emanating from low-lying swampland. | *This is a fact. Likely either background or premise.* | Euros in HK: Poison gas → malaria |
| --- | --- | --- |
| In the 1880s, however, doctors determined that Anopheles mosquitoes were responsible for transmitting the disease to humans after observing that **the female of the species can carry a parasitic protozoan that is passed on to unsuspecting humans when a mosquito feasts on a person's blood**. | *Okay, this is still a fact, but it's the conclusion of the story. They used to think it was one thing, and then they figured out it was really the mosquitoes. The boldface language, in particular, is the evidence used to show that it was mosquitoes. That's a premise.* | But 1880s MDs: mosq bite, pass parasite blood Want: P |

Step 3: State the Goal

*The question specifically asks me what role this information plays: the female carries a parasite that is passed to humans when a mosquito bites someone. Because of that, the scientists decided that the mosquitoes were transmitting the disease. That's the most like a P—a premise that supports some further conclusion.*

*I need to find the abstract language that indicates some kind of premise or support.*

**18**

Step 4: Work from Wrong to Right

| | | |
|---|---|---|
| (A) It provides support for the explanation of a particular phenomenon. | Support—*that's good—for a* phenomenon. *Okay, that's just fancy-speak for: Provides support for something that happened. That sounds okay. Leave it in.* | A̰ |
| (B) It presents evidence that contradicts an established fact. | Evidence—*that's also good. And that evidence does contradict what the earlier settlers thought! Oh, wait—was that an established fact? Let me look at the first sentence again. No, they thought that, but the argument doesn't say it was an* established fact. *Cross this one off.* | ~~B~~ |
| (C) It offers confirmation of a contested assumption. | Confirmation *is also good…of a* contested assumption. *I'm not quite sure what they're referring to when they say* assumption, *but nothing was contested here. First, some people thought one thing, and later, new evidence led some doctors to conclude something else. No.* | ~~C~~ |
| (D) It identifies the cause of an erroneous conclusion. | *No—the only thing we might be able to describe as an erroneous conclusion is what the early settlers thought. But the bold stuff supports the doctors' conclusion.* | ~~D~~ |
| (E) It proposes a new conclusion in place of an earlier conjecture. | *Oh, yes, a new conclusion. Yes, that's exactly what the argument says! Oh, wait—I labeled the boldface stuff a P, not a C. Why was that? Oh, I see—tricky. The first half of the sentence, the non-bold part, is the new conclusion. The bold part is the evidence supporting that. This isn't it after all!* | ~~E~~ |

5. Digital Marketing: The correct answer is **(E)**.

Step 1: Identify the Question

| Carlos responds to Sania by | *The "two person" structure and the focus on how Carlos responds indicate that this is a Describe the Argument question.* | DA<br>A<br>B<br>C<br>D<br>E |
|---|---|---|

Step 2: Deconstruct the Argument

| Sania: The newest workers in the work-force are the most effective digital marketing employees because they are more likely to use social networking websites and tools themselves. | *Sania claims that the workers who use certain online tools are also the most effective at digital marketing and that those people are the newest workers.* | Sania: New empl use soc nw → most eff dig mktg ⓒ |
|---|---|---|
| Carlos: But effective digital marketing also requires very technical expertise, such as search engine optimization, that is best learned on the job via prolonged exposure and instruction. | *Carlos doesn't dispute Sania's evidence, but he brings up a new point: You also need these other skills to be a good digital marketer…and those skills are learned on the job over a long (prolonged) time…which hurts Sania's claim that the newest workers are the most effective.* | Carlos: But eff dig mktg needs tech expertise, best learned on job |

Step 3: State the Goal

*I need to articulate how Carlos responds to Sania. He doesn't say that she's wrong about the newest workers using social networking tools. Rather, he says that digital marketers also need this other skill that takes a long time to learn on the job. If that's the case, this weakens Sania's claim that the newest workers are the most effective.*

18

Step 4: Work from Wrong to Right

| (A) demonstrating that Sania's conclusion is based upon evidence that is not relevant to the given situation | *Carlos doesn't say anything negative about Sania's evidence; rather, he introduces new evidence that attacks Sania's assumption that her piece of evidence is the most important thing to consider.* | ~~A~~ |
|---|---|---|
| (B) questioning the accuracy of the evidence presented by Sania in support of her conclusion | *This is similar to choice (A); Carlos doesn't question Sania's evidence.* | ~~B~~ |
| (C) reinforcing Sania's argument by contributing an additional piece of evidence in support of her conclusion | *Carlos does contribute an additional piece of evidence, but his new evidence hurts Sania's argument. Carlos doesn't support Sania's conclusion.* | ~~C~~ |
| (D) pointing out differences in the qualifications desired by different employers seeking digital marketing employees | *Carlos does point out a different way to assess the effectiveness of digital marketing employees, but he doesn't mention employers at all or differences among different employers.* | ~~D~~ |
| (E) providing an additional piece of evidence that undermines a portion of Sania's claim | *Bingo. This is exactly what Carlos does—a new piece of information that hurts the* newest workers *portion of Sania's claim.* | E ~ |

~~A~~     ~~B~~     ~~C~~     ~~D~~     (E ~)

18

6.  Innovative Design: The correct answer is **(B)**.

Step 1: Identify the Question

| In the argument above, the two portions in boldface play which of the following roles? | *This is a Role question. The question contains the word* boldface, *and I'm asked to find the* role *of each bold statement.* | R<br>A<br>B<br>C<br>D<br>E |
|---|---|---|

Step 2: Deconstruct the Argument

| Products with innovative and appealing designs relative to competing products can often command substantially higher prices in the marketplace. | *Sort of between a fact and a claim. Probably a premise.* | Innov designs → ↑↑ $ |
|---|---|---|
| **Because design innovations are quickly copied by other manufacturers**, many consumer technology companies charge as much as possible for their new designs to extract as much value as possible from them. | *Getting more toward claim-based material, with the first half of the sentence providing support for the second half. I'm not sure yet whether this is the conclusion though.* | Because others copy<br>many co's charge ↑↑ $ |
| But large profits generated by the innovative designs give competitors stronger incentives to copy the designs. | *BUT signals a contrast. Oh, so there's actually a drawback to making a lot of money: Competitors will copy even faster so I guess that could hurt market share. That's interesting.* | BUT ↑↑ prof → incent to copy |
| Therefore, **the best strategy to maximize overall profit from an innovative new design is to charge less than the greatest possible price**. | *Here we go, the conclusion. The person's claiming that companies actually shouldn't charge the largest possible price and this will actually help maximize profits in the end. The second boldface is the conclusion; that gets a C. The first boldface is a premise that supports a strategy the argument disagrees with (that companies should charge the greatest possible price for an ID).* | Ⓒ to max prof<br>charge < than max price<br>Want: X C |

Step 3: State the Goal

*The question asks me to determine the role played by each of two boldface statements. I've decided the second one is the conclusion and the first is a premise supporting an alternate strategy, so I want to find an answer that gives this combo: X C (in that order).*

Step 4: Work from Wrong to Right

| | | |
|---|---|---|
| (A) The first is an assumption that supports a described course of action; the second provides a consideration to support a preferred course of action. | *Hmm, they call the first an assumption, not a premise, but I suppose that's okay; they do say it* supports *something. The second, though, is the actual conclusion—but this answer choice makes the second sound like another premise. I don't think so.* | ~~A~~ |
| (B) The first is a consideration that helps explain the appeal of a certain strategy; the second presents an alternative strategy endorsed by the argument. | *The wording for the first statement is a little strange, but I suppose that could be considered a premise. And it does support the greatest possible price strategy. The second boldface is the strategy the argument supports. Keep this one.* | B<br>~ |
| (C) The first is a phenomenon that makes a specific strategy unlikely to be successful; the second is that strategy. | *The first boldface provides support for the first strategy. It definitely doesn't weaken the author's strategy. Eliminate this answer choice.* | ~~C~~ |
| (D) The first is a consideration that demonstrates why a particular approach is flawed; the second describes a way to amend that approach. | *No, the first supports the alternate strategy— it doesn't illustrate a flaw. I don't even need to read the second half of this choice.* | ~~D~~ |
| (E) The first is a factor used to rationalize a particular strategy; the second is a factor against that strategy. | *Something used to* rationalize *a strategy? Yes, that could be describing a premise that supports the alternate strategy. Oh, but the second goes against the strategy? No! The second is actually the author's strategy.* | ~~E~~ |

7. Gray Wolf Population: The correct answer is (**A**).

Step 1: Identify the Question

| | | |
|---|---|---|
| The environmentalist challenges the government representative's argument by doing which of the following? | *There's a 2-person-talking structure, and I'm asked how the second person responds; this is a Describe the Argument question.* | DA<br><br>A<br>B<br>C<br>D<br>E |

Step 2: Deconstruct the Argument

| | | |
|---|---|---|
| Government representative: Between 1996 and 2005, the gray wolf population in Minnesota grew nearly 50 percent; the gray wolf population in Montana increased by only 13 percent during the same period. | *This is just a straight fact. The Minnesota wolf population grew a lot faster in that time period than the Montana wolf population.* | Gov rep: 96-05, wolf in Minn ↑ 50 percent, in Mont only ↑ 13 percent |
| Clearly, the Minnesota gray wolf population is more likely to survive and thrive long term. | *Conclusion! Claiming that Minnesota wolves are more likely to survive and thrive. Certainly, the Minnesota wolf population grew more… but does that automatically mean they're more likely to survive and thrive?* | ©️ Minn > likely to survive/ thrive |
| Environmentalist: But the gray wolf population in Montana is nearly 8 times the population in Minnesota; above a certain critical breeding number, the population is stable and does not require growth in order to survive. | *Ah, okay. The environmentalist is pointing out that they're not necessarily the same thing. Once the population is large enough, it's already stable, so growth isn't necessarily critical to survival.* | Enviro: BUT Mont 8x Minn; when ↑ enough, pop = stable |

Step 3: State the Goal

*The gov rep concludes that the Minnesota wolves are more likely to survive and thrive because the growth rate was a lot higher, but the environmentalist responds that the Montana population was already a lot larger, so growth might not have been necessary to keep the population thriving. The Montana population might already have been stable in the first place.*

*I need to find something that explains this response in a more abstract way: A new piece of evidence changes the way someone would think about the issue addressed in the conclusion (surviving and thriving).*

Step 4: Work from Wrong to Right

| | | |
|---|---|---|
| (A) Introducing additional evidence that undermines an assumption made by the representative | *This sounds pretty good. The environmentalist's statement is a new piece of evidence, and it does undermine the government rep's assumption that growth is a good indicator of likelihood to survive and thrive.* | A ∼ |
| (B) Challenging the representative's definition of a critical breeding number | *The environmentalist challenges the rep's assumption about what it takes to survive and thrive, but the environmentalist can't challenge the rep on* critical breeding number, *because the rep never mentions this concept.* | B̶ |
| (C) Demonstrating that the critical breeding number of the two wolf populations differs significantly | *The environmentalist mentions the concept of* critical breeding number, *but establishes only that the number of wolves in each population differs significantly, not that the number of wolves needed to achieve the critical breeding number is different.* | C̶ |
| (D) Implying that the two populations of wolves could be combined in order to preserve the species | *This might be an interesting strategy, but the environmentalist never mentions it.* | D̶ |
| (E) Suggesting that the Montana wolf population grew at a faster rate than stated in the representative's argument | *This is tricky. The environmentalist introduces a new figure, but that figure has to do with the size of the two populations, not the rate of growth. The environmentalist does not dispute the rep's figures for rate of growth.* | E̶ |

18

# The Assumption Family: Find the Assumption

## In This Chapter:

- How Assumptions Work

- Excercise: Brainstorm Assumptions

- Assumption Family Questions

- Find the Assumption Questions

- The Negation Technique

- Find the Assumption Cheat Sheet

**In this chapter, you will learn** the role that assumptions play in arguments and how to answer the first of five question types that all rely on assumptions somehow.

# CHAPTER 19 The Assumption Family: Find the Assumption

**Assumptions** were introduced briefly in the first two chapters of this unit, but did not play a role in Structure Family questions. They are the key to the largest family of questions, the Assumption Family; all five question types in this family contain arguments that involve at least one assumption made by the author. (The *author* refers to the hypothetical person who is "arguing" the argument and believes that argument to be valid.)

## How Assumptions Work

An assumption is something that *the author must believe to be true* in order to draw a certain conclusion; however, the author *does not state* the assumption in the argument. The assumption itself might not necessarily be true in the real world; rather, the *author* believes that it is true in order to make his or her argument.

For example, what does the author of the following argument assume must be true?

> No athletes under the age of 14 can qualify for Country Y's Olympic team. Therefore, Adrienne can't qualify for Country Y's Olympic team.

*therefore*

No athlete under 14 can qualify
for Olymp from Y.

(premise)

Adrienne can't qual for Y's
Olymp team.

(conclusion)

The author assumes that this premise applies to Adrienne—in other words, that she is an athlete from Country Y and that she is under the age of 14. There may be other reasons she would not qualify for the Olympic team (perhaps her sport is not included), but if she can't qualify *for this reason*, then it must be because she is otherwise qualified (that is, she is an athlete from Country Y) but is too young.

The diagram above represents the **core** of the argument. The core consists of the conclusion and the main premise or premises that lead to that conclusion, as well as the unstated *assumption(s)*. You need assumptions as much as you need any other piece of the argument to make the whole thing work. After all, if Adrienne were *not* under 14, then the argument above would make no sense.

Assumptions fill at least part of a gap in the argument; the gap is represented by the arrow in the diagram above. If you insert a valid assumption into the argument, it makes the argument much better:

> No athletes under the age of 14 can qualify for Country Y's Olympic team. *Adrienne is an athlete from Country Y who is under the age of 14.* Therefore, Adrienne can't compete for Country Y's Olympic team.

| No athlete under 14 can qualify for Olymp from Y. | *therefore* ⟹ | Adrienne can't qual for Y's Olymp team. |
|:---:|:---:|:---:|
| (premise) | | (conclusion) |

*Adrienne is an athlete from Country Y who is under the age of 14.*

(assumption)

The argument above has a single obvious assumption that fills the gap on its own. Most GMAT arguments contain multiple assumptions, none of which individually fill the gap. Any one assumption will not automatically make the argument airtight, but it will make the argument more likely to be true, and the argument will depend on each of those assumptions. Take any assumption away and the argument collapses.

In order to train yourself to notice the presence of assumptions, think of the person in your life with whom you argue or disagree the most. Whenever you talk to him or her, your brain is already on the offensive. "Really? I'm not so sure about that. You've failed to consider…" Pretend this person is the one making the argument to you. How would you try to pick it apart? You'll be attacking assumptions.

Okay, are you ready? Brainstorm some assumptions for the following argument:

> Thomas's football team lost in the championship game last year. The same two teams are playing in the championship game again this year, and the players on Thomas's team have improved. Therefore, Thomas's team will win the championship game this year.

Picture that person with whom you argue; what would you say? Maybe something such as the following: "You're just *assuming* that Thomas's team has improved enough to be competitive with last year's winning team! You're also assuming that last year's winning team has *not* improved enough to keep themselves clearly ahead of Thomas's team!" As you brainstorm, however, remember that on the GMAT, you never have to come up with any assumption in a vacuum. After all, the test is multiple choice! If you are asked to find an assumption one of the choices will be a valid assumption and the other four choices will not be. So, while it's worth reading critically to poke holes in weak arguments, don't spend too much time thinking up assumptions on your own.

Here are a couple of important strategies for dealing with assumptions on the test:

| Do | | Don't |
|---|:---:|---|
| Notice gaps and articulate assumptions you can think of relatively easily. | **but** | Don't spend more than about 20 seconds brainstorming up front. |
| Look for your brainstormed assumptions in the answers. | **but** | Don't eliminate answers just because they don't match any of your brainstormed assumptions. |
| Choose an answer that the author must believe to be true in order to draw the conclusion. | **but** | Don't hold out for something that makes the conclusion "perfect" or definitely true. |

**19**

Try inserting a brainstormed assumption into the football argument to see how it works:

> Thomas's football team lost in the championship game last year. The same two teams are playing in the championship game again this year, and the players on Thomas's team have improved enough to be competitive with the defending champion team. Therefore, Thomas's team will win the championship game this year.

If the author is going to claim that the improvement will lead to a victory for Thomas's team, then it is *necessary* for the author to believe that this improvement was enough to put that team at least at the same level as the defending champion team. Otherwise, it wouldn't make sense to say that, because these players have improved, they will win this year.

It is still not a foregone conclusion that Thomas's team will definitely win, even though the author clearly believes so. There are too many other potential factors involved; the author is making many assumptions, not just one. It is only necessary to find one assumption, though; it is not necessary to make the argument foolproof.

# Exercise: Brainstorm Assumptions

Brainstorm at least one assumption that must be true. If you like, you can draw out the argument core.

1. Over 30 percent of students at an elementary school failed the state reading test last year. In order to reduce the failure rate, the school plans to offer free reading tutoring after school.

2. The employees of Quick Corp's accounting department consistently show a significant jump in productivity in the two weeks before taking vacation. Clearly, the knowledge that they are about to go on vacation motivates the employees to be more productive.

3. Mayor: The Acme Factory has developed a new manufacturing process that uses chemical Q, the residue of which is toxic to babies. In order to protect our children, we need to pass a law banning the use of this chemical.

## Answers to Exercise

Possible assumptions are noted in italics below the arrow. You may brainstorm different assumptions from the ones shown. Other assumptions are acceptable as long as they represent something that MUST be true in order to make the given argument.

1.

*therefore*

Offer free tutoring  Reduce reading test failure

*Student will go. Tutoring will help pass.*

The author argues that offering free after-school tutoring will reduce the failure rate on the test. The plan must work as expected for that conclusion to hold. Students, especially those who are likely to fail the test, must actually attend the tutoring sessions. Also, the tutoring must help students pass the test. If, for example, the tutoring focused on material that was not on the test, it might not make much difference for failure rates.

2.

*therefore*

2 wks b4 vaca:
h ↑ prod

⇒

emp choose >> prod
b4 vaca

*They didn't plan vacation to
occur right after a big deadline
or other busy time.*

The author concludes that employees decide to be more productive *because* they'll be taking vacation soon; this is a **causation** argument. Perhaps it's the case, instead, that the employees choose to take vacation right after they know they'll be *forced* to work harder for some other reason. For example, maybe everyone in the accounting department takes vacation right after the annual financial report is due. The author is assuming that *other* causes of the jump in productivity don't apply in this case.

3.

*therefore*

Acme using Q,
toxic baby

⇒

to protect kids,
ban Q

*If Acme uses Q, then kids will
somehow come into contact
with Q.*

The mayor assumes that use of chemical Q in the production process will somehow eventually expose babies to the chemical residue. Maybe the chemical is used only for something that never comes into contact with the final product and will never come into contact with kids.

## Assumption Family Questions

There are five types of Assumption questions. The first major type, Find the Assumption, is covered in this chapter. In the next chapter, you'll learn about the next two major types: Strengthen the Argument and Weaken the Argument. Later, you'll be introduced to the two remaining types in the Assumption Family: Evaluate the Argument and Find the Flaw.

Each type of question has its own key characteristics and goals, but some characteristics are common to all five types. There will always be a conclusion, so you definitely want to look for it. In addition, *while* you read, try to notice any gaps, indicating assumptions, that jump out at you (but don't take much longer than you normally take to read the argument itself).

19

# Find the Assumption Questions

**Find the Assumption (FA) questions** ask you to, well, find an assumption that the author must believe to be true in order to make the argument. If the correct answer were *not* true, the argument would not be valid.

Your task is to figure out which answer choice represents something that must hold true according to the author. Note one especially tricky aspect of these problems: The assumption itself might only be true in the mind of the author. You might think, "Well, is that really true in the real world? I don't think that has to be true." Don't ask that question! The only issue is whether the *author* must believe it to be true in order to arrive at his or her conclusion. If the argument is "Planets are wonderful; therefore, Pluto is wonderful," then the assumption is that Pluto is a planet (whether you still think it is or not).

## Identifying the Question

These questions are usually easy to identify, because the question stem will use some form of the noun *assumption* or the verb *to assume*. Occasionally, the question may ask for a new premise or a new piece of information that is required or necessary to draw the conclusion. Here are a couple of examples:

> Which of the following is an *assumption* on which the argument depends?

> Which of the following is *required* for the mayor's plan to succeed?

Try this sample argument:

> When news periodicals begin forecasting a recession, people tend to spend less money on nonessential purchases. Therefore, the perceived threat of a future recession decreases the willingness of people to purchase products that they regard as optional or luxury goods.

> Which of the following is an assumption on which the argument depends?

Do the first couple of steps before looking at the answer choices:

## Step 1: Identify the Question

| Which of the following is an assumption on which the argument depends? | *The question stem uses the word* assumption, *so it is the Assumption type. Write* FA *on the scrap paper and then the answer choice letters.* | FA<br>A<br>B<br>C<br>D<br>E |
| --- | --- | --- |

19

**Step 2: Deconstruct the Argument**

| | | |
|---|---|---|
| When news periodicals begin forecasting a recession, people tend to spend less money on nonessential purchases. | *This sounds like a premise, though I suppose it could be a conclusion. The news periodicals predict a recession, and then people spend less money.* | Periodicals forecast recess → ppl spend ↓ $ non-ess |
| Therefore, the perceived threat of a future recession decreases the willingness of people to purchase products that they regard as optional or luxury goods. | *This is the conclusion. The premise above tells what people do—spend less money. The conclusion tries to claim* why *they do it—a perceived future threat.* | ©<br><br>Perceived threat → ppl spend ↓ $ lux |
| | *What is the author assuming? That people are actually reading or hearing about the forecasts. That the recession hasn't already started and that's* why *people are spending less money—maybe the periodicals are just slow in forecasting something that has already started. Also, the author assumes that* nonessential *and* luxury *mean the same thing.* | |

Did you come up with any other assumptions? The key is to get your brain thinking about these things, but there are almost always multiple possible assumptions; you may not brainstorm the exact one that will show up in the answers.

**Step 3: State the Goal**

When you state your goal, you want to think about how the question type should be applied to the argument you just read. To do this, it can be helpful to articulate the core to yourself. You don't necessarily need to write/draw it out unless you want to.

*therefore*

Periodicals forecast:
recess! ↓ spend non-ess

Perceived threat → spend lux $ ↓

*People reading/hearing info from periodicals.*
*Threat only perceived today;*
*recession hasn't already started.*

19

State your goal. What has to be true for the forecasts of a recession to result in decreased spending on luxury goods?

Take a look at the full problem now:

> When news periodicals begin forecasting a recession, people tend to spend less money on nonessential purchases. Therefore, the perceived threat of a future recession decreases the willingness of people to purchase products that they regard as optional or luxury goods.
>
> Which of the following is an assumption on which the argument depends?
>
> (A) People do not always agree as to which goods should be considered luxury goods.
>
> (B) Many more people read news periodicals today than five years ago.
>
> (C) Most people do not regularly read news periodicals.
>
> (D) Decreased spending on nonessential goods does not prompt news periodicals to forecast a recession.
>
> (E) At least some of the biggest spenders prior to the recession were those who curtailed their spending after the recession began.

## Step 4: Work from Wrong to Right

As you move to the answer choices, look for the assumptions you brainstormed but also be flexible; you might not have thought of the assumption in the correct answer, or the assumption you thought of may be phrased differently than you imagined. On FA questions, traps often involve an answer that is not tied to the conclusion, an answer that makes the argument weaker, not stronger, or an answer that makes an irrelevant distinction or comparison. (Note: You'll learn more about trap answers later in the chapter.)

| | | |
|---|---|---|
| (A) People do not always agree as to which goods should be considered luxury goods. | *I can believe that this is true in the real world, but this is irrelevant to the conclusion. The argument is not based upon whether people agree as to how to classify certain goods.* | ~~A~~ |
| (B) Many more people read news periodicals today than five years ago. | *This sounds a little bit like one of my brainstormed assumptions—the argument assumes that people are actually reading those periodicals. I'm not so sure about the more today than five years ago part, though. You don't absolutely have to believe that in order to draw that conclusion. I'll keep it in for now, but maybe I'll find something better.* | B̰ |
| (C) Most people do not regularly read news periodicals. | *This is also about reading the periodicals…but it's the opposite of what I want! The argument needs to assume that people DO read the periodicals; if they don't, then how can they be influenced by what the periodicals forecast?* | ~~C~~ |
| (D) Decreased spending on nonessential goods does not prompt news periodicals to forecast a recession. | *Let's see. This choice is saying that the drop in spending is not itself causing the forecasts. That's good, because the argument is that the causality runs the other way: The forecasts cause the drop in spending. This one is looking better than answer (B). I can cross off (B) now.* | D̰ |
| (E) At least some of the biggest spenders prior to the recession were those who curtailed their spending after the recession began. | *Hmm. This one sounds good, too. Maybe if some of the biggest spenders keep spending during the recession, then the overall amount of money being spent won't go down that much…although the argument doesn't really seem to depend on how much it goes down. Oh, wait: This says* after the recession began*—but the conclusion is about a perceived threat of a* future *recession. Nice trap!* | ~~E~~ |

~~A~~    B̰    ~~C~~    Ⓓ    ~~E~~

There were a couple of good brainstormed assumptions, but none that matched the exact assumption contained in the correct answer, (D). That's okay; be prepared to be flexible!

Note that answer choice (C) contained an "opposite" answer: It weakened the conclusion rather than making it stronger.

# The Negation Technique

On harder questions, you might find yourself stuck between two answer choices. To unstick yourself, try the **Negation Technique**.

On Find the Assumption questions, the correct answer will be something that the author must believe to be true in order to make his or her argument. As a result, if you were to turn the correct answer around to make the opposite point, then the author's argument should be harmed. Negating the correct answer should weaken the author's conclusion.

Try it out on the *News Periodicals* problem from above. Say that you narrowed the answers to (B) and (D):

(B) Many more people read news periodicals today than five years ago.

(D) Decreased spending on nonessential goods does not prompt news periodicals to forecast a recession.

Recall the argument itself as mapped out above:

Periodicals forecast recess → ppl spend ↓ $ non-ess

Perceived threat → ppl spend ↓ $ lux

The author argues that when the periodicals forecast a recession, people perceive a future threat, and so people choose to spend less money on luxury goods.

What if answer choice (B) were NOT true? It would say something like:

(B) The same number or fewer people read news periodicals today than five years ago.

Does this weaken the author's conclusion? Not really. While the argument does assume that at least some people are reading news periodicals, it doesn't discuss what used to happen five years ago, nor does it hinge on any sort of change over time.

Try negating answer (D):

(D) Decreased spending on nonessential goods DOES prompt news periodicals to forecast a recession.

Hmm. If spending goes down and then the news periodicals react by forecasting a recession…then the author has it backwards! The news periodicals aren't causing a behavior change in consumers. Rather, they're reacting to something the consumers are already doing. Thus, the argument no longer works. Negating this answer breaks down the author's argument, so this choice is the right answer.

A word of warning: Don't use this technique on every answer choice or you'll be in danger of spending too much time. However, when you're stuck, the Negation technique can be a big help. And if *that* doesn't work, as always, you know what to do: Guess and move on.

## Right Answers

For Find the Assumption questions, the right answer is necessary to the conclusion. Generally, you will not see a lot of new language or new ideas different from what was in the argument: The exception is assumptions that exclude another possibility. Take a look at this argument you saw in a previous chapter:

**19**

> Metropolis has experienced an increase in the amount of trash in its city parks. In order to reduce the amount of litter in the parks, Metropolis plans to double the number of trash cans in each city park.
>
> Which of the following is an assumption on which the argument depends?
>
> (A) Trash will not blow into the park from the streets and sidewalks surrounding the park.
>
> (B) Some people still choose to litter even if there is a trash receptacle within 20 feet of their location.

This argument is a plan: put more trash cans in parks to reduce litter. You are looking for an assumption: What is necessary for the increase in trash cans to reduce litter in the parks?

Answer (A) might have given you pause because it introduces something not discussed in the argument: trash from the surrounding streets and sidewalks. But answer (A) is actually excluding the possibility. The plan presented can only reduce litter coming from inside the park because that is where there will be more trash cans. Answer (A) is the correct answer and an example of an assumption that excludes a possibility, and thus may have new ideas or language. If you were wondering, answer (B) actually makes the argument worse, suggesting people may still litter even with more trash cans.

Below are some common assumptions for different argument types. Note that some arguments will have unique assumptions that do not match the categories described:

- **Causation:** In an argument that concludes that X causes Y, assumptions often exclude reverse causation (Y causes X) or outside causes (Z causes both X and Y).
- **Plan:** In a plan, an assumption may validate that the steps of the plan will work as expected or exclude a previously unmentioned detriment to the plan (see park litter example above).
- **Prediction:** In order for a prediction to come true, you have to assume that no other future events beyond those mentioned in the argument will intervene.
- **Profit:** For profit to move in the direction predicted by the argument, there cannot be some other factor that outweighs the predicted outcome. For example, a conclusion that states profit will increase assumes there is not some hidden cost that exceeds the benefit.

## Common Trap Answers

On many Find the Assumption questions, a trap answer won't actually address the conclusion. Because the question specifically asks you to find an assumption necessary to draw that conclusion, an answer that has **No Tie to the Conclusion** must be wrong. Answer (A) in the problem above is a good example. The conclusion does not depend upon whether different people would agree to classify the same item as a luxury good. Rather, the conclusion is about what causes someone to spend less money on anything that that individual believes to be a luxury good.

Trap answers can also use **Reverse Logic**, as in answer choice (C). Reverse logic does the opposite of what you want; in this case, answer (C) actually makes the argument worse, but an assumption should make the argument a bit stronger.

Answers (B) and (E) are examples of another trap: making an **Irrelevant Distinction or Comparison**. The argument does not hinge upon whether people read more now than they did five years ago. Nor does it depend upon the highest spending consumers doing something different from the rest of consumers. Rather, all consumers are lumped together in the argument.

**Find the Assumption Cheat Sheet**

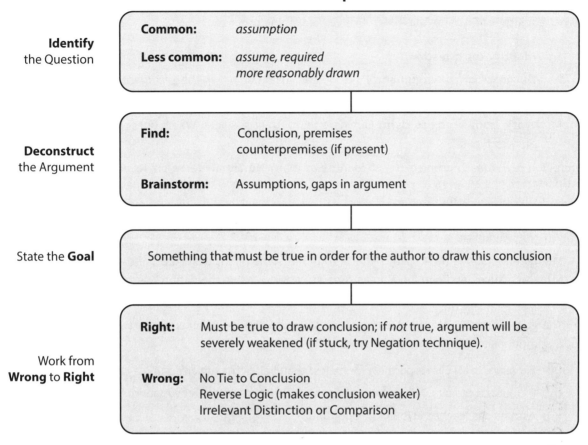

Take a picture of this page and keep it with the review sheets you're creating as you study. Better yet, use this page as a guide to create your own review sheet—you'll remember the material better if you write it down yourself.

# Problem Set

Answer each question using the 4-step Critical Reasoning process.

1. **Identify the question.**

2. **Deconstruct the argument:** Find the conclusion and map the argument on your paper.

3. **State the goal:** What will the right answer need to do?

4. **Work from wrong to right:** Eliminate four wrong answers. Watch out for common wrong answer types.

Before you review each problem, try to identify as many **No Tie**, **Reverse Logic**, and **Irrelevant Distinction** wrong answers as you can. There will be at least one common wrong answer type in each problem, and probably more!

1. *MTC and Asthma*

   Methyltetrachloride (MTC) is a chemical found in some pesticides, glues, and sealants. Exposure to MTC can cause people to develop asthma. In order to halve the nation's asthma rate, the government plans to ban all products containing MTC.

   The government's plan to halve the nation's asthma rate relies on which of the following assumptions?

   (A) Exposure to MTC is responsible for no less than half of the nation's asthma cases.

   (B) Products containing MTC are not necessary to the prosperity of the American economy.

   (C) Asthma has reached epidemic proportions.

   (D) After MTC is used in an area, residual amounts of the chemical can be detected months or years later.

   (E) Dust mites and pet dander can also cause asthma.

2. *Oil and Ethanol*

   Country N's oil production is not currently sufficient to meet its domestic demand. In order to sharply reduce its dependence on foreign sources of oil, Country N recently began requiring all automobiles produced in the country to use a blend of gasoline and ethanol, rather than gasoline alone. Country N produces enough ethanol from agricultural by-products to make up for the gap between its domestic oil production and its current demand for energy.

   Which of the following must be assumed in order to conclude that Country N will succeed in its plan to reduce its dependence on foreign oil?

   (A) Electric power is not a superior alternative to ethanol in supplementing automobile gasoline consumption.

   (B) In Country N, domestic production of ethanol is increasing more quickly than domestic oil production.

   (C) Ethanol is suitable for the heating of homes and other applications aside from automobiles.

   (D) In Country N, oil consumption is not increasing at a substantially higher rate than domestic oil and ethanol production.

   (E) Ethanol is as efficient as gasoline in terms of mileage per gallon when used as fuel for automobiles.

3. *Exchange Student*

   Student Advisor: One of our exchange students faced multiple arguments with her parents over the course of the past year. Not surprisingly, her grade point average (GPA) over the same period showed a steep decline. This is just one example of a general truth: Problematic family relationships can cause significant academic difficulties for our students.

   Which of the following is required for the student advisor to conclude that problematic family relationships can cause academic difficulties?

   (A) Last year, the exchange student reduced the amount of time spent on academic work, resulting in a lower GPA.

   (B) The decline in the GPA of the exchange student was not the reason for the student's arguments with her parents.

   (C) School GPA is an accurate measure of a student's intellectual ability.

   (D) The student's GPA is lower than the average GPA for exchange students at the university.

   (E) Fluctuations in academic performance are typical for many students.

4. *Genetics*

   Two genes, BRCA1 and BRCA2, are linked to hereditary breast cancer. Genetic testing, which can detect these genes, is increasing in both accuracy and prevalence. The test is also less painful and invasive than a mammogram, which is typically used to detect early signs of breast cancer. Therefore, we can expect the percentage of women who undergo mammograms each year to decrease.

   Which of the following is an assumption on which the argument depends?

   (A) Some women who are tested for BRCA1 and BRCA2 will choose not to undergo a mammogram.

   (B) The percentage of women undergoing mammograms each year has remained consistent over the last decade.

   (C) Aside from BRCA1 and BRCA2, there are no other genes that are strongly linked to breast cancer.

   (D) Doctors will continue to recommend regular mammograms for all women at risk of breast cancer, regardless of the results of genetic testing.

   (E) A significant percentage of cases of breast cancer are linked to BRCA1 or BRCA2.

19

## Solutions

1.  MTC and Asthma: The correct answer is **(A)**. Try to spot any **No Tie to the Conclusion**, **Reverse Logic**, or **Irrelevant Distinction or Comparison** wrong answers before you keep reading!

Step 1: Identify the Question

| The government's plan to halve the nation's asthma rate relies on which of the following assumptions? | *Asks for the* assumption; *this is a Find the Assumption question.* | FA<br><br>A<br>B<br>C<br>D<br>E |
| --- | --- | --- |

Step 2: Deconstruct the Argument

| Methyltetrachloride (MTC) is a chemical found in some pesticides, glues, and sealants. | *This is just a fact—background or maybe a premise.* | MTC = chem |
| --- | --- | --- |
| Exposure to MTC can cause people to develop asthma. | *Another fact but it's specifically a bad fact. This is likely a premise.* | Can → asthma |
| In order to halve the nation's asthma rate, the government plans to ban all products containing MTC. | *Okay, the government has a plan to ban MTC, and the result will be (they claim) that the asthma rate will be cut in half. There are no numbers or anything to support that. Are a lot of people exposed now? What percentage of those who develop asthma were exposed? Etc.* | Ⓒ Gov plan: ban MTC to ½ asthma rate |

Step 3: State the Goal

*The government claims that it can halve the asthma rate by banning MTC, but it gives absolutely no evidence or numbers to support* halving *the rate.*

*I need to find an answer that supports the idea that they can halve the asthma rate—maybe that a very large percentage of people who develop asthma were exposed to MTC or something like that.*

19

Step 4: Work from Wrong to Right

| | | |
|---|---|---|
| (A) Exposure to MTC is responsible for no less than half of the nation's asthma cases. | *This sounds similar to what I said. Let's see. If MTC actually is responsible for at least half of asthma cases, then getting rid of it would get rid of all those cases as well. This one looks pretty good.* | A<br>~ |
| (B) Products containing MTC are not necessary to the prosperity of the American economy. | ***No tie.*** *This is a deceptive wrong answer. It says that these products aren't economically important, but the conclusion isn't about economics! The conclusion talks about whether the plan will halve the asthma rate, regardless of the economic effects.* | ~~B~~ |
| (C) Asthma has reached epidemic proportions. | ***No tie.*** *This answer choice explains why we might want to reduce the asthma rate. But it doesn't address the specific plan at all.* | ~~C~~ |
| (D) After MTC is used in an area, residual amounts of the chemical can be detected months or years later. | ***Reverse logic.*** *This actually weakens the government's proposal. Since MTC sticks around long after the chemicals are actually used, banning the chemicals now may not reduce the asthma rate.* | ~~D~~ |
| (E) Dust mites and pet dander can also cause asthma. | ***Irrelevant distinction.*** *Sure, there are other things that can cause asthma. But the argument isn't about these things—it's specifically about MTC. The fact that other things can also cause asthma doesn't change anything about the MTC situation.* | ~~E~~ |

19

2. Oil and Ethanol: The correct answer is (**D**). Try to spot any **No Tie to the Conclusion**, **Reverse Logic**, or **Irrelevant Distinction or Comparison** wrong answers before you keep reading!

Step 1: Identify the Question

| Which of the following must be assumed in order to conclude that Country N will succeed in its plan to reduce its dependence on foreign oil? | *Contains the phrase* must be assumed—*this is a Find the Assumption question.* | FA<br>A<br>B<br>C<br>D<br>E |
|---|---|---|

Step 2: Deconstruct the Argument

| Country N's oil production is not currently sufficient to meet its domestic demand. | *They produce oil but can't make enough for their own needs. That must mean they have to import some oil.* | N oil prod < dom demand |
|---|---|---|
| In order to sharply reduce its dependence on foreign sources of oil, Country N recently began requiring all automobiles produced in the country to use a blend of gasoline and ethanol, rather than gasoline alone. | *They're requiring cars to use ethanol, and they think that'll lead to having to use less foreign oil. It sounds like the cars can still use gas, though...* | To ↓ for. oil, N reqs ethanol in cars |
| Country N produces enough ethanol from agricultural by-products to make up for the gap between its domestic oil production and its current demand for energy. | *Okay, so they do make enough ethanol PLUS oil combined to satisfy their own needs currently. The question is whether people are actually going to use ethanol for their cars or whether they'll want to keep using gasoline. And what if demand changes in future?* | N eth + oil = curr demand |

Step 3: State the Goal

*Country N thinks it can* sharply reduce *the amount of foreign oil it needs if it starts making people own cars that use ethanol. Will the plan really work that way? They're assuming people really will start to use the ethanol. They're also assuming they'll continue to produce enough oil and ethanol in the future.*

*I need to find an answer that must be true in order to allow the author to draw the conclusion above.*

Step 4: Work from Wrong to Right

| | | |
|---|---|---|
| (A) Electric power is not a superior alternative to ethanol in supplementing automobile gasoline consumption. | ***Irrelevant distinction.*** *Comparing ethanol to electric power doesn't tell me anything useful about ethanol, which is what I really care about. We're supposed to find something that goes with the plan stated in the argument, and that plan mentions nothing about electric power.* | A̶ |
| (B) In Country N, domestic production of ethanol is increasing more quickly than domestic oil production. | *If this is true, then switching stuff to ethanol seems like a good call. Does it have to be true in order to draw the conclusion? What if the two were increasing at the same rate? That would be fine, actually. This doesn't have to be true—so it isn't a necessary assumption.* | B̶ |
| (C) Ethanol is suitable for the heating of homes and other applications aside from automobiles. | ***Irrelevant distinction.*** *The argument only talks about a plan to have cars start using ethanol. Whether the plan will also work for homes doesn't have anything to do with cars.* | C̶ |
| (D) In Country N, gasoline consumption is not increasing at a substantially higher rate than domestic oil and ethanol production. | *Hmm. The argument is assuming in general that the ethanol + oil production can keep up with the country's demand. So, yes, the author would have to assume that gas consumption isn't increasing at a much faster rate than production.*<br><br>*Let's try negating this one: If gas consumption were increasing at a much higher rate, what would happen? Oh, they might have to get more from foreign sources— bingo! Negating this does weaken the conclusion.* | D̰ |
| (E) Ethanol is as efficient as gasoline in terms of mileage per gallon when used as fuel for automobiles. | ***No tie.*** *The conclusion isn't about gas mileage, it's about reducing foreign oil dependency. There isn't necessarily a link between those two things. Maybe people will use more ethanol than gas if it's less efficient, but maybe they won't.* | E̶ |

3. Exchange Student: The correct answer is (B). Try to spot any **No Tie to the Conclusion**, **Reverse Logic**, or **Irrelevant Distinction or Comparison** wrong answers before you keep reading!

Step 1: Identify the Question

| Which of the following is required for the student advisor to claim that problematic family relationships can cause academic difficulties? | *This is an unusual question stem. It doesn't include the word* assumption, *but it does include a synonymous idea: What is required to draw the conclusion? This is an assumption question.* | FA<br>A<br>B<br>C<br>D<br>E |
|---|---|---|

Step 2: Deconstruct the Argument

| Student Advisor: One of our exchange students faced multiple arguments with her parents over the course of the past year. | *This is a fact—background or a premise.* | Advisor: student had args w parents |
|---|---|---|
| Not surprisingly, her grade point average (GPA) over the same period showed a steep decline. | *Not only did the student's GPA go down, but the advisor says* not surprisingly. *Sounds like the advisor is going to conclude a causal relationship.* | GPA ↓↓ |
| This is just one example of a general truth: Problematic family relationships can cause significant academic difficulties for our students. | *Here we go: The advisor claims that this student's family problems* caused *the academic problems. Maybe there was a different cause.* | ↓<br><br>© Fam probs → acad probs |

Step 3: State the Goal

*I need to find an answer that the author must believe to be true in order to draw this conclusion. The only thing I can think of right now is very general: If the advisor is assuming the family problems were what caused the academic problems, then the advisor is also assuming there wasn't something else causing the academic problems.*

Step 4: Work from Wrong to Right

| | | |
|---|---|---|
| (A) Last year, the exchange student reduced the amount of time spent on academic work, resulting in a lower GPA. | *Reverse logic. This actually works against the advisor's conclusion. It suggests a different reason that the student's grades decreased. If this different reason is correct, then the advisor's reasoning is incorrect. An assumption always has to support the conclusion and can't work against it.* | ~~A~~ |
| (B) The decline in the GPA of the exchange student was not the reason for the student's arguments with her parents. | *Let's see. This is kind of what I said before—there is not a different cause for the decline of her GPA.*<br><br>*Let's try negating this. If the student's GPA went down first and then her parents got mad at her for that reason, then you can't claim that the family problems caused the lower GPA. The advisor's argument would fall apart. This choice looks good.* | B̰ |
| (C) School GPA is an accurate measure of a student's intellectual ability. | *No tie. The conclusion has nothing to do with intellectual ability! It discusses academic difficulties and their relationship to GPA and does not draw any comparison to the student's intellectual ability.* | ~~C~~ |
| (D) The student's GPA is lower than the average GPA for exchange students at the university. | *Irrelevant distinction. The argument deals with a decrease in a single exchange student's GPA. It isn't necessary to compare that student to other students in order to explain the decrease in her own GPA.* | ~~D~~ |
| (E) Fluctuations in academic performance are typical for many students. | *Reverse logic. This actually works against the advisor's conclusion. The advisor argues that the problematic family relationship caused the student's difficulties. However, this answer choice suggests that the student's GPA decrease was actually due to random fluctuation. An assumption will never work against the conclusion.* | ~~E~~ |

19

4. Genetics: The correct answer is (**A**).

Step 1: Identify the Question

| | | |
|---|---|---|
| Which of the following is an assumption on which the argument depends? | *The word* assumption *indicates that this is a Find the Assumption question.* | FA<br><br>A<br>B<br>C<br>D<br>E |

Step 2: Deconstruct the Argument

| | | |
|---|---|---|
| Two genes, BRCA1 and BRCA2, are linked to hereditary breast cancer. | *A fact about genes and cancer.* | 2 genes linked to b-cancer |
| Genetic testing, which can detect these genes, is increasing in both accuracy and prevalence. | *We're getting better at testing for these genes, and we're doing it more often.* | testing: acc & freq ↑ |
| The test is also less painful and invasive than a mammogram, which is typically used to detect early signs of breast cancer. | *Now the argument is comparing this testing to an alternative test for breast cancer. Looks like the genetic test has some advantages, although I still don't know if it's as good at detecting cancer.* | genetic test vs mammo.: less pain, less invasive |
| Therefore, we can expect the percentage of women who undergo mammograms each year to decrease. | *Here's the conclusion: It's a prediction about the future. Since genetic testing has these advantages, a smaller percentage of women will have mammograms in the future.* | ⓒ<br><br>mammo. % ↓ |

Step 3: State the Goal

*The author claims that the percentage of women who have mammograms will decrease. I know that mammograms have some disadvantages compared to genetic testing, but the author is making a big assumption in concluding that fewer people will actually have them! The right answer is something that must be true in order for the author to reach this conclusion.*

19

Step 4: Work from Wrong to Right

| | | |
|---|---|---|
| (A) Some women who are tested for BRCA1 and BRCA2 will choose not to undergo a mammogram. | *If at least some women get tested and then don't have a mammogram, then that would help to reduce the percentage of mammograms. But does this have to be true? Actually, I think it does. For fewer women to have mammograms, at least some women must be changing their minds about having one.* | A̰ |
| (B) The percentage of women undergoing mammograms each year has remained consistent over the last decade. | **No tie.** *The conclusion deals with what will happen in the immediate future: The percentage of women undergoing mammograms each year will decrease. This answer choice describes something that happened in the past. I don't know whether the past and the future are related here.* | ~~B~~ |
| (C) Aside from BRCA1 and BRCA2, there are no other genes that are strongly linked to breast cancer. | **Irrelevant distinction.** *Comparing those two genes to a third gene doesn't tell me anything about the mammogram situation. The argument is only about the results of genetic testing for those two genes, not about breast cancer more broadly.* | ~~C~~ |
| (D) Doctors will continue to recommend regular mammograms for all women at risk of breast cancer, regardless of the results of genetic testing. | **Reverse logic.** *If anything, this suggests that the prevalence of mammograms will stay the same, since genetic testing won't change doctors' recommendations. An assumption always has to support the conclusion.* | ~~D~~ |
| (E) A significant percentage of cases of breast cancer are linked to BRCA1 or BRCA2. | **No tie.** *This doesn't tell me anything about who will undergo a mammogram. If I assume that women who discover that they have this gene will choose not to have a mammogram, this might cause a decline in the number of mammograms. But I'd have to make my own assumptions in order to use that reasoning and that isn't allowed.* | ~~E~~ |

# The Assumption Family: Strengthen and Weaken

## In This Chapter:

- Strengthen and Weaken: The Basics
- Strengthen the Argument Questions
- Weaken the Argument Questions
- EXCEPT Questions
- Strengthen the Argument Cheat Sheet
- Weaken the Argument Cheat Sheet

**In this chapter, you will learn** how to recognize and answer the second and third of the five question types in the Assumption Family: Strengthen and Weaken.

# CHAPTER 20 The Assumption Family: Strengthen and Weaken

In the previous chapter, you learned about the first major question type in the Assumption Family: Find the Assumption. If you haven't read the previous chapter yet, please do so before reading this chapter.

To recap briefly:

- Assumptions are something an author must believe to be true in order to draw his or her conclusion. These assumptions are not stated explicitly in the argument.
- All assumption arguments will contain a "core": a conclusion and the major premise or premises that lead to it.
- All assumption arguments will include at least one (and probably more than one) unstated assumption.

This chapter addresses the next two Assumption Family question types: **Strengthen the Argument** and **Weaken the Argument**. Like Find the Assumption, these two types are commonly tested on the GMAT. They also hinge upon identifying an assumption.

## Strengthen and Weaken: The Basics

Both Strengthen and Weaken questions ask you to find a *new* piece of information that, if added to the existing argument, will make the conclusion either more likely to be true (strengthen) or less likely to be true (weaken).

In the case of a Strengthen, the new piece of information will typically provide evidence to support an assumption. In the case of a Weaken, the new piece of info will attack an assumption: It will serve as evidence that the assumption is invalid.

How does this work? Let's look at one of the arguments from the last chapter again:

> Thomas's football team lost in the championship game last year. The same two teams are playing in the championship game again this year, and the players on Thomas's team have improved. Therefore, Thomas's team will win the championship game this year.

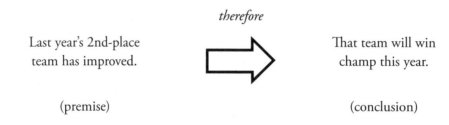

Last year's 2nd-place team has improved.

*therefore*

That team will win champ this year.

(premise)

(conclusion)

If you were asked a Find the Assumption question, the answer might be something like this: Thomas's team has improved enough to be competitive with the defending champions. In order for the author to draw this conclusion, that point must be assumed. If Thomas's team hasn't improved enough to be (at minimum) competitive with last year's first-place team, then it wouldn't make any sense to say that *because* they have improved, they will win this year.

If you're asked a Strengthen question, how does the answer change? A Strengthen answer provides some new piece of information that does not have to be true, but *if it is true*, that information does make the conclusion more likely to be valid. For example:

> The star quarterback on the defending champion team will miss the game due to an injury.

*Must* it be true that the star quarterback will miss the game in order for the author to believe that Thomas's team will win? No. If that information *is* true, though, then the conclusion is more likely to be true. Thomas's team is more likely to win if a star player on the opposing team can't play.

What happens if you're asked a Weaken question? Similarly, a Weaken answer provides a new piece of information that does not have to be true, but *if it is true*, then the conclusion is a bit less likely to be valid. For example:

> The players on the defending champion team train more than the players on any other team.

That specific fact does not have to be true in order for you to doubt the claim that Thomas's team will win—there are lots of reasons to doubt the claim—but *if it is true* that the defending champion team trains more than all of the other teams, then the author's conclusion just got weaker.

Note that Strengthen and Weaken question stems include the words *if true* or an equivalent variation. In other words, you are explicitly told to accept the information in the answer as true.

Finally, there are three possible ways that an answer choice could affect the argument on both Strengthen and Weaken questions: The answer *strengthens* the argument, the answer *weakens* the argument, or the answer *does nothing* to the argument. One of your tasks will be to classify each answer choice into one of these three buckets.

20

# Strengthen the Argument Questions

Strengthen questions ask you to find a *new* piece of information that, if added to the existing argument, will make the argument somewhat more likely to be true.

Most often, Strengthen questions will contain some form of the words *strengthen* or *support*, as well as the phrase *if true*. Here are some typical examples:

> Which of the following, if true, most strengthens the argument above?

> Which of the following, if true, most strongly supports the mayor's claim?

Strengthen questions will sometimes use synonyms in place of the strengthen/support language. These synonyms may do the following:

- Provide the best basis *or* the best reason for
- Provide justification for
- Provide evidence in favor of (a plan or a conclusion)

Strengthen questions may occasionally lack the exact phrase *if true*, but some other wording will provide a similar meaning. That wording might be something quite similar, such as *if feasible* (in reference to a plan). Alternatively, the wording might indicate that the answer can be *effectively achieved* or *successfully accomplished* (indicating that the information would become true).

Try this short example:

> At QuestCorp, many employees have quit recently and taken jobs with a competitor. Shortly before the employees quit, QuestCorp lost its largest client. Clearly, the employees were no longer confident in QuestCorp's long-term viability.
>
> Which of the following, if true, most strengthens the claim that concerns about QuestCorp's viability caused the employees to quit?
>
> (A) Employees at QuestCorp's main competitor recently received a large and well-publicized raise.
> (B) QuestCorp's largest client accounted for 40 percent of sales and nearly 60 percent of the company's profits.
> (C) Many prospective hires who have interviewed with QuestCorp ultimately accepted jobs with other companies.

The question stem indicates that this is a Strengthen question. Deconstruct the argument. The core might be:

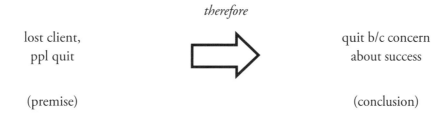

Remember, you can write the core down or you can just articulate the core to yourself mentally. Whichever path works best for you is fine.

Make sure that you understand what the argument is trying to say. The author claims that, because the company lost its largest client, some employees lost confidence in the company, so they quit. The author assumes that losing that client will be a significant blow to the company. What if the company has many clients and the largest client only represented a very small fraction of the business? The author also assumes there aren't other reasons why employees quit.

State your goal: How would you strengthen this particular conclusion?

> *This is a Strengthen question, so I have to find some evidence that supports the claim that people quit specifically because they lost confidence in the company after it lost its largest client.*

| (A) Employees at QuestCorp's main competitor recently received a large and well-publicized raise. | *Wouldn't that make QuestCorp's employees jealous—maybe they'd expect more money? That'd make it more likely that they quit because of pay issues rather than a loss of confidence in the company. If anything, this weakens the conclusion; I want a strengthen answer.* | A̶ |
|---|---|---|
| (B) QuestCorp's largest client accounted for 40 percent of sales and nearly 60 percent of the company's profits. | *Ouch. Then losing this client would be a pretty serious blow to the company. This is a fact that helps make the conclusion a little more likely; I'll keep it in.* | B ∼ |
| (C) Many prospective hires who have interviewed with QuestCorp ultimately accepted jobs with other companies. | *Hmm.* Prospective hires *are not employees. I was asked to strengthen the part about* employees losing confidence in the company. I could speculate that maybe something is wrong with QuestCorp if people take other jobs…but the answer doesn't even tell me why *these people took other jobs. Maybe QuestCorp rejected them!* | C̶ |

The correct answer is (B).

Answer choice (A) represents one common trap on Strengthen questions: The answer does the opposite of what you want. That is, it weakens the conclusion rather than strengthening it.

Answer choice (C) represents another common trap: The answer addresses (and sometimes even strengthens) something other than what you were asked to address. In this case, the answer does seem to imply that there's something not so great about QuestCorp, but it discusses the wrong group of people (prospective hires) and doesn't actually provide any information that allows you to assess what they think of QuestCorp's viability. (Again, that last part doesn't matter in the end, because it's already talking about the wrong group of people.)

## Putting It All Together

Try a full problem now:

> Donut Chain, wishing to increase the profitability of its new store, will place a coupon in the local newspaper offering a free donut with a cup of coffee at its grand opening. Donut Chain calculates that the cost of the advertisement and the free donuts will be more than compensated for by the new business generated through the promotion.
>
> Which of the following, if true, most strengthens the prediction that Donut Chain's promotion will increase the new store's profitability?

— (A) Donut Chain has a loyal following in much of the country.

— (B) Donut Chain has found that the vast majority of new visitors to its stores become regular customers.

— (C) One donut at Donut Chain costs less than a cup of coffee.

— (D) Most of the copies of the coupon in the local newspaper will not be redeemed for free donuts.

— (E) Donut Chain's stores are generally very profitable.

### Step 1: Identify the Question

| Which of the following, if true, most strengthens the prediction that Donut Chain's promotion will increase the new store's profitability? | *The language* if true *and* most strengthens the prediction that… *indicates that this is a Strengthen the Argument question. Also, the question stem tells me the conclusion I need to address: The plan will lead to better profitability.* | S<br>A<br>B<br>C<br>D<br>E<br>ⓒ promo → ↑<br>proof |
| --- | --- | --- |

### Step 2: Deconstruct the Argument

| Donut Chain, wishing to increase the profitability of its new store, will place a coupon in the local newspaper offering a free donut with a cup of coffee at its grand opening. | *Donut Chain thinks that giving away a free donut will lead to increased profitability.* | promo = free coupon |
| --- | --- | --- |
| Donut Chain calculates that the cost of the advertisement and the free donuts will be more than compensated for by the new business generated through the promotion. | *It costs $ to place the ad and give away free donuts, but Donut Chain thinks it'll get enough new business to offset those costs. Still, does that lead to better profitability?* | $ spent < $ new biz |
| (brainstorm assumptions) | *The argument isn't 100 percent clear that the profitability part is the conclusion, but the question stem also said so. The author is assuming that giving away a free donut once will lead to increased revenues over time (what if they never come back?), and that will then lead to increased profits (more revenues don't necessarily equal more profits).* | |

## Step 3: State the Goal

*I need to strengthen the claim that a particular plan is going to lead to increased profitability. The plan is to distribute coupons to give away free donuts.*

*I need to find an answer that makes it a little more likely that this plan will lead to more profits.*

## Step 4: Work from Wrong to Right

| | | |
|---|---|---|
| (A) Donut Chain has a loyal following in much of the country. | *This is good for Donut Chain. Does that mean it will* increase *profitability though? No. It's already an established fact. Plus, it only says that Donut Chain enjoys a loyal following in* much *of the country, not necessarily where the new store is located.* | ~~A~~ |
| (B) Donut Chain has found that the vast majority of new visitors to its stores become regular customers. | *So if Donut Chain can get people to visit once, they'll usually keep coming back. That sounds pretty good for Donut Chain's plan, which is all about getting people to visit the first time for that free donut.* | B ~ |
| (C) One donut at Donut Chain costs less than a cup of coffee. | *This tells me nothing about profits or revenues or how much they could sell or anything, really. This doesn't address the argument.* | ~~C~~ |
| (D) Most of the copies of the coupon in the local newspaper will not be redeemed for free donuts. | *If this happens, then Donut Chain's plan is really unlikely to work—it spends money on the ads, but never gets the new customers to come in. That* weakens *the conclusion.* | ~~D~~ |
| (E) Donut Chain's stores are generally very profitable. | *It's good that Donut Chain stores are usually profitable; that means this new one is likely to be profitable, too. The conclusion, though, specifically talks about* increasing *the store's profitability—and the question specifically asks whether this plan* will *accomplish that goal. This choice looks tempting at first, but it doesn't address whether this plan will increase profitability.* | ~~E~~ |

~~A~~    (B ~)    ~~C~~    ~~D~~    ~~E~~

# Where's the Conclusion?

In the Donut Chain argument above, you might have noticed the question provided additional information about the conclusion (that the coupon would increase profitability). Read this argument and question, and try to find the conclusion:

> Average customer wait times at the registry of motor vehicles (RMV) in Starton have increased by 30 minutes in the last year. The RMV recently developed a smartphone application that allows customers to view current wait times and predicted wait times later in the day.

> Which of the following, if true, most strengthens the claim that the smartphone application will decrease average wait times at the RMV?

The question asks you to support the claim that the app will decrease wait times. So that claim is the conclusion of the argument. But is that conclusion ever in the argument? No: The first statement says that wait times are a problem, but the possibility of reducing them is not in the argument.

Be aware that sometimes the conclusion of the argument is never stated in the argument but is instead found in the question. When you do step 1, look out for language in the question about a specific claim or prediction you are trying to support (or refute, depending on the argument type). Sometimes the GMAT hides the conclusion in the question, most frequently on Strengthen, Weaken, and Evaluate the Argument questions.

## Right Answers

On Strengthen questions, right answers need to provide additional information that makes the conclusion more likely. Do not eliminate an answer just because you see a new word or idea; consider whether the answer is logically connected to the conclusion.

In the Donut Chain example, the right answer talked about *regular customers*. Although regular customers are not mentioned in the argument, such customers have a link to profitability and thus are relevant to strengthening the conclusion.

## Common Trap Answers

One of the most common traps is the Reverse Logic answer: The question asks you to strengthen, but a trap answer choice weakens the conclusion instead. You saw an example of this with answer choice (D) in the Donut Chain problem. These can be especially tricky if you misread the conclusion or otherwise get turned around while evaluating the argument.

Most of the wrong answers will have no tie to the argument—they will neither strengthen nor weaken the argument. Some of these will be more obviously wrong, but these answers can also be quite tricky. A No Tie trap might address something in a premise without actually affecting the conclusion; answer choice (E) in the Donut Chain problem is a good example. Notice that it says something positive about Donut Chain, but not anything that addresses the specific chain of logic in the argument.

## Strengthen Variant: Fill in the Blank

Contrary to popular belief, **Fill in the Blank (FitB) questions** are not actually a separate question type; rather, any of the existing question types can be presented in FitB format. In practice, most FitB questions are Strengthen questions; occasionally, they are Inference or Find the Assumption questions.

Look at an example:

> Which of the following most logically completes the argument below?
>
> XYZ Industries sells both a premium line of televisions and a basic line. The higher-end line sells at a 20 percent premium over the basic line and accounts for about half of the company's revenues. The company has announced that it will stop producing premium televisions and sell only the basic line in the future. This plan will help to improve profitability, since _____.

Right away, you'll notice that there is no question stem after the argument—but there is a question above. The location of the question stem (and the blank at the end of the argument) indicates that you have the FitB structure. But which type of question is it?

The clue to help you identify the question will be just before the blank. In the vast majority of these problems, the word *since* or *because* will be just before the blank, in which case you have a Strengthen question.

20

The author claims that *this plan will help to improve profitability*. As with any Strengthen question, your task is to find an answer that will make this claim more likely to be true.

For the example above, for instance, a correct answer might read:

> premium televisions cost 40 percent more to produce and market than do basic televisions

If the company charges 20 percent more for a premium television, but has to pay 40 percent more to produce and market it, then it's more likely that the company makes less money on premium televisions than it does on basic ones. (This is not an absolute slam dunk, but that's okay. You just have to make the argument more likely to be valid.) Given this, the plan to drop the premium televisions and sell only the basic ones is more likely to improve profitability, strengthening the author's case.

On some FitB questions, the correct answer reinforces or even restates a premise already given in the argument. Most of the time, though, the correct answer will introduce a new premise, as with regular Strengthen questions. Either way, the result will be the same: The answer will make the author's argument at least a little more likely to be true.

## Negatively Worded Claims

Many FitB questions introduce a negatively worded twist. Take a look at this variation on the original argument:

> Which of the following most logically completes the argument below?
>
> XYZ Industries sells both a premium line of televisions and a basic line. The higher-end line sells at a 20 percent premium but also costs 40 percent more to produce and market. Producing more televisions from the basic line, however, will not necessarily help to improve profitability, since
>
> _____.

This is still a Strengthen question because the word *since* is just before the underline. The conclusion is that last sentence: A particular plan will *not* necessarily help to improve profitability. Why? Consider this possible correct answer:

> the market for basic televisions is shrinking

In other words, producing more TVs doesn't necessarily mean the company can *sell* more TVs, and it would have to sell them in order to make money. If the market for basic TVs is shrinking, then producing more of those TVs won't necessarily be beneficial for the company's profitability.

If you see *since* _____ in a FitB question, your goal is to strengthen the conclusion that comes before, even if that conclusion contains a *not* or is otherwise worded negatively.

## Alternative Wording

The *since* _____ or *because* _____ variations are the two most common ways in which FitB questions can be presented. There are a few alternative examples, however, that might pop up. Students aiming for 90th percentile or higher on the Verbal section may want to be prepared for these rare variations; otherwise, it's fine to skip this section.

The rare variants will still typically include the conclusion or claim in the final sentence with the blank, but the "lead-in" wording to the blank will be different, signaling a different question type as shown below:

| "Lead-In" Wording | Answer Choice Should | Question Type |
|---|---|---|
| If (some claim is true), "it should be expected that" _____ | represent something that must be true given the information in the argument | Inference |
| (In order for some claim to be true), "it must be shown that" _____ | represent something that must be true given the information in the argument | Inference |
| (Something is true) "assuming that" _____ | articulate an assumption used to draw the conclusion | Find the Assumption |

## Common Trap Answers

The common trap answers will mirror the trap answers given on the regular question type. For example, if the question is a Strengthen, then expect to see the same trap answers that you see on regular Strengthen questions: Reverse Logic (weakens rather than strengthens) and No Tie to the Argument.

# Weaken the Argument Questions

Weaken the Argument questions ask you to find a *new* piece of information that, if added to the existing argument, will make the argument less likely to be valid. Your goal, then, is to *attack* the argument. The correct answer will generally attack some assumption made by the author.

Most Weaken question stems contain either the word *weaken* or a synonym of it. You will also typically see the phrase *if true* and question stems similar to these examples:

- Which of the following, if true, most seriously weakens the conclusion?
- Which of the following, if true, would cast the most serious doubt on the validity of the argument?
- Which of the following, if true, would raise the most serious doubt regarding the conclusion of the argument?
- Which of the following, if true, most strongly calls into question the author's conclusion?
- Which of the following, if true, most seriously undermines the mayor's claim?

Sometimes, the question stem will contain more unusual language, such as the words in quotes below:

- Find a "disadvantage" or what is "damaging" to the argument
- A plan is "ill-suited" or otherwise unlikely to succeed
- Find a "criticism" of the argument

Now, try the same short argument about QuestCorp from earlier in the chapter, but with a different question stem and answers:

> At QuestCorp, many employees have quit recently and taken jobs with a competitor. Shortly before the employees quit, QuestCorp lost its largest client. Clearly, the employees were no longer confident in QuestCorp's long-term viability.
>
> Which of the following, if true, most seriously undermines the claim that concerns about QuestCorp's viability caused the employees to quit?
>
> (A) A new competitor in the same town provides health insurance for its employees, a benefit that QuestCorp lacks.
>
> (B) QuestCorp is unlikely to be able to replace the lost revenue via either an increase in existing client sales or the attraction of new clients.
>
> (C) Many prospective hires who have interviewed with QuestCorp ultimately accepted jobs with other companies.

The question stem indicates that this is a Weaken question. In your mind or on your paper, the argument core might look like this:

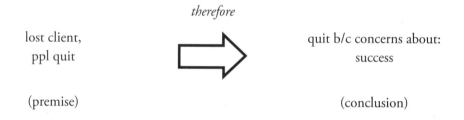

*therefore*

lost client,　　　　　　　　　　　　quit b/c concerns about:

ppl quit　　　　　　　　　　　　　　success

(premise)　　　　　　　　　　　　　(conclusion)

As always, make sure that you understand what the argument is trying to say. The author claims that losing this client caused employees to lose confidence in QuestCorp, leading them to quit. The author is assuming that losing this one client was serious enough to result in a major problem for the company. Is that necessarily the case?

Remind yourself of your goal:

*This is a Weaken question, so I have to find some evidence that makes it* less *likely that people quit for that reason. That could be because it wasn't really a big problem, or it could be that there was some other reason that people quit.*

| | | |
|---|---|---|
| (A) A new competitor in the same town provides health insurance for its employees, a benefit that QuestCorp lacks. | *The argument claims that people left for one reason, but this answer actually provides an alternative. Maybe people quit because they could get better benefits at the other company. This would weaken the claim that people quit specifically because of concerns over QuestCorp's viability as a company.* | A ~ |
| (B) QuestCorp is unlikely to be able to replace the lost revenue via either an increase in existing client sales or the attraction of new clients. | *So QuestCorp lost its largest client, which means a loss of revenue, and the company probably can't find a way to make up that revenue through other sales. That definitely reinforces the problem described in the argument. This actually strengthens the argument; that's the opposite of what I want.* | B̶ |
| (C) Many prospective hires who have interviewed with QuestCorp ultimately accepted jobs with other companies. | *Hmm. Prospective hires* are not *employees. I was asked to weaken the part about employees losing confidence in QuestCorp. I could speculate that maybe something is wrong with the company if people take other jobs…but the answer doesn't even tell me* why *these people took other jobs. Maybe QuestCorp rejected them!* | C̶ |

The correct answer is (A).

Answer (B) repeats the common Reverse Logic trap discussed earlier: It strengthens the argument. Answer (C) attempts to distract you by talking about a different part of the argument—perhaps you'll reason that, if interviewees took different jobs, then they didn't believe QuestCorp was a good company. You have no idea why these prospective hires ended up working for another company, though—it's entirely possible that QuestCorp didn't extend a job offer to these people.

Note that the problem used the exact same answer choice (C) for both the Strengthen and Weaken versions of this QuestCorp problem. If a choice is irrelevant to the argument, as choice (C) is, then it doesn't matter whether you're asked to strengthen or weaken the argument. An irrelevant choice doesn't affect the argument at all.

Try this full example:

> The national infrastructure for airport runways and air traffic control requires immediate expansion to accommodate the increase in smaller private planes. To help fund this expansion, the Federal Aviation Authority has proposed a fee for all air travelers. However, this fee would be unfair, as it would impose costs on all travelers to benefit only the few who utilize the new private planes.
>
> Which of the following, if true, would cast the most doubt on the claim that the proposed fee would be unfair?
>
> (A) The existing national airport infrastructure benefits all air travelers.
> (B) The fee, if imposed, will have a negligible impact on the overall volume of air travel.
> (C) The expansion would reduce the number of delayed flights resulting from small private planes congesting runways.
> (D) Travelers who use small private planes are almost uniformly wealthy or traveling on business.
> (E) A substantial fee would need to be imposed in order to pay for the expansion costs.

20

## Step 1: Identify the Question

| | | |
|---|---|---|
| Which of the following, if true, would cast the most doubt on the claim that the proposed fee would be unfair? | *The language* cast the most doubt on the claim *indicates that this is a Weaken question. Attack: The proposed fee would be unfair.* | W<br><br>A<br>B<br>C<br>D<br>E<br><br>Ⓒ fee = unfair |

## Step 2: Deconstruct the Argument

| | | |
|---|---|---|
| The national infrastructure for airport runways and air traffic control requires immediate expansion to accommodate the increase in smaller, private planes. | *This is written as a fact and appears to be stating something that has already been established; I'm guessing it's background info, not the conclusion, but I'm not 100 percent sure.* | To handle more small priv planes → must expand infra |
| To help fund this expansion, the Federal Aviation Authority has proposed a fee for all air travelers. | *Okay, here's a plan. It could be the conclusion. The FAA wants to charge a fee to pay for the expansion.* | FAA: fee → fund exp |
| However, this fee would be unfair, as it would impose costs on all travelers to benefit only the few who utilize the new private planes. | *Change of direction! The author disagrees with the plan, claiming it's unfair. The author's reasoning: Everyone would have to pay the fee, but only a few people would benefit.*<br><br>*Why wouldn't everyone benefit? If there's more space, then all the planes will be able to take off more quickly. The author is assuming the benefit is only for the people flying in small planes.* | BUT fee = unfair b/c all pay to benef few |

## Step 3: State the Goal

The airports are congested because there are so many small planes, and the FAA wants to charge a fee to expand the airports. The author claims that this is unfair because the fee would be paid by all but the expansion would only benefit a few.

*I want to weaken the author's conclusion, so I need to find some reason why it really isn't unfair. One possibility: Maybe more people will benefit than just the small plane people.*

## Step 4: Work from Wrong to Right

| | | |
|---|---|---|
| (A) The existing national airport infrastructure benefits all air travelers. | *This sounds like what I was thinking before—everyone benefits, so why is it unfair for everyone to pay? Great; I'll leave it in.* | A ~ |
| (B) The fee, if imposed, will have a negligible impact on the overall volume of air travel. | *A* negligible impact *means it won't really change anything. The fee won't change the volume of planes trying to fly…but that was never the plan. The plan was to raise money to expand the infrastructure—then they'll be able to handle more volume. This answer doesn't address the right thing.* | ̶B̶ |
| (C) The expansion would reduce the number of delayed flights resulting from small private planes congesting runways. | *Hmm. This is another potential benefit for everyone—a reduction in the number of flight delays. I'll leave this one in, too.* | C ~ |
| (D) Travelers who use small private planes are almost uniformly wealthy or traveling on business. | *That's nice for them, but what does it have to do with this argument? Maybe you could say, "So they can afford to pay more," but that isn't the point of the argument. The point of the argument is that it's unfair to make the regular travelers pay for something that doesn't benefit them (according to the author).* | ̶D̶ |
| (E) A substantial fee would need to be imposed in order to pay for the expansion costs. | *So the fee would have to be pretty large. If anything, doesn't that make it even more unfair? Though, actually, I don't think it really addresses the fairness at all. Either it is fair, in which case the size of the fee doesn't matter, or it isn't fair…in which case the size of the fee still doesn't matter.* | ̶E̶ |
| Examine (A) and (C) again. | *Compare choices (A) and (C). Both say that this expansion would benefit everyone…wait a second. Choice (C) does explicitly mention the expansion, but (A) says* the existing…infrastructure. *Existing? Of course, the existing structure benefits everyone who uses it—the argument isn't about that. It's about whether the* expansion *would benefit everyone. Only choice (C) actually says that; I missed that the first time around.* | ̶A̶ ~ Ⓒ |

A̶    B̶    Ⓒ    D̶    E̶

## Right Answers

As discussed with Strengthen questions, for Weaken questions, look for an answer that has a logical connection to the conclusion, in this case one that makes the conclusion less likely to be true. You will often see new language and ideas in correct answers because one way to weaken an argument is to bring up an issue that the author did not discuss. For example, in the previous example, the author had not discussed flight delays in the original argument. Below are some common ways to weaken different argument types:

- **Causation:** Provide an alternate cause for the situation.

- **Plan:** Present an unexpected cost of the plan or reason the plan will not work as expected.

- **Prediction:** Discuss additional circumstances or future changes that might affect the prediction.

- **Profit:** Provide additional information about costs or revenues (often the one not discussed in the argument). Be careful about how the direction of a change relates to the conclusion (e.g., an answer that provides a reason that costs may increase weakens an argument that profits will increase).

An argument of each of type is provided below. For each argument, first identify the argument type. Second, find a way to weaken the argument in the manner described above.

1. This year's spring festival takes place next weekend. A large number of attendees at last year's festival have recently shared positive posts about the festival on social media. Also, the advertising budget for the festival is 50 percent higher than last year's budget. Therefore, attendance at this year's spring festival will exceed attendance at last year's festival.

2. Jitters Coffee Shop offers free WiFi for use by its customers. The manager is concerned that the free WiFi results in customers sitting at tables for extended periods, driving away new customers who cannot find a table. In order to increase sales, the manager plans to limit WiFi use to 30 minutes per session.

3. A teacher observed that students who consistently sat in the first three rows of the classroom scored an average of 12 points higher on the final exam than students who consistently sat in the last three rows. Thus, sitting in the front of the classroom causes enhanced retention of course material.

4. Workers at Tangerine Corporation receive overtime pay equal to one and a half times their normal hourly pay when they work more than 40 hours in a given week. Recently, Tangerine implemented a policy requiring approval from a manager for any employee to exceed the 40-hour threshold. By limiting overtime pay, this policy will increase profits for Tangerine.

Take a look at the suggested answers below. There are multiple ways to weaken any argument, so you may have thought of a different answer.

1. **Prediction.** This conclusion is a prediction about increased attendance at the festival. The premises in the argument only discuss publicity via both social media and advertising. You can weaken this argument by providing any other issue that might decrease attendance (bad weather, fewer attractions at this year's festival). For example, a major snowstorm is predicted for the weekend of the festival this year.

2. **Plan.** The manager provides a plan to increase sales: limit WiFi to 30 minutes so more customers can sit down. You can weaken this argument by providing reasons this plan might not increase sales or even decrease sales. For example, most customers who use the WiFi for over an hour make multiple purchases during their stay. If this were the case, the plan could actually lead to losing some sales.

20

3.  **Causation.** The teacher has made an observation that two things occur together: sitting in the front and higher test scores. The conclusion introduces causation: Sitting in front causes enhanced retention of the course material. You can weaken this argument by providing another cause for the teacher's observation: either reverse causation or an outside cause for both factors. Reverse causation in this case would mean high test grades are causing students to sit in the front of the room. While that idea doesn't make complete sense, it might get you thinking about what types of students might choose to sit in the front. For example, students who report studying more hours per week tend to select seats in the front of the classroom.

4.  **Profit** (also a Plan). The argument states that profits will increase, but the information provided only discusses potentially reducing costs through limiting overtime pay. You can weaken this plan by providing a reason that the plan may reduce revenues (or a reason it might not reduce costs). For example, most overtime work results in additional sales to new clients.

## Common Trap Answers

Weaken questions contain the same kind of common trap answers that show up on Strengthen questions.

One of the trickiest types is the Reverse Logic trap: The question asks you to weaken, but a trap answer choice strengthens the argument instead. You will also again see the No Tie to the Argument traps—choices that might discuss something in a premise but don't affect the argument.

The most tempting wrong answer in the last problem, answer choice (A), is actually a No Tie trap. Almost everything in the choice was addressing the right thing, but one word made it wrong: *existing*. The conclusion was about the future infrastructure, after an expansion, so limiting the answer to the existing infrastructure meant that the information didn't affect the conclusion after all.

# EXCEPT Questions

Assumption Family questions may also be presented in a "negative" form that is commonly referred to as EXCEPT questions.

A regular Weaken question might read:

> Which of the following, if true, most seriously weakens the conclusion?

A Weaken EXCEPT question might read:

> Each of the following, if true, weakens the conclusion EXCEPT:

What is the difference in wording between those two questions?

The first one indicates that one answer choice, and only one, weakens the argument. You want to pick that choice.

The second one indicates that four answer choices weaken the argument. These four are all wrong answers. What about the fifth answer—what does that one do?

Many people assume that the fifth one must do the opposite: strengthen the argument. *This is not necessarily true.* The fifth one certainly does not weaken the argument, but it may not strengthen the argument either. It might have no impact whatsoever on the argument.

For these negatively worded questions, use the "odd one out" strategy. Four of the answer choices will do the same thing; in the case of the example above, four answers will weaken the argument. The fifth choice, the correct one, will do something else. It doesn't matter whether the fifth one strengthens the argument or does nothing—all that matters is that it is the odd one out, the one that does *not* weaken. In order to keep track of the four similar answers versus the odd one out, label the choices as you assess them with an S for Strengthen, a W for Weaken, and an N for Neutral or "does Nothing."

Try this example:

> Supporters of a costly new Defense Advanced Research Projects Agency (DARPA) initiative assert that the project will benefit industrial companies as well as the military itself. In many instances, military research has resulted in technologies that have fueled corporate development and growth, and this pattern can be expected to continue.
>
> Each of the following, if true, serves to weaken the argument above EXCEPT:
>
> (A) The research initiative will occupy many talented scientists, many of whom would otherwise have worked for private corporations.
>
> (B) In the past decade, DARPA has adopted an increasingly restrictive stance regarding the use of intellectual property resulting from its research.
>
> (C) If the DARPA initiative hadn't been approved, much of the funding would instead have been directed toward tax breaks for various businesses.
>
> (D) At any given time, DARPA is conducting a wide variety of costly research projects.
>
> (E) The research initiative is focused on specific defense mechanisms that would be ineffective for private corporations.

## Step 1: Identify the Question

| | | |
|---|---|---|
| Each of the following, if true, serves to weaken the argument above EXCEPT: | *The language* serves to weaken *indicates that this is a Weaken question. The word* EXCEPT *indicates that the four wrong answers will weaken, and I want to pick the "odd one out" answer.* | WEx<br><br>A<br><br>B<br><br>C<br><br>D<br><br>E |

## Step 2: Deconstruct the Argument

| | | |
|---|---|---|
| Supporters of a costly new Defense Advanced Research Projects Agency (DARPA) initiative assert that the project will benefit industrial companies as well as the military itself. | *The supporters of DARPA think that this costly project will be good for companies and for the military.* | ©<br><br>Supporters:<br>Costly proj will benef co's & mil |
| In many instances, military research has resulted in technologies that have fueled corporate development and growth, and this pattern can be expected to continue. | *Research has helped companies in the past, and the author claims this will keep happening in the future. That all supports the claim of the supporters: that the specific DARPA project will be beneficial for companies.* | Past: mil research → techs help co's, will cont |

## Step 3: State the Goal

In the past, military research has helped companies, and the claim is that this DARPA project will also help companies.

*I want to find four answers that weaken the argument. The answer that doesn't weaken—the odd one out—is the correct answer.*

## Step 4: Work from Wrong to Right

| | | |
|---|---|---|
| (A) The research initiative will occupy many talented scientists, many of whom would otherwise have worked for private corporations. | *This benefits the military and specifically does not benefit the companies. That does weaken the idea that companies will benefit.* | ~~A~~ W |
| (B) In the past decade, DARPA has adopted an increasingly restrictive stance regarding the use of intellectual property resulting from its research. | *Hmm. Restrictive makes it sound like DARPA doesn't let others use its research as much. If that's the case, then that would weaken the idea that companies will benefit. I'm not totally sure that's what this means though—the wording is tricky—so I'm going to give this a question mark and come back to it later.* | B W ? |
| (C) If the DARPA initiative hadn't been approved, much of the funding would instead have been directed toward tax breaks for various businesses. | *A tax break is a good thing. This choice is saying that the funding for the DARPA project would instead have been spent on tax breaks, which is a definite benefit. So not giving those tax breaks is a bad thing for the companies; this does weaken the argument.* | ~~C~~ W |
| (D) At any given time, DARPA is conducting a wide variety of costly research projects. | *This choice talks about all research projects DARPA is conducting. Hmm. The argument makes a claim only about one specific project. Does this information make that claim more or less likely to be valid? I can't really see how it affects the argument's conclusion at all.* | D N |
| (E) The research initiative is focused on specific defense mechanisms that would be ineffective for private corporations. | *The key here is the language ineffective for private corporations. If the private companies can't make effective use of the results of this particular research, then that weakens the claim that the DARPA research will benefit companies.* | ~~E~~ W |
| Examine (B) and (D) again. | *I need to compare answers (B) and (D). I thought (B) might weaken a little bit, and I thought (D) didn't do anything to the argument. Between those two, I should choose the one that doesn't weaken at all, so I'm going to choose choice (D).* | ~~B~~ Ⓓ W N |

The correct answer is (D).

The biggest trap answer on an EXCEPT question is simply to forget halfway through that you're working on an EXCEPT question. If this happens, you might accidentally pick a Weaken answer or pick the answer that you think *most* weakens the argument. The *W* labels under your weaken answers will help to remind you that multiple answers weaken, so that is not what you want to pick.

## Strengthen the Argument Cheat Sheet

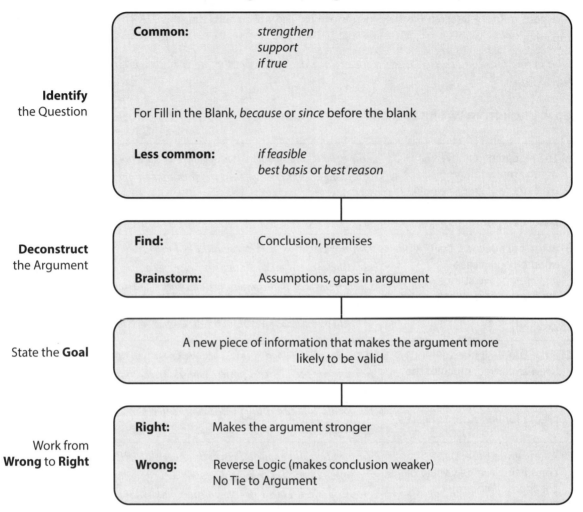

**Identify** the Question

**Common:**
*strengthen*
*support*
*if true*

For Fill in the Blank, *because* or *since* before the blank

**Less common:**
*if feasible*
*best basis* or *best reason*

**Deconstruct** the Argument

**Find:** Conclusion, premises

**Brainstorm:** Assumptions, gaps in argument

State the **Goal**

A new piece of information that makes the argument more likely to be valid

Work from **Wrong** to **Right**

**Right:** Makes the argument stronger

**Wrong:** Reverse Logic (makes conclusion weaker)
No Tie to Argument

Note: Fill in the Blank is almost always Strengthen, because the blank is usually preceded by *since* or *because*. When in doubt, assume that the question type is Strengthen.

Take a picture of this page and keep it with the review sheets you're creating as you study. Better yet, use this page as a guide to create your own review sheet—you'll remember the material better if you write it down yourself.

**Weaken the Argument Cheat Sheet**

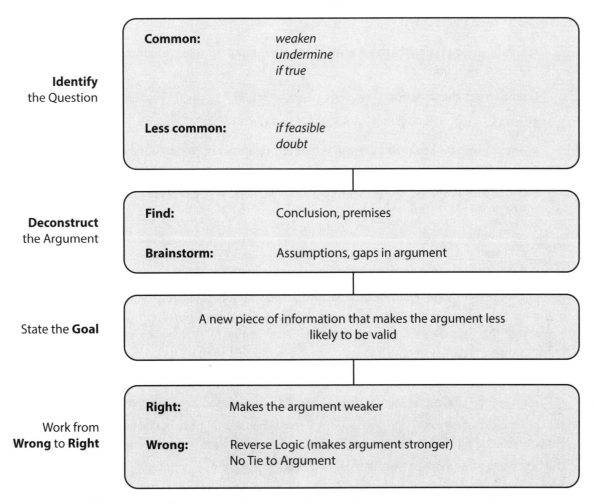

Take a picture of this page and keep it with the review sheets you're creating as you study. Better yet, use this page as a guide to create your own review sheet—you'll remember the material better if you write it down yourself.

# Problem Set

Answer each question using the 4-step Critical Reasoning process.

1. **Identify the question:** Is this a Strengthen the Argument question or a Weaken the Argument question?

2. **Deconstruct the argument:** Find the conclusion and map the argument on your paper.

3. **State the goal:** What will the right answer need to do?

4. **Work from wrong to right:** Eliminate four wrong answers. Watch out for common wrong answer types.

Before you check your answers, identify as many Reverse Logic wrong answers as you can in each problem. Every problem has at least one!

1. *Motor City*

    Which of the following best completes the passage below?

    A nonprofit organization in Motor City has proposed that local college students be given the option to buy half-price monthly passes for the city's public transportation system. The nonprofit claims that this plan will reduce air pollution in Motor City while increasing profits for the city's public transportation system. However, this plan is unlikely to meet its goals, since _____.

    (A) most college students in Motor City view public transportation as unsafe

    (B) most college students in Motor City view public transportation as prohibitively expensive

    (C) college students typically do not have the 9-to-5 schedules of most workers, and can thus be expected to ride public transportation at times when there are plenty of empty seats

    (D) a bus produces more air pollution per mile than does a car

    (E) a large proportion of the college students in Motor City live off campus

2. *Smithtown Theatre*

    The Smithtown Theatre, which stages old plays, has announced an expansion that will double its capacity along with its operating costs. The theatre is only slightly profitable at present. In addition, all of the current customers live in Smithtown, and the population of the town is not expected to increase in the next several years. Thus, the expansion of the Smithtown Theatre will prove unprofitable.

    Which of the following, if true, would most seriously weaken the argument?

    (A) A large movie chain plans to open a new multiplex location in Smithtown later this year.

    (B) Concession sales in the Smithtown Theatre comprise a substantial proportion of the theatre's revenues.

    (C) Many recent arrivals to Smithtown are students who are less likely to attend the Smithtown Theatre than are older residents.

    (D) The expansion would allow the Smithtown Theatre to stage larger, more popular shows that will attract customers from neighboring towns.

    (E) The Board of the Smithtown Theatre often solicits input from residents of the town when choosing which shows to stage.

3.  *Books and Coffee*

    The owners of a book store and a nearby coffee shop have decided to combine their businesses. Both owners believe that this merger will increase the number of customers and therefore the gross revenue, because customers who come for one reason may also decide to purchase something else.

    Which of the following, if true, most weakens the owners' conclusion that a merger will increase revenue?

    (A) Books and drinks can both be considered impulse purchases; often, they are purchased by customers without forethought.

    (B) Profit margins at a coffee shop are generally significantly higher than profit margins at a book store.

    (C) People who are able to read the first chapter of a book before buying are more likely to decide to buy the book.

    (D) A large majority of the book store's current customer base already frequents the coffee shop.

    (E) A combination book store and coffee shop that opened in a neighboring city last year has already earned higher than expected profits.

4.  *Teacher Compensation*

    Traditionally, public school instructors have been compensated according to seniority. Recently, education experts have criticized the system as one that rewards lackadaisical teaching and reduces motivation to excel. Instead, these experts argue that, to retain exceptional teachers and maintain quality instruction, teachers should receive salaries or bonuses based on performance rather than seniority.

    Which of the following, if true, most weakens the argument of the education experts?

    (A) Some teachers express that financial compensation is not the only factor contributing to job satisfaction and teaching performance.

    (B) School districts will develop their own unique compensation structures that may differ greatly from those of other school districts.

    (C) Upon leaving the teaching profession, many young, effective teachers cite a lack of opportunity for more rapid financial advancement as a primary factor in the decision to change careers.

    (D) In school districts that have implemented pay for performance compensation structures, standardized test scores have dramatically increased.

    (E) A merit-based system that bases compensation on teacher performance reduces collaboration, which is an integral component of quality instruction.

5. *Machu Picchu*

In 2001, the Peruvian government began requiring tourists to buy permits to hike the Inca Trail to the ancient city of Machu Picchu. Only 500 people per day are given permission to hike the Inca Trail, whereas before 2001 daily visitors numbered in the thousands. The Peruvian government claims that this permit program has successfully prevented deterioration of archaeological treasures along the Inca Trail.

Which of the following, if true, most strengthens the argument above?

 (A) Since 2001, Incan ruins similar to Machu Picchu but without a visitor limit have disintegrated at a significantly greater rate than those on the Inca Trail.

 (B) Villages near Machu Picchu have experienced declines in income, as fewer tourists buy fewer craft goods and refreshments.

 (C) Many of the funds from the sale of Inca Trail permits are used to hire guards for archaeological sites without permit programs.

 (D) Since 2001, tourist guides along the Inca Trail have received 50 percent to 100 percent increases in take-home pay.

 (E) Due to limited enforcement, the majority of tourists hiking the Inca Trail currently do so without a permit.

6. *Digital Video Recorders*

Advertising Executive: More than 10 million households now own digital video recorders that can fast-forward over television commercials; approximately 75 percent of these households fast-forward over at least one commercial per 30-minute program. Because television commercials are not as widely watched as they used to be, they are much less cost-effective today.

Which of the following is required in order for the advertising executive to claim that television commercials are less cost-effective today?

(A) Product placement within television programs is a viable alternative to traditional television commercials.

(B) The television programs preferred by consumers without digital video recorders are similar to those preferred by consumers with the devices.

(C) Prior to the advent of digital video recorders, very few television viewers switched channels or left the room when commercials began.

(D) The cost-effectiveness of television advertising is based less upon how many people watch a particular commercial and more upon the appropriateness of the demographic.

(E) The amount that television channels charge for advertisers to air commercials on their channel has increased steadily over the last decade.

20

7. *APR*

CEO: Over the past several years, we have more than doubled our revenues, but profits have steadily declined because an increasing number of customers have failed to pay their balances. In order to compensate for these higher default rates, we will increase the interest charged on outstanding balances from an annual percentage rate (APR) of 9.5 percent to an APR of 12 percent. This increase will be sufficient to compensate for the current rate of defaults and allow us to increase our profits.

Which of the following statements, if true, would most seriously undermine a plan to increase interest rates in order to spur profitable growth?

(A) Many other companies have experienced a similar trend in their default rates.

(B) The company's operating expenses are above the industry average and can be substantially reduced, thus increasing margins.

(C) The increase in default rates was due to a rise in unemployment, but unemployment rates are expected to drop in the coming months.

(D) The proposed increase in the APR will, alone, more than double the company's profit margins.

(E) An increase in the APR charged on credit card balances often results in higher rates of default.

8. *Jupiter vs. Mars*

Scientists suspect that Europa, a moon orbiting Jupiter, may contain living organisms. However, the government recently scrapped an unmanned science mission to Europa and replaced it with a project aimed at landing an astronaut on Mars. Polls show that the public is far more fascinated by space travel than by discovering life elsewhere in the universe. Critics argue that the government's decision-making process places a greater emphasis on popularity than it does on the importance of scientific research.

Which of the following, if true, would most strengthen a contention by the government that the critics' accusation is incorrect?

(A) In the first year of the project, the government will spend 30 percent of its total budget on developing a space shuttle that can travel to Mars; that figure is expected to drop to 0 percent after five years.

(B) The government cannot be absolutely certain of the chances for success of either project.

(C) Some scientists are convinced that a mission to Europa would add immeasurably to our understanding of the universe.

(D) A new telescope that has just become available to scientists promises to yield more information than the planned mission to Europa was designed to provide.

(E) Most people feel that a shuttle to Mars would represent a first step toward an extensive program of space travel.

9.   *Deep-Brain Stimulation*

Which of the following most logically completes the argument given below?

Deep-brain stimulation is a new technique for combating severe depression. In a recent experiment, electrodes were implanted into the brains of six patients who had not responded to any currently approved treatment for depression. When an electrical current to the electrodes was switched on, four of the patients reported feeling a dramatic reduction in depressive symptoms. The long-term prospects of the new treatment are not promising, however, because _____.

(A)   other treatments for depression may also be effective

(B)   the other two patients reported only a slight reduction of depressive symptoms during the treatment

(C)   deep-brain stimulation relies on the expertise of highly skilled physicians

(D)   when the electrical current is interrupted, the effects of the treatment are reversed

(E)   in a subsequent experiment, a one-hour treatment with the electrodes resulted in a sustained remission from depression in the four patients for six months

# Solutions

1. Motor City: The correct answer is **(A)**. Remember to identify any Reverse Logic answers before you read the explanation!

Step 1: Identify the Question

| Which of the following best completes the passage below? | *The blank at the end signals a Fill in the Blank format. The word* since *just before the blank indicates that this is a Strengthen question.* | S<br>A<br>B<br>C<br>D<br>E |
|---|---|---|

Step 2: Deconstruct the Argument

| A nonprofit organization in Motor City has proposed that local college students be given the option to buy half-price monthly passes for the city's public transportation system. | *This is a fact—the organization has proposed this plan.* | Nonprof: give coll stud 1/2 off pub trans |
|---|---|---|
| The nonprofit claims that this plan will reduce air pollution in Motor City while increasing profits for the city's public transportation system. | *Okay, the nonprofit claims something, but I'm not labeling this the conclusion, because the conclusion is supposed to be in the final sentence of CA questions.* | → ↓ air poll, ↑ prof |
| However, this plan is unlikely to meet its goals, since_____. | *This is the conclusion. The author thinks the plan won't work. Why?* | ©️ BUT unlikely to work |

Step 3: State the Goal

*The author believes that the nonprofit's plan is not going to work, and I need to find a reason that supports this author's belief. The plan is to let college students buy public transportation passes for half price in order to reduce air pollution and increase profits. Which answer choice supports the idea that this plan will* not *work?*

Step 4: Work from Wrong to Right

| | | |
|---|---|---|
| (A) most college students in Motor City view public transportation as unsafe | *If this is the case, then the students wouldn't want to use public transport at all, even if they were given a discount. That would make the plan unlikely to succeed. This might be it!* | A $\sim$ |
| (B) most college students in Motor City view public transportation as prohibitively expensive | ***Reverse logic.** Giving the students a discount is likely to make them use public transport more. This makes the plan more likely to succeed, not less likely.* | ~~B~~ |
| (C) college students typically do not have the 9-to-5 schedules of most workers, and can thus be expected to ride public transportation at times when there are plenty of empty seats | ***Reverse logic.** If this were true, it'd be good news for the public transport's profits—the students would be filling what are currently empty seats.* | ~~C~~ |
| (D) a bus produces more air pollution per mile than does a car | *At first, this sounds good—if a bus produces more air pollution than a car, then using more buses would create more air pollution, which would hurt the plan. But the plan isn't to add more buses; it's to put more people on the already-running buses. Plus, one car won't be replaced with one bus! A bus might replace 10 or more cars.* | ~~D~~ |
| (E) a large proportion of the college students in Motor City live off campus | ***Reverse logic.** This makes it likely that the students need some method of transportation to get to school—if they're using cars now and switch to buses, then the plan just might work.* | ~~E~~ |

2. Smithtown Theatre: The correct answer is (**D**). Remember to identify any Reverse Logic answers before you read the explanation!

Step 1: Identify the Question

| Which of the following, if true, would most seriously weaken the argument? | *The words* if true *and* weaken *tell me that this is a Weaken question.* | W<br>A<br>B<br>C<br>D<br>E |
|---|---|---|

Step 2: Deconstruct the Argument

| The Smithtown Theatre, which stages old plays, has announced an expansion that will double its capacity along with its operating costs. | *They have a plan. It's future, so it could be the conclusion, but I'm guessing there'll be more of a claim like "The theatre will (or will not) be successful with its plan" or something like that.* | Theatre: expand to ↑↑ cap & cost |
|---|---|---|
| The theatre is only slightly profitable at present. | *This is a fact. I wonder: If the theatre expands, will it get enough new business to continue covering costs?* | Now: barely prof |
| In addition, all of the current customers live in Smithtown, and the population of the town is not expected to increase in the next several years. | *The first half is a fact; the second half is a future prediction. So far, the case for the theatre's new plan doesn't sound very good.* | Cust live in S, prob won't be more from S |
| Thus, the expansion of the Smithtown Theatre will prove unprofitable. | *Okay, here's the conclusion. The author thinks the plan will fail and provides some pieces of evidence to support that claim.* | Ⓒ<br>Theatre expansion unprof |

Step 3: State the Goal

*The theatre has a plan to expand, but the author claims that the plan will fail. The author reasons that the theatre is only barely profitable right now, and it doesn't seem like there are a lot more opportunities to get new customers.*

*I want something that will weaken the author's claim. I have to be careful here: I should weaken the idea that the plan will fail, not weaken the plan itself. The right answer will actually strengthen the plan and show that the expansion may work.*

Step 4: Work from Wrong to Right

| | | |
|---|---|---|
| (A) A large movie chain plans to open a new multiplex location in Smithtown later this year. | ***Reverse logic.*** *If anything, you'd have to say that the new movie theatre would take business from the theatre, which would strengthen the author's claim that the theatre will fail.* | ~~A~~ |
| (B) Concession sales in the Smithtown Theatre comprise a substantial proportion of the theatre's revenues. | *How would this change if the theatre expanded? That still depends upon whether they can get more people to come to the theatre, so this doesn't really tell me anything new.* | ~~B~~ |
| (C) Many recent arrivals to Smithtown are students who are less likely to attend the Smithtown Theatre than are older residents. | ***Reverse logic.*** *The new people moving to town are people who aren't likely to start going to the theatre. That strengthens the author's claim that ST's expansion is going to fail.* | ~~C~~ |
| (D) The expansion would allow the Smithtown Theatre to stage larger, more popular shows that will attract patrons from neighboring towns. | *Hmm. This basically means that the expansion would attract a greater audience—that helps! If they have more people, they can fill the larger theatre and make more money. This one is looking good as a weakener for the claim that the expansion will fail.* | D ~ |
| (E) The Board of the Smithtown Theatre often solicits input from residents of the town when choosing which shows to stage. | *This is how they do things now. Would it stay the same or change when they expand? I have no idea.* | ~~E~~ |

3. Books and Coffee: The correct answer is (**D**). Remember to identify any Reverse Logic answers before you read the explanation!

Step 1: Identify the Question

| | | |
|---|---|---|
| Which of the following, if true, most weakens the owners' conclusion that a merger will increase revenue? | *The words* if true *and* weakens *tell me that this is a Weaken question. Further, I now know the conclusion: Some merger will result in increased revenue.* | W<br><br>A<br>B<br>C<br>D<br>E<br><br>© Merger<br>→ ↑ rev |

Step 2: Deconstruct the Argument

| | | |
|---|---|---|
| The owners of a book store and a nearby coffee shop have decided to combine their businesses. | *This is a fact; they have already made this decision, although it sounds like they haven't actually merged yet.* | Book + coffee combining |
| Both owners believe that this merger will increase the number of customers and therefore the gross revenue, | *This is the same thing the Q stem said: The merger will increase revenue.* | Will → ↑ cust, rev |
| because customers who come for one reason may also decide to purchase something else. | *According to the owners, the individual customers of each store will end up buying both books and coffee, so there'll be more customers for both, which means more revenue for both.* | B/c cross-sell |

Step 3: State the Goal

*The owners think that merging will lead to increased revenue because it'll increase the number of customers and the customers will buy more stuff. This assumes that the same customers weren't already going to both stores and buying stuff.*

*This is a Weaken question, so I need to find something that will make the conclusion less likely to be valid. The right answer will show that revenue might not increase.*

Step 4: Work from Wrong to Right

| | | |
|---|---|---|
| (A) Books and drinks can both be considered impulse purchases; often, they are purchased by customers without forethought. | ***Reverse logic.*** *If people normally just buy coffee but see a book they like, maybe they'll be more likely to buy. That would strengthen the plan to merge, but I want to weaken the plan.* | A̶ |
| (B) Profit margins at a coffee shop are generally significantly higher than profit margins at a book store. | *That might make the coffee shop owner not want to merge, but it doesn't address the revenue side of the equation at all—and the conclusion has to do with revenues, not profits.* | B̶ |
| (C) People who are able to read the first chapter of a book before buying are more likely to decide to buy the book. | ***Reverse logic.*** *This helps the owners' argument again! If I can sit there and read while having my coffee, then I'm more likely to buy the book, which would increase revenues.* | C̶ |
| (D) A large majority of the book store's current customer base already frequents the coffee shop. | *Most of the people who shop at the book store also already go to the coffee shop. That's bad for the owner's plan—it means that they're not going to pick up as many new customers as I might have thought before.* | D ~ |
| (E) A combination book store and coffee shop that opened in a neighboring city last year has already earned higher than expected profits. | *Two problems here. One, the author's not talking about the same book store and coffee shop. Two, this choice talks about profits, not revenues.* | E̶ |

A̶     B̶     C̶     Ⓓ͌     E̶

4.  Teacher Compensation: The correct answer is **(E)**. Remember to identify any Reverse Logic answers before you read the explanation!

Step 1: Identify the Question

| | | |
|---|---|---|
| Which of the following, if true, most weakens the argument of the education experts? | *The language* if true *and* weakens *tells me this is a Weaken question. In addition, the question tells me that I need to look for a reference to* education experts *because whatever they claim is the conclusion.* | W<br>A<br>B<br>C<br>D<br>E |

Step 2: Deconstruct the Argument

| | | |
|---|---|---|
| Traditionally, public school instructors have been compensated according to seniority. | *Fact: Teachers have been getting paid based upon how long they've worked.* | Trad: Pub school teachers = $ by seniority |
| Recently, education experts have criticized the system as one that rewards lackadaisical teaching and reduces motivation to excel. | *Supposedly, paying teachers by seniority makes them less likely to work hard.* | Experts: ↓ motiv |
| Instead, these experts argue that, to retain exceptional teachers and maintain quality instruction, teachers should receive salaries or bonuses based on performance rather than seniority. | *The experts want to base compensation on performance, and they claim this will lead to better teachers and instruction. This is the conclusion.* | ©️ Base comp on perform → keep great teachers |

Step 3: State the Goal

*Teachers normally get paid based on seniority, but these experts think that paying them based on performance will help teacher quality.*

*I need to find something that weakens this plan. The right answer should show that paying teachers based on performance* won't *get us better teachers.*

Step 4: Work from Wrong to Right

| | | |
|---|---|---|
| (A) Some teachers express that financial compensation is not the only factor contributing to job satisfaction and teaching performance. | *This answer is going in the right direction. If financial compensation isn't the only factor, then maybe paying teachers based on performance won't make them perform better. But there are a few problems: First, this answer says it isn't the only factor. But if it isn't the only factor, that means compensation is still a factor! Plus, this is just about what some teachers say. Even if some teachers claim to disagree, they might not be right, and they might not represent the majority.* | ~~A~~ |
| (B) School districts will develop their own unique compensation structures that may differ greatly from those of other school districts. | *The argument isn't claiming that every school district has to be identical. It just makes a recommendation that compensation be tied to performance in general.* | ~~B~~ |
| (C) Upon leaving the teaching profession, many young, effective teachers cite a lack of opportunity for more rapid financial advancement as a primary factor in the decision to change careers. | ***Reverse logic.*** *This shows that teachers do care about the financial side of things. So, paying effective teachers more will probably help schools hang on to them.* | ~~C~~ |
| (D) In school districts that have implemented pay for performance compensation structures, standardized test scores have dramatically increased. | ***Reverse logic.*** *If paying for teacher performance helps the students, then the experts' plan is probably a good one.* | ~~D~~ |
| (E) A merit-based system that bases compensation on teacher performance reduces collaboration, which is an integral component of quality instruction. | *The experts' plan has a drawback: It reduces something that is considered an integral component of good teaching. If that's true, it could hurt the idea that basing compensation on performance will result in maintaining good instruction.* | E ~ |

~~A~~    ~~B~~    ~~C~~    ~~D~~    Ⓔ

20

5.   Machu Picchu: The correct answer is **(A)**. Remember to identify any Reverse Logic answers before you read the explanation!

Step 1: Identify the Question

| Which of the following, if true, most strengthens the argument above? | *The words* if true *and* strengthens the argument *indicate that this is a Strengthen question.* | S A B C D E |
| --- | --- | --- |

Step 2: Deconstruct the Argument

| In 2001, the Peruvian government began requiring tourists to buy permits to hike the Inca Trail to the ancient city of Machu Picchu. | *This is a fact. People now have to pay to hike the Inca Trail.* | 2001 Peru gov: req permits to hike Inca Trail |
| --- | --- | --- |
| Only 500 people per day are given permission to hike the Inca Trail, whereas before 2001 daily visitors numbered in the thousands. | *More facts. Now, only 500 people a day are allowed; before, there were thousands a day.* | Now: 500/day (old = 1000's) |
| The Peruvian government claims that this permit program has successfully prevented deterioration of archaeological treasures along the Inca Trail. | *Here's the claim: The PG specifically says that the permit program is responsible for preventing deterioration along the trail.* | ©Gov: permits → ↓ damage |

Step 3: State the Goal

*The Peruvian government claims that its permit program has been responsible for preventing deterioration along the Inca Trail. This is a cause-and-effect relationship. Since I need to strengthen the argument, the right answer should show that the permit program probably has reduced the damage.*

Step 4: Work from Wrong to Right

| | | |
|---|---|---|
| (A) Since 2001, Incan ruins similar to Machu Picchu but without a visitor limit have disintegrated at a significantly greater rate than those on the Inca Trail. | *This sounds promising. The government's assumption was that the visitor limit helped prevent deterioration, so showing that other sites without limits did experience deterioration would make it more likely that the government's reasoning is valid. I'll definitely keep this one in.* | A̰ |
| (B) Villages near Machu Picchu have experienced declines in income, as fewer tourists buy fewer craft goods and refreshments. | *This sounds bad for the villages, but it doesn't impact the specific claim about preventing deterioration along the trail.* | B̶ |
| (C) Many of the funds from the sale of Inca Trail permits are used to hire guards for archaeological sites without permit programs. | *All this tells me is that* other *sites are better protected due to the guards. It doesn't tell me whether the program is protecting the Inca Trail itself.* | C̶ |
| (D) Since 2001, tourist guides along the Inca Trail have received 50 percent to 100 percent increases in take-home pay. | *This doesn't tell me anything about the damage to the trail.* | D̶ |
| (E) Due to limited enforcement, the majority of tourists hiking the Inca Trail currently do so without a permit. | ***Reverse logic.*** *This one makes me think that even though only 500 people per day are allowed on the trail, the actual number is much higher. So, the permit program probably isn't working very well.* | E̶ |

20

6. Digital Video Recorders: The correct answer is **(C)**.

Did this one seem a little different from all of the others? We set a trap for you! This is a Find the Assumption question, not a Strengthen or a Weaken. We discussed Find the Assumption questions in the previous chapter (though we used a less common variant for the question wording, just to see whether you were paying attention). We did warn you at the beginning of this chapter to read the previous chapter first!

On the real test, you'll never have the luxury of knowing that the next question will be a certain type. Be prepared for *anything*.

Step 1: Identify the Question

| Which of the following is required in order for the advertising executive to claim that television commercials are less cost-effective today? | *The words* required in order to claim *indicate that this is a Find the Assumption question.* | FA<br>A<br>B<br>C<br>D<br>E |
|---|---|---|

Step 2: Deconstruct the Argument

| Advertising Executive: More than 10 million households now own digital video recorders that can fast-forward over television commercials; | *This is just a fact.* | Exec: 10 mill + HH's = DVR |
|---|---|---|
| approximately 75 percent of these households fast-forward over at least one commercial per 30-minute program. | *Another fact. I don't think I need to write down the exact numerical details right now, but I'll note that there are numerical details with a # just to remind myself.* | 75 percent skip ads (#) |
| Because television commercials are not as widely watched as they used to be, they are much less cost-effective today. | *This contains another premise and the conclusion. The premise: TV ads aren't as widely watched today. The conclusion: TV ads are much less cost-effective than they used to be.* | B/c ads now watched less, ads = less cost eff |

Step 3: State the Goal

*Okay, the advertising executive claims that TV ads are not as cost-effective specifically because people aren't watching them as much, and that is specifically because a lot of people fast-forward over at least some commercials. I want an answer that the author must believe to be true in order to draw that conclusion. What assumptions are being made?*

*Let's see. They're assuming that people really did watch TV commercials more before, instead of changing channels or something. They're also assuming that if fewer people are watching, that's actually hurting the cost-effectiveness. Maybe commercials are worth more per viewer these days?*

Step 4: Work from Wrong to Right

| | | |
|---|---|---|
| (A) Product placement within television programs is a viable alternative to traditional television commercials. | *That's nice for the advertisers who want to make money, but this doesn't have to be true in order to claim that TV commercials are less cost-effective now.* | ~~A~~ |
| (B) The television programs preferred by consumers without digital video recorders are similar to those preferred by consumers with the devices. | *The DVR thing was used as evidence to show how some people are skipping commercials. I don't think making a distinction about people with or without the DVRs really tells us anything. The conclusion is about commercials, not what programs people watch.* | ~~B~~ |
| (C) Prior to the advent of digital video recorders, very few television viewers switched channels or left the room when commercials began. | *That's interesting. People didn't used to change channels or leave the room, so maybe they really were watching more TV commercials. If I negate this answer, then it would say that people* did *switch channels or leave the room. If that were the case, then it'd be tough to claim that people watch fewer commercials nowadays. This choice looks good.* | C ~ |
| (D) The cost-effectiveness of television advertising is based less upon how many people watch a particular commercial and more upon the appropriateness of the demographic. | *Hmm. They're saying that cost-effectiveness isn't measured based on how many people watch the commercials. That actually hurts the argument! If viewing doesn't matter for cost-effectiveness, then cost-effectiveness probably isn't going down. An assumption will never hurt the argument, so I can eliminate this.* | ~~D~~ |
| (E) The amount that television channels charge for advertisers to air commercials on their channel has increased steadily over the last decade. | *This definitely helps the argument, since it makes it seem like the commercials are less cost-effective now. But it isn't an assumption, because it doesn't have to be true for the argument to make sense. It would be helpful if it* was *true, but it's not a big deal if it isn't.* | ~~E~~ |

~~A~~     ~~B~~     Ⓒ     ~~D~~     ~~E~~

20

7. APR: The correct answer is **(E)**. Remember to identify any Reverse Logic answers before you read the explanation!

Step 1: Identify the Question

| Which of the following statements, if true, would most seriously undermine a plan to increase interest rates in order to spur profitable growth? | *The* undermine *and if true* language *indicates that this is a Weaken question. Further, the question stem tells me the conclusion: There's a plan to increase interest rates that will supposedly cause profits to grow.* | W A B C D E © Plan: ↑ int rats → ↑ prof growth |
|---|---|---|

Step 2: Deconstruct the Argument

| CEO: Over the past several years, we have more than doubled our revenues, but profits have steadily declined because an increasing number of customers have failed to pay their balances. | *Several facts here. Revenues have gone up but profits have gone down because the customers aren't paying what they owe.* | CEO: 2x rev but ↓ prof b/c cust not pay bills |
|---|---|---|
| In order to compensate for these higher default rates, we will increase the interest charged on outstanding balances from an annual percentage rate (APR) of 9.5 percent to an APR of 12 percent. | *Okay, here's the plan. They'll charge more interest to everyone to compensate for the people who aren't paying their bills.* | ↑ percent int rate to comp |
| This increase will be sufficient to compensate for the current rate of defaults and allow us to increase our profits. | *Hmm. They're claiming that 12 percent will be enough to compensate for the* current *rate of people who don't pay so that they can increase profits (which is the conclusion I already wrote down). They're assuming that the current rate isn't going to get worse in the future.* | 12 percent will be enough |

Step 3: State the Goal

*The company plans to charge higher interest rates in order to become profitable again. This is a Weaken question, so the right answer should show that this might not actually help profits.*

Step 4: Work from Wrong to Right

| | | |
|---|---|---|
| (A) Many other companies have experienced a similar trend in their default rates. | *This doesn't address the company's plan to fix the problem: increasing the interest rate. This doesn't impact the conclusion at all.* | ~~A~~ |
| (B) The company's operating expenses are above the industry average and can be substantially reduced, thus increasing margins. | *If the company does this, it could increase profits, which is the company's goal…but the conclusion is that the plan to increase interest rates will improve profits. The right answer needs to weaken that specific plan, not the company's goal in general.* | ~~B~~ |
| (C) The increase in default rates was due to a rise in unemployment, but unemployment rates are expected to drop in the coming months. | ***Reverse logic.*** *If unemployment caused people not to pay their bills, and fewer people are going to be unemployed, then maybe more will pay their bills? That would help the company, but I want something that will weaken the conclusion. This isn't even a great strengthener, since it doesn't talk about the actual plan in the argument.* | ~~C~~ |
| (D) The proposed increase in the APR will, alone, more than double the company's profit margins. | ***Reverse logic.*** *This supports the company's claim that increasing the interest rate will help raise profits. I want something that weakens that claim.* | ~~D~~ |
| (E) An increase in the APR charged on credit card balances often results in higher rates of default. | *Okay, if they do increase the APR, then more people may stop paying their bills as a result! The conclusion specifically said that raising the APR would compensate for the current rate of defaults, so if the rate goes up, then the company is less likely to increase its profits. This does weaken the conclusion.* | E ~ |

20

8.  Jupiter vs. Mars: The correct answer is **(D)**. Remember to identify any Reverse Logic answers before you read the explanation!

Step 1: Identify the Question

| Which of the following, if true, would most strengthen a contention by the government that the new project is a better use of its funds? | *The words* if true *and* strengthen a contention *indicate that this is a Strengthen question. The conclusion is also in the question stem: that the critics are wrong.* | S<br>A<br>B<br>C<br>D<br>E<br><br>© Gov: critics wrong |
|---|---|---|

Step 2: Deconstruct the Argument

| Scientists suspect that Europa, a moon orbiting Jupiter, may contain living organisms. | *There is a fact: Scientists suspect something is true. I don't actually know whether it's true, though.* | Sci: Europa may have life |
|---|---|---|
| However, the government recently scrapped an unmanned science mission to Europa and replaced it with a project aimed at landing an astronaut on Mars. | *There was a project to send an unmanned mission to Europa, but that was replaced by another project to send a person to Mars. More facts.* | © BUT gov replaced w/ Mars proj |
| Polls show that the public is far more fascinated by space travel than by discovering life elsewhere in the universe. | *More facts—a survey showed that people like space travel more.* | Ppl like space travel more |
| Critics argue that the government's decision-making process places a greater emphasis on popularity than it does on the importance of scientific research. | *This is a counterconclusion. The critics say that the government is just paying attention to popularity of projects, but the question stem told me that the government claims that the new project is a better use of funds.* | Critics: gov cares more ab popularity |

Step 3: State the goal.

*There are two opposing points of view, the government and the critics. The government claims that the critics are wrong. So, the government is claiming that it doesn't actually care more about popularity than about science. I need to strengthen that claim by showing that the government actually does care about science. I should be really careful not to strengthen the critics' claim, which is that the government cares more about popularity!*

Step 4: Work from wrong to right.

| | | |
|---|---|---|
| (A) In the first year of the project, the government will spend 30 percent of its total budget on developing a space shuttle that can travel to Mars; that figure is expected to drop to 0 percent after five years. | *This doesn't give me any additional information as to why the Mars project is better than the Europa project. I don't know whether they'd be spending more or less on the Europa project, nor do I know what kind of good research they'll expect to get in return.* | ~~A~~ |
| (B) The government cannot be absolutely certain of the chances for success of either project. | *Was there anything in the argument that hinged on being absolutely certain of success? No. If they told me that the Mars project has a greater chance for success, that would be good—but knowing that, I don't know the chances for either project...that doesn't add anything.* | ~~B~~ |
| (C) Some scientists are convinced that a mission to Europa would add immeasurably to our understanding of the universe. | ***Reverse logic.*** *This one tells me that the Europa mission is important for science. But, the government didn't fund it! That makes it more likely that the government only cares about popularity. So, this strengthens the critics' argument, not the government's.* | ~~C~~ |
| (D) A new telescope that has just become available to scientists promises to yield more information than the planned mission to Europa was designed to provide. | *Now they have a new telescope that they can use to get even more research than they would have if they sent an unmanned mission? It looks like the government canceled the Europa mission because it wasn't the best choice for science, not because it was less popular! Maybe the government really does care about science.* | D $\sim$ |
| (E) Most people feel that a shuttle to Mars would represent a first step towards an extensive program of space travel. | *This explains why people find the shuttle to Mars interesting, but it doesn't actually tell me anything new about the government's decision. It still looks like the government picked this program because it was popular with many people, regardless of the reason that it was popular.* | ~~E~~ |

~~A~~    ~~B~~    ~~C~~    (D)    ~~E~~

9. Deep-Brain Stimulation: The correct answer is (**D**). Remember to identify any Reverse Logic answers before you read the explanation!

Step 1: Identify the Question

| | | |
|---|---|---|
| Which of the following most logically completes the argument given below? | *The blank at the end signals a Fill in the Blank format. The word* because *just before the blank indicates that this is a Strengthen question.* | S<br>A<br>B<br>C<br>D<br>E |

Step 2: Deconstruct the Argument

| | | |
|---|---|---|
| Deep-brain stimulation is a new technique for combating severe depression. | *Straight fact.* | Deep-brain stim combats depression |
| In a recent experiment, electrodes were implanted into the brains of six patients who had not responded to any currently approved treatment for depression. | *This tells me how it works and that they tested it on six people.* | Tested on 6 ppl |
| When an electrical current to the electrodes was switched on, four of the patients reported feeling a dramatic reduction in depressive symptoms. | *And four of the people got a lot better.* | 4 better |
| The long-term prospects of the new treatment are not promising, however, because _____. | *Oh, but the author thinks the treatment's not really going to work long-term. Why?* | © BUT probably won't work, b/c … |

Step 3: State the Goal

*The author describes a new medical treatment but says it's probably not going to be good long-term; I need to find a reason why. The right answer should say something negative about the treatment's long-term prospects.*

Step 4: Work from Wrong to Right

| | | |
|---|---|---|
| (A) other treatments for depression may also be effective | *Talking about other treatments doesn't explain why deep-brain stimulation won't be a good treatment long-term. The conclusion is only about deep-brain stimulation, not about depression treatment in general.* | ~~A~~ |
| (B) the other two patients reported only a slight reduction of depressive symptoms during the treatment | *This looks like a negative at first glance, but then I remembered that the first four patients were helped dramatically. Technically, the treatment helped every patient! That doesn't hurt the treatment's prospects.* | ~~B~~ |
| (C) deep-brain stimulation relies on the expertise of highly skilled physicians | *This is probably true, but the right answer needs to be a downside of the treatment. Is relying on the expertise of physicians a downside? Possibly, but it's a real stretch. I'd have to assume that requiring skilled physicians has other consequences, like increasing the cost—and I don't know that.* | ~~C~~ |
| (D) when the electrical current is interrupted, the effects of the treatment are reversed | *When the current is on, the symptoms go away, but when the current is off, the depression comes back. That means they'd have to be connected to some machine all the time—they couldn't just get a treatment once a week or once a month. That definitely makes the treatment less practical and promising. Unless choice (E) is better, this looks like the answer.* | D ~ |
| (E) in a subsequent experiment, a one-hour treatment with the electrodes resulted in a sustained remission from depression in the four patients for six months | ***Reverse logic.*** *This is almost the opposite of choice (D). If you get a one-hour treatment, then the symptoms go away for 6 months— that's great for deep-brain stimulation! This can't be the right answer.* | ~~E~~ |

~~A~~     ~~B~~     ~~C~~     (D̰)     ~~E~~

# The Assumption Family: Evaluate the Argument and Find the Flaw

## In This Chapter:

**In this chapter, you will learn** how to apply your knowledge of Strengthen and Weaken questions to the fourth type of Assumption question: Evaluate. You will also learn how to address the final (and not very common) Assumption question type: Flaw.

# Chapter 21 The Assumption Family: Evaluate the Argument and Find the Flaw

In the previous two chapters, you learned about the three major question types in the Assumption Family: Find the Assumption, Strengthen, and Weaken. If you haven't read those chapters yet, please do so before reading this chapter.

In addition, think about how much time you want to put into this chapter. **Evaluate the Argument** questions are somewhat uncommon—you'll most likely see just one or two. **Find the Flaw** questions are even rarer. If you have a very high Verbal goal (90th percentile or higher), then study these two question types. If your Verbal score goal is lower, consider guessing on Flaw questions. If you struggle with Evaluate questions, you might want to guess on those as well.

The Assumption lessons you learned earlier still apply to Evaluate and Flaw questions:

- Assumptions are something an author must believe to be true in order to draw his or her conclusion. These assumptions are not stated explicitly in the argument.

- All assumption arguments will contain a core: a conclusion and the major premise or premises that lead to it.

- All assumption arguments will include at least one (and probably more than one) unstated assumption.

## Evaluate the Argument Questions

For Evaluate questions, your first step is still to find an assumption, but you have to do a little more work to get to the answer. At heart, you are asked what additional information would help to determine whether the assumption is valid or invalid.

Most Evaluate question stems will contain one or more of the following:

- The word *evaluate* or a synonym
- The word *determine* or a synonym
- Language asking what would be *useful to know* (or *establish*) or *important to know*

For example, an Evaluate question stem might ask:

> Which of the following must be studied in order to evaluate the argument?

> Which of the following would it be most useful to know in determining whether the mayor's plan is likely to be successful?

Occasionally, an Evaluate question will use other wording, but the question will still get at the same overall idea—what information would help to evaluate the given argument? That information, if made available, would either strengthen or weaken that argument.

# The Strengthen/Weaken Strategy

Evaluate answer choices will often be in the form of a question or in the form of a "one way or the other" statement. Imagine you have to take a stand on whether you agree with the conclusion of the argument: What question would you ask the author to help your decision? For example, say you're asked to evaluate this argument:

> In order to increase its profits, MillCo plans to reduce costs by laying off any nonessential employees.

Hmm. According to the argument:

> MillCo will lay off nonessential employees → reduce costs → increase profits

Does that sound like a good plan? What additional information would help you evaluate this plan?

Profits are equal to revenues minus costs. The argument says costs will go down, but no information is given about revenues. It seems pretty important to have some information about revenues to draw a conclusion about profits. One question might be: How will revenues be affected by this plan?

The question associated with the argument and the correct answer might read:

> Which of the following would be most important to determine to evaluate the argument?

> Whether revenues will be affected adversely enough to threaten MillCo's profit structure

This *whether* does something very interesting to the argument. Imagine that you could find out whether revenues will be affected adversely. The argument would be strengthened one way and weakened the other. Take a look:

> Yes, the plan *will* affect MillCo's revenues adversely enough to threaten profits. In this case, the plan to increase profits is less likely to work, so the argument is weakened.

> No, the plan *won't* affect MillCo's revenues adversely enough to threaten profits. In this case, the plan to increase profits is a little more likely to work, so the argument is strengthened.

If the answer goes one way, the argument is strengthened, and if it goes the other way, the argument is weakened.

The correct answer will be structured in such a way that these two possible "paths" exist, one strengthening and one weakening the argument.

The incorrect answers will be presented in a similar format, but won't actually test the strength of the argument. What if you had the following answer choice?

> Whether MillCo might reduce its costs more by eliminating some health insurance benefits for the remaining employees

Evaluate the two paths:

> Yes, MillCo can reduce costs more by eliminating some health benefits. How will this affect the given plan to lay off employees? Technically, this doesn't impact whether laying off certain employees will improve profits. It is true that reducing costs could help to increase profits, but the argument specifies that MillCo will reduce costs specifically by laying off nonessential employees. Whether the company could also reduce costs in some other way has no bearing on this specific argument.

> No, MillCo cannot reduce costs more by eliminating some health benefits. This certainly doesn't strengthen the argument. It doesn't weaken the argument either, though, since the argument hinges on laying off employees. This path does nothing to the argument.

This incorrect answer choice is trying to distract you by offering a different way to increase profits, but you aren't asked to find alternative ways to increase profits. You're asked to evaluate whether the *existing argument* involving this particular path to profits is valid. The answer doesn't provide a strengthen/weaken pair here, so the choice cannot be the right answer.

On Evaluate questions, after reading the question, you're going to focus on the argument:

> First, find the core (conclusion plus major premises).

> Second, briefly think about the questions you have or additional information you would want in order to evaluate the conclusion.

As you move to the answer choices, look for an answer similar to the questions you identified. Make sure to be flexible because the correct answer may not be something you identified. The correct answer should offer two different paths: one that would make the argument stronger and one that would make the argument weaker.

Try a full example; set your timer for 2 minutes. If you get stuck, pick an answer before you read the explanation. During the real test, you'll have to pick an answer in order to move on, so practice letting go and guessing.

> Food allergies account for more than 30,000 emergency room visits each year. Often, victims of these episodes are completely unaware of their allergies until they experience a major reaction. Studies show that 90 percent of food allergy reactions are caused by only eight distinct foods. For this reason, parents should feed a minuscule portion of each of these foods to their children to determine whether the children have these particular food allergies.

> Which of the following must be studied in order to evaluate the recommendation made in the argument?

> (A) The percentage of allergy victims who were not aware of the allergy before a major episode

> (B) The percentage of the population that is at risk for allergic reactions

> (C) Whether some of the eight foods are common ingredients used in cooking

> (D) Whether an allergy to one type of food makes someone more likely to be allergic to other types of food

> (E) Whether ingesting a very small amount of an allergen is sufficient to provoke an allergic reaction in a susceptible individual

**21**

Step 1: Identify the Question

| Which of the following must be studied in order to evaluate the recommendation made in the argument? | *The words* must be studied *and* evaluate *indicate that this is an Evaluate question.* | Ev<br>A<br>B<br>C<br>D<br>E |
|---|---|---|

Step 2: Deconstruct the Argument

| Food allergies account for more than 30,000 emergency room visits each year. | *This is a fact.* | Food allerg → 30k ER/yr |
|---|---|---|
| Often, victims of these episodes are completely unaware of their allergies until they experience a major reaction. | *Fact, but more fuzzy. A lot of people don't know they're allergic till they have a major reaction.* | Ppl unaware till have rxn |
| Studies show that 90 percent of food allergy reactions are caused by only eight distinct foods. | *More facts! That's interesting. Only eight foods cause most allergic reactions.* | Only 8 foods → 90 percent rxn |
| For this reason, parents should feed a minuscule portion of each of these foods to their children to determine whether the children have these particular food allergies. | *This is the conclusion. The author's saying parent should give a tiny bit of these eight foods to see what happens.* | ©Give child tiny bit of 8 foods to test |

Step 3: State the Goal

*This is an Evaluate question, so I need to find an answer that will help to determine whether or not the conclusion is likely to be valid. The correct answer will have two paths: one path will make the conclusion a little more likely to be valid and the other will make the conclusion a little less likely to be valid.*

*In this case, the author recommends that we all try tiny bits of these eight foods to see whether we're allergic. What will help determine if this is a good idea? Could these tests actually cause harm if children have severe reactions to the sample amounts? Will these tests actually work? How much do you need to eat to cause an allergic reaction (are the minuscule bits enough)?*

Step 4: Work from Wrong to Right

| (A) The percentage of allergy victims who were not aware of the allergy before a major episode | *The argument said that victims* often *aren't aware of the allergy beforehand. If I knew that 90 percent weren't aware, that would go along with what the argument already says. If I knew that 50 percent weren't aware...hmm, that wouldn't change the argument. In general, knowing the exact percentage doesn't change anything.* | A̶ |
|---|---|---|

| (B) The percentage of the population that is at risk for allergic reactions | *If a really high percentage is at risk for allergies, then it's probably important to figure out whether people are allergic…but that doesn't mean that the specific recommendation in the conclusion here is a good one or bad one. Also, this answer choice doesn't specifically limit itself to food allergies; it mentions all allergies in general.* | ~~B~~ |
| --- | --- | --- |
| (C) Whether some of the eight foods are common ingredients used in cooking | *If yes, then many people may have already tried small amounts of these foods. That doesn't actually tell me, though, whether the recommendation is a good one. If no, then it doesn't affect the conclusion at all—I still don't know whether it's a good recommendation.* | ~~C~~ |
| (D) Whether an allergy to one type of food makes someone more likely to be allergic to other types of food | *If yes or if no, I'd still want to test people to see whether they're allergic to anything. This choice doesn't have two paths that lead to alternate outcomes.* | ~~D~~ |
| (E) Whether ingesting a very small amount of an allergen is sufficient to provoke an allergic reaction in a susceptible individual | *If yes, then the author's plan will work: Children will be able to try small amounts and determine whether they're allergic. If no, then the author's plan is not a good one: Trying small amounts won't actually help you tell whether a child is allergic.* | E ~ |

~~A~~    ~~B~~    ~~C~~    ~~D~~    (Ḛ)

In the prior example, although the student brainstormed a relevant question in step 3, it was not available as an answer choice. Make sure not to get hung up on the specific questions you thought of when working through the answers; most arguments have multiple relevant questions and only one will be in the answer choices.

## Correct Answers

The correct answer will be information important to determining if the the conclusion is valid. You don't get follow-up questions on the GMAT. The answer to the question in the correct answer choice must help you evaluate the conclusion on its own without any additional information or clarification. One answer to the question posed in the correct answer will clearly strengthen the argument and the other will clearly weaken it.

## Common Trap Answers

The incorrect answers are very tricky. How do the test writers get you to pick trap answers on Evaluate questions?

### No Effect on the Conclusion

Answer (C) presented something that seemed like it would matter: Maybe lots of people have already tried the eight foods. What does that mean for the recommendation? Maybe some people have already had reactions to some foods. But some people might have tried only six of the eight, so maybe they should still try the other two. Or, maybe…You could speculate endlessly, but all paths lead to the same place: This choice doesn't impact whether the specific recommendation made is good or bad.

The correct answer should *clearly strengthen* the conclusion if it goes one way and *clearly weaken* if it goes the other. Be careful of answers that only *might strengthen* or *might weaken* or *might do nothing*, especially if you need additional information to make the determination.

### Irrelevant Distinction or Comparison

You saw this trap for the first time in the Find the Assumption chapter. In the problem above, answer (D) does discuss something mentioned by the argument—allergies—but tries to talk about whether someone might have more than one allergy; this is not at issue in the argument. The argument only distinguishes those with allergies and those without.

## Find the Flaw Questions

**Find the Flaw questions** are the least common of the five Assumption Family question types. The question stems will almost always contain some form of the word *flaw*, but be careful: Weaken the Argument questions also might contain the word *flaw* in the question stem.

Here's how to tell the difference. Weaken questions will also contain *if true* language. Flaw questions will *not* contain this language. Take a look at the chart below:

| Flaw | Weaken |
|------|--------|
| *Look for this first:* | |
| Contains the word *flaw* but NOT *if true* language. | Contains the word *flaw* AND the words *if true* (or an equivalent synonym). |
| *If you're still not sure, try this:* | |
| Answer choices are a bit more abstract, similar to but not as abstract as Structure Family questions. | Answer choices represent a new piece of information (as described in the discussion of the Weaken question type). |
| *Example:* | |
| Which of the following indicates a *flaw* in the reasoning above? | Which of the following, *if true*, would indicate a *flaw* in the teacher's plan? |

On occasion, a Flaw question may contain a synonym of the word *flaw*, such as *vulnerable to criticism*.

As with the other Assumption Family questions, Find the Flaw questions will contain an argument core, and it's great if you notice assumptions that the author makes. The correct answer, though, will be essentially the opposite of the correct answer on a Find the Assumption question. On Find the Assumption, you pick an answer that articulates an assumption that is necessary to the argument. On Flaw questions, by contrast, you are looking for wording that indicates why it is *flawed* thinking to believe that this assumption is true.

For example:

> Pierre was recovering from the flu when he visited Shelley last week, and now Shelley is showing signs of the flu. If Pierre had waited until he was no longer contagious, Shelley would not have become ill.

The author is assuming that Pierre was definitely the one to infect Shelley. The author is also assuming that there is no other way Shelley could have gotten sick. Perhaps it is flu season, and many people with whom Shelley came in contact had the flu!

The correct answer might be something like:

> The author fails to consider that there are alternate paths by which Shelley could have become infected.

Contrast that language with the assumption itself: The author assumes that only Pierre could have infected Shelley. If that's true, then that piece of information at least partially fixes the author's argument. When you take the same information, though, and flip it around into a flaw, you harm the author's argument:

| Pierre was recovering from the flu when he visited Shelley last week, and now Shelley is showing signs of the flu. If Pierre had waited until he was no longer contagious, Shelley would not have become ill. ||
| --- | --- |
| *Assumption* | *Flaw* |
| Only Pierre could have infected Shelley. | The author fails to consider that there are alternate paths by which Shelley could have become infected. |
| *The argument is made stronger.* | *The argument is made weaker.* |

In sum, think of Flaw questions as the "reverse" of Assumption questions. The answer still hinges on an assumption, but the correct answer will word that assumption in a way that hurts the argument.

In addition, the answer choice language may be a bit more abstract than the answer choices on other Assumption Family questions. Often, the answer choices will talk about what the author "fails to consider (or establish)," "does not specify (or identify)," or something along those lines.

Try this full example:

> Environmentalist: Bando Inc.'s manufacturing process releases pollution into the atmosphere. In order to convince the company to change processes, we will organize a boycott of the product that represents its highest sales volume, light bulbs. Because Bando sells more light bulbs than any other product, a boycott of light bulbs will cause the most damage to the company's profits.
>
> The environmentalist's reasoning is flawed because it fails to

(A) allow for the possibility that Bando may not want to change its manufacturing process

(B) supply information about other possible ways for Bando to reduce pollution

(C) consider that the relative sales volumes of a company's products are not necessarily proportional to profits

(D) identify any alternate methods by which to convince Bando to change its manufacturing process

(E) consider that a boycott may take too long to achieve its purpose

Step 1: Identify the Question

| The environmentalist's reasoning is flawed because it fails to | *The word* flawed *indicates that this is either a Flaw or a Weaken question. If* true *does not appear, so this is a Flaw question. I'll write down "Fl" on my scrap paper.* | Fl<br>A<br>B<br>C<br>D<br>E |
| --- | --- | --- |

Step 2: Deconstruct the Argument

21

| Environmentalist: Bando Inc.'s manufacturing process releases pollution into the atmosphere. | *This is a fact (assume the environmentalist is telling the truth).* | Environ-ist: manuf → atmo pollutn |
|---|---|---|
| In order to convince the company to change processes, we will organize a boycott of the product that represents its highest sales volume, light bulbs. | *Okay, here's a plan, so it's likely a conclusion. They think if they boycott something, this company might change its manufacturing process. So they're going to boycott light bulbs because Bando sells more light bulbs than anything else.* | boyc bulbs (↑ sales) → so company Δ manuf |
| Because Bando sells more light bulbs than any other product, a boycott of light bulbs will cause the most damage to the company's profits. | *Another claim. Because they sell more light bulbs than anything else, the environmentalist figures that a boycott of light bulbs will do the most damage to profits. Profits? How profitable are the light bulbs?*<br><br>*Okay, the conclusion was the previous sentence, because all of this is designed to convince Bando to change its manufacturing process.* | Bando sells ↑ bulbs → boyc → ↑ damage to prof |

Step 3: State the Goal

*The environmentalist doesn't like that Bando pollutes. Bando sells more light bulbs than any other product, so the environmentalist wants to boycott those bulbs to do the most damage to Bando's profits (according to this environmentalist, anyway), and then the hope is that this will all cause the company to change its manufacturing process.*

*I need to find an answer that will articulate a flaw in that reasoning. I've already thought of one. The environmentalist is assuming that just because Bando sells more light bulbs than anything else, the company is also earning the most profits from those products. But there's no evidence to support that. Also, consumers might not actually agree to boycott Bando.*

Step 4: Work from Wrong to Right

| (A) allow for the possibility that Bando may not want to change its manufacturing process | *If anything, it could be argued that the environmentalist is already assuming the company will not want to change—that's why the environmentalist thinks he or she has to organize a boycott to change the company's mind!* | ~~A~~ |
|---|---|---|
| (B) does not supply information about other possible ways for Bando to reduce pollution | *In the real world, I agree that environmentalists should explore all possible ways...but the question asks me to find a flaw in this particular plan about the boycott. This doesn't apply to that plan.* | ~~B~~ |

| (C) consider that the relative sales volumes of a company's products are not necessarily proportional to profits | *This sounds kind of like what I said before. It's a little abstract, so I'm not sure I fully understand all of it, but it does say that sales aren't necessarily proportional to profits. I'll keep this one in.* | C̰ |
| (D) identify any alternative methods by which to convince Bando to change its manufacturing process | *This is like choice (B). It'd be good in general for the environmentalist to do this…but this doesn't help me figure out a flaw in the boycott plan specifically.* | ~~D~~ |
| (E) consider that a boycott may take too long to achieve its purpose | *I think what really matters is whether the plan is going to work at all, not how long it takes. The argument doesn't have any requirements about how long it will take to get Bando to change its process.* | ~~E~~ |

~~A~~   ~~B~~   Ⓒ   ~~D~~   ~~E~~

## Common Trap Answers

### Irrelevant Distinction or Comparison

This trap discusses alternative plans or paths when you were asked to comment on the given plan, similar to answers (B) and (D) in the example above. A choice can also bring up a detail or distinction that does not actually affect the argument, similar to choice (E) in the problem above.

Flaw questions may also occasionally use Reverse Logic, similar to answer choice (A) in the example above.

**21**

## Evaluate the Argument Cheat Sheet

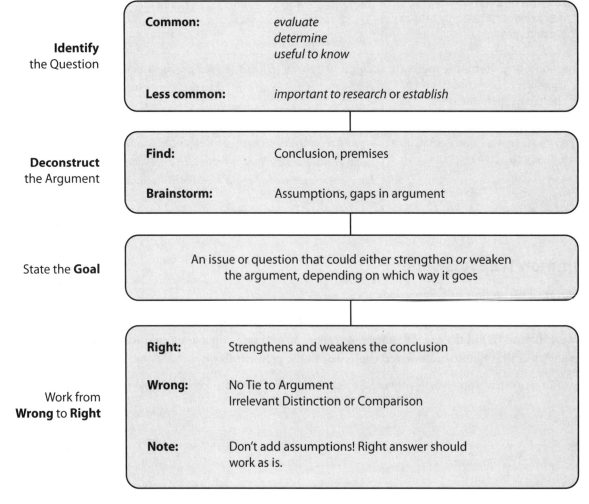

**Identify**
the Question

| Common: | *evaluate* |
| | *determine* |
| | *useful to know* |
| Less common: | *important to research* or *establish* |

**Deconstruct**
the Argument

| Find: | Conclusion, premises |
| Brainstorm: | Assumptions, gaps in argument |

State the **Goal**

An issue or question that could either strengthen *or* weaken the argument, depending on which way it goes

Work from
**Wrong** to **Right**

| Right: | Strengthens and weakens the conclusion |
| Wrong: | No Tie to Argument |
| | Irrelevant Distinction or Comparison |
| Note: | Don't add assumptions! Right answer should work as is. |

Take a photo of this page and keep it with the review sheets you're creating as you study. Better yet, use this page as a guide to create your own review sheet—you'll remember the material better if you write it down yourself.

## Find the Flaw Cheat Sheet

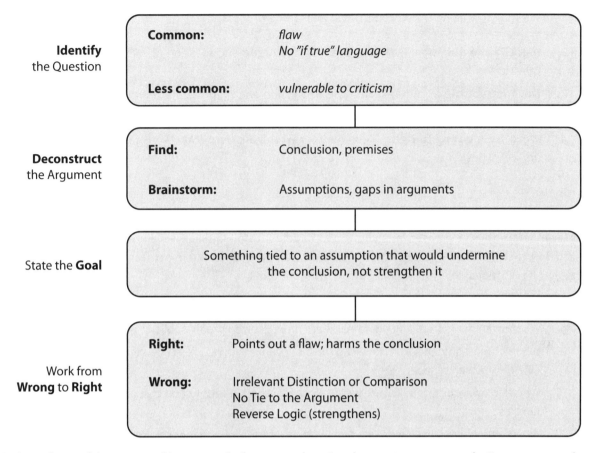

**Identify** the Question

| **Common:** | *flaw* |
| | *No "if true" language* |
| **Less common:** | *vulnerable to criticism* |

**Deconstruct** the Argument

| **Find:** | Conclusion, premises |
| **Brainstorm:** | Assumptions, gaps in arguments |

State the **Goal**

Something tied to an assumption that would undermine the conclusion, not strengthen it

Work from **Wrong** to **Right**

| **Right:** | Points out a flaw; harms the conclusion |
| **Wrong:** | Irrelevant Distinction or Comparison |
| | No Tie to the Argument |
| | Reverse Logic (strengthens) |

Take a photo of this page and keep it with the review sheets you're creating as you study. Better yet, use this page as a guide to create your own review sheet—you'll remember the material better if you write it down yourself.

## Problem Set

Answer each question using the 4-step Critical Reasoning process.

1. **Identify the question:** Is this an Evaluate the Argument question or a Find the Flaw question?
2. **Deconstruct the argument:** Find the conclusion and map the argument on your paper.
3. **State the goal:** What will the right answer need to do?
4. **Work from wrong to right:** Eliminate four wrong answers. Watch out for common wrong answer types.

1. *Tuition*

   Recently, the tuition at most elite private high schools has been rising more quickly than inflation. Even before these increases, many low- and middle-income families were unable to afford the full tuition costs for their children at these schools. With the new tuition increases, these schools will soon be attended solely by students from affluent families.

   Which of the following would it be most useful to determine in order to evaluate the argument?

   (A) Whether students from affluent families are more likely to prefer public or private high schools

   (B) Whether most students from low- and middle-income families are academically qualified to attend elite private high schools

   (C) Whether low-income families are less likely to be able to afford tuition costs than middle-income families

   (D) Whether graduates of elite private high schools typically earn higher salaries as adults than do people who did not graduate from these schools

   (E) Whether grants or scholarships are available for students from economically disadvantaged families

2. *Charity*

   Studies show that impoverished families give away a larger percentage of their income in charitable donations than do wealthy families. As a result, fundraising consultants recommend that charities direct their marketing efforts toward individuals and families from lower socioeconomic classes in order to maximize the dollar value of incoming donations.

   Which of the following best explains why the consultants' reasoning is flawed?

   (A) Marketing efforts are only one way to solicit charitable donations.

   (B) Not all impoverished families donate to charity.

   (C) Some charitable marketing efforts are so expensive that the resulting donations fail to cover the costs of the marketing campaign.

   (D) Percentage of income is not necessarily indicative of absolute dollar value.

   (E) People are more likely to donate to the same causes to which their friends donate.

3. *CostMart*

Editorial: To avoid increasing the unemployment rate in the city of Dorwall, a CostMart warehouse department store should not be permitted to open within city limits. In the past, when CostMart has opened a new warehouse department store in a city, up to 20 percent of local retailers—which, in Dorwall, primarily employ local residents—have closed within the next three years.

Which of the following questions would be most useful for evaluating the conclusion of the editorial?

(A) Does the bankruptcy rate of local retailers in a city generally stabilize several years after a CostMart warehouse department store opens?

(B) Are the majority of residents of Dorwall currently employed within the city limits?

(C) Will the number of jobs created by the opening of the CostMart warehouse store be greater than the number of jobs that will be lost when local retailers close?

(D) Have other cities that have permitted CostMart warehouse stores to open within city limits experienced an increase in unemployment within the city?

(E) Does CostMart plan to hire employees exclusively from within Dorwall for the proposed warehouse department store?

4. *Bicycle Manufacturing*

Bicycle Manufacturer: Switching our focus from building aluminum bicycles to primarily building carbon-fiber bicycles will reduce the time taken by our manufacturing process. Although the initial construction of aluminum bicycle frames was significantly faster and simpler than the construction of carbon-fiber frames, each weld in an aluminum frame then needed to be individually checked for integrity. This required that substantial time be spent on quality control to avoid shipping out any defective frames.

Which of the following would be most useful in evaluating the claim made in the argument?

(A) Whether factory workers will require additional training in order to manufacture carbon bicycle frames

(B) Whether the carbon manufacturing process is likely to require time-consuming quality checks

(C) Whether aluminum bicycle frames with defective welds can be fixed or must be thrown away

(D) Whether there are improvements that could be introduced that would significantly reduce the rate of defects in aluminum bicycle frames

(E) Whether the demand for carbon-fiber bicycles is as high as the demand for aluminum bicycles

5.   *Ethanol*

Ethanol, a fuel derived from corn, can be used alone to power vehicles or along with gasoline to reduce the amount of gasoline consumed. Compared with conventional gasoline, pure ethanol produces significantly less pollution per gallon used. In order to combat pollution, many individuals advocate the increased usage of ethanol as a fuel source for vehicles in conjunction with or in place of gasoline.

In evaluating the recommendation to increase the use of ethanol, it would be most important to research which of the following?

(A)   Whether the majority of existing vehicles are capable of using ethanol for fuel, either alone or in conjunction with gasoline

(B)   Whether the process of growing corn to produce ethanol results in significant amounts of pollution

(C)   Whether completely replacing gasoline with ethanol results in less pollution than using ethanol in conjunction with gasoline

(D)   Whether ethanol is more expensive to produce than conventional gasoline

(E)   Whether there are some vehicles in which using ethanol fuel would not result in a significant reduction in pollution compared to conventional gasoline

# Solutions

1. Tuition: The correct answer is (**E**).

Step 1: Identify the Question

| Which of the following would it be most useful to determine in order to evaluate the argument? | *Contains the words* evaluate *and* useful to determine—*this is an Evaluate question.* | Ev<br>A<br>B<br>C<br>D<br>E |
|---|---|---|

Step 2: Deconstruct the Argument

| Recently, the tuition at most elite private high schools has been rising more quickly than inflation. | *Fact: Tuition at this specific type of school has been going up even faster than inflation.* | ↑ priv HS tuit > infl |
|---|---|---|
| Even before these increases, many low- and middle-income families were unable to afford the full tuition costs for their children at these schools. | *And many people without much money already couldn't afford these schools, even before the tuition went up. Another fact.* | B4: mid inc fams can't afford |
| With the new tuition increases, these schools will soon be attended solely by students from affluent families. | *This must be the conclusion because the other two were facts, and this is a prediction about the future. Basically, they're saying that only wealthy students are going to be able to afford these schools now.* | © Priv HS will have only rich students |

Step 3: State the Goal

*This is an Evaluate question, so I need to find an answer that will help to determine whether or not the conclusion is likely to be valid. The correct answer will have two paths: One path will make the conclusion a little more likely to be valid and the other will make the conclusion a little less likely to be valid.*

*The conclusion is that* only *wealthy students are going to be able to go to these elite private high schools. What is the author assuming? That there's no way that students from lower-income families can attend these schools: Their families can't take out loans, they can't receive scholarships, etc.*

Step 4: Work from Wrong to Right

| | | |
|---|---|---|
| (A) Whether students from affluent families are more likely to prefer public or private high schools | *The conclusion is that private high schools will only have wealthy students, not that all wealthy students will go to private schools. Even if most wealthy students go to public schools, private schools won't suddenly become affordable for other students. So, this doesn't affect the conclusion.* | ~~A~~ |
| (B) Whether most students from low- and middle-income families are academically qualified to attend elite private high schools | *This is interesting. Maybe the lower-income students aren't actually qualified to go to these schools. But on the other hand, regardless of whether they're qualified, they won't be able to afford them! So the conclusion is equally strong either way: If the low-income students are qualified, they can't afford the schools, so they won't attend. And if they aren't qualified, they also won't attend. Either way, these high schools will only be attended by students from wealthy families.* | ~~B~~ |
| (C) Whether low-income families are less likely to be able to afford tuition costs than middle-income families | *This answer makes a distinction between low- and middle-income families, but the argument doesn't distinguish between these two groups—it combines them. Logically, it would make sense that the less money a family has, the less likely it could afford the tuition…but this doesn't change anything about the basic argument that low- and middle-income families can't afford the tuition.* | ~~C~~ |
| (D) Whether graduates of elite private high schools typically earn higher salaries as adults than do people who did not graduate from these schools | *This answer choice discusses the consequences of attending one of these private high schools. However, the conclusion deals with whether certain students can attend these schools in the first place. The outcome of attending a private school doesn't influence whether a student will be able to afford to attend.* | ~~D~~ |
| (E) Whether grants or scholarships are available for students from economically disadvantaged families | *If there are grants and scholarships for lower-income students, then perhaps they can afford to attend these schools—this hurts the argument's conclusion. If there are no grants and scholarships for these students, then the argument's conclusion is more likely to be true: These students won't be able to afford these schools. This answer can either strengthen or weaken the argument, so it's correct.* | E ~ |

2. Charity: The correct answer is **(D)**.

Step 1: Identify the Question

| Which of the following best explains why the consultants' reasoning is flawed? | *The word* flawed *indicates that this is either a Flaw or Weaken question. The lack of the words* if true *(or an equivalent) means that this is a Flaw question.* | F<br>A<br>B<br>C<br>D<br>E |
|---|---|---|

Step 2: Deconstruct the Argument

| Studies show that impoverished families give away a larger percentage of their income in charitable donations than do wealthy families. | *This is a fact. It's impressive that the poor donate anything, but if they do donate anything, then this fact makes sense because donating $100 is a much greater percentage of your income if you don't have much income.* | Poor donate > % inc than rich |
|---|---|---|
| As a result, fundraising consultants recommend that charities direct their marketing efforts toward individuals and families from lower socioeconomic classes in order to maximize the dollar value of incoming donations. | *This is the conclusion. Based on the percentage info, the consultants are saying that the charities should focus on lower-income people…but the consultants are assuming that greater percentage equals more money. A very rich person might donate $10 million, a small percentage of income but a very large sum.* | ©Consultants: to get most $, char shld focus on ↓ inc ppl |

Step 3: State the Goal

*For Flaw questions, it's important to find the conclusion and brainstorm any assumptions, if I can. I need to find an answer that hurts the argument or shows why the argument is not a good argument.*

*In this case, the fundraising consultants are recommending that the charities target lower-income families in order to maximize the number of dollars they get in donations. I've identified one potential assumption: The consultants assume that donating a greater percentage of income also means donating a greater dollar amount collectively. If that's not actually the case, then that's a flaw.*

21

Step 4: Work from Wrong to Right

| (A) Marketing efforts are only one way to solicit charitable donations. | *This might be true, but it just indicates that there might be other ways, in addition to marketing efforts, to raise money. That doesn't affect the consultants' recommendation to target lower-income families in particular.* | A̶ |
| --- | --- | --- |
| (B) Not all impoverished families donate to charity. | *I'm sure this is true, but how does it affect the conclusion? It doesn't. The argument never claims that ALL impoverished families donate to charity—only that, in general, they donate a larger percentage of income to charity.* | B̶ |
| (C) Some charitable marketing efforts are so expensive that the resulting donations fail to cover the costs of the marketing campaign. | *Oh, maybe this is it. If you spend more on the marketing than you make from donations, that can't be a very successful marketing campaign. What was the conclusion again? Oh, wait,* to maximize the dollar value of donations. *Whether the marketing covered costs isn't part of the conclusion—it just depends on how much money they get in donations. Tricky, but not correct.* | C̶ |
| (D) Percentage of Income is not necessarily indicative of absolute dollar value. | *This is what I was saying before about the really rich person donating $10 million! You can have a bunch of low-income people give 10 percent of their income and one billionaire give 9 percent of her income…and the billionaire could be giving more in terms of absolute dollars. This indicates the flawed assumption made by the fundraising consultants.* | D ~ |
| (E) People are more likely to donate to the same causes to which their friends donate. | *I can believe that this is true, but the argument doesn't address which causes people choose for charity. Rather, the argument talks about amount of money donated.* | E̶ |

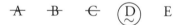 A̶  B̶  C̶  (D)  E

3. CostMart: The correct answer is (**C**).

Step 1: Identify the Question

| Which of the following questions would be most useful for evaluating the conclusion of the editorial? | *The language* most useful *and* evaluating *indicates that this is an Evaluate question.* | Ev<br>A<br>B<br>C<br>D<br>E |
|---|---|---|

Step 2: Deconstruct the Argument

| Editorial: To avoid increasing the unemployment rate in the city of Dorwall, a CostMart warehouse department store should not be permitted to open within city limits. | *This seems like the conclusion: It's telling me what Dorwall should do. Also, it doesn't just say that Dorwall should ban CostMart. The conclusion is specifically about unemployment.* | © Dorwall shld ban CostMart in city → unempl. not ↑ |
|---|---|---|
| In the past, when CostMart has opened a new warehouse department store in a city, up to 20 percent of local retailers—which, in Dorwall, primarily employ local residents—have closed within the next three years. | *The author is explaining why CostMart will increase unemployment. A lot of local stores will close, so locals will lose their jobs.* | new store → 20 percent of local stores close |

Step 3: State the Goal

*I need to find an answer that will have two possible paths—one way will strengthen the author's claim and the other way will weaken it. The author's claim is that banning CostMart will prevent an increase in unemployment. One path will show that CostMart might cause unemployment and the other path will show that it might not.*

Step 4: Work from Wrong to Right

**21**

| | | |
|---|---|---|
| (A) Does the bankruptcy rate of local retailers in a city generally stabilize several years after a CostMart warehouse department store opens? | *If yes, then unemployment wouldn't continue to worsen over time…but it would still happen in the first place! Even if the bankruptcy rate stabilizes, the editorial still has a good point.* | ~~A~~ |
| (B) Are the majority of residents of Dorwall currently employed within the city limits? | *If yes, then…I'm not sure what this has to do with the conclusion. The argument says that local retailers primarily employ Dorwall residents. Even if most of the other residents are employed outside of the city, the ones who work at local retailers are at risk of losing their jobs.* | ~~B~~ |
| (C) Will the number of jobs created by the opening of the CostMart warehouse store be greater than the number of jobs that will be lost when local retailers close? | *If yes, then the opening of CostMart will result in a net gain in jobs within the Dorwall city limits. That weakens the author's point about unemployment. If no, then some of the residents who lose their jobs might not be able to find new ones, which makes the author's point stronger.* | C ~ |
| (D) Have other cities that have permitted CostMart warehouse stores to open within city limits experienced an increase in unemployment within the city? | *This could be right. If CostMart has increased unemployment in other cities, isn't it more likely to increase unemployment in Dorwall? Well, not necessarily—there's no way to know whether the other cities had the same economic situation as Dorwall. We just knew that their local retailers closed; if that happened in Dorwall, jobs would be lost.* | ~~D~~ |
| (E) Does CostMart plan to hire employees exclusively from within Dorwall for the proposed warehouse department store? | *This one could be good, too. If yes, then that would reduce unemployment! If no, then…hmm…it's not bad necessarily but it's not good either, so I'll have to be sure.* | E ~ |
| Compare (C) and (E). | *Wait. (C) specifically says that the number of jobs created will be greater than the ones that are lost. (E) doesn't demonstrate this. Maybe CostMart will only hire Dorwall employees, but there still won't be enough jobs for all of them. Or, maybe CostMart will hire a few people from outside of Dorwall, but there will be enough jobs for the Dorwall residents, too.* | C E ~ ~ |

4.  Bicycle Manufacturing: The correct answer is **(B)**.

Step 1: Identify the Question

| Which of the following would be most useful in evaluating the claim made in the argument? | *The language* most useful in evaluating *indicates that this is an Evaluate question.* | Ev<br>A<br>B<br>C<br>D<br>E |
|---|---|---|

Step 2: Deconstruct the Argument

| Bicycle Manufacturer: Switching our focus from building aluminum bicycles to primarily building carbon-fiber bicycles will reduce the time taken by our manufacturing process. | *This looks like a prediction. It's probably the manufacturer's conclusion.* | $\text{\textcircled{C}}$ Alum $\rightarrow$ CF = time $\downarrow$ |
|---|---|---|
| Although the initial construction of aluminum bicycle frames was significantly faster and simpler than the construction of carbon-fiber frames, each weld in an aluminum frame then needed to be individually checked for integrity. | *Now I know why it took longer to make the aluminum bikes. They were faster to make, but the quality control took a long time.* | Alum: faster originally, but QC = time $\uparrow$ |
| This required that substantial time be spent on quality control to avoid shipping out any defective frames. | *This really just confirms what we found out in the last sentence! Since we had to check all of those welds, QC took forever.* | |

Step 3: State the Goal

*The right answer will have two possible paths. One should show that switching to carbon manufacturing might save time. The other should show that it won't actually save time. There might be a drawback to the carbon manufacturing process: Maybe some other part of it actually takes extra time?*

Step 4: Work from Wrong to Right

**21**

| | | |
|---|---|---|
| (A) Whether factory workers will require additional training in order to manufacture carbon bicycle frames | *This seems reasonable. If it takes extra training to make the new frames, it'll probably take more time.* | A $\sim$ |
| (B) Whether the carbon manufacturing process is likely to require time-consuming quality checks | *Okay, this directly addresses the time issue! If it goes one way, then carbon manufacturing might actually take longer. If it goes the other way, carbon should save time. This is stronger than (A), because it definitely affects the time spent. I don't have to just guess that it'll take more time.* | B $\sim$ |
| (C) Whether aluminum bicycle frames with defective welds can be fixed or must be thrown away | *This might explain why aluminum manufacturing took a long time, but it doesn't say anything about whether switching to carbon would help.* | C̶ |
| (D) Whether there are improvements that could be introduced that would significantly reduce the rate of defects in alumi-num bicycle frames | *Interesting. If this is true, then maybe the aluminum process could be made faster. But the problem is, the conclusion is about whether switching to carbon would help or not. It's not about whether something else could help.* | D̶ |
| (E) Whether the demand for carbon-fiber bicycles is as high as the demand for aluminum bicycles | *This doesn't mention manufacturing time at all. If I wanted to relate it to time, I'd need to make some serious assump-tions.* | E̶ |

5. Ethanol: The correct answer is (**B**).

Step 1: Identify the Question

| In evaluating the recommendation to increase the use of ethanol, it would be most important to research which of the following? | *This question asks me to evaluate a recommendation, so it's an Evaluate question.* | Ev<br>A<br>B<br>C<br>D<br>E |
|---|---|---|

Step 2: Deconstruct the Argument

| Ethanol, a fuel derived from corn, can be used alone to power vehicles or along with gasoline to reduce the amount of gasoline consumed. | *This is a fact. Ethanol, alone or with gas, can power vehicles.* | Eth OR eth + gas can power veh. |
|---|---|---|
| Compared with conventional gasoline, pure ethanol produces significantly less pollution per gallon used. | *Another fact. This is just about pure ethanol, though. Weren't we just talking about combining it with gasoline?* | PURE eth = pollution < than gas |
| In order to combat pollution, many individuals advocate the increased usage of ethanol as a fuel source for vehicles in conjunction with or in place of gasoline. | *Here's the conclusion. It's very specific: In order to combat pollution, we should use more ethanol, alone or with gas.* | © Eth or eth + gas → pollution ↓ |

Step 3: State the Goal

*This is an Evaluate question, so the right answer will be able to both strengthen and weaken the argument. It has to show that the ethanol plan might decrease pollution, but on the other hand, it might not. I'll have to avoid trap answer choices that don't mention pollution, though.*

21

Step 4: Work from Wrong to Right

| | | |
|---|---|---|
| (A) Whether the majority of existing vehicles are capable of using ethanol for fuel, either alone or in conjunction with gasoline | *If most vehicles can use ethanol, the plan is good to go. What if most vehicles can't use ethanol? Well, switching as many as possible over to ethanol would still reduce pollution. This doesn't say that switching wouldn't reduce pollution! It just says that switching might be difficult.* | ~~A~~ |
| (B) Whether the process of growing corn to produce ethanol results in significant amounts of pollution | *This is a drawback to using ethanol! If making ethanol fuel produces a lot of pollution, then switching won't actually cut down on pollution. But if it can be produced cleanly, the switch will cut pollution a lot. It can go either way, so it might be right.* | B ~ |
| (C) Whether completely replacing gasoline with ethanol results in less pollution than using ethanol in conjunction with gasoline | *The conclusion combines these two things together, but the answer choice splits them up. Even if one produces less pollution than the other, they might or might not make less pollution than pure gasoline. There's no way to know, so it's wrong!* | ~~C~~ |
| (D) Whether ethanol is more expensive to produce than conventional gasoline | *Cost might be a drawback to ethanol in general, but the conclusion is about pollution, not cost.* | ~~D~~ |
| (E) Whether there are some vehicles in which using ethanol fuel would not result in a significant reduction in pollution compared to conventional gasoline | *This talks about some vehicles. Okay, if switching won't cut pollution from some vehicles, will the overall switch still cut pollution? I don't know, since I don't know how many vehicles we're talking about. This doesn't tell me that the switch would or wouldn't work.* | ~~E~~ |

# Evidence Family

## In This Chapter:

**In this chapter, you will learn** how to recognize and answer two question types that differ from the rest in one crucial way: Evidence Family arguments typically do *not* contain conclusions. You will also learn how to distinguish Inference questions from Strengthen questions, allowing you to avoid traps.

# CHAPTER 22 Evidence Family

The **Evidence Family** of questions is the third main family. Here's a short recap of what you learned about this family earlier in the book:

- There are no conclusions. Evidence Family questions are made up entirely of premises.
- There are no assumptions either! Just premises.
- There are two main question types: **Inference** and **Explain a Discrepancy**.

Inference questions require you to find a piece of information that *must be true* according to the premises given in the argument.

Explain a Discrepancy questions require you to identify some kind of paradox or puzzling result in an argument and find an answer that explains, or resolves, the puzzling part of the argument. Before delving further into each type, let's talk about what inferences are on the GMAT.

## What Are Inferences?

In GMAT world, an inference is something that absolutely *must* be true according to the evidence given in the argument. You don't usually think of inferences this way; rather, in the real world, inferences are *likely* to be true based on the available evidence, but they don't absolutely have to be true. In the real world, an inference is a good guess or conjecture. In GMAT world, an inference is a bulletproof logical consequence.

For example, if a friend tells you that chocolate is her favorite flavor of ice cream, what kind of real-world inferences might you make? You might infer that she likes chocolate in general and that she likes ice cream in general. Maybe she likes all desserts in general—perhaps she has a sweet tooth. All of these things are perfectly reasonable to infer in the real world, but not a single one *has* to be true. It's possible that she likes chocolate only when it's in the form of ice cream or that she likes ice cream only when it's chocolate. The kinds of answers discussed in this paragraph would be tempting *incorrect* answers on the GMAT.

What would be good GMAT inferences? Well, what *must* be true? She can't like vanilla ice cream better than she likes chocolate ice cream—if chocolate is her *favorite* flavor of ice cream, then by definition she doesn't like any other flavor better. She has to have tried at least one other flavor of ice cream at some point in her life—she has to have had the ability to compare with at least one other flavor in order to decide that chocolate is her *favorite* flavor. These kinds of inferences would be correct answers on the GMAT.

All inference lessons refer to the GMAT's definition: something that *must* be true based on the available evidence.

# Inference Questions

**Inference questions** require you to find an answer that must be true according to the information in the argument.

Most Inference question stems contain some form of the words *conclude* or *infer*, although some variations don't include those specific words. Here are examples of phrasing in Inference questions:

> Which answer can be "logically concluded"?
>
> The "statements above most strongly support which of the following conclusions"?
>
> Which answer can be "properly inferred"?
>
> The statements above "best support" which of the following "assertions"?
>
> Which answer "must be true" based upon the statements above?

Note: Inference question stems can contain the language "most strongly support," which you also saw on Strengthen questions.

The diagram below shows how to tell whether the word *support* indicates Strengthen or Inference. On Inference questions, the argument (above) is used to support the correct answer (below). On Strengthen questions, the correct answer (below) is used to support the conclusion of the argument (above):

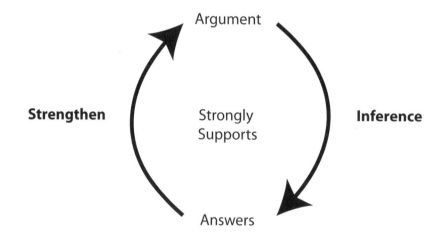

Inference questions will ask you to **use the argument to support an answer choice**. Also, Inference arguments will *not* contain a conclusion in the argument or question stem; they will consist only of premises.

By contrast, Strengthen questions will ask you to **use an answer to support the argument**. The correct answer would serve as an additional premise to support the argument's conclusion. Also, Strengthen questions will contain a conclusion in the argument or question stem.

Try this short example:

> Both enrollment and total tuition revenue at Brownsville University have increased during each of the last four years. During the same period, enrollment at Canterbury University has steadily decreased, while total tuition revenue has remained constant.
>
> Which of the following hypotheses is best supported by the statement given?
>
> (A) Brownsville University now collects more total revenue from tuition than does Canterbury University.
>
> (B) The per-student tuition at Canterbury University has risen over the last four years.
>
> (C) Brownsville University will continue to increase its revenues as long as it continues to increase enrollment.

The question stem uses the word *hypotheses* instead of the more common *conclusions*, but it signals the same thing: an Inference question. Your notes might look like this:

4 yrs:

BU: enrol, tuit ↑

CU: enrol ↓, tuit =

(premise)

There are two schools but different trends are happening. BU's enrollment and tuition revenues are both going up. CU's enrollment is going down, but tuition revenues are the same.

State your goal: *This is an Inference question, so I have to find an answer that must be true according to the premises.*

| (A) Brownsville University now collects more total revenue from tuition than does Canterbury University. | *Things have certainly been looking up for BU lately, but the argument says nothing about the actual dollar values that the schools are collecting. It's entirely possible that CU still collects more money than BU.* | ~~A~~ |
| --- | --- | --- |
| (B) The per-student tuition at Canterbury University has risen over the last four years. | *Let's see. Per-student tuition = revenues/# of students. CU has the same revenues today, so the numerator stays the same, but fewer students, so the denominator gets smaller. Dividing by a smaller number = a larger number. This must be true! I'll check (C), just in case.* | B̰ |
| (C) Brownsville University will continue to increase its revenues as long as it continues to increase enrollment. | *This might be reasonable to believe in the real world, but it doesn't have to be true. A trend never absolutely has to continue in the future.* | ~~C~~ |

~~A~~   (B̰)   ~~C~~

The argument provides several fact-based premises. (It is also possible to have premises that are somewhat more claim-based.) The correct answer must be true based on those premises, though in this case, you only needed to use the information about Canterbury in order to draw the correct conclusion. Answer (B) didn't use the Brownsville data at all. That's perfectly acceptable; you may need to use only some of the information in the argument, not all of it.

Answer (A) tried to trap you into concluding something based on information you don't have (actual dollar values). Answer (C) is a classic Real-World Distraction trap—it might be reasonable to believe that the trend will continue, but nothing says that a trend must continue in the future.

Quick quiz! What can you infer in the situation described below?

> Imagine two ice cream companies, X and Y. Chocolate ice cream represents 60 percent of Company X's sales and 50 percent of Company Y's sales. Clearly, Company X sells more chocolate ice cream than Company Y.

60 percent of sales      50 percent of sales

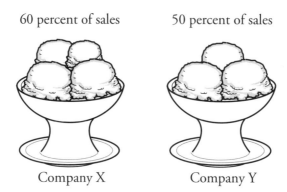

Company X         Company Y

The conclusion above is not necessarily true. You know nothing about the actual sales' numbers, nor about how those percentages relate to each other. What if company Y has $1 million in annual revenues and company X has only $10,000 in annual revenues? In that case, company Y sells a lot more chocolate ice cream than company X. You can't conclude anything about actual dollar amounts from this limited information about percentages.

Choc = $6,000      Choc = $500,000

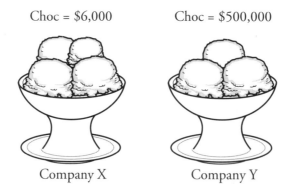

Company X         Company Y

Try this problem:

> A particular company sells only vanilla and chocolate ice cream. Last year, 55 percent of the company's profits were derived from chocolate ice cream sales and 40 percent of the revenues were derived from vanilla ice cream sales. What can you infer?
>
> (A) Chocolate ice cream is more popular than vanilla ice cream.
> (B) The company's vanilla ice cream produces more profit per dollar of sales than does the company's chocolate ice cream.

Yes, they might actually test your math skills on critical reasoning! Because you know that the company sells only these two products, you can figure out two additional percentages. If 55 percent of profits came from chocolate, then 45 percent of profits came from vanilla. If 40 percent of revenues came from vanilla, then 60 percent of revenues came from chocolate. These things must be true, but these inferences are probably too easy for any GMAT question. What else can you infer?

The company earned 60 percent of its revenues, but only 55 percent of its profits, from chocolate. By contrast, the company earned 40 percent of its revenues and a *higher* percentage of its profits, 45 percent, from vanilla. That's interesting. The company made more profit on vanilla and less profit on chocolate than you might have expected based on the percentage of revenues that each product generates. *Profitability* is a measure of profit per dollar of revenues. The vanilla ice cream product is more *profitable* than the chocolate ice cream product. That must be true, so answer (B) is correct.

What doesn't have to be true? It doesn't have to be true that vanilla will continue to be more profitable in the future. The trend might not continue. It also doesn't have to be true that more chocolate ice cream is more popular or even that more is sold by the industry in general—maybe this company makes a fantastic chocolate ice cream, but some other company makes a much better vanilla. Notice that answer (A) focuses on how popular chocolate ice cream is in general, not just this company's chocolate ice cream. You don't have any information about how popular chocolate ice cream is overall.

When you are given numbers, proportions, or any other mathematical information, do two things:

1. Confirm whether you have real numbers or percentages.

2. Figure out any other values or relationships that must be mathematically true.

Try a full example. Set your timer for 2 minutes:

> Reducing government spending has been demonstrated to raise the value of a country's currency over time. However, many economists no longer recommend this policy. A currency of lesser value causes a country's exports to be more competitive in the international market, encouraging domestic industries and making the economy more attractive to foreign investment.
>
> The statements above most strongly support which of the following inferences?
>
> (A) Limited government spending can also lead to a reduction in the national deficit.
> (B) Reducing government spending can make a country's exports less competitive.
> (C) Many economists now recommend higher levels of government spending.
> (D) An increase in the value of a currency will result in reduced government spending.
> (E) Competitive exports indicate a weak currency.

Step 1: Identify the Question

| The statements above most strongly support which of the following inferences? | *They're asking to support something below (in the answers), and they use the word inference. This is an Inference question.* | In<br>A<br>B<br>C<br>D<br>E |
|---|---|---|

Step 2: Deconstruct the Argument

| | | |
|---|---|---|
| Reducing government spending has been demonstrated to raise the value of a country's currency over time. | *This is a fact (that is, I should take it as one in the world of this argument). One thing demonstrably leads to another.* | ↓ gov spend → ↑ val curr |
| However, many economists no longer recommend this policy. | *Hmm. According to the first sentence, raising the value of currency sounds like a good thing, so why wouldn't the economists want to do that?* | BUT econs no longer rec |
| A currency of lesser value causes a country's exports to be more competitive in the international market, encouraging domestic industries and making the economy more attractive to foreign investment. | *Oh, okay, so there are some good reasons to have a lower currency value. I guess the economists think these benefits outweigh the lower value.* | ↓ val curr → exports more > compet → various benefits |

Step 3: State the Goal

Reducing government spending will increase currency value. It seems like it would be good to have a high currency value, but some economists disagree, because there are other benefits involved in having a lower currency value.

*I need to find an answer that must be true given the information in the argument. I don't need to use all of the info in the argument, though I may.*

Step 4: Work from Wrong to Right

| | | |
|---|---|---|
| (A) Limited government spending can also lead to a reduction in the national deficit. | *Deficit? This might be reasonable to believe in the real world, but there was nothing about the deficit in the argument—there's no evidence to support this statement.* | ~~A~~ |
| (B) Reducing government spending can make a country's exports less competitive. | *Let's see. The author said that reducing spending leads to a higher currency value. And then the economists said that a lower currency value makes exports more competitive. If that's true, then a higher currency value could make exports less competitive . . . so it is actually the case that reducing spending might lead to less competitive exports! Keep this one in.* | B ~ |
| (C) Many economists now recommend higher levels of government spending. | *The argument says* many economists *and the answer says* many economists, *so that part is okay. If you tell someone not to lower their spending, is that the same thing as telling them to increase their spending? No. You could also recommend spending the same amount. Tricky! This one isn't a "must be true" statement.* | ~~C~~ |
| (D) An increase in the value of a currency will result in reduced government spending. | *This one feels similar to (B)—language pretty similar to the argument, and I have to figure out what leads to what. The author said that X (reducing spending) will lead to Y (a higher currency value). This answer reverses the direction: Y will lead to X. That's not what the author said!* | ~~D~~ |

22

| | | |
|---|---|---|
| (E) Competitive exports indicate a weak currency. | *The economists said that a lower currency value leads to more competitive exports. Hmm. These things do seem to go together, according to the argument. I'll leave this one in and compare it to answer (B).* | $\underset{\sim}{E}$ |
| Compare (B) and (E). | *Now I need to compare (B) and (E). I'll check the wording of the answers to make sure I'm reading them correctly. Oh, I see. Answer (B) says that reducing spending can make exports less competitive, which is true, while (E) says that competitive exports indicate a weak currency. The argument says that a weaker currency leads to more competitive exports, but it doesn't say that the ONLY way to competitive exports is to have a weak currency. Maybe you can have competitive exports by investing in great research and development nationally or in some other fashion, so (E) isn't necessarily true and I can eliminate it.* | $\underset{\sim}{B}$ $\underset{\sim}{\bar{E}}$ |

## Right Answers

Right answers on Inference questions must be entirely supported by the information provided in the argument. Often, the right answer will bring together two or more of the premises in the argument, but not necessarily all the premises. This was the case in the prior example where the right answer linked reduced government spending (first sentence) to exports (last sentence). Occasionally, you may see a right answer that only draws from one premise in the argument.

## Common Trap Answers

### Real-World Distraction

The most tempting wrong answers on Inference questions tend to revolve around Real-World Distractions—things that you would reasonably assume to be true in the real world, but that don't absolutely have to be true. Some of these trap answers may quite obviously go way too far, but the trickiest ones will seem very reasonable…until you ask yourself whether that answer *must* be true.

Choices (C) and (E) from the last problem both seem reasonable in the real world, but neither one has to be true. The argument said merely that economists no longer recommend a policy to *reduce* spending. That doesn't necessarily mean that the economists recommend *higher* spending, as choice (C) says. There's also a third option: maintaining the same level of spending. Choice (E) didn't qualify the claim with a *could* or *can*. It isn't the case that competitive exports must always indicate a weak currency; they might have been caused by something else.

### Reverse Logic

Other trap answers will use language very similar to the language in the argument but will reverse the proper direction of the information. If you're told that eating honey causes people to hiccup, then a wrong answer might say that hiccupping causes people to eat honey. In the last problem, choice (D) used Reverse Logic, as did answer choice (E).

### Too Broad

If you're told that the flu often results in weight loss, then a trap answer might say that illness causes people not to be hungry. All illnesses? The flu is just one example; it isn't reasonable to conclude something about illnesses in general. (In addition, perhaps people are hungry when they have the flu, but they feel so nauseous that they can't eat!). Often, wrong answers on the GMAT will include a claim that is broader than the information in the argument; these broader claims, although common when making inferences in the real world, are not valid GMAT inferences.

## Explain a Discrepancy

As with Inference questions, **Discrepancy questions** consist only of premises, mostly on the fact-based side (though it is possible to have more claim-like premises). Most of the time, two sets of premises will be presented, and those premises will seem to be contradictory in some way. They won't "make sense" together. Sometimes, the argument will include indicator words such as *surprisingly* or *yet*.

Most Discrepancy question stems will include some form of the words *explain* or *resolve*, and the vast majority will also contain the words *if true*. Here are two typical examples:

> Which of the following, if true, most helps to resolve the paradox described above?

> Which of the following, if true, best explains the fact that many economists no longer recommend reducing spending in order to increase currency values?

Your task on Discrepancy questions is to find an answer that *resolves* or *fixes* the discrepancy—that is, all of the information now makes sense together. If you leave the argument as is, people should say, "Wait. That doesn't make sense." If you add the correct answer into the argument, people should say, "Oh, I see. That makes sense now."

Take a look at this short example:

> According to researchers, low dosages of aspirin taken daily can significantly reduce the risk of heart attack or stroke. Yet doctors have stopped recommending daily aspirin for most patients.

> Which of the following, if true, most helps to explain why doctors no longer recommend daily low dosages of aspirin?

> (A) Only a small percentage of patients have already experienced a heart attack or stroke.

> (B) Patients who are at low risk for heart attack or stroke are less likely to comply with a doctor's recommendation to take aspirin daily.

> (C) Aspirin acts as a blood thinner, which can lead to internal bleeding, particularly in the stomach or brain.

The question stem asks you to *explain* something that doesn't make sense: Aspirin is apparently beneficial, but "doctors have *stopped* recommending" its use for most people (implying that they used to recommend it more). Why would they do that? You might sketch or think of the info visually in this way:

daily aspirin ↓        *BUT*        Drs stop recomm
heart attack, stroke                    for most

WHY?

You're trying to highlight the apparent discrepancy between the two facts: On the one hand, daily aspirin is beneficial, and, on the other, doctors have stopped recommending it.

Go back to step 3, and state the goal:

*So far, they've told me something really good about taking aspirin daily: It significantly reduces the risk of some pretty bad things. The fact that the doctors have stopped recommending it means that they used to recommend it, so why would they stop doing so? Maybe there's something else that's bad about taking aspirin daily.*

| (A) Only a small percentage of patients have already experienced a heart attack or stroke. | *So maybe this means the doctors think it won't help that many people? Wait. The purpose of taking the aspirin is to try to prevent a heart attack or stroke. If most people haven't had a heart attack or stroke, you'd want them to do something that would help lower the risk.* | ~~A~~ |
|---|---|---|
| (B) Patients who are at low risk for heart attack or stroke are less likely to comply with a doctor's recommendation to take aspirin daily. | *I can believe this is true in the real world, but is a doctor really going to say, "Oh, I know a lot of people won't take the life-saving medication properly, so I just won't bother to prescribe it." I hope not! Plus, why would they recommend aspirin to people who are at low risk?* | ~~B~~ |
| (C) Aspirin acts as a blood thinner, which can lead to internal bleeding, particularly in the stomach or brain. | *Oh, this is a bad thing about aspirin—it can cause you to bleed! Yeah, if it could make your brain start bleeding, I can imagine that doctors would want to avoid prescribing it unless there was a really good reason to do so.* | C~ |

~~A~~     ~~B~~     Ⓒ

Answer (C) indicates a bad consequence that can result from taking aspirin. If you add it to the argument, now it's understandable why doctors might be reluctant to have people take aspirin regularly.

Answer (A) talks about the wrong group. The argument talks about preventing heart attacks or strokes in the general population, not only among those who have already experienced these maladies.

Answer (B) might be true, but this doesn't explain why doctors would stop recommending aspirin in general. In addition, this choice limits itself to those who are at low risk for heart attack or stroke—why would doctors need to recommend daily aspirin for a group that doesn't have the risk factors?

As you read that argument, the surprising finding (aspirin no longer recommended) may have seemed a lot like what has previously been classified as a conclusion. It is not actually a conclusion because there was nothing in the existing argument to support that claim; a claim is only a conclusion if it is supported by at least one premise. In fact, the only information in the argument went against that claim. Once you add the answer choice, you actually do have an argument with a counterpremise, premise (the answer), and conclusion. This approach provides another way to think about answering Discrepancy questions: Find a premise to support the surprising claim in the argument.

Try another example:

> In a recent poll, 71 percent of respondents reported that they cast votes in the most recent national election. Voting records show, however, that only 60 percent of eligible voters actually voted in that election.
>
> Which of the following pieces of evidence, if true, would provide the best explanation for the discrepancy?
>
> (A) The margin of error for the survey was plus or minus 5 percentage points.
>
> (B) Fifteen percent of the survey's respondents were living overseas at the time of the election.
>
> (C) Prior research has shown that people who actually do vote are also more likely to respond to polls than those who do not vote.
>
> (D) Some people who intend to vote are prevented from doing so by last-minute conflicts or other complications.
>
> (E) People are less likely to respond to a voting poll on the same day that they voted.

### Step 1: Identify the Question

| Which of the following pieces of evidence, if true, would provide the best explanation for the discrepancy? | *The question stem uses the word* explanation *and explicitly mentions a* discrepancy, *so this is an Explain the Discrepancy question.* | ED A B C D E |
|---|---|---|

### Step 2: Deconstruct the Argument

| In a recent poll, 71 percent of respondents reported that they cast votes in the most recent national election. | *Pure fact. There was a poll, and 71 percent of the people who responded said they voted in the last election.* | Poll: 71 percent voted |
|---|---|---|
| Voting records show, however, that only 60 percent of eligible voters actually voted in that election. | *Okay, that's strange. Records show that only 60 percent of people who were allowed to vote actually voted.* | BUT records: only 60 percent of elig voters voted |

### Step 3: State the Goal

*How can it be the case that, when asked, 71 percent of the people said they voted, but records show only 60 percent of those who were allowed to vote actually voted? I don't think it would be because some people voted who weren't allowed to—that would technically resolve the discrepancy, but I doubt the GMAT is going to say that. So what could it have been? Maybe some people are remembering incorrectly or mixing up the election in question. Oh, I know! Polls always have a margin of error, so maybe the margin of error accounts for the discrepancy.*

*Okay, I need to find something that will make the whole thing make sense—it'll explain why 71 percent said they voted but records showed that only 60 percent actually voted.*

Step 4: Work from Wrong to Right

| (A) The margin of error for the survey was plus or minus 5 percentage points. | *Margin of error, bingo! Excellent. So the real percentage could've been anywhere from…71 percent + 5 percent to 71 percent − 5 percent, which is still 66 percent. This doesn't go far enough. Still, it's about margin of error. I'm going to keep this one and come back to it later.* | A̰ |
| --- | --- | --- |
| (B) Fifteen percent of the survey's respondents were living overseas at the time of the election. | *This percentage is larger than the 11 percent discrepancy mentioned in the argument. But what group are they talking about? Are these the people who did vote, or didn't vote, or some mix of the two? And what does living overseas imply? This country might allow people to vote by absentee ballot. This doesn't resolve anything.* | B̶ |
| (C) Prior research has shown that people who actually do vote are also more likely to respond to polls than those who do not vote. | *People who vote are also more likely to respond to a survey. What does that mean? Of the people who responded, more were likely to have been voters than is represented in the overall population. Oh, I see—the survey group was skewed toward those who voted. That's why 71 percent of that subgroup could have voted while only 60 percent of the overall population of eligible voters voted. That's better than (A)—I'll get rid of (A).* | C̰ |
| (D) Some people who intend to vote are prevented from doing so by last-minute conflicts or other complications. | *I'm sure this is true in the real world. How does it affect this argument? The survey took place after the election; it asked people whether they had voted in the past. It doesn't address what people intended to do before the election.* | D̶ |
| (E) People are less likely to respond to a voting poll on the same day that they voted. | *I have no idea when the poll was taken, so I can't do much with this. Even if the poll was done the same day as the election, this just highlights the discrepancy—it's even more puzzling now. I would expect the percentage of people who said they voted to be lower than the real percentage because those who didn't vote that day would be more likely to agree to participate in the poll.* | E̶ |

On the first pass through the answers, both (A) and (C) seemed possible, but choice (A) didn't explain far enough, especially when compared with (C). The correct answer is (C).

A̰    B̶    (C)    D̶    E̶

# Right Answers

The right answer on a Discrepancy question should provide an explanation for the surprising finding presented in the argument. New language, information, and ideas are common in right answers because the finding was not explained by the original information in the argument.

### Common Trap Answers

### Half Way

One common wrong answer trap will seem to be on topic because it will address one of the premises, but it won't actually resolve the discrepancy between the two premises. Thus, this trap answer only goes Half Way. Some of these will more obviously fall short, such as answer (D), while others will be trickier because they just don't go quite far enough, such as answer (A). If answer (A) had said that the margin of error was plus or minus 15 percentage points, it could have been the correct answer.

### Reverse Logic

You may also see Reverse Logic traps, where the answer choice actually highlights or even heightens the discrepancy—that is, the choice makes the surprise even more surprising. Answer (E) could fall into this category: If the poll was taken the same day as the election, then the fact that the numbers don't match would be even more puzzling. People probably wouldn't have forgotten how they just voted, so did some of them lie?

## EXCEPT Questions

As with Assumption Family questions, Evidence Family questions can also be presented in the negative EXCEPT format. These are more likely to occur on Discrepancy questions than on Inference questions.

A regular Discrepancy question might read:

> Which of the following, if true, would best help to explain the surprising finding?

An EXCEPT Discrepancy question might read:

> Each of the following, if true, could help to explain the surprising finding EXCEPT

What is the difference in wording between those two questions?

The first one indicates that one answer choice, and only one, explains the discrepancy. That is the answer choice that you want to pick.

The second one indicates that four answer choices explain the discrepancy. These four are all wrong answers. The fifth answer will *not* explain or resolve the discrepancy. This is the odd one out and the correct answer.

Similarly, on an Inference EXCEPT question, four answer choices will represent things that must be true according to the argument; eliminate these four. One answer will represent something that does not have to be true. This is the odd one out; pick it.

## Inference Cheat Sheet

**Identify**
the Question

| | |
|---|---|
| **Common:** | *conclude* <br> *infer* |
| **Less common:** | *assertion* <br> *hypothesis* <br> *must be true* |
| **Infer:** | Use argument to support answer. |
| **Strengthen:** | Use answer to support conclusion in argument. |

**Deconstruct**
the Argument

**Find:**   Premises
(No conclusion! No assumptions!)

If not sure whether Infer or Strengthen, check the argument for a conclusion. No conclusion = infer.

State the **Goal**

Must be true based on the information given in the argument.
Does not need to use all of argument info.

Work from
**Wrong** to **Right**

**Right:**   Must be true given the info in the argument.

**Wrong:**   Real-World Distraction (logical in real world, but not necessarily true based on argument)

Reverse Direction (says X leads to Y, when really Y leads to X)

Switch Terms (leads to different meaning: not the right group, object, or idea)

Take a picture of this page and keep it with the review sheets you're creating as you study. Better yet, use this page as a guide to create your own review sheet—you'll remember the material better if you write it down yourself.

## Explain a Discrepancy Cheat Sheet

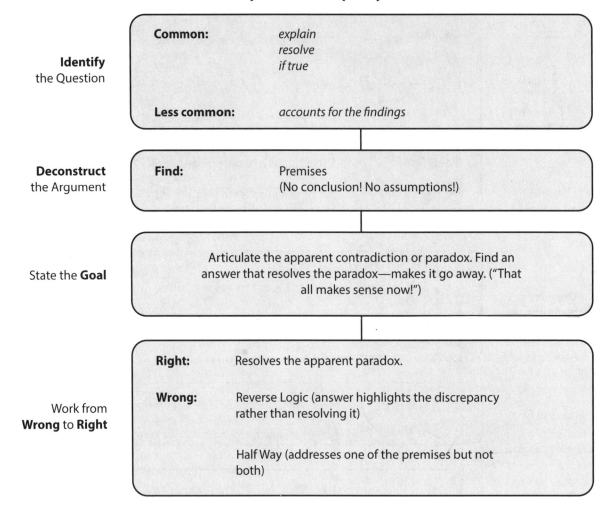

**Identify**
the Question

**Common:**  *explain*
*resolve*
*if true*

**Less common:**  *accounts for the findings*

**Deconstruct**
the Argument

**Find:**  Premises
(No conclusion! No assumptions!)

State the **Goal**

Articulate the apparent contradiction or paradox. Find an answer that resolves the paradox—makes it go away. ("That all makes sense now!")

Work from
**Wrong** to **Right**

**Right:**  Resolves the apparent paradox.

**Wrong:**  Reverse Logic (answer highlights the discrepancy rather than resolving it)

Half Way (addresses one of the premises but not both)

Take a picture of this page and keep it with the review sheets you're creating as you study. Better yet, use this page as a guide to create your own review sheet—you'll remember the material better if you write it down yourself.

# Problem Set

Answer each question using the 4-step Critical Reasoning process.

1. **Identify the question:** Is this an Inference question or an Explain the Discrepancy question?

2. **Deconstruct the argument:** Map the argument on your paper. Remember that there won't be a conclusion.

3. **State the goal:** What will the right answer need to do?

4. **Work from wrong to right:** Eliminate four wrong answers. Watch out for common wrong answer types.

1. *Mycenaean Vase*

   Museum A will display only objects that are undamaged and that have been definitively proven to be authentic. Doubts have been raised about the origins of a supposedly Mycenaean vase currently on display in the museum's antiquities wing. The only way to establish this vase's authenticity would be to pulverize it, then subject the dust to spectroscopic analysis.

   The claims above, if true, most strongly support which of the following conclusions?

   (A) Authentic Mycenaean vases are valuable and rare.
   (B) Museum A was not sufficiently diligent in establishing the authenticity of the vase before displaying it.
   (C) The vase in question will no longer be displayed in Museum A.
   (D) Spectroscopic analysis is the only method used by Museum A to establish the authenticity of objects.
   (E) Many of the world's museums unknowingly display forgeries.

2. *Gas Mileage*

   The average fuel efficiency of vehicles sold nationwide during the period 2000–2004 was 25 miles per gallon; the corresponding figure during the period 1995–1999 was 20 miles per gallon. The national average price of gasoline during the period 2000–2004 was $2 per gallon; the corresponding figure during the period 1995–1999 was $1.60 per gallon.

   The statements above, if true, best support which of the following conclusions?

   (A) The average fuel efficiency of vehicles sold nationwide should reach 30 miles per gallon for the period 2005–2009.
   (B) The cost of gasoline for an average trip in a vehicle was higher during the period 1995–1999 than during the period 2000–2004.
   (C) Rising gasoline prices lead consumers to purchase more fuel-efficient cars.
   (D) The ratio of average fuel efficiency to average price of gasoline from the 1995–1999 period was roughly equal to the ratio from the 2000–2004 period.
   (E) Consumers spent more money on gasoline during the period 2000–2004 than during the period 1995–1999.

3. *CarStore*

   CarStore's sales personnel have an average of 15 years' experience selling automobiles, and for the last 5 years, they have sold more cars each year than other local dealers. Despite this, CarStore management has decided to implement a mandatory training program for all sales personnel.

   Which of the following, if true, best explains the facts given above?

   (A) Sales personnel at CarStore earn significantly more money than those who work for other local dealers.

   (B) Within the last 5 years, a number of other local dealers have implemented mandatory training programs.

   (C) It is common for new or less experienced employees to participate in training programs.

   (D) A website has recently released confidential pricing information for the cars sold by CarStore, and customers have begun trying to negotiate lower prices using this data.

   (E) Several retailers that compete directly with CarStore use "customer-centered" sales approaches.

4. *Stem Cell Research*

   Government restrictions have severely limited the amount of stem cell research U.S. companies can conduct. Because of these restrictions, many U.S. scientists who specialize in the field of stem cell research have signed long-term contracts to work for foreign companies. Recently, Congress has proposed lifting all restrictions on stem cell research.

   Which of the following statements can most properly be inferred from the information above?

   (A) Some foreign companies that conduct stem cell research work under fewer restrictions than some U.S. companies do.

   (B) Because U.S. scientists are under long-term contracts to foreign companies, there will be a significant influx of foreign professionals into the U.S.

   (C) In all parts of the world, stem cell research is dependent on the financial backing of local government.

   (D) In the near future, U.S. companies will no longer be at the forefront of stem cell research.

   (E) If restrictions on stem cell research are lifted, many of the U.S. scientists will break their contracts to return to U.S. companies.

5. *Hunting Season*

In an effort to reduce the number of deer, and therefore decrease the number of automobile accidents caused by deer, the government lengthened the deer hunting season earlier this year. Surprisingly, the number of accidents caused by deer has increased substantially since the introduction of the longer hunting season.

All of the following, if true, help to explain the increase in traffic accidents caused by deer EXCEPT

(A) The presence of humans in the woods causes the deer to move to new areas, which causes the deer to cross roads more frequently than normal.

(B) In the area where the deer live, the lengthened hunting season attracted a significantly greater amount of traffic than usual this year.

(C) Most automobile accidents involving deer result from cars swerving to avoid deer, and they leave the deer in question unharmed.

(D) Deer tend to bolt when hearing gunshots or other loud sounds and are more likely to run across a road without warning.

(E) A new highway was recently built directly through the state's largest forest, which is the primary habitat of the state's deer population.

6. *World Bank*

In 2010, China comprised about 10 percent of the world's gross domestic product (GDP), and its voting share in the World Bank was increased from less than 3 percent to 4.4 percent. During the same time frame, France comprised about 4 percent of the world's GDP and saw its voting share in the World bank drop from 4.3 percent to 3.8 percent.

Which of the following can be logically concluded from the passage above?

(A) Prior to 2010, China comprised less than 10 percent of the world's GDP.

(B) Voting share in the World Bank is not directly proportional to each country's share of the world's GDP.

(C) China's share in the world's GDP is increasing more rapidly than France's share.

(D) The Chinese government is likely to be dissatisfied with the degree of the increase in its voting share.

(E) World Bank voting shares are allocated based upon each country's share of the world's GDP during previous years, not during the present year.

7. *Barcodes*

Two-dimensional barcodes are omni-directional; that is, unlike one-dimensional barcodes, they can be scanned from any direction. Additionally, two-dimensional barcodes are smaller and can store more data than their one-dimensional counterparts. Despite such advantages, two-dimensional barcodes account for a much smaller portion of total barcode usage than one-dimensional barcodes.

**22**

Which of the following, if true, most helps to resolve the apparent paradox?

(A) Many smaller stores do not use barcodes at all because of the expense.

(B) For some products, the amount of data necessary to be coded is small enough to fit fully on a one-dimensional barcode.

(C) Two-dimensional barcodes are, on average, less expensive than one-dimensional barcodes.

(D) Two-dimensional barcodes can also be scanned by consumer devices, such as cell phones.

(E) One-dimensional barcodes last longer and are less prone to error than two-dimensional barcodes.

# Solutions

1.  Mycenaean Vase: The correct answer is (**C**).

    Step 1: Identify the Question

    | The claims above, if true, most strongly support which of the following conclusions? | *The language* strongly support *could indicate an Inference or a Strengthen question. Since the question stem says* which of the following conclusions, *the conclusion will be in the answer choices, not in the argument. This is an Inference problem.* | In<br>A<br>B<br>C<br>D<br>E |
    | --- | --- | --- |

    Step 2: Deconstruct the Argument

    | Museum A will display only objects that are undamaged and that have been definitively proven to be authentic. | *This is a fact—all objects have to be perfect and authenticated for this museum to display them.* | Mus: only perfect, auth objects |
    | --- | --- | --- |
    | Doubts have been raised about the origins of a supposedly Mycenaean vase currently on display in the museum's antiquities wing. | *Another fact: They're not sure whether this vase is authentic.* | Doubts about Myc vase |
    | The only way to establish this vase's authenticity would be to pulverize it, then subject the dust to spectroscopic analysis. | *That's interesting and kind of sad. In order to prove whether the vase is authentic, they've got to destroy it!* | To auth, must destroy! |

    Step 3: State the Goal

    *This is an Inference question; I need to find something that must be true according to the info given in the argument. In this case, they're not sure whether this vase is authentic and the only way to establish its authenticity is to destroy it. What follows logically from that? They can't display a fake vase, and they can't display a pulverized vase, so they won't be able to display it at all.*

Step 4: Work from Wrong to Right

| | | |
|---|---|---|
| (A) Authentic Mycenaean vases are valuable and rare. | *This might be true, but I can't prove it using only what's in the argument.* | ~~A~~ |
| (B) Museum A was not sufficiently diligent in establishing the authenticity of the vase before displaying it. | *That seems a little judgmental, but reasonable. The museum only wants to display authentic objects, so why were they displaying this vase?* | B̰ |
| (C) The vase in question will no longer be displayed in Museum A. | *I can prove that this answer choice is true! Since they only display objects they know are authentic, if they want to display the vase, they have to authenticate it. But to authenticate it, they have to destroy it! No matter what, they won't be able to display the vase. This is better than (B), since it's something I can prove using logic, not a value judgment.* | C̰ |
| (D) Spectroscopic analysis is the only method used by Museum A to establish the authenticity of objects. | *That's not necessarily true. They have to use it for this vase, but they might have other methods for other objects.* | ~~D~~ |
| (E) Many of the world's museums unknowingly display forgeries. | *This makes sense in the real world, but I can't prove it using only the information here. I only know about one museum and one object, not many of the world's museums.* | ~~E~~ |

~~A~~   B̰   Ⓒ   ~~D~~   ~~E~~

2.  Gas Mileage: The correct answer is (**D**).

    Step 1: Identify the Question

    | The statements above, if true, best support which of the following conclusions? | *The language* best support *could indicate an Inference or a Strengthen question. The rest of the question says that the conclusion will be one of the answer choices, so this is an Inference question.* | In<br>A<br>B<br>C<br>D<br>E |
    |---|---|---|

    Step 2: Deconstruct the Argument

    | The average fuel efficiency of vehicles sold nationwide during the period 2000–2004 was 25 miles per gallon; the corresponding figure during the period 1995–1999 was 20 miles per gallon. | *These are all facts, which I'm expecting because this is an Inference question. They're talking about time periods and figures, so maybe a table is the best way to keep track.* | **95–99** | **00–04** |
    |---|---|---|---|
    | | | Fuel eff<br>20 mpg | 25 |
    | The national average price of gasoline during the period 2000–2004 was $2 per gallon; the corresponding figure during the period 1995–1999 was $1.60 per gallon. | *Yep, a table was a good idea! More facts and figures for the same time frame.* | $1.60 per gal | $2 |

    Step 3: State the Goal

    *This is an Inference question, so I'm looking for something that must be true based on all this data. I was given specific figures for average fuel efficiency and average gas price for two time periods. Both went up over time. I imagine that I'll need to make a mathematical inference.*

Step 4: Work from Wrong to Right

| | | |
|---|---|---|
| (A) The average fuel efficiency of vehicles sold nationwide should reach 30 miles per gallon for the period 2005–2009. | *Should reach? That doesn't have to be true. Who knows what's going to happen in the future?* | ~~A~~ |
| (B) The cost of gasoline for an average trip in a vehicle was higher during the period 1995–1999 than during the period 2000–2004. | *Interesting. Gas efficiency was lower in the first time period, but gas also cost less. On top of that, I don't know whether the number or length of trips changed. I don't have enough information to prove this.* | ~~B~~ |
| (C) Rising gasoline prices lead consumers to purchase more fuel-efficient cars. | *This statement is logical, but I can't prove it using only what's in the argument, and I'm not allowed to use outside knowledge. The argument doesn't say anything about why consumers decide to purchase certain cars.* | ~~C~~ |
| (D) The ratio of average fuel efficiency to average price of gasoline from the 1995–1999 period was roughly equal to the ratio from the 2000–2004 period. | *The ratio? Hmm. I don't know, but I can calculate based on the figures I was already given. In the first period, the fuel efficiency number was 20 miles per gallon, and the cost of gas was $1.60. $20/\$1.60 = 20/(8/5) = 400/8 = 12.5$. In the second period, the numbers were 25 and $2. That's also a ratio of 12.5. They're equal!* | $\underset{\sim}{D}$ |
| (E) Consumers spent more money on gasoline during the period 2000–2004 than during the period 1995–1999. | *Tricky! This one seems pretty good at first glance, but average price per gallon is not the same thing as total amount of money spent. It's true that the average price was higher, but maybe people bought fewer gallons of gasoline (especially because fuel efficiency was better!). This one might be true, but it doesn't have to be.* | ~~E~~ |

3. CarStore: The correct answer is (**D**).

Step 1: Identify the Question

| Which of the following, if true, best explains the facts given above? | *The language best explains the facts is slightly unusual. But since I need to explain something, it's a Discrepancy problem.* | ED<br>A<br>B<br>C<br>D<br>E |
|---|---|---|

Step 2: Deconstruct the Argument

| CarStore's sales personnel have an average of 15 years' experience selling automobiles, and for the last 5 years, they have sold more cars each year than other local dealers. | *CarStore's people have 15 years' experience on average, and they sell more cars than the competition. These are facts.* | Sales ppl: avg 15y exper, sell more than comp<br><br>~ |
|---|---|---|
| Despite this, CarStore has recently implemented a mandatory training program for all sales personnel. | *Here's the contrast. Why are they going to make them all go through training? Maybe something has changed in the marketplace?* | BUT store now req training for all |

Step 3: State the Goal

*This is a Discrepancy question, so I need to find an answer that explains the surprise. What is the reason for the new training?*

Step 4: Work from Wrong to Right

| (A) Sales personnel at CarStore earn significantly more money than those who work for other local dealers. | *Maybe they want to train their employees because they're investing a lot of money into them? No, that's too much of a stretch. It doesn't clearly explain why management suddenly made this decision.* | ~~A~~ |
|---|---|---|
| (B) Within the last 5 years, a number of other local dealers have implemented mandatory training programs. | *This would be a good explanation if I didn't know that CarStore employees were selling more cars than employees at other dealers. But, the argument makes it sound like if this is true, then the training programs at the other dealerships don't work. Why would CarStore copy them?* | ~~B~~ |
| (C) It is common for new or less experienced employees to participate in training programs. | *This makes sense, but doesn't explain why the employees who average 15 years' experience need training. The argument said that all sales personnel have to undergo the training, not just the new ones.* | ~~C~~ |
| (D) A website has recently released confidential pricing information for the cars sold by CarStore, and customers have begun trying to negotiate lower prices using this data. | *This describes a change, which is promising. A change in the situation might explain why management wants to train the sales personnel now. And this change makes sense, too: Customers are using a new negotiating tactic, so CarStore employees should be trained to respond to it.* | D |
| (E) Several retailers that compete directly with CarStore use "customer-centered" sales approaches. | *The other retailers aren't doing as well as CarStore is, so this doesn't explain why the CarStore employees need training. We also don't know whether CarStore already uses this approach or whether it has something better.* | ~~E~~ |

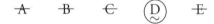

4.   Stem Cell Research: The correct answer is **(A)**.

Step 1: Identify the Question

| Which of the following statements can most properly be inferred from the information above? | *The word* inferred *indicates that this is an Inference question.* | In<br>A<br>B<br>C<br>D<br>E |
|---|---|---|

Step 2: Deconstruct the Argument

| Government restrictions have severely limited the amount of stem cell research U.S. companies can conduct. | *This is a fact. The U.S. government restricts this stem cell research.* | In A B C D E<br>Stem cell res restrict by U.S. gov |
|---|---|---|
| Because of these restrictions, many U.S. scientists who specialize in the field of stem cell research have signed long-term contracts to work for foreign companies. | *Because of that—so the first sentence leads to the second sentence.* | → U.S. sci work foreign coms instead |
| Recently, Congress has proposed lifting all restrictions on stem cell research. | *Still a fact: The government is considering lifting the restrictions. Maybe that'll bring the scientists back to work for U.S. companies?* | U.S. gov: maybe lift restrict? |

Step 3: State the Goal

*This is an Inference question, so I need to find something that's definitely true based on the information so far. The U.S. government restricts a certain kind of research, so many U.S. scientists who do this type of research are working for foreign companies instead. Congress might lift the restrictions.*

Step 4: Work from Wrong to Right

| | | |
|---|---|---|
| (A) Some foreign companies that conduct stem cell research work under fewer restrictions than some U.S. companies do. | *If the researchers decided to work for foreign companies specifically* because *the U.S. companies had restrictions, then that would mean that at least some foreign companies did have fewer restrictions. Yes, this one must be true! I'll check the other answers just in case, though.* | A ~ |
| (B) Because U.S. scientists are under long-term contracts to foreign companies, there will be a significant influx of foreign professionals into the U.S. | *This might be true, but it certainly doesn't have to be true. The argument doesn't say anything about foreign professionals coming into the United States.* | B̶ |
| (C) In all parts of the world, stem cell research is dependent on the financial backing of local government. | *The argument doesn't say anything about how this type of research gets its financial backing. This doesn't have to be true.* | C̶ |
| (D) In the near future, U.S. companies will no longer be at the forefront of stem cell research. | *Irrelevant. The argument doesn't discuss who is or will be at the forefront of this kind of research.* | D̶ |
| (E) If restrictions on stem cell research are lifted, many of the U.S. scientists will break their contracts to return to U.S. companies. | *This might happen, but we can't necessarily predict what will happen in the future.* | E̶ |

5. Hunting Season: The correct answer is **(C)**.

Step 1: Identify the Question

| All of the following, if true, help to explain the increase in traffic accidents caused by deer EXCEPT | *The language* help to explain *indicates that this is a Discrepancy question. This is also an EXCEPT question.* | ED<br>Ex<br>A<br>B<br>C<br>D<br>E |
| --- | --- | --- |

Step 2: Deconstruct the Argument

| In an effort to reduce the number of deer, and therefore decrease the number of automobile accidents caused by deer, the government lengthened the deer hunting season earlier this year. | *Multiple levels here. First, the government lengthened the hunting season, which is supposed to reduce the number of deer, which is then supposed to reduce the number of car accidents caused by deer.* | Gov: ↑ hunt seas → ↓ deer → ↓ car acc |
| --- | --- | --- |
| Surprisingly, the number of accidents caused by deer has increased substantially since the introduction of the longer hunting season. | *That's weird. The exact opposite has happened: There have been more car accidents caused by deer!* | BUT # car acc ↑ |

Step 3: State the Goal

*This is a Discrepancy EXCEPT question. Normally on Discrepancy questions, I'm looking for the answer that makes the contradictory evidence make sense. On this one, though, all four wrong answers will fix the discrepancy. The odd one out—the one that doesn't fix the discrepancy—will be the right answer.*

*So I need to find (and cross off) four things that explain why there have been even more car accidents caused by deer.*

Step 4: Work from Wrong to Right

| | | |
|---|---|---|
| (A) The presence of humans in the woods causes the deer to move to new areas, which causes the deer to cross roads more frequently than normal. | *If hunting season is lengthened, then there will be people in the woods for a longer period of time. According to this choice, that means the deer are going to cross the roads more frequently than they otherwise would have. That could increase the likelihood of accidents due to deer, which explains the discrepancy. Cross this one off.* | A̶ |
| (B) The lengthened hunting season attracted a significantly greater amount of traffic than usual to the area this year. | *Oh, this makes sense. The lengthened hunting season actually caused more traffic, so there are more chances for accidents between cars and deer where the deer live. This explains the discrepancy, too.* | B̶ |
| (C) Most automobile accidents involving deer result from cars swerving to avoid deer, and they leave the deer in question unharmed. | *This one is tricky! It explains how the accidents happen, which makes sense. But the right answer has to explain why there are* more *accidents. This doesn't show anything about the number of accidents.* | C̰ |
| (D) Deer tend to bolt when hearing gunshots or other loud sounds and are more likely to run across a road without warning. | *If there are gunshots for a longer length of time, then there are more chances for the deer to bolt and cross the road suddenly. . .increasing the chances of an accident.* | D̶ |
| (E) A new highway was recently built directly through the state's largest forest, which is the primary habitat of the state's deer population. | *The situation has changed from the year before: A new highway was built right through the area where the deer live. So it would make sense that there are now more accidents caused by deer.* | E̶ |

  Ⓒ

6. World Bank: The correct answer is **(B)**.

Step 1: Identify the Question

| Which of the following can be logically concluded from the passage above? | *The language* logically concluded *indicates that this is an Inference question.* | In<br>A<br>B<br>C<br>D<br>E |
|---|---|---|

Step 2: Deconstruct the Argument

| In 2010, China comprised about 10 percent of the world's gross domestic product (GDP), and its voting share in the World Bank was increased from less than 3 percent to 4.4 percent. | *A bunch of stats about China in 2010. I just need to keep this straight because, glancing down, I can see the next sentence has more numbers.* | <table><tr><td>2010</td><td>GDP</td><td>Vote Share</td></tr><tr><td>China</td><td>10</td><td>&lt;3 → 4.4</td></tr></table> |
|---|---|---|
| During the same time frame, France comprised about 4 percent of the world's GDP and saw its voting share in the World bank drop from 4.3 percent to 3.8 percent. | *Same type of stats, but about France this time. Same time frame.* | <table><tr><td>Fra</td><td>4</td><td>4.3 → 3.8</td></tr></table> |

Step 3: State the Goal

*This is an Inference question, so I need to find something that must be true based upon the info given so far. There are a lot of numbers to keep straight, but generally, China has a larger share of the world GDP than France. China used to have a lower voting share than France, but now it has a higher share.*

Step 4: Work from Wrong to Right

| | | |
|---|---|---|
| (A) Prior to 2010, China comprised less than 10 percent of the world's gross domestic product. | *China's voting share increased in 2010. Maybe that happened because its GDP was lower than 10 percent, and then it increased? On the other hand, I don't actually know that the voting share is based on the GDP. They could have nothing to do with each other. This doesn't have to be true.* | A̶ |
| (B) Voting share in the World Bank is not directly proportional to each country's share of the world's GDP. | *If they were directly proportional, a country with twice the GDP would also have twice the voting share. But China's GDP is more than twice France's and their voting shares are almost the same. The voting share must not be directly proportional! This is probably right.* | B ~ |
| (C) China's share in the world's gross domestic product is increasing more rapidly than France's share. | *China's share is higher now, but I don't actually know whether France's share is increasing or how quickly.* | C̶ |
| (D) The Chinese government is likely to be dissatisfied with the degree of the increase in its voting share. | *There's no way to know this using only the information in the argument. I don't even know whether an increase from 3 percent to 4.4 percent is considered small or large.* | D̶ |
| (E) World Bank voting shares are allocated based upon each country's share of the world's GDP during previous years, not during the present year. | *I could speculate that this was true, but I can't prove it. I don't have enough information to tell where these numbers came from.* | E̶ |

7.  Barcodes: The correct answer is **(E)**.

Step 1: Identify the Question

| Which of the following, if true, most helps to resolve the apparent paradox? | *The word* paradox *indicates that this is a Discrepancy question.* | ED<br>A<br>B<br>C<br>D<br>E |
| --- | --- | --- |

Step 2: Deconstruct the Argument

| Two-dimensional barcodes are omni-directional; that is, unlike one-dimensional barcodes, they can be scanned from any direction. | *Okay, so 2D barcodes have a better feature than 1D barcodes.* | 2D barcodes scan any dir, unlike 1D |
| --- | --- | --- |
| Additionally, two-dimensional barcodes are smaller and can store more data than their one-dimensional counterparts. | *Even more advantages for the 2D barcodes.* | Also 2D smaller, more data |
| Despite such advantages, two-dimensional barcodes account for a much smaller portion of total barcode usage than one-dimensional barcodes. | *But the 1D barcodes are used a lot more—why? There must be some advantages to the 1Ds or disadvantages to the 2Ds that I don't yet know about.* | BUT 1D is used >> |

Step 3: State the Goal

*I need to find something that fixes the discrepancy described in the argument: The 2D barcodes have a bunch of advantages, but people mostly still use the 1D barcodes. Why? Maybe the 2D ones are super-expensive or something like that.*

Step 4: Work from Wrong to Right

| | | |
|---|---|---|
| (A) Many smaller stores do not use barcodes at all because of the expense. | *Expense—does this explain why 1D barcodes are still being used? No, wait—this says the stores aren't using any type of barcode at all. So that doesn't explain why the ones that do use barcodes seem to prefer the 1D models.* | ~~A~~ |
| (B) For some products, the amount of data necessary to be coded is small enough to fit fully on a one-dimensional barcode. | *Okay, so some products might not need the 2D barcodes. Except, this only mentions* some *products, while the argument says that the 2D barcodes are a much smaller* portion of total usage. *This doesn't fully explain the discrepancy.* | ~~B~~ |
| (C) Two-dimensional barcodes are, on average, less expensive than one-dimensional barcodes. | *Less expensive, this is it! Wait a second. No, this says the 2D barcodes are less expensive—that gives them yet another advantage! If they're less expensive, I'd expect people to use them more. This isn't it.* | ~~C~~ |
| (D) Two-dimensional barcodes can also be scanned by consumer devices, such as cell phones. | *This sounds like yet another advantage of the 2D barcodes. This isn't it either!* | ~~D~~ |
| (E) One-dimensional barcodes last longer and are less prone to error than two-dimensional barcodes. | *Here are two advantages of the 1D barcodes. If it's true that they last longer and are less prone to error, then that would explain why people would want to use them rather than the 2D barcodes.* | E ~ |

# APPENDIX A

# Idioms

# Idioms

This appendix contains idioms that have been tested on the GMAT in the past but that are not among the most commonly tested idioms. The list is quite long; we don't recommend memorizing every idiom here.

Rather, use this appendix as a reference. If you miss a problem that uses one of these idioms, check the entry to learn the acceptable uses of the idiom.

| Label | Definition |
|---|---|
| RIGHT: | Expressions that the GMAT considers correct. |
| SUSPECT: | *Expressions that the GMAT seems to avoid if possible. They occasionally show up in a correct answer, but only when the other four choices are clearly wrong. These expressions are sometimes grammatically correct, but they may be wordy, controversial, or simply less preferred than other forms.* |
| WRONG: | *Expressions that the GMAT considers incorrect.* |

## ACT

| | |
|---|---|
| RIGHT: | The bay ACTED AS a funnel for the tide. (functioned as)<br>My friend ACTED LIKE a fool. (behaved in a similar manner) |
| SUSPECT: | *The bay ACTED LIKE a funnel for the tide.*<br>Note: At least one official explanation for an *Official Guide* problem claims that ACT LIKE must be used only with people. This claim is contradicted by other published problems. The way to resolve this issue is to ask whether the author intends *metaphorical comparison* (LIKE) or *actual function* (AS). If actual function is possible, use AS. |

## AFFECT/EFFECT

| | |
|---|---|
| RIGHT: | The new rules will AFFECT our performance. |
| WRONG: | *The new rules will CAUSE AN EFFECT ON our performance.* |

### AFTER

| | |
|---|---|
| RIGHT: | AFTER the gold rush, the mining town collapsed. |

*FOLLOWING the gold rush, the mining town collapsed.* (Ambiguous: Could be interpreted to mean that the mining town was following the gold rush in a metaphorical way.)

SUSPECT: *FOLLOWING the gold rush, the mining town collapsed.* (Ambiguous: Could be interpreted to mean that the mining town was following the gold rush in a metaphorical way.)

### AGGRAVATE

RIGHT: His behavior AGGRAVATED the problem. (made worse)

WRONG: *His behavior WAS AGGRAVATING TO the problem.* (was annoying to)

### AGREE

RIGHT: They AGREE THAT electrons EXIST.

Electrons are particles THAT physicists AGREE EXIST.

WRONG: *They AGREE electrons EXIST.* (*THAT* is required.)

*There is AGREEMENT AMONG them TO THE FACT THAT electrons exist.*

*Electrons are particles physicists AGREE THAT EXIST.*

*Electrons are particles physicists AGREE TO EXIST.*

*Electrons are particles THAT physicists AGREE ON AS EXISTING.*

### AID

RIGHT: She AIDS her neighbor.

She provides AID TO victims.

AID FOR victims is available.

Her AID IN WALKING the dog was appreciated.

WRONG: *Her AID TO WALK the dog was appreciated.*

### AIM

RIGHT: We adopted new procedures AIMED AT REDUCING theft.

We adopted new procedures WITH THE AIM OF REDUCING theft.

WRONG: *We adopted new policies WITH THE AIM TO REDUCE theft.*

### AMONG

See BETWEEN.

## ANXIETY

RIGHT:    His ANXIETY ABOUT his company's future is ill-founded.

His ANXIETY THAT his company MAY BE SOLD is ill-founded.

......................................................................................................

WRONG:    *His ANXIETY ABOUT his company MAY BE SOLD is ill-founded.*

## APPEAR

RIGHT:    Imperfections APPEAR AS tiny cracks. (show up as)

He APPEARS CONFUSED. (seems)

The dinosaurs APPEAR TO HAVE BEEN relatively smart.

IT APPEARS THAT the dinosaurs WERE smart.

......................................................................................................

WRONG:    *He APPEARS AS confused.*

*The dinosaurs APPEARED AS smart.*

## APPLY

RIGHT:    The rules APPLY TO all of us.

......................................................................................................

WRONG:    *All of us ARE SUBJECT TO THE APPLICABILITY OF the rules.*

## AS LONG AS

RIGHT:    I will leave, AS LONG AS it IS safe.

I will leave, SO LONG AS it IS safe.

I will leave, PROVIDED THAT it IS safe.

......................................................................................................

SUSPECT:    *I will leave, BUT it HAS TO BE safe.*

......................................................................................................

WRONG:    *I will leave, BUT it BE safe.*

*I will leave, AS (or SO) LONG AS it BE safe.*

## AS ... SO

RIGHT:    AS you practice, SO shall you play. (in the same way or manner)

JUST AS you practice, SO shall you play. (in the same way or manner)

JUST AS you practice piano regularly, you should study regularly. (in the same way; the situations are analogous)

......................................................................................................

WRONG:    *You practice, SO shall you play.*

*JUST LIKE you practice, SO shall you play.*

## ASK

| | |
|---|---|
| RIGHT: | I ASKED FOR his AID. |
| | He ASKED her TO GO to the store. |
| | He ASKED THAT she GO to the store. (subjunctive) |

| | |
|---|---|
| WRONG: | *He ASKED THAT she SHOULD GO to the store.* |

## ATTRIBUTE

| | |
|---|---|
| RIGHT: | We ATTRIBUTE the uprising TO popular discontent. |

| | |
|---|---|
| WRONG: | *We ATTRIBUTE the uprising AS popular discontent.* |

## AVERAGE

| | |
|---|---|
| RIGHT: | Tech COMPANIES are as likely as the AVERAGE COMPANY to fail. |
| | ON AVERAGE, 3 out of 10 new small businesses fail during their first two years. |

| | |
|---|---|
| WRONG: | *AT AVERAGE, 3 out of 10 new small businesses fail during their first two years.* |

## AWARE

| | |
|---|---|
| RIGHT: | AWARE OF the danger, he fled. |
| | AWARE THAT danger was near, he fled. |

| | |
|---|---|
| WRONG: | *WITH AN AWARENESS THAT danger was near, he fled.* |
| | *WITH AN AWARENESS OF the danger, he fled.* |

## BAN

| | |
|---|---|
| RIGHT: | They passed a BAN PROHIBITING us FROM CARRYING bottles. |

| | |
|---|---|
| WRONG: | *They passed a BAN that we CANNOT CARRY bottles.* |

## BASED ON

| | |
|---|---|
| RIGHT: | The verdict was BASED ON the evidence. |
| | The jury reached a verdict BASED ON the evidence. |

| | |
|---|---|
| WRONG: | *BASED ON the evidence, the jury reached a verdict.* (The jury was not itself BASED ON the evidence.) |

## BEGIN

RIGHT: The movement BEGAN AS a protest. (started as a protest, became a movement)

The movement BEGAN WITH a protest. (A protest was the first event of the movement.)

The protest BEGAN a movement. (The protest caused a movement.)

...............................................................................................................

WRONG: *The movement WAS BEGUN FROM a protest.*

## BETWEEN

RIGHT: An argument ensued BETWEEN the CEO AND the marketing director.

A skirmish ensued AMONG the attendees of the game. (Use AMONG for more than two parties.)

...............................................................................................................

WRONG: *An argument ensued BETWEEN the CEO WITH the marketing director.*

*An argument ensued AMONG the CEO AND the marketing director.*

*An argument ensued AMONG the CEO WITH the marketing director.*

## BORDERS

RIGHT: WITHIN the BORDERS of a country.

...............................................................................................................

WRONG: *IN the BORDERS of a country.*

*INSIDE the BORDERS of a country.*

## CHANCE

RIGHT: I have ONE CHANCE IN A THOUSAND OF WINNING tonight.

...............................................................................................................

WRONG: *I have ONE CHANCE IN A THOUSAND FOR WINNING tonight.*

*I have ONE IN A THOUSAND CHANCES TO WIN tonight.*

*I have ONE CHANCE IN A THOUSAND THAT I WILL WIN tonight.*

*I have ONE CHANCE IN A THOUSAND FOR ME TO WIN tonight.*

## CLAIM

RIGHT: They CLAIM THAT they CAN read minds.

They CLAIM TO BE ABLE to read minds.

...............................................................................................................

WRONG: *They CLAIM BEING ABLE to read minds.*

## COMPARABLE

RIGHT:        Costs are rising, but incomes have not increased COMPARABLY.

...................................................................................................

SUSPECT:    *Costs are rising, but incomes have not increased TO A COMPARABLE EXTENT.*

## COMPARED/COMPARISON

RIGHT:        IN COMPARISON WITH (or TO) horses, zebras are vicious.

A zebra can be COMPARED TO a horse in many ways.

COMPARED WITH a horse, a zebra is very hard to tame.

Note: The GMAT ignores the traditional distinction between COMPARED TO (emphasizing similarities) and COMPARED WITH (emphasizing differences).

...................................................................................................

WRONG:      *WHEN COMPARED TO horses, zebras are vicious.*

*Zebras are MORE vicious COMPARED TO horses.*

## CONCEIVE

RIGHT:        He CONCEIVES OF architecture AS a dialogue.

...................................................................................................

SUSPECT:    *His CONCEPTION OF architecture IS AS a dialogue.*

...................................................................................................

WRONG:      *He CONCEIVES OF architecture TO BE a dialogue.*

## CONFIDENCE

RIGHT:        We have CONFIDENCE THAT the market WILL RECOVER.

...................................................................................................

SUSPECT:    *We have CONFIDENCE IN the market's ABILITY TO RECOVER.*

...................................................................................................

WRONG:      *We have CONFIDENCE IN the market TO RECOVER.*

## CONNECTION

RIGHT:        There is a strong CONNECTION BETWEEN his grades AND his effort.

...................................................................................................

WRONG:      *There is a strong CONNECTION OF his grades AND his effort.*

## CONTEND

RIGHT:  They CONTEND THAT they can decipher the code.

........................................................................................

WRONG:  *They CONTEND they can decipher the code. (THAT is required.)*

*They CONTEND the code TO BE decipherable.*

*They CONTEND the ABILITY to decipher the code.*

## CONTRAST

RIGHT:  IN CONTRAST WITH the zoo, the park charges no admission.

IN CONTRAST TO the zoo, the park charges no admission.

UNLIKE the zoo, the park charges no admission.

........................................................................................

WRONG:  *AS CONTRASTED WITH the zoo, the park charges no admission.*

*IN CONTRAST TO the zoo CHARGING admission, the park does not.*

## CONVINCE

RIGHT:  She was CONVINCED THAT she had been robbed.

........................................................................................

SUSPECT:  *She was OF THE CONVICTION THAT she had been robbed.*

## COST

RIGHT:  Pollution COSTS us billions IN increased medical bills.

........................................................................................

WRONG:  *The COST OF pollution TO us is billions IN increased medical bills.*

*Increased medical bills COST us billions BECAUSE OF pollution.*

## COULD

RIGHT:  You COULD DO anything you want.

........................................................................................

SUSPECT:  *You HAVE (or MAY HAVE) THE POSSIBILITY OF DOING anything you want.*

........................................................................................

WRONG:  *You COULD POSSIBLY DO anything you want. (redundant)*

## CREATE

RIGHT:  We WILL CREATE a team TO LEAD the discussion.

........................................................................................

WRONG:  *We WILL CREATE a team FOR LEADING the discussion.*

## CREDIT

RIGHT:          Hugo CREDITS Sally WITH good taste.

Sally IS CREDITED WITH good taste.

..................................................................................................................

WRONG:      *Sally IS CREDITED FOR good taste.*

*Sally IS CREDITED FOR HAVING good taste.*

*Sally IS CREDITED AS a person with good taste.*

*Sally IS CREDITED AS HAVING good taste.*

*Sally IS CREDITED TO BE a person with good taste.*

## DANGER

RIGHT:          We ARE IN DANGER OF FORGETTING the past. (Forgetting is possible or likely.)

..................................................................................................................

SUSPECT:     *We ARE ENDANGERED BY FORGETTING the past.* (Forgetting causes us to be in danger.)

..................................................................................................................

WRONG:      *We ARE IN DANGER TO FORGET the past.*

*We HAVE A DANGER OF FORGETTING the past.*

*We HAVE A DANGER TO FORGET the past.*

## DATE

RIGHT:          They DATED the artifact AT three centuries old.

The artifact WAS DATED AT three centuries old.

..................................................................................................................

WRONG:      *The artifact WAS DATED TO BE three centuries old.*

*The artifact WAS DATED AS BEING three centuries old.*

## DECIDE

RIGHT:          She DECIDED TO START a company.

..................................................................................................................

SUSPECT:     *Her DECISION WAS TO START a company.*

## DECLARE

RIGHT:  I DECLARED the election a fraud.

I DECLARED the referendum invalid.

I DECLARED invalid the referendum that the new regime imposed.

They DECLARED THAT the election was a fraud.

.................................................................................

SUSPECT:  *They DECLARED the election was a fraud.* (*DECLARE THAT* is preferred.)

*The judge DECLARED the election TO BE a fraud.*

.................................................................................

WRONG:  *The judge DECLARED the election AS a fraud.*

## DECLINE

See also NUMBER.

RIGHT:  The DECLINE IN the price of oil was unexpected.

Bee populations are IN DECLINE.

Oil DECLINED in price.

My friend's reputation DECLINED.

.................................................................................

WRONG:  *My friend DECLINED in reputation.*

## DEMAND

RIGHT:  They DEMANDED THAT the store BE closed.

Their DEMAND THAT the store BE closed was not met.

.................................................................................

WRONG:  *They DEMANDED the store TO BE closed.*

*They DEMANDED THAT the store SHOULD BE closed.*

## DESIGN

RIGHT:  This window IS DESIGNED TO OPEN.

.................................................................................

WRONG:  *This window IS DESIGNED SO THAT IT OPENS.*

*This window IS DESIGNED SO AS TO OPEN.*

## DETERMINE

RIGHT:  The winner was DETERMINED BY a coin toss.

.................................................................................

WRONG:  *The winner was DETERMINED THROUGH a coin toss.*

*The winner was DETERMINED BECAUSE OF a coin toss.*

*The winner was DETERMINED FROM a coin toss.*

*The winner was DETERMINED AS A RESULT OF a coin toss.*

## DEVELOP

RIGHT:    The executive DEVELOPED her idea INTO a project.

The idea DEVELOPED INTO a project.

..................................................................................................

WRONG:    *An idea DEVELOPED ITSELF INTO a project.*

## DIFFER/DIFFERENT

RIGHT:    My opinion DIFFERS FROM yours.

My opinion IS DIFFERENT FROM yours.

..................................................................................................

WRONG:    *My opinion IS DIFFERENT IN COMPARISON TO yours.*

## DIFFERENCE

RIGHT:    There is a DIFFERENCE IN ability BETWEEN us.

There is a DIFFERENCE BETWEEN what you can do AND what I can do.

There are DIFFERENCES IN what you and I can do.

..................................................................................................

WRONG:    *There are DIFFERENCES BETWEEN what you and I can do.*

## DIFFICULT

RIGHT:    Quantum mechanics is DIFFICULT TO STUDY.

..................................................................................................

WRONG:    *Quantum mechanics is DIFFICULT FOR STUDY.*

## DISCOVERY

RIGHT:    I love the DISCOVERY THAT carbon CAN form soccer-ball molecules.

..................................................................................................

SUSPECT:    *I love the DISCOVERY OF carbon's ABILITY TO form soccer-ball molecules.*

..................................................................................................

WRONG:    *I love the DISCOVERY OF carbon BEING ABLE TO form soccer-ball molecules.*

## DISINCLINED

RIGHT:    She IS DISINCLINED TO WRITE to her parents.

..................................................................................................

WRONG:    *She HAS A DISINCLINATION TO WRITE to her parents.*

*There IS A DISINCLINATION ON HER PART TO WRITE to her parents.*

*Her busy schedule BRINGS OUT A DISINCLINATION IN HER TO WRITE to her parents.*

## DISTINGUISH/DISTINCTION

RIGHT:
The investor DISTINGUISHED BETWEEN trends AND fads.

There is a DISTINCTION BETWEEN trends AND fads.

...................................................................................................................................

WRONG:
*The investor DISTINGUISHED trends AND fads.*

*The investor DISTINGUISHED BETWEEN trends FROM fads.*

*There is a DISTINCTION BETWEEN trends WITH fads.*

*There is a DISTINCTION OF trends TO fads.*

*Trends HAVE a DISTINCTION FROM fads.*

## DO

RIGHT:
I did not eat the cheese, but my mother DID (or DID SO).

...................................................................................................................................

WRONG:
*I did not eat the cheese, but my mother DID IT (or DID THIS).*

## DOUBLE

See TWICE.

## DOUBT

RIGHT:
We DO NOT DOUBT THAT the apples are ripe.

We HAVE NO DOUBT THAT the apples are ripe.

She DOUBTS WHETHER Jan will arrive on time.

...................................................................................................................................

SUSPECT:
*She DOUBTS THAT Jan will arrive on time.*

Note: An official GMAT explanation states that DOUBT, used in a positive statement without NOT or NO, should be followed by WHETHER or IF, not THAT. It is unclear, however, whether the GMAT always holds to this statement.

...................................................................................................................................

WRONG:
*We DO NOT DOUBT WHETHER the apples are ripe.*

*We HAVE NO DOUBT WHETHER the apples are ripe.*

## DUE TO

RIGHT:
The deficit IS DUE TO overspending. (results from)

Our policy will not cover damage DUE TO fire. (resulting from)

BECAUSE politicians SPEND money, we have a deficit.

...................................................................................................................................

WRONG:
*DUE TO politicians SPENDING money, we have a deficit.*

*DUE TO THE FACT THAT politicians SPEND money, we have a deficit.*

### ECONOMIC and ECONOMICAL

RIGHT: The rise in gasoline prices has an ECONOMIC impact on consumers. (financial)

Our new car is more ECONOMICAL than our last. (efficient)

.....................................................................................................

WRONG: *The rise in gasoline prices has an ECONOMICAL impact on consumers.*

### EFFECT

See AFFECT.

### ELECT

RIGHT: She ELECTED TO WITHDRAW her money early.

.....................................................................................................

SUSPECT: *She ELECTED early WITHDRAWAL OF her money.*

.....................................................................................................

WRONG: *She ELECTED WITHDRAWING her money early.*

### ENOUGH

See also SO/THAT.

RIGHT: The book was SHORT ENOUGH TO READ in a night.

The book was SHORT ENOUGH FOR me TO READ in a night.

The power plant manager has found a way to generate more energy, ENOUGH TO POWER an entire city.

.....................................................................................................

SUSPECT: *The power plant manager has found a way to generate energy at an unprecedented scale, ENOUGH FOR powering an entire city.*

.....................................................................................................

WRONG: *The book was SHORT ENOUGH THAT I could read it in a night.*

*The book was SHORT ENOUGH FOR IT TO BE read in a night.*

*The book was SHORT ENOUGH SO THAT I could read it in a night.*

*The book was SHORT ENOUGH AS TO BE read in a night.*

### ENSURE

RIGHT: He ENSURES THAT deadlines ARE met.

He ENSURES THAT deadlines WILL BE met.

.....................................................................................................

WRONG: *He ENSURES THAT deadlines MUST BE met.*

*He ENSURES THAT deadlines SHOULD BE met.*

## EQUIPPED

RIGHT:    They are EQUIPPED TO FIGHT on any terrain.

...............................................................................................

WRONG:    *They are EQUIPPED FOR FIGHTING on any terrain.*

## ESTIMATE

RIGHT:    She ESTIMATES the cost TO BE 10 dollars.

The cost IS ESTIMATED TO BE 10 dollars.

With a temperature ESTIMATED AT 100 degrees, boiling water can cause severe burns.

She ESTIMATES the cost TO BE 10 percent less than it was last year.

...............................................................................................

WRONG:    *She ESTIMATES the cost AT 10 percent less than it was last year.*

## EVEN

RIGHT:    The company is EVEN MORE PROFITABLE THAN Apple.

I earn AS MUCH acclaim AS EVEN the most famous athlete.

...............................................................................................

WRONG:    *The company is MORE PROFITABLE EVEN THAN Apple.*

*I earn EVEN AS MUCH acclaim AS the most famous athlete.*

## EVER

RIGHT:    The economy is MORE fragile THAN EVER BEFORE.

...............................................................................................

WRONG:    *The economy is MORE fragile THAN NEVER BEFORE.*

*The economy is MORE fragile AS NEVER BEFORE.*

*The economy is MORE THAN EVER BEFORE fragile.*

## EVERY

RIGHT:    FOR EVERY dollar SAVED, THREE dollars ARE WASTED.

...............................................................................................

SUSPECT:    *FOR EVERY dollar SAVED, you WASTE THREE dollars.*

...............................................................................................

WRONG:    *FOR EVERY dollar SAVED WASTES THREE dollars.*

## EXCEPT

RIGHT:    EXCEPT FOR a final skirmish, the war was over.

...................................................................

SUSPECT:    *BESIDES a final skirmish, the war was over.*
*WITH THE EXCEPTION OF a final skirmish, the war was over.*
*EXCEPTING a final skirmish, the war was over.*

## EXPEND

RIGHT:    We EXPEND energy ON neighborhood development.

...................................................................

WRONG:    *We EXPEND energy FOR neighborhood development.*

## EXTENT

RIGHT:    We enjoyed the film TO some EXTENT.
The EXTENT TO WHICH we enjoyed the film was moderate.
TO the EXTENT THAT your example is relevant, it supports my conclusion.

...................................................................

WRONG:    *The EXTENT THAT we enjoyed the film was moderate.*

## FAULT

RIGHT:    The criminals ARE AT FAULT FOR BREAKING the law.

...................................................................

SUSPECT:    *BREAKING the law IS THE FAULT OF the criminals.*

...................................................................

WRONG:    *THAT the criminals BROKE the law IS AT FAULT.*
*IT IS THE FAULT OF the criminals WHO BROKE the law.*

## FIND

RIGHT:    The scientist FOUND THAT the reaction WAS unusual.

...................................................................

SUSPECT:    *The scientist FOUND the reaction TO BE unusual.*

...................................................................

WRONG:    *The scientist FOUND the reaction WAS unusual. (THAT is required.)*

## FORBID

RIGHT:    The law FORBIDS any citizen TO VOTE twice.

..........................................................................................................

WRONG:    *The law FORBIDS any citizen FROM VOTING twice.*

## GOAL

RIGHT:    The GOAL IS TO EXPAND the company.

..........................................................................................................

SUSPECT:    *The GOAL IS EXPANSION OF the company.*

..........................................................................................................

WRONG:    *The GOAL IS EXPANDING the company.*

## HEAR

RIGHT:    She HEARD THAT her investment HAD PAID off.

..........................................................................................................

WRONG:    *She HEARD OF her investment PAYING off.*

## HELP

RIGHT:    He HELPS RAKE the leaves.

He HELPS TO RAKE the leaves.

He HELPS me RAKE the leaves.

He HELPS me TO RAKE the leaves.

His HELP IN RAKING the leaves has been appreciated.

..........................................................................................................

WRONG:    *He HELPS me IN RAKING the leaves.*

*I need him AS HELP TO RAKE the leaves.*

## HOLD

RIGHT:    The law HOLDS THAT jaywalking is illegal.

..........................................................................................................

SUSPECT:    *The law HOLDS jaywalking TO BE illegal.*

..........................................................................................................

WRONG:    *The law HOLDS jaywalking is illegal.*

### INFLUENCE

RIGHT:        His example INFLUENCED me.

.................................................................................................

WRONG:        *His example WAS AN INFLUENCE ON me.*
              *His example WAS INFLUENTIAL ON me.*

### INSTANCE

RIGHT:        We cook often; FOR INSTANCE, last week we cooked every night.

.................................................................................................

WRONG:        *We cook often; AS AN INSTANCE, last week we cooked every night.*

### INSTEAD

RIGHT:        They avoided the arcade and INSTEAD went to a movie.

.................................................................................................

WRONG:        *They avoided the arcade and RATHER went to a movie.*
              *They avoided the arcade, RATHER going to a movie.*

### INTERACT

RIGHT:        These groups often INTERACT WITH ONE ANOTHER (or EACH OTHER).

.................................................................................................

WRONG:        *These groups often INTERACT AMONG ONE ANOTHER.*
              *These groups often INTERACT WITH THEMSELVES.*

### INTERACTION

RIGHT:        The INTERACTION OF two nuclei COLLIDING releases energy.

.................................................................................................

SUSPECT:      *The INTERACTION BETWEEN two nuclei COLLIDING releases energy.*

.................................................................................................

WRONG:        *The INTERACTION WHERE two nuclei COLLIDE releases energy.*

### INVEST

RIGHT:        She INVESTED funds IN research TO STUDY cancer.

.................................................................................................

WRONG:        *She INVESTED funds INTO research TO STUDY cancer.*
              *She INVESTED funds FOR research TO STUDY cancer.*
              *She INVESTED funds IN research FOR STUDYING cancer.*

## ISOLATED

RIGHT: The culture was ISOLATED FROM outside contact.

IN ISOLATION, his reaction is puzzling, but it makes sense in context.

..................................................................................................

SUSPECT: *The culture was IN ISOLATION.*

..................................................................................................

WRONG: *The culture was IN ISOLATION FROM outside contact.*

## JUST AS ... SO     See AS ... SO.

## KNOW

RIGHT: We KNOW her TO BE brilliant.

She is KNOWN TO BE brilliant.

We KNOW him AS "Reggie."

He is KNOWN AS "Reggie."

..................................................................................................

WRONG: *We KNOW her AS brilliant.* (*KNOW AS* means named; not used for a description.)

## LACK

RIGHT: Old gadgets ARE LACKING IN features.

Old gadgets LACK features.

The LACK OF features is upsetting.

..................................................................................................

SUSPECT: *There is A LACK OF engineers TO BUILD new gadgets.*

..................................................................................................

WRONG: *Old gadgets LACK OF features.*

*It is hard to build bridges LACKING engineers.*

## LESS     See also THAN.

RIGHT: Our utility bills add up to LESS THAN 10 percent of our income.

..................................................................................................

WRONG: *Our utility bills add up to LOWER THAN 10 percent of our income.*

## LET

RIGHT: My doctor LETS me SWIM in the ocean.

..................................................................................................

WRONG: *My doctor LEAVES me SWIM in the ocean.*

*The surgery WILL LEAVE me TO SWIM in the ocean.*

## LIE

RIGHT:      Our strength LIES IN numbers. (resides in/comes from)

Yesterday, our strength LAY IN numbers.

Tomorrow, our strength WILL LIE IN numbers.

I lose my books whenever I LAY them down. (present tense of different verb)

......................................................................................................................

WRONG:      *Tomorrow, our strength WILL LAY IN numbers.*

## LIKELY

RIGHT:      My friend IS LIKELY TO EAT worms.

IT IS LIKELY THAT my friend WILL EAT worms.

My friend is MORE LIKELY THAN my enemy [is] TO EAT worms.

My friend is TWICE AS LIKELY AS my enemy [is] TO EAT worms.

MORE THAN LIKELY, my friend WILL EAT worms.

......................................................................................................................

WRONG:      *My friend IS LIKELY THAT he WILL EAT worms.*

*RATHER THAN my enemy, my friend is THE MORE LIKELY to EAT worms.*

## LOSS

RIGHT:      I have suffered a LOSS OF strength. (decline of a quality)

They have suffered a LOSS IN the euro. (decline of an investment)

......................................................................................................................

WRONG:      *I have suffered a LOSS IN strength.*

## MAKE

RIGHT:      The leader MADE the resistance POSSIBLE.

The leader MADE IT POSSIBLE TO RESIST oppression.

The leader MADE IT POSSIBLE FOR us TO RESIST oppression.

Windshields ARE MADE resistant to impact.

......................................................................................................................

SUSPECT:      *The leader MADE POSSIBLE the resistance.*

......................................................................................................................

WRONG:      *The leader MADE POSSIBLE TO RESIST oppression.*

## MANDATE

| | |
|---|---|
| RIGHT: | The general MANDATED THAT a trench BE dug. (subjunctive) |

---

| | |
|---|---|
| SUSPECT: | *We HAVE A MANDATE TO CALL an election soon.* (have authority) |

---

| | |
|---|---|
| WRONG: | *The general MANDATED a trench TO BE dug.* |
| | *The general MANDATES THAT a trench WILL BE dug.* |
| | *We HAVE A MANDATE FOR an election in the near future.* |

## MASS

| | |
|---|---|
| RIGHT: | The truck HAS 10 TIMES THE MASS of a small car. |

---

| | |
|---|---|
| WRONG: | *The truck IS 10 TIMES THE MASS of a small car.* |

## MAYBE

| | |
|---|---|
| | See PROBABLY. |

## MEANS

| | |
|---|---|
| RIGHT: | Music education is A MEANS TO improved cognition. |

---

| | |
|---|---|
| WRONG: | *Music education is A MEANS OF improved cognition.* |
| | *Music education is A MEANS FOR improved cognition.* |

## MISTAKE

| | |
|---|---|
| RIGHT: | My waiter HAS MISTAKEN me FOR a celebrity. |

---

| | |
|---|---|
| WRONG: | *My waiter HAS MISTAKEN me AS a celebrity.* |
| | *My waiter HAS MISTAKEN me TO a celebrity.* |

## MORE

| | |
|---|---|
| | See also THAN. |
| RIGHT: | We observed A 10 percent INCREASE IN robberies last month. |
| | MORE AND MORE, we have observed violent robberies on weekends. |
| | INCREASINGLY, we have observed violent robberies on weekends. |

---

| | |
|---|---|
| SUSPECT: | *We observed 10 percent MORE robberies last month.* |

## MOST

RIGHT:  OF ALL the Greek gods, Zeus was THE MOST powerful. (superlative)

He was THE SECOND MOST attractive AND THE MOST powerful.

......................................................................................................................................................

WRONG:  *OF ALL the Greek gods, Zeus was THE MORE powerful.*

*He was THE SECOND MOST attractive AND MOST powerful.*

## NATIVE

RIGHT:  The kangaroo is NATIVE TO Australia. (said of animals, plants)

My friend is A NATIVE OF Australia. (said of people)

......................................................................................................................................................

WRONG:  *The kangaroo is NATIVE IN Australia.*

## NUMBER

RIGHT:  A NUMBER OF dogs ARE barking.

THE NUMBER OF dogs IS large.

THE NUMBER OF dogs HAS FALLEN, but THE NUMBER OF cats HAS RISEN.

The grey oyster nearly vanished, but ITS NUMBERS have rebounded.

......................................................................................................................................................

WRONG:  *THE NUMBERS OF dogs HAVE fallen.*

*Dogs HAVE FALLEN IN NUMBER, but cats HAVE RISEN IN NUMBER.*

## ONCE

RIGHT:  We might ONCE have seen that band.

......................................................................................................................................................

WRONG:  *We might AT ONE TIME have seen that band.*

## ONLY

RIGHT:  Her performance is exceeded ONLY by theirs. (modifies *by theirs*)

......................................................................................................................................................

WRONG:  *Her performance is ONLY exceeded by theirs.* (technically modifies *exceeded*)

Note: ONLY should be placed just before the words it is meant to modify. In both speech and writing, ONLY is often placed before the verb, but this placement is generally wrong, according to the GMAT, since we rarely mean that the verb is the only action ever performed by the subject.

## OR

RIGHT: I do NOT want water OR milk.

SUSPECT: *I do NOT want water AND milk.* (implies the combination)

## ORDER

RIGHT: The state ORDERS THAT the agency COLLECT taxes. (subjunctive)

The state ORDERS the agency TO COLLECT taxes.

WRONG: *The state ORDERS THAT the agency SHOULD COLLECT taxes.*

*The state ORDERS the agency SHOULD COLLECT taxes.*

*The state ORDERS the agency WOULD COLLECT taxes.*

*The state ORDERS the agency COLLECTING taxes.*

*The state ORDERS the agency the COLLECTION OF taxes.*

*The state ORDERS the COLLECTION OF taxes BY the agency.*

*The state ORDERS taxes collected.*

## OWE

RIGHT: He OWES money TO the government FOR back taxes.

SUSPECT: *He OWES money TO the government BECAUSE OF back taxes.*

## PAY

RIGHT: The employer PAYS the same FOR this JOB as for that one.

WRONG: *The employer PAYS the same IN this JOB as in that one.*

**PERHAPS** See PROBABLY.

## PERSUADE

RIGHT: He PERSUADED her TO GO with him.

WRONG: *He PERSUADED her IN GOING with him.*

*He PERSUADED THAT she GO with him.*

*He PERSUADED THAT she SHOULD GO with him.*

## POTENTIALLY

RIGHT:        A tornado IS POTENTIALLY overwhelming.

................................................................................

WRONG:      *A tornado CAN POTENTIALLY BE overwhelming.* (redundant)

## PROBABLY

RIGHT:        This situation IS PROBABLY as bad as it can get.

                     This situation MAY BE as bad as it can get. (less certain than PROBABLY)

                     PERHAPS (or MAYBE) this situation IS as bad as it can get.

................................................................................

SUSPECT:     *IT MAY BE THAT this situation IS as bad as it can get.*

................................................................................

WRONG:      *This situation IS MAYBE as bad as it can get.*

## PROHIBIT

RIGHT:        The law PROHIBITS any citizen FROM VOTING twice.

................................................................................

WRONG:      *The law PROHIBITS any citizen TO VOTE twice.*

                     *The law PROHIBITS THAT any person VOTE (or VOTES) twice.*

## PRONOUNCE

RIGHT:        She PRONOUNCED the book a triumph.

................................................................................

SUSPECT:     *She PRONOUNCED the book AS a triumph.*

## PROPOSE

RIGHT:        The attorneys PROPOSED THAT a settlement BE reached. (subjunctive)

                     The attorneys PROPOSED a new venue.

                     The attorneys PROPOSED TO MEET for lunch.

................................................................................

WRONG:      *The attorneys PROPOSED THAT a settlement IS reached.*

                     *The attorneys PROPOSED a settlement BE reached.*

                     *The attorneys PROPOSED a settlement TO BE reached.*

                     *The attorneys PROPOSED a settlement IS TO BE reached.*

## PROVIDED THAT    See IF.

**RAISE**        See RISE.

**RANK**

RIGHT:        This problem RANKS AS one of the worst we have seen.

........................................................................

WRONG:        *This problem HAS THE RANK OF one of the worst we have seen.*

**RATE**

RIGHT:        The RATES FOR bus tickets are good for commuters. (prices)

              The RATE OF theft has fallen. (frequency or speed)

........................................................................

WRONG:        *The RATES OF bus tickets are good for commuters.*

              *The RATE FOR theft has fallen.*

**REASON**

RIGHT:        I have A REASON TO DO work today.

              She has A REASON FOR the lawsuit.

              This observation indicates a REASON THAT he is here.

........................................................................

SUSPECT:      *This observation indicates a REASON WHY he is here.*

........................................................................

WRONG:        *This observation indicates a REASON he is here.*

              *The REASON he is here IS BECAUSE he wants to be.*

**REBEL**

RIGHT:        The colonists REBELLED AGAINST tyranny.

........................................................................

SUSPECT:      *The colonists' REBELLION WAS AGAINST tyranny.*

**RECOGNIZE**

RIGHT:        They RECOGNIZED THAT the entrance fee WAS a bargain.

              They RECOGNIZED the entrance fee TO BE a bargain.

              They RECOGNIZED the entrance fee AS a bargain.

........................................................................

WRONG:        *They RECOGNIZED the entrance fee AS BEING a bargain.*

### RECOMMEND

| | |
|---|---|
| RIGHT: | We RECOMMENDED THAT the shelter BE opened. (subjunctive) |

...........................................................................................................................

| | |
|---|---|
| WRONG: | *We RECOMMENDED THAT the shelter SHOULD BE opened.* |

### REDUCE

| | |
|---|---|
| RIGHT: | The coalition REDUCED prices. |
| | The coalition was considering A REDUCTION IN prices. |

...........................................................................................................................

| | |
|---|---|
| SUSPECT: | *The coalition MADE A REDUCTION IN prices.* |
| | *The coalition CAUSED A REDUCTION IN prices.* |

...........................................................................................................................

| | |
|---|---|
| WRONG: | *The coalition MADE A REDUCTION OF prices.* |

### REFER

| | |
|---|---|
| RIGHT: | This term REFERS TO a kind of disease. |
| | REFERRING TO the controversy, the politician asked for calm. |

...........................................................................................................................

| | |
|---|---|
| SUSPECT: | *This term IS USED TO REFER TO a kind of disease.* |

...........................................................................................................................

| | |
|---|---|
| WRONG: | *This term IS IN REFERENCE TO a kind of disease.* |
| | *IN REFERENCE TO the controversy, the politician asked for calm.* |

### REGARD

| | |
|---|---|
| RIGHT: | He REGARDS the gold ring AS costly. |
| | The gold ring IS REGARDED AS costly. |
| | He IS REGARDED AS HAVING good taste. |

...........................................................................................................................

| | |
|---|---|
| WRONG: | *The gold ring IS REGARDED THAT IT IS costly.* |

### RELUCTANT

| | |
|---|---|
| RIGHT: | They were RELUCTANT TO SAY anything. |

...........................................................................................................................

| | |
|---|---|
| WRONG: | *They were RELUCTANT ABOUT SAYING anything.* |

## REPORT

RIGHT: A study HAS REPORTED THAT bees ARE DISAPPEARING rapidly.

................................................................

WRONG: *A study HAS REPORTED bees AS DISAPPEARING rapidly.*

## REQUEST

RIGHT: I REQUEST THAT he BE removed. (subjunctive)

................................................................

WRONG: *I REQUEST him TO BE removed.*

## REQUIRE

RIGHT: She REQUIRES time TO WRITE (or IN ORDER TO WRITE).

She REQUIRES her friend TO DO work.

Her friend IS REQUIRED TO DO work.

She REQUIRES THAT her friend DO work. (subjunctive)

She REQUIRES OF her friend THAT work BE done. (subjunctive)

................................................................

SUSPECT: *In this hostel, there is a REQUIREMENT OF work.*

*There is a REQUIREMENT THAT work BE done.*

................................................................

WRONG: *She REQUIRES her friend DO work (or MUST DO work).*

*She REQUIRES her friend TO HAVE TO DO work.*

*She REQUIRES OF her friend TO DO work.*

*She REQUIRES THAT her friend DOES work (or SHOULD DO work).*

*She REQUIRES THAT her friend IS TO DO work.*

*She REQUIRES DOING work (or THE DOING OF work).*

*She REQUIRES her friend DOING work.*

*In this hostel, there is a REQUIREMENT OF work BY guests.*

## RESEMBLE

RIGHT: A neighbor of mine RESEMBLES my father.

................................................................

SUSPECT: *A neighbor of mine HAS A RESEMBLANCE TO my father.*

## RESTRICTION

RIGHT: The government imposed RESTRICTIONS ON the price of gasoline.

................................................................

WRONG: *The government imposed RESTRICTIONS FOR the price of gasoline.*

## RESULT

RIGHT:     Success RESULTS FROM hard work.

Hard work RESULTS IN success.

Success IS A RESULT OF hard work.

Success comes AS A RESULT OF hard work.

AS A RESULT OF our hard work, we became successful.

The RESULT OF our hard work WAS THAT we became successful.

......

WRONG:     *We worked hard WITH THE RESULT OF success.*

*We worked hard WITH A RESULTING success.*

*RESULTING FROM our hard work, we became successful.*

*BECAUSE OF THE RESULT OF our hard work, we became successful.*

*The RESULT OF our hard work WAS we became successful. (THAT is needed.)*

## REVEAL

RIGHT:     The analysis REVEALED THAT the comet WAS mostly ice.

......

WRONG:     *The analysis REVEALED the comet WAS mostly ice. (THAT is needed.)*

*The analysis REVEALED the comet TO HAVE BEEN mostly ice.*

## RISE

RIGHT:     Oil prices ROSE sharply last year.

A RISE IN oil prices has led to inflation. (The article *A* before *RISE* signals a noun, not a verb.)

RISING prices at the gas pump are hurting consumers.

The RISING OF the SUN always lifts my spirits.

......

WRONG:     *A RAISE IN oil prices has led to inflation.*

*A RISING OF PRICES at the gas pump is hurting consumers.*

## RULE

RIGHT:     The judge RULED THAT the plaintiff WAS in contempt.

......

SUSPECT:   *The judge RULED the plaintiff WAS in contempt.*

......

WRONG:     *The judge RULED the plaintiff TO BE in contempt.*

*The judge RULED ON the plaintiff WHO WAS in contempt.*

## SAME

RIGHT:     The car looks THE SAME TO me AS TO you.

I drove to the store AT THE SAME TIME AS you [did].

...................................................................................................

WRONG:     *The car looks THE SAME TO me AS you.* (ambiguous)

*I drove to the store AT THE SAME TIME you did.*

## SECURE

RIGHT:     Our authority IS SECURE.

...................................................................................................

WRONG:     *We ARE SECURE ABOUT our authority.*

## SEEM

RIGHT:     This result SEEMS TO DEMONSTRATE the new theory.

IT SEEMS THAT this result DEMONSTRATES the new theory.

IT SEEMS AS IF this result DEMONSTRATES the new theory.

...................................................................................................

SUSPECT:     *This result SEEMS TO BE A DEMONSTRATION OF the new theory.*

*This result SEEMS DEMONSTRATIVE OF the new theory.*

*This result SEEMS LIKE A DEMONSTRATION OF the new theory.*

...................................................................................................

WRONG:     *This result SEEMS AS IF IT DEMONSTRATES the new theory.*

*This result SEEMS LIKE IT DEMONSTRATES the new theory.*

## SHOULD

RIGHT:     A car SHOULD BE TAKEN to the mechanic frequently. (obligation)

...................................................................................................

WRONG:     *A car SHOULD PASS every two hours.* (probability)

*The owner REQUESTED THAT the car SHOULD BE TAKEN to the mechanic.* (Use the subjunctive *BE TAKEN* instead.)

**SHOW**

| | |
|---|---|
| RIGHT: | A discovery SHOWS THAT an object IS strange. |
| | A discovery SHOWS an object TO BE strange. |

........................................................................................................................

| | |
|---|---|
| SUSPECT: | *A discovery SHOWS an object IS strange.* |

........................................................................................................................

| | |
|---|---|
| WRONG: | *A discovery SHOWS an object AS strange* (or *AS BEING strange*). |

**SIGNIFICANT**

| | |
|---|---|
| RIGHT: | Your edits HAVE SIGNIFICANTLY IMPROVED the book. |

........................................................................................................................

| | |
|---|---|
| SUSPECT: | *Your edits HAVE MADE A SIGNIFICANT IMPROVEMENT IN the book.* |

........................................................................................................................

| | |
|---|---|
| WRONG: | *Your edits HAVE BEEN SIGNIFICANT IN IMPROVING the book.* |
| | *Your edits HAVE BEEN SIGNIFICANT IN AN IMPROVEMENT OF the book.* |

**SIMILAR**

| | |
|---|---|
| RIGHT: | ALL companies HAVE SIMILAR issues. (Comparison requires plural.) |

........................................................................................................................

| | |
|---|---|
| WRONG: | *EACH company HAS SIMILAR issues.* |
| | *EVERY company HAS SIMILAR issues.* |

**SINCE**

| | |
|---|---|
| RIGHT: | Xingo is THE MOST successful new product SINCE 1997. (up to now) |
| | It is the best new beverage SINCE Prune Cola. |

........................................................................................................................

| | |
|---|---|
| SUSPECT: | *Xingo is the best new beverage FOLLOWING Prune Cola.* |

........................................................................................................................

| | |
|---|---|
| WRONG: | *Xingo is THE MOST successful new product AFTER 1997.* |

**SO LONG AS**   See AS LONG AS.

## SO TOO

RIGHT:   Bellbottoms ARE coming back in style, and SO TOO ARE vests.

........................................................................................................

SUSPECT:   *Bellbottoms ARE coming back in style, and ALSO vests.*

........................................................................................................

WRONG:   *Bellbottoms ARE coming back in style, and SO TOO vests.*

## SUBSTITUTE

RIGHT:   We SUBSTITUTED Parmesan cheese FOR mozzarella.

........................................................................................................

WRONG:   *We SUBSTITUTED Parmesan cheese IN PLACE OF mozzarella.*

## SUCCEED

RIGHT:   She SUCCEEDED IN REACHING the summit.

........................................................................................................

WRONG:   *She SUCCEEDED TO REACH the summit.*

## SUCH

RIGHT:   You may enjoy chemistry and physics, but I hate SUCH subjects.
You may enjoy chemistry and physics, but I hate THESE subjects.
Note: THESE means "these specifically." SUCH is more general.

........................................................................................................

WRONG:   *You may enjoy chemistry and physics, but I hate subjects OF THIS KIND.*
*You may enjoy chemistry and physics, but I hate subjects LIKE THESE.*

## SUGGEST

RIGHT:   A study SUGGESTS THAT more work IS needed.
A study SUGGESTS THAT more work WILL BE needed.
We SUGGEST THAT he BE promoted. (subjunctive)
This artwork SUGGESTS great talent.

........................................................................................................

SUSPECT:   *This artwork IS SUGGESTIVE OF great talent.*

## SURFACE

RIGHT: Craters have been seen ON THE SURFACE OF the moon.

......................................................................................

SUSPECT: *Craters have been seen AT THE SURFACE OF the moon.*

## TARGETED

RIGHT: This intervention is TARGETED AT a specific misbehavior.

......................................................................................

WRONG: *This intervention is TARGETED TO a specific misbehavior.*

## THINK

RIGHT: She THINKS OF them AS heroes.

She IS THOUGHT TO BE secretly wealthy.

......................................................................................

WRONG: *They ARE THOUGHT OF BY her AS heroes.*

*She THINKS OF them TO BE heroes.*

*She THINKS OF them BEING heroes.*

**TO + verb**    See IN ORDER TO.

## TRAIN

RIGHT: She WAS TRAINED TO RUN a division.

......................................................................................

WRONG: *She WAS TRAINED FOR RUNNING a division.*

*She WAS TRAINED IN RUNNING a division.*

## TRY

RIGHT: They WILL TRY TO BUILD a company. (intent or purpose)

......................................................................................

SUSPECT: *We TRIED BREAKING the door down. (experiment)*

......................................................................................

WRONG: *They WILL TRY AND BUILD a company.*

*They WILL TRY THAT THEY BUILD a company.*

## TWICE

RIGHT:    He is TWICE AS tall AS Alex [is].

Leaves fall TWICE AS quickly AS they grow.

Naomi wrote TWICE AS MANY letters AS Sara [did].

Naomi wrote 10 letters, DOUBLE THE NUMBER THAT Sara wrote.

Naomi's income DOUBLED in three years.

Naomi DOUBLED her income in three years.

......................................................................................................................

WRONG:    *He is TWICE AS tall THAN Alex [is].*

*Leaves fall TWICE AS quickly AS their rate of growth.*

*Naomi wrote DOUBLE THE LETTERS THAT Sara did.*

*Naomi's income INCREASED BY TWICE in three years.*

## USE

RIGHT:    He USES the hammer AS a weapon.

He USES the hammer TO BREAK a board.

He BREAKS a board WITH the hammer.

......................................................................................................................

WRONG:    *He USES a hammer FOR BREAKING a board.*

*He USES the hammer LIKE a weapon.*

*He USES the hammer TO BE a weapon.*

## VARIATION

RIGHT:    There are VARIATIONS IN sunspot frequency and strength over time.

......................................................................................................................

WRONG:    *There are VARIATIONS OF sunspot frequency and strength over time.*

*There are VARIATIONS AMONG sunspot frequency and strength over time.*

## VIEW

RIGHT:    I VIEWED this process AS a mistake.

......................................................................................................................

WRONG:    *I VIEWED this process TO BE a mistake.*

*I VIEWED this process LIKE a mistake.*

### WAY

RIGHT:  We proposed a WAY OF REACHING the goal.

     The WAY IN WHICH we discussed the idea was positive.

     The best WAY TO REACH the goal IS TO FOCUS one's energy.

     This process was developed TO ACHIEVE the target.

     ...........................................................................................................

SUSPECT:  *This process was developed AS A WAY OF ACHIEVING the target.*

     ...........................................................................................................

WRONG:  *We proposed a WAY FOR REACHING the goal.*

     *The best WAY TO REACH the goal IS FOCUSING one's energy.*

### WEIGH

RIGHT:  My laptop WEIGHS LESS THAN a suitcase.

     My laptop IS LIGHTER THAN a suitcase.

     ...........................................................................................................

WRONG:  *My laptop WEIGHS LIGHTER THAN a suitcase.*

### WHERE

RIGHT:  Sussex is the only county WHERE pomegranates grow in this state.

     Sussex is the only county IN WHICH pomegranates grow in this state.

     This incident represents a case IN WHICH I would call the police.

     ...........................................................................................................

WRONG:  *This incident represents a case WHERE I would call the police.*

### WHOSE/WHOM

RIGHT:  The officer WHOSE task was to be here did not show up.

     The company WHOSE growth leads the industry is XYZ, Inc.

     The board consists of 12 members, EACH OF WHOM is responsible for following the law and supervising the management team.

     The teachers, MOST OF WHOM have tenure, are negotiating their contract.

     ...........................................................................................................

WRONG:  *The officer, THE task OF WHOM was to be here, did not show up.*

## WITH

RIGHT:     The lions growled, WITH their fur STANDING on end.

................................................................................................

WRONG:     *WITH only 25 percent of the student body, seniors get 50 percent of the resources.*

## WORRY

RIGHT:     The committee was WORRIED ABOUT increased prices.

................................................................................................

WRONG:     *The committee was WORRIED OVER increased prices.*

# APPENDIX B

# Glossary

# Glossary

The following is a list of grammatical terms used in this guide.

## Absolute Phrase

A phrase is a group of words that modifies a whole clause or sentence. An absolute phrase cannot stand alone as a sentence, but it often expresses an additional thought. An absolute phrase is separated from the main clause by a comma; it may come before or after that main clause. See also **Modifier**.

> The car fell into the lake, the cold water filling the compartment.

> His arm in pain, Guillermo strode out of the building.

## Action Noun

A noun that expresses an action. Action nouns are often derived from verbs. In general, action nouns can be parallel to other action nouns (including gerunds), but not to person-place-thing nouns. Also, if a particular noun has both action and gerund forms, the action form is typically preferred (e.g., *the eruption of the volcano* is typically preferred over *the erupting of the volcano*).

| | |
|---|---|
| verb + –TION: | construction, pollution, redemption |
| verb + –AL: | arrival, reversal |
| verb + –MENT: | development, punishment |
| Same as verb: | change, rise, struggle |

## Active Voice

The form of a verb in which the subject is doing the action expressed by the verb.

> The driver swerved.

> The tires exploded.

> They broke the lamp.

## Additive Phrase

Modifier phrases that add nouns onto another noun. However, additive phrases are not part of the main subject of a sentence.

<u>along with</u> me                 <u>in addition to</u> the memo      <u>as well as</u> a dog

<u>accompanied by</u> her            <u>together with</u> the others      <u>including</u> them

## Adjective

A word that modifies a noun.

<u>wonderful</u> food                 <u>forest</u> fire

<u>green</u> eyes                     the <u>changing</u> seasons

## Adverb

A word that modifies a verb, an adjective, another adverb, or even a whole clause. Most adverbs end in –*ly*, but not all.

The stone fell <u>slowly</u>.

A <u>swiftly</u> frozen lake appears cloudy.

We ran <u>very</u> quickly.

## Adverbial Modifier

A word, phrase, or clause that describes a verb or clause.

Adverb:                      He walked <u>energetically</u>.

Prepositional phrase:        He walked <u>toward the building</u>.

Subordinate clause:          He walked <u>because he was thirsty</u>.

Present participle:          He walked ahead, <u>swinging</u> his arms.

Infinitive:                  He walked <u>to buy</u> a drink.

Preposition + simple gerund: He walked <u>by putting</u> one foot in front of the other.

## Antecedent

The noun that a pronoun refers to.

The ROWERS lifted the BOAT and flipped <u>it</u> over <u>their</u> heads.

(*Rowers* is the antecedent of *their*. *Boat* is the antecedent of *it*.)

## Appositive

A noun or noun phrase that is placed next to another noun to identify it. Often separated from the rest of the sentence by commas.

> The coach, <u>an old classmate of mine</u>, was not pleased.

> (*An old classmate of mine* is an appositive phrase to the noun *coach*.)

## Article

The words *a*, *an*, or *the*. An article must be followed by a noun (perhaps with modifiers in between). Articles can be considered special adjectives.

> <u>a</u> CAT          <u>the</u> board MEETING
>
> <u>an</u> APPLE          <u>an</u> important but often overlooked RULE

## Bare Form (of verb)

The dictionary form of a verb (what you would look up in a dictionary). A bare form has no endings added on, such as –*s*, –*ed*, or –*ing*. The bare form is the infinitive without the *to* in front.

> assess          call          command
>
> decide          furnish          gather

## Bossy Verb

A verb that tells someone to do something. Bossy verbs are paired with one of two tenses, depending on the specific verb: the command subjunctive or an infinitive. (Some bossy verbs are flexible and can be paired with either of those forms.)

> Bossy + infinitive:          I TOLD him <u>to run</u>.
>
> Bossy + subjunctive:          He REQUESTED that the bus <u>wait</u> another minute.
>
> Bossy + either form:          I ASKED him <u>to finish</u> the report by tomorrow.
> I ASKED that he <u>finish</u> the report by tomorrow.

## Case

The grammatical role that a noun or pronoun plays in a sentence.

> Subject case (subject role):          I, you, she, he, it, we, they
>
> Object case (object role):          me, you, her, him, it, us, them
>
> Possessive case (ownership role):          my/mine, your(s), her(s), his, its, our(s), their(s)

Nouns show the possessive case by adding *'s* for singular nouns (Mary's car) or *s'* for plural nouns (the executives' conference call).

### Clause

A group of words that contains a subject and a working verb.

> Main or independent clause:
>
> > The company is successful.
> >
> > Yesterday I ate a pizza in haste.
>
> Subordinate or dependent clause:
>
> > Yesterday I ate a pizza that I did not like.
> >
> > When I think about that pizza, I feel ill.

### Collective Noun

A noun that looks singular (it does not end in –s) but that refers to a group of people or things. Usually considered singular on the GMAT (but look for clues in the sentence!).

> The army is recruiting again.
>
> This team was eliminated during the semifinal round.

### Command Subjunctive

Subjunctive form used with certain bossy verbs and similar constructions. Same in form as a direct command. See also **Subjunctive Mood** and **Bossy Verb**.

> The draft board required that he register for selective service.

### Comparative Form

Form of adjectives and adverbs used to compare two things or people. Regular comparative forms are either the base word plus –*er* (e.g., *greener*) or the base word preceded by *more* (e.g., *more intelligent*). Common irregular forms are listed in the table:

| Adjective or Adverb | Comparative |
| --- | --- |
| good/well | better |
| bad/badly | worse |
| much, many | more |
| little, few | less, fewer |
| far | farther, further |

### Comparisons

Structures by which we compare things or people in sentences. Usually marked with signal words such as *like*, *unlike*, *as*, or *than*. Comparisons can be between two things or people (comparative) or among three or more things or people (superlative).

## Complex Gerund

A gerund is an *–ing* form of a verb that functions as a noun; a complex gerund includes an article or something similar to indicate that the *–ing* word is definitely functioning as a noun. In general, complex gerunds can be put in parallel with action nouns, but simple gerunds should not be. See also **Simple Gerund**.

> The running of the bulls is a tradition in Spain.

> The volcanic eruption resulted in the melting of the iceberg.

## Concrete Noun

A noun that does not represent an action. Concrete nouns refer to things, people, places, and even time periods or certain events. Generally, concrete nouns are not logically parallel to action nouns.

| | | |
|---|---|---|
| hole | manager | month |
| proton | area | inauguration |

## Conditional Tense

A verb tense formed by combining the helping verb *would* with the base form of the verb. See also **Tense**.

> Future as seen from the past:

> > He said that he would write.

> Hypothetical result of unlikely condition:

> > If she liked pizza, she would like this restaurant.

## Conjunction

A word that joins two parts of a sentence together. Coordinating and correlative conjunctions give the two parts equal weight. Subordinating conjunctions put one part in a logically junior role, in relation to the other part.

| | |
|---|---|
| Coordinating (Co): | and, but, or (less common: for, nor, so, yet) |
| Correlative (Cor): | either X or Y; neither X nor Y; not X but Y; not only X but also Y |
| Subordinating (Sub): | after, although, because, before, if, since, when |

## Conjunctive Adverb

A transition word or phrase that is used after a semicolon to help connect two main clauses. Conjunctive adverbs are not true conjunctions.

> therefore, thus, consequently, however, nevertheless, furthermore, etc.

> The general was stuck in traffic; therefore, the ceremony started late.

## Connecting Punctuation

The comma (,), the semicolon (;), the colon (:), and the em dash (—). Used to link parts of a sentence.

## Connecting Words

Conjunctions, conjunctive adverbs, and relative pronouns. Used to link parts of a sentence.

## Countable Noun

A noun that can be counted in English. For example, you can say *one hat, two hats, three hats.* Countable nouns can be made singular or plural.

> hat/hats      thought/thoughts
>
> month/months    person/people

## Dangling Modifier

A noun modifier that does not properly modify or describe any noun in the sentence. In fact, the noun that should be modified has been omitted from the sentence. Likewise, a verb modifier that requires a subject but lacks one in the sentence is considered dangling. Dangling modifiers are always incorrect. See also **Modifier**.

> Walking along the river bank, the new tower can be seen.
>
> (The modifier *walking along the river bank* has no subject. The sentence could be rewritten as follows: *Walking along the river bank, one can see the new tower.*)

## Demonstrative Pronoun

The pronouns *this*, *that*, *these*, and *those*. Demonstrative pronouns can be used as adjectives (*these plants, that company*). They can also be used in place of nouns, but they must be modified in some way, according to the GMAT. See also **Pronoun**.

> The strategy taken by Livonia is preferable to that taken by Khazaria.
>
> (The demonstrative pronoun *that* properly stands for the noun *strategy*. The pronoun *that* is modified by the phrase *taken by Khazaria*.)

## Dependent Clause

A clause that cannot stand alone without a main or independent clause. A dependent clause is led by a subordinator. Also known as a subordinate clause. See also **Clause** and **Subordinator**.

## Direct Object

The noun that is acted upon by a verb in the active voice. Can be a pronoun, a noun phrase, or a noun clause.

> I broke the lamp.
>
> Who let the big dogs out?
>
> I believe that you are right.

## Essential Modifier

A modifier that provides necessary information. Use an essential modifier to identify the particular noun out of many possibilities or to create a permanent description of the noun. Do not use commas to separate an essential modifier from the modified noun. See also **Modifier**.

> I want to sell the car that my sister drove to the city.

## Fragment

A group of words that does not work as a stand-alone sentence, either because it is begun by a subordinator or because it lacks a subject or a verb. See also **Subordinator**.

> Although he bought a pretzel. (*Although* is a subordinator.)

> The device developed by scientists. (*Developed by scientists* is a noun modifier; the subject *the device* lacks a verb.)

## Future Tense

The form of a verb that expresses action in the future. Also known as simple future. See also **Tense**.

> The driver will swerve.

> The tires will be punctured.

> They will break the lamp.

## Gerund

An *–ing* form of a verb used as a noun.

> Skiing is fun.

> She enjoys snowboarding.

> She often thinks about sledding.

## Gerund Phrase

A phrase centered on an *–ing* form of a verb used as a noun.

> Simple:        Skiing difficult trails is fun.

> Complex:    We discussed the grooming of the horses.

### Helping Verb

A verb used with another verb. Helping verbs create various grammatical structures or provide additional shades of meaning. The most common are the three primary helping verbs.

| | |
|---|---|
| be: | I am working. |
| do: | The company does follow safety rules. |
| have: | The team has succeeded. |

There are also modal helping verbs, such as *can, could, may, might, must, shall, should, will,* and *would.* These words qualify the main verb (He *may* accept the job) or convey a judgment (He *should* accept the job).

### Hypothetical Subjunctive

Subjunctive form that indicates unlikely or unreal conditions. This form is used in some cases after the words *if, as if,* or *as though,* or with the verb *to wish.* The hypothetical subjunctive is equivalent to the simple past tense of every verb, except the verb *to be*: The hypothetical subjunctive of *be* is *were* for every subject. See also **Subjunctive Mood.**

If he <u>were</u> in better shape, he would win the race.

### Idiom

An expression that has a unique form. Idioms do not follow general rules; rather, they must simply be memorized.

### *If–Then* Statement

A sentence that contains both a condition (marked by an *if* ) and a result (possibly marked by a *then*). Either the condition or the result may be written first in the sentence. The verbs in *if–then* statements follow particular patterns of tense and mood.

If he were in better shape, he would win the race.

They get sick if they eat dairy products.

If she swims, then she will win.

### Imperative Mood

The form of a verb that expresses direct commands. Identical to the bare form of the verb as well as to the command subjunctive. See also **Mood.**

<u>Go</u> to the store and <u>buy</u> me an ice cream cone.

### Indefinite Pronoun

A pronoun that does not refer to a specific noun. Most indefinite pronouns are singular.

| | |
|---|---|
| anyone, anybody, anything | no one, nobody, nothing |
| each, every (as pronouns) | someone, somebody, something |
| everyone, everybody, everything | whatever, whoever |
| either, neither (may require a plural verb if paired with *or/nor*) | |

A few indefinite pronouns are always plural.

> both, few, many, several

The SANAM pronouns (some, any, none, all, more/most) can be either singular or plural, depending on the noun in the *of* phrase that follows the pronoun.

> None of the RECORDS <u>have been</u> updated. (plural)

> Most of the COFFEE <u>was spilled</u> down the stairs. (singular)

## Independent Clause

A clause that can stand alone as a grammatical sentence. Contains its own subject and verb. Also known as a <u>Main Clause</u>.

## Indicative Mood

The form of a verb that expresses facts or beliefs. Most verbs in most English sentences are in the indicative mood. See also **Mood**.

> I <u>went</u> to the store and <u>bought</u> an ice cream cone.

> I <u>will do</u> so again.

## Indirect Object

The noun that expresses the recipient or the beneficiary of some action. Can be a <u>Pronoun</u>, a <u>Noun Phrase</u>, or a <u>Noun Clause</u>.

> I gave <u>him</u> the lamp.

> She found <u>the man</u> a good book.

## Infinitive

The bare form of the verb plus the marker *to*. Used as a noun or as a modifier within a sentence.

> I prefer <u>to read</u> novels.

> She drove many miles in order <u>to see</u> her uncle.

## *–ing* Form

The bare form of the verb plus the ending *–ing*. When used as a noun, the *–ing* form is called a gerund. When used as a modifier or as part of the progressive tense, the *–ing* form is called a present participle.

| | |
|---|---|
| Present participle (part of verb): | I am <u>eating</u> an apple. |
| Gerund (noun): | <u>Eating</u> an apple is good for you. |
| Present participle (noun modifier): | The man <u>eating</u> an apple is my friend. |
| Present participle (adverbial modifier): | I sat on the porch, <u>eating</u> an apple. |

### Intransitive Verb

A verb that does not take a direct object. Intransitive verbs cannot be put in the passive voice.

> I <u>went</u> to the library.

> The driver <u>swerved</u>.

> (Intransitive verb –*ing* forms followed by nouns are usually adjectives: *The <u>swerving driver</u> came to a stop on the sidewalk.*)

### Linking Verb

A verb that expresses what a subject is, rather than what it does. The most important linking verb is *to be*. Often, linking verbs are followed by adjectives that describe the subject.

> Our academic adviser <u>is</u> happy.

> My sister's dog <u>is</u> devoted to her.

### Main Clause

A clause that can stand alone as a grammatical sentence. A main clause contains its own subject and verb and is not introduced by a subordinator. Also known as an <u>Independent Clause</u>.

> <u>I prefer to read novels.</u>

> While eating lunch, <u>she finished reading the report</u>.

### Marker

Words that serve as clues that the GMAT is testing a particular issue. For example, *and* is a parallelism marker and *which* is a modifier marker.

### Middleman

Words that the GMAT inserts between the subject and the verb to hide the subject. Middlemen are usually modifiers of various types.

### Misplaced Modifier

A noun modifier that is not positioned next to the noun it needs to describe in the sentence. Misplaced modifiers are incorrect. See also **Modifier**.

> Misplaced: I collapsed onto the sofa <u>exhausted by a long day of work</u>.

> Corrected: *Exhausted by a long day of work, I collapsed on the sofa.*

> (In the misplaced example, the modifier *exhausted by a long day of work* refers to *sofa*, but a sofa can't be exhausted.)

### Modal Helping Verb

See **Helping Verb**.

## Modifier

Words, phrases, or clauses that describe other parts of the sentence. Noun Modifiers modify nouns. Adverbial Modifiers modify anything other than nouns (verbs, clauses, adjectives, etc.).

## Mood

The form of the verb that indicates the attitude of the speaker toward the action.

> Indicative: I drive fast cars. We drove to Las Vegas.
>
> Imperative: Drive three blocks and turn left.
>
> Command Subjunctive: I suggested that he drive three blocks.
>
> Hypothetical Subjunctive: If he drove three blocks, he would see us.

## Nonessential Modifier

A modifier that provides extra information. If this modifier were removed from the sentence, the core meaning of the sentence would still make sense. Use commas to separate a nonessential modifier from the modified noun. See also **Modifier**.

> I want to sell this beat-up old car, which my sister drove to the city.

## Noun

A word that means a person, place, or thing. Nouns can be the subject of a verb, the direct or indirect object of a verb, or the object of a preposition. Nouns can be modified by an adjective or another noun modifier.

## Noun as Adjective

A noun that is placed in front of another noun and that functions as an adjective.

> A government survey; the stone wall
>
> (*A government survey* is a type of survey; a *stone wall* is a type of wall.)

## Noun Clause

A subordinate clause (with its own subject and verb) that acts as a noun in the sentence. That is, it is the subject of a verb, the object of a verb, or the object of a preposition. Led by relative pronouns *which*, *what*, *when*, *why*, *whether*, or *that*.

> I care about what he thinks. (object of the preposition *about*)
>
> Whether I stay or go is unimportant. (subject of the verb *is*)
>
> I believe that you are right. (object of the verb *believe*)

## Noun Modifier

A word, phrase, or clause that describes a noun.

| | |
|---|---|
| Adjective: | <u>This big</u> window needs to be replaced. |
| Past participle: | The window <u>broken during the storm</u> needs to be replaced. |
| Present participle: | The window <u>rattling against the sill</u> needs to be replaced. |
| Prepositional phrase: | The window <u>on the right</u> needs to be replaced. |
| Appositive: | This window, <u>an original installation</u>, needs to be replaced. |
| Infinitive: | The window <u>to replace</u> is on the second floor. |
| Relative clause: | The window <u>that needs to be replaced</u> has a missing pane. |

## Noun Phrase

A phrase that acts as a noun in the sentence. A noun phrase typically consists of a noun and its modifiers.

<u>A new government SURVEY of taxpayers</u> is planned.

(The subject of the sentence is the noun phrase consisting of the noun *survey* and its modifiers: *a*, *new*, *government*, and *of taxpayers*.)

## Object Case

The form of a pronoun used as the object of a verb or of a preposition. Nouns do not change form in the object case. See also **Case**.

## Opening Modifier

A phrase or clause at the beginning of a sentence that does not contain the noun or subject it refers to. An opening modifier is always followed by a comma. The main noun/subject after the comma has to be the noun to which the opening modifier was referring.

<u>Intrigued by the opportunity</u>, the manager approached her supervisor to inquire about the requirements for the new position.

## Parallel Element

A part of a sentence made parallel to another part or parts of the sentence through the use of parallel markers.

We will invite both <u>his friends</u> and <u>her family</u>.

## Parallel Marker

The words that link or contrast parts of a sentence, forcing them to be parallel.

We will invite both his friends <u>and</u> her family.

## Parallelism Category

A type of word, phrase, or clause. Something in one parallelism category can be made parallel to something else of the same type, but it should not be made parallel to anything in another category.

| | |
|---|---|
| Concrete nouns: | I like to eat <u>peanut butter</u> and <u>ice cream</u>. |
| Action nouns and complex gerunds: | I like to watch <u>the release of the doves</u> and <u>the changing of the guard</u>. |
| Simple gerunds: | I like <u>eating ice cream</u> and <u>watching birds</u>. |
| Working verbs: | I like <u>eating ice cream</u> and <u>watching birds</u>. |
| Infinitives: | I prefer either <u>to eat</u> ice cream or <u>to watch</u> birds. |
| Adjectives and participles: | I like ice cream, either <u>frozen</u> or <u>warm</u>. |
| Clauses: | She knows <u>that I like ice cream</u> and <u>that I hate sorbet</u>. |

## Participle

One of two kinds of words derived from verbs. Present participles typically end in –*ing* and can be used as a verb, a noun, a noun modifier, or an adverbial modifier. Present participles typically indicate ongoing action (though not necessarily in the present). Past participles typically end in –*ed* (though there are lots of irregular forms) and can be used as a verb, a noun modifier, or an adverbial modifier. Past participles tend to indicate a completed action relative to the given time frame in the sentence.

| | **Form** | **Example** |
|---|---|---|
| **Present Participle** | Verb: | She will be <u>hiking</u> next week. |
| | Noun: | <u>Studying</u> for the GMAT is fun. |
| | Noun mod: | The man <u>running</u> down the hall is late for his meeting. |
| | Adverbial mod: | He missed the deadline, <u>hurting</u> his standing with his boss. |
| **Past Participle** | Verb: | The tires were <u>punctured</u>. |
| | Noun mod: | The tire <u>punctured</u> by the nail needs to be repaired. |
| | Adverbial mod: | <u>Punctured</u> by a nail, the tire slowly deflated. |

## Parts of Speech

The basic kinds of words. A word's part of speech is determined both by what the word means and by what role or roles the word can play in a sentence.

| | |
|---|---|
| Noun: | peanut, lake, vacuum, considerations, opportunity |
| Verb: | swim, proceed, execute, went, should |
| Adjective: | wonderful, blue, helpful |
| Adverb: | slowly, very, graciously |
| Preposition: | of, for, by, with, through, during, in, on |
| Conjunction: | and, but, or, although, because |

## Passive Voice

The form of a verb in which the subject is receiving the action expressed by the verb.

> The driver <u>was thrown</u> from the car.

> The crystal vases <u>have been broken</u> by the thieves.

## Past Participle

The participle used in perfect tenses and passive voice. A past participle may also be used as an adjective. Past participles tend to indicate completed action, although not necessarily in the past (relative to now).

> The tires will be <u>punctured</u>. (passive voice)

> They have <u>broken</u> the lamp. (present perfect tense)

> A <u>frozen</u> lake. (adjective)

Regular past participles are formed by adding –*d* or –*ed* to the base form of the verb. Many irregular past participles are listed below, together with irregular past tense forms. Sometimes the past tense form and the past participle are identical. Non-native English speakers should study this list. Native English speakers likely already know most or all of these forms.

| **Base Form** | **Past Tense** | **Past Participle** |
|---|---|---|
| be | was, were | been |
| become | became | become |
| begin | began | begun |
| break | broke | broken |
| bring | brought | brought |
| build | built | built |
| buy | bought | bought |
| catch | caught | caught |
| choose | chose | chosen |
| come | came | come |
| cost | cost | cost |
| cut | cut | cut |
| do | did | done |
| draw | drew | drawn |
| drink | drank | drunk |
| drive | drove | driven |
| eat | ate | eaten |
| fall | fell | fallen |
| fight | fought | fought |
| find | found | found |
| forget | forgot | forgotten |

| Base Form | Past Tense | Past Participle |
|---|---|---|
| freeze | froze | frozen |
| give | gave | given |
| go | went | gone |
| grow | grew | grown |
| hold | held | held |
| keep | kept | kept |
| know | knew | known |
| lead | led | led |
| lose | lost | lost |
| make | made | made |
| pay | paid | paid |
| put | put | put |
| rise | rose | risen |
| say | said | said |
| see | saw | seen |
| seek | sought | sought |
| sell | sold | sold |
| send | sent | sent |
| set | set | set |
| show | showed | shown |
| shrink | shrank | shrunk |
| speak | spoke | spoken |
| spend | spent | spent |
| spread | spread | spread |
| stand | stood | stood |
| steal | stole | stolen |
| strike | struck | struck |
| sweep | swept | swept |
| take | took | taken |
| teach | taught | taught |
| tell | told | told |
| think | thought | thought |
| throw | threw | thrown |
| understand | understood | understood |
| win | won | won |
| write | wrote | written |

## Past Perfect Tense

The form of a verb that expresses action that takes place before another past action or time marker. The past perfect tense is formed with the verb *had* and the past participle.

> The officer said that the driver <u>had swerved</u>.

> By 2005, she <u>had visited</u> India three times.

## Past Tense

The form of a verb that expresses action in the past. See also **Tense**.

> The driver <u>swerved</u>.

> The tires <u>were punctured</u>.

> They <u>broke</u> the lamp.

> (Common irregular past tense forms are listed under the entry for <u>Past Participles</u>.)

## Person

Indicates whether the word refers to the speaker or writer (first person), the listener or reader (second person), or someone/something else (third person). Personal pronouns are marked for person. Present tense verbs in the third person singular add an *–s*: *The doctor writes*.

> First person: I, me, my, we, us, our

> Second person: you, your

> Third person: she, he, it, its, they, them, their

## Phrase

A group of words that has a particular grammatical role in the sentence. The type of phrase is often determined by one main word within the phrase. A phrase can contain other phrases. For example, a noun phrase can contain a prepositional phrase.

| | |
|---|---|
| Noun phrase: | <u>The short **chapter** at the end of the book</u> is important. |
| Verb phrase: | The computer <u>must have been **broken**</u> in the move. |
| Adjective phrase: | The employee <u>most **reluctant** to volunteer</u> was chosen. |
| Prepositional phrase: | The wolf <u>**in** the cage</u> has woken up. |

## Plural

A category of number that indicates more than one. Nouns, pronouns, and verbs can be made plural. See also **Singular**.

> <u>Many dogs are</u> barking; <u>they are</u> keeping me awake.

## Possessive Case

The form of a pronoun or a noun that owns another noun. In possessive case, nouns add *–'s* or *–s'*. See also **Case**.

## Preposition

A word that indicates a relationship between the object (usually a noun) and something else in the sentence. In some cases, prepositions can consist of more than one word.

> of, in, to, for, with, on, by, at, from, as, into, about, like, after,
>
> between, through, over, against, under, out of, next to, upon

## Prepositional Phrase

A prepositional phrase consists of a preposition and an object (a noun). The preposition indicates a relationship between that object and something else in the sentence.

> I would like a drink of water. (*Of water* modifies *drink*.)
>
> The man in the gray suit is the CEO. (*In the gray suit* modifies *man*.)

## Present Participle

The participle used in progressive tenses. A present participle may also be used as a noun, a noun modifier, or a verb modifier. Present participles tend to indicate ongoing action, although not necessarily at the present moment. To form a present participle, add *–ing* to the base form of the verb, possibly doubling the verb's last consonant.

> The tires were rolling.
>
> She jumped into the swimming pool.
>
> Hiking is great.

## Present Perfect Tense

The form of a verb that expresses action that began in the past and continues to the present or whose effect continues to the present. The present perfect tense is formed with the verb *has* or *have* and the past participle.

> The tires have been punctured. (The tires were punctured in the past, and it is still true in the present that they are punctured.)
>
> You have broken my lamp! (The lamp was broken in the past, and it is still broken now.)

## Present Tense

The form of a verb that expresses action in the present. The simple present (nonprogressive) often indicates general truths. See also **Tense**.

> The driver swerves.
>
> The tires are on the car.
>
> They speak English. (general truth; not necessarily speaking English right now)

## Primary Helping Verb

See **Helping Verb**.

### Progressive Tense

The form of a verb that expresses ongoing action in the past, present, or future. See also **Tense**.

> The driver <u>is swerving</u>.

> The tires <u>were rolling</u>.

> They <u>will be running</u>.

### Pronoun

A pronoun stands in for another noun elsewhere in the sentence or for an implied noun. The noun is called the antecedent.

> When Amy fell, <u>she</u> hurt <u>her</u> knee. (*She* and *her* refer to the antecedent *Amy*.)

> When it started to rain, the tourists pulled out <u>their</u> umbrellas. (*Their* refers to *tourists*.)

> The term bibliophile refers to <u>someone who</u> loves books. (*Someone* is a pronoun but does not need to have a specific antecedent; *who* refers to *someone*.)

### Relative Clause

A subordinate clause headed by a relative pronoun. Relative clauses may act as noun modifiers or, more infrequently, as nouns.

> The professor <u>who spoke</u> is my mother.

> <u>What you see</u> is <u>what you get</u>.

### Relative Pronoun

A pronoun that connects a subordinate clause to a sentence. The relative pronoun plays a grammatical role in the subordinate clause (e.g., subject, verb, object, or prepositional object). If the relative clause is a noun modifier, the relative pronoun also refers to the modified noun. If the relative clause is a noun clause, then the relative pronoun does not refer to a noun outside the relative clause.

> The professor <u>who</u> spoke is my mother.

> (The relative pronoun *who* is the subject of the clause *who spoke*. *Who* also refers to *professor*, the noun modified by the clause *who spoke*.)

> <u>What you see</u> is a disaster waiting to happen.

> (The relative pronoun *what* is the object of the clause *what you see*. *What* does not refer to a noun outside the clause; rather, the clause *what you see* is the subject of the sentence.)

### Reporting Verb

A verb, such as *indicate*, *claim*, *announce*, or *report*, that in fact reports or otherwise includes a thought or belief. A reporting verb should be followed by *that* on the GMAT.

> The survey <u>indicates</u> that CFOs are feeling pessimistic.

## Run-On Sentence

A sentence incorrectly formed out of two main clauses joined without proper punctuation or a proper connecting word, such as a coordinator or subordinator. Also called a comma splice.

| | |
|---|---|
| Wrong: | The film was great, I want to see it again. |
| Right: | The film was great; I want to see it again. |
| Right: | The film was great, and I want to see it again. |
| Right: | Because the film was great, I want to see it again. |

## SANAM Pronouns

An indefinite pronoun that can be either singular or plural, depending on the object of the *of* phrase that follows. The SANAM pronouns are *some, any, none, all, more/most.*

Some of the milk has gone bad.

Some of the children are angry.

## Sentence

A complete grammatical utterance. Sentences contain a subject and a verb in a main clause. Some sentences contain two main clauses linked by a coordinating conjunction, such as *and*. Other sentences contain subordinate clauses tied to the main clause in some way.

My boss is angry. (This sentence contains one main clause. The subject is *boss*; the verb is *is*.)

He read my blog, and I saw the comments that he posted. (This sentence contains two main clauses linked by *and*. In the first, the subject is *he* and the verb is *read*. In the second, the subject is *I* and the verb is *saw*. There is also a subordinate clause, *that he posted*, describing *comments*.)

## Simple Gerund

A gerund is an *–ing* form of a verb that functions as a noun. A simple gerund typically does not include an article or something similar (as a complex gerund does).

Swimming is fun.

She likes running and hiking.

(In general, simple gerunds should not be put in parallel with action nouns. Complex gerunds can be put in parallel with action nouns. See also **Complex Gerund**.)

## Singular

A category of number that indicates one. Nouns, pronouns, and verbs can be made singular. See also **Plural**.

A dog is barking; it is keeping me awake.

## Split

Differences in the answer choices. When working on a Sentence Correction problem, compare the answers to find splits; these differences will help you determine what the problem is testing.

### State Verb

A verb that expresses a condition of the subject, rather than an action that the subject performs. State verbs are rarely used in progressive tenses.

> Her assistant <u>knows</u> Russian.
>
> I <u>love</u> chocolate.
>
> This word <u>means</u> "hello."

### Subgroup Modifier

A type of modifier that describes a smaller subset within the group expressed by the modified noun.

> French wines, <u>many of which I have tasted</u>, are superb.

### Subject

The noun or pronoun that goes with the verb and that is required in every GMAT sentence. The subject performs the action expressed by an active-voice verb; in contrast, the subject receives the action expressed by a passive-voice verb. The subject and the verb must agree in number (singular or plural).

> The <u>market</u> closed.
>
> <u>She</u> is considering a new job.
>
> <u>They</u> have been seen.

### Subjunctive Mood

One of two verb forms indicating desires, suggestions, or unreal or unlikely conditions.

> Command subjunctive: She requested that he <u>stop</u> the car.
>
> Hypothetical subjunctive: If he <u>were</u> in charge, he would help us.

### Subordinate Clause

A clause that cannot stand alone without a main or independent clause. A subordinate clause is led by a subordinator. Also known as a dependent clause. See also **Clause**.

> Her dog, <u>which is brown</u>, is friendly.
>
> <u>Although he barely studied</u>, he scored well on the test.

### Subordinator

A word that creates a subordinate clause. Relative pronouns typically introduce noun modifiers. Subordinating conjunctions typically introduce adverbial modifiers.

| | |
|---|---|
| Relative pronoun: | which, that, who, whose, whom, what |
| Subordinating conjunction: | although, because, while, whereas |

## Superlative Form

Form of adjectives and adverbs used to compare three or more things or people. The reference group may be implied. Regular superlative forms are either the base word plus *–est* (e.g., *greenest*) or the base word preceded by *most* (e.g., *most intelligent*). Irregulars are listed below.

| Adjective or Adverb | Superlative |
|---|---|
| good/well | best |
| bad/badly | worst |
| much, many | most |
| little, few | least, fewest |
| far | farthest, furthest |

## Tense

The form of the verb that indicates the time of the action (relative to the present time). The completed or ongoing nature of the action may also be indicated.

| Present: | She <u>speaks</u> French. |
|---|---|
| Past: | She <u>spoke</u> French. |
| Future: | She <u>will speak</u> French. |
| Present progressive: | She <u>is speaking</u> French. |
| Past progressive: | She <u>was speaking</u> French. |
| Future progressive: | She <u>will be speaking</u> French. |
| Present perfect: | She <u>has spoken</u> French. |
| Past perfect: | By 2018, she <u>had spoken</u> French for half her life. |

## *That* Clause

A clause that begins with the word *that*. The *that* clause can be a standard noun modifier.

> The suggestion <u>that he made</u> is bad.

A *that* clause can also be part of a Subject–Verb–THAT–Subject–Verb(–Object) sentence structure. In this case, the entire *that* clause is considered the object of the first subject–verb pairing

> He suggested <u>that the world is flat</u>.

## Transitive Verb

A verb that takes a direct object; if the sentence doesn't have that object, it is incomplete.

> Wrong: The company <u>makes</u>.

> Right: The company <u>makes</u> computer chips.

Some verbs can be either transitive or intransitive. In particular, verbs that indicate changes of state can be either.

> The lamp <u>broke</u>.

> I <u>broke</u> the lamp.

Transitive verbs can usually be put in the passive voice, which turns the object into the subject.

> The agent <u>observed</u> the driver.

> The driver <u>was observed</u> by the agent.

Transitive verb *–ing* forms followed by nouns are usually simple gerund phrases.

> The agent was paid for <u>observing the driver</u>.

This duality means that some *–ing* forms in isolation can be ambiguous. The phrase *melting snow* could mean "the act of causing snow to melt" or "snow that is melting." Use context to resolve the ambiguity.

## Uncountable Noun

A noun that cannot be counted in English. For instance, you cannot say *one patience, two patiences, three patiences*. Most uncountable nouns exist only in the singular form and cannot be made plural.

| | | |
|---|---|---|
| patience | milk | information |
| furniture | rice | chemistry |

## Verb

The word or words that express the action of the sentence. The verb indicates the time of the action (tense), the attitude of the speaker (mood), and the role of the subject (voice). The verb may also reflect the number and person of the subject. Every sentence must have a verb.

## Verbal

A word or phrase that is derived from a verb and that functions as a different part of speech in the sentence: as a noun, as an adjective (noun modifier), or as an adverb (verb modifier).

| | |
|---|---|
| Infinitive: | He likes <u>to walk</u> to the store. |
| Gerund: | I enjoy <u>walking</u>. |
| Present participle: | The man <u>walking</u> toward us is my father. |
| Past participle: | The facts <u>given</u> in the case are clear. |

## Voice

The form of the verb that indicates the role of the subject as performer of the action (active voice) or recipient of the action (passive voice).

| | |
|---|---|
| Active voice: | She <u>threw</u> the ball. |
| Passive voice: | The ball <u>was thrown</u> by her. |

## Warm-Up

Words that the GMAT inserts at the beginning of the sentence to hide the subject in question. Warm-ups are modifiers of various types, including <u>Opening Modifiers</u>.

## Working Verb

A verb that could be the main verb of a grammatical sentence. A working verb shows tense, mood, and voice, as well as number and person in some circumstances. The use of this term helps to distinguish working verbs from verbals, which cannot by themselves be the main verb of a sentence.

# Go beyond books.
# Try us for free.

### In-Person

Find a GMAT course near you
and attend the first session
free, no strings attached.

### Online

Enjoy the flexibility of prepping
from home or the office with
our online course.

### On-Demand

Prep where you are, when you
want with GMAT Interact™ –
our on-demand course.

**Try our classes and on-demand products for free at manhattanprep.com/gmat.**

# Not sure which is right for you? Try all three! Or give us a call and we'll help you figure out which program fits you best.

# Prep made personal.

Whether you want quick coaching in a particular GMAT subject area or a comprehensive study plan developed around your goals, we've got you covered. Our expert GMAT instructors can help you hit your top score.

## CHECK OUT THESE REVIEWS FROM MANHATTAN PREP STUDENTS.

## Contact us at 800-576-4628 or gmat@manhattanprep.com
for more information about your GMAT study options.